...en biographies of Bruce Chatwin,
...vell. Born in Liverpool, he now
...es.

D1628302

By the same auth

BRUCE CH

A LIFE OF MAT

AFTER ARNOLD: CULTURE AND ACCESSIBILITY

WORLD ENOUGH AND TIME: THE LIFE
OF ANDREW MARVELL

Poetry

PLAUSIBLE FICTIONS

Fiction

A SHORT BOOK ABOUT LOVE

ALDOUS HUXLEY

An English Intellectual

NICHOLAS MURRAY

BLACKBURN COLLEGE LIBRARY

NOT TO BE REMOVED FROM THE LIBRARY

An *Abacus* Book

First published in Great Britain in 2002 by Little, Brown
This edition published by Abacus 2003

Copyright © 2002 Nicholas Murray

The moral right of the author has been asserted.

All rights reserved. No part of this publication may be
reproduced, stored in a retrieval system, or transmitted, in
any form or by any means, without the prior permission in
writing of the publisher, nor be otherwise circulated in any
form of binding or cover other than that in which it is
published and without a similar condition including this
condition being imposed on the subsequent purchaser.

A CIP catalogue record for this book is available
from the British Library.

ISBN 0 349 11348 3

Typeset in Minion by M Rules
Printed and bound in Great Britain by
Clays Ltd, St Ives plc

BLACKBURN COLLEGE

Ac BB19332

Ci HSC 823·912 mur

D   17/1/09

Abacus
An imprint of
Time Warner Books UK
Brettenham House
Lancaster Place
London WC2E 7EN

www.TimeWarnerBooks.co.uk

To Sue

Contents

The man of letters is tempted to live too exclusively
in only a few of the universes to which,
as a multiple amphibian, he has access.

Aldous Huxley 'Foreword' to *You are not the Target*
by Laura Archera Huxley

Meanwhile, one must be content to go on piping up for
reason and realism and a certain decency.

Aldous Huxley, 'Introduction' to *Texts and Pretexts*

I

Aldous

'Born into the rain,' Aldous Huxley told the *New York Herald Tribune* in 1952, 'I have always felt a powerful craving for light.'[1] Huxley had in mind his lifelong struggle with defective eyesight, which sent him first to the Mediterranean and then to Southern California. But the wider metaphor is irresistible. His life was a constant search for light, for understanding, of himself and his fellow men and women in the twentieth century. This intellectual ambition – not unknown but rare in English novelists – sent him far beyond the confines of prose fiction into history, philosophy, science, politics, mysticism, psychic exploration. He offered as his personal motto the legend hung around the neck of a ragged scarecrow of a man in a painting by Goya: *aun aprendo*. I am still learning. Grandson of the great Victorian scientist Thomas Henry Huxley – 'Darwin's bulldog' – he had a lifelong passion for truth, artistic and scientific. His field of interest, declared Isaiah Berlin after his death, was nothing less than 'the condition of men in the twentieth century'.[2]

Like an eighteenth century *philosophe*, a modern Voltaire – though in truth he found that historical epoch lacking in depth and resonance – he took the whole world as his province, and like those urbane thinkers he did it with consummate clarity and grace, was frequently iconoclastic, and struck many of his contemporaries in the early decades of the twentieth century as a liberator and a herald of the modern age of secular enlightenment and scientific progress. He was also an often disturbingly accurate prophet who became steadily more disillusioned with the uses to which science was being put in his time. His was an early voice in the ecological movement, which gathered pace after his death. He warned against the dangers of nuclear weapons, over-population, exhaustion of the world's natural resources, militarism and destructive nationalism. His subtler messages – about the corrosive effects of modern consumer capitalism and brainwashing by advertising, about the slow surrender of freedom – have made his most famous work, Brave New World, in many ways a more accurate prophecy than Orwell's 1984. From a certain point of view, it is true, Huxley's brand of high amateurism might look a little anachronistic in an era of intense academic specialisation – he loved to mock 'the professors' (not least when he became a 'Visiting Professor of Nothing in Particular' himself) and considered no subject, however abstruse, alien to him. The wide-ranging intellectual, acknowledging no disciplinary barriers, nor feeling the need to kow-tow to the appointed custodians of this or that area of knowledge, if not extinct is certainly an endangered species. The example of Huxley – who constituted what Rosamund Lehmann called 'a luminous intelligence incarnate'[3] – serves as a reminder of what might be at stake were the species to disappear for good.

But Huxley was never – in spite of his prodigious intellectual gifts – a mere desiccated calculating machine. It is true that he confessed to 'a fear of the responsibilities of relationships'.[4] And he admitted: 'I know how to deal with abstract ideas but not people'.[5] In spite of his exceptional intelligence and his frequent impatience with human stupidity (expressed more at a theoretical than at a personal level) Huxley was a surprisingly modest and self-effacing man. He showed an exceptionally acute perception of his own shortcomings as a man and as a writer. In the 1940s, Huxley was smitten by the classification of human types drawn up by Dr William Sheldon in The Varieties of Human Physique and The Varieties of Temperament. In this scheme, Huxley was a 'cerebrotonic', a term that would crop up regularly in his later works. In an article which appeared in Harper's Magazine in

November 1944, with droll illustrations by James Thurber, Huxley explained the characteristics of his own type:

> The cerebrotonic is the over-alert, over-sensitive introvert, who is more concerned with the inner universe of his own thoughts and feelings and imagination than with the external world . . . In posture and movements, the cerebrotonic person is tense and restrained. His reactions may be unduly rapid and his physiological responses uncomfortably intense . . . Extreme cerebrotonics . . . have a passion for privacy, hate to make themselves conspicuous . . . In company they tend to be shy and unpredictably moody . . . Their normal manner is inhibited and restrained and when it comes to the expression of feelings they are outwardly so inhibited that viscerotonics suspect them of being heartless.[6]

Huxley, however, was not 'heartless'. As a young writer in the twenties, he was seen as a cold-eyed and ruthless satirist, disgusted by human folly, but the underlying humanity was always there, and keener readers noticed it.

One sticky afternoon in Los Angeles in the early part of the year 2000, I was taken by a gentle Armenian taxi-driver – with perfect manners and an imperfect grasp of the street-plan of Hollywood – to the house in Mulholland Highway in the Hollywood Hills where Huxley ended his life and where his second wife, Laura Archera Huxley, still lives. Sitting on the verandah at the back of the house, in view of the famous white HOLLYWOOD letters erected on the hillside at what seemed only a stone's throw away, I found myself asking Mrs Huxley at one point in our conversation about the view of Huxley that had been disseminated widely towards the end of his life: that he had been transformed into an other-worldly sage, abstracted, almost ethereal, his moorings cut loose from the world. It is a common view of Huxley in the 1950s and 1960s. Laura Huxley dissented vigorously: 'He was very *present* and light and amused,' she insisted. We had been talking for more than an hour. The light had

begun to fade and a cool breeze bringing the scent of vegetation was
blowing gently in from the hills. Mosquitoes, like tiny paratroopers
landing on an enemy beach, were dropping in at angles. There was a
long pause:

> I cannot tell you how gentle and tender the man was:
> accepting and tender and caring.

Laura Huxley's comments echo many of the tributes made at the time
of his death. Testimonies to what Leonard Woolf called his 'essential
gentleness and sweetness'[7] abounded. For Osbert Sitwell he was 'that
rare thing, a good man' and for Isaiah Berlin 'a wholly civilised, good
and scrupulous man'.[8]

Present-day criticism and biography is not at ease with this way of
speaking about writers. Until very recently critics were pre-occupied
with formal and theoretical questions. The writer's moral stance was
considered, in Derrida's words 'hors-texte' – beyond the text and therefore irrelevant. But nothing dates more quickly than critical fashion
and there are growing signs of dissatisfaction with such narrow
approaches. We are perhaps now ready again for Huxley and writers
like him. On the other hand, those who have called Huxley a secular
saint (when coined by Gladstone to describe John Stuart Mill, that
epithet was intended to carry an ambivalent charge) run the risk of
inviting a sceptical reaction. Yet even the unillusioned Cyril Connolly,
interviewing Huxley for *Picture Post* in 1948, was forced to conclude
that the man he had met at Claridges during the West End run of one
of his plays was qualitatively different from the general run of contemporary authors:

> If one looks at his face one gets first an impression of
> immense intelligence, but this is not unusual among
> artists. What is much more remarkable and almost
> peculiar to him is the radiance of serenity and loving-
> kindness on his features; one no longer feels 'what a
> clever man' but 'what a good man,' a man at peace with
> himself and plunged as well – indeed, fully engaged – in

the eternal conflict between good and evil, awareness and stupidity.'[9]

Huxley's philosophy might be summed up as: the world can be made better, but only if we make ourselves better. He was not an ideologist, a writer of manifestos, a practical politician. But he wanted to change minds – or to release their potential. His intelligence roamed freely and was uninterested in boundaries. In California, he gave lunch to L. Ron Hubbard, founder of the batty science of dianetics – for the simple reason that he wanted to find out what he had to say – and when a friend wrote about flying saucers he confessed that he had 'no settled opinion so far' about whether or not they existed.[10] An open mind is such a rarity that perhaps we should hesitate to censure it.

But, in addition to the intellect and the moral vision, there was the physical man. Huxley was immensely tall – six feet four-and-a half inches – and the near-blindness that afflicted him for much of his life sometimes gave him an air of strangeness, perhaps intimidating for those who met him for the first time. For Christopher Isherwood who knew him in his southern California years he was 'too tall. I felt an enormous zoological separation from him. There is a very, very great chasm between the tall and the short.'[11] For the scallywags of Hampstead where Huxley lived in a tiny flat just after he was married in 1919, he was the spindly Old Etonian toff they would tease in the street by shouting up to him: 'Is it cold up there, guv?'[12] Virginia Woolf confided to her diary after her first meeting that he was 'infinitely long'. It was on the lawn at Garsington, while scanning the manuscripts of Gerald Manley Hopkins which Robert Bridges had just handed to her, that she looked up at 'that gigantic grasshopper Aldous folded up in a chair close by'. A few years later she met him at a concert 'more of a windmill and a scarecrow, more highbrow, pur-blind and pallid and spavined than ever'.[13] The zoological comparisons proliferate. Sybille Bedford noticed at her first meeting with him: 'the apartness, the vulnerability, the curious young bird's unprotectedness that has caught so many women'.[14] Then there were the botanical analogies: to Frieda Lawrence he was a 'weed'[15] and to Sewell Stokes 'like a tall sad tulip, whose head rests a little too heavily on its stalk'.[16] To the children of St John and Mary Hutchinson, he was 'the Quangle-Wangle'.[17] Anita Loos, a close friend of Huxley in Southern California, was struck by his 'physical beauty . . . the head of an angel drawn by William Blake. His faulty sight even intensified Aldous's majesty, for he appeared to be looking at things above and beyond what other people saw.'[18] Mary Hutchinson was struck by his physical appearance: 'so long and gentle and languid suggesting untouchable withdrawn snail's horns in strange contrast to his flowing outgoing mind'.[19]

And there was the famous voice: beautifully modulated, silvery, precise. Listening to a recording of himself, pressed on vinyl in the summer of 1949, when he had lived in Southern California for more than a decade, Huxley reflected:

> Language is perpetually changing; the cultivated English
> I listened to as a child is not the same as the cultivated
> English spoken by young men and women today. But
> within the general flux there are islands of linguistic
> conservatism; and when I listen to myself objectively,
> from the outside, I perceive that I am one of those
> islands. In the Oxford of Jowett and Lewis Carroll, the
> Oxford in which my mother was brought up, how did
> people speak the Queen's English? I can answer with a
> considerable degree of confidence that they spoke almost
> exactly as I do. These recordings of 1950 are at the same
> time documents from the seventies and eighties of the
> last century.[20]

Locked for a day in a booth at the National Sound Archive in London, listening to that voice – unaltered by years of residence in the United States – 'neat as a seamstress's stitching'[21] as his friend Gerald Heard put it, one can testify to the accuracy of another friend, Raymond Mortimer's, judgement that, 'his voice and articulation remained the most exquisite I have ever known.'[22] His conversation was peppered with 'how *extraordinary*' and '*fascinating*', and with casual references to leading contemporary authorities on this or that

branch of knowledge and effortlessly deployed allusions to past masters ('There's a very *striking* phrase in Spinoza . . .'). Just occasionally,
that easeful, liquid articulation, the tone almost of languor, rises a
little to a degree that could become, were it to be taken a little further,
querulousness, as if the speaker cannot quite comprehend the sheer
enormity of human folly in his time, falling back exhausted at the
spectacle. Yet the speaking voice was the man and Yehudi Menuhin
declared, 'he had made himself into an instrument of music . . . his
voice was the gentlest melody.'[23]

'Aldous,' observed his nephew, Francis Huxley. 'How well the name
suited him, and how often have I heard people refer to him with
familiar reverence by that name alone, as though there were but one
Aldous in the history of the world!'[24]

Aldous Huxley was born in 1894, when Queen Victoria was on the
throne of England. As a child he glimpsed the Queen in old age,
taking carriage exercise in Windsor Great Park, attended by her faith-
ful servant John Brown.[25] He died in Hollywood, in 1963, a few hours
after the fatal shots rang out from the Texas Book Depository in
Dallas which killed President John F. Kennedy. He was the grandson
of a great Victorian scientist and the great-nephew of the Victorian
poet and critic, Matthew Arnold. He was thus a kind of conduit or
link between the world of high Victorian liberal intellectualism and
the world of the twentieth century, whose course those ardent, pro-
gressively-minded meliorists could not have predicted. It was this
aspect of Huxley which first drew me to him, for I had written the life
of Matthew Arnold, and was curious to explore the ways in which that
nineteenth century tradition of the writer and thinker as enlightened
public intellectual had persisted into the modern era. In his youth,
Huxley was seen by his contemporaries as the opponent of that
Victorian inheritance, a defiantly modern figure who was breaking
free – and encouraging others to break free – from what was perceived
as a stuffy, reactionary order of society. The eponymous heroine of
Two or Three Graces (1926) knows what she is up against:

> As for Grace's parents, they were only a generation away;
> but, goodness knows, that was far enough. They had

opinions about socialism and sexual morality, and
gentlemen, and what ought or ought not to be done by
the best people – fixed, unalterable, habit-ingrained and
by now almost instinctive opinions that made it
impossible for them to understand or forgive the
contemporary world.[26]

Seen in a wider context, however, profounder continuities can be
seen at work. Huxley's passion both for science (even though he was
painfully aware of the misuses of science in his time) and for communicating to a large public recall his grandfather's determination to
bring scientific knowledge to ordinary people, in plain language, in
his lectures at the Royal Institution, attended by working men and
cab-drivers, one of whom famously refused to accept a fare in gratitude for what he had heard. On his mother's side, the Arnoldian
inheritance of urbane public discourse and a love and practice of
poetry is plain. Huxley had no time for those who would erect barriers between art and science, knowing them to be two complementary
modes of knowing, as Thomas Henry Huxley and Matthew Arnold
had agreed them to be a century before, when Arnold vigorously
insisted to his friend, Huxley, that his famous definition of culture as
'the best that has been thought and said in the world' embraced scientific knowledge and culture.[27]

Two principal obstacles face anyone seeking to write a life of
Aldous Huxley. The first is the fire that swept through his home in
1961, destroying papers, letters, and diaries belonging to Huxley, but
also letters from others, including family members and relatives who
had deposited material with him after he indicated that he was contemplating some form of autobiographical writing. Huxley, however,
like most of his literary contemporaries, was a prolific letter writer
and this book draws on the hundreds of unpublished letters which
survive and which are scattered throughout library collections in
Britain, the United States and Europe. The second cause for hesitation
given to anyone contemplating a new life is the authorised biography
of Huxley by Sybille Bedford, published in two volumes in 1973 and
1974. One of the outstanding post-war literary biographies in English,

this book is more than a biography: periodically it acquires the special authority and richness of a memoir – for Sybille Bedford was an intimate of the Huxleys for many years. It is also an eloquent honouring of a life, and a way of life, that she seemed peculiarly well-equipped to perform. I am especially grateful to Sybille Bedford for the long conversations that I was able to have with her at her London home in the summer of 2000 and for her kindness and encouragement.

A new life, however, needs no justification. The last thirty years have seen the publication of many collected editions of letters and diaries of those who knew Huxley – Lawrence, Woolf and many others. In addition, as my acknowledgements indicate, there is now a wealth of unpublished material, which necessitates a bringing up to date of the Huxley story. Inevitably this means that the intimate life of Aldous Huxley and his remarkable wife, Maria, can now be more fully documented. Maria's bisexuality, the extraordinary *ménage à trois* in the 1920s of Aldous, Maria and Mary Hutchinson – absent for obvious reasons from previous biographical accounts – are described here for the first time. Not the least of the many paradoxes of Aldous Huxley's life was the co-existence of this complete sexual freedom and a long and loving marriage: what Huxley described, in a letter that has only recently come to light, as 'thirty-five years of being two in one'.[28] The Huxleys matriculated in sexual ethics at Garsington. They had an easy and civilised enjoyment of the sensual life. They loathed the 'smut hounds' whom Huxley angrily denounced for snapping at the heels of his friend D.H. Lawrence. Whatever is revealed of the private life of the Huxleys, their marriage remains one of the most extraordinary and sustaining literary marriages of the twentieth century.

At the centenary of Huxley's birth in 1994, much emphasis was laid on Huxley's early politics – in particular his supposed democratic lapses during a brief period in the very early 1930s. Two years earlier, a book by John Carey, *The Intellectuals and the Masses* (1992), had enjoyed considerable acclaim for its thesis that many leading twentieth century intellectuals imagined 'the masses' as 'ripe for extermination' as part of a 'cult of the Nietzschean Superman, which found its ultimate exponent in Hitler' – to quote from its excited blurb. The immediate success of this book was not hard to understand. It told conservative English opinion what it wanted to hear: that the high-toned progressives were no better than they ought to be. *The Daily Mail* was delighted. The Carey thesis – from which, in relation to Huxley, I wholly dissent – had an unfortunate influence on the centenary, including an hour-long BBC2 *Bookmark* programme about the writer which dutifully reflected the new orthodoxy.

What effect these passing media trends, however, have had on long-term assessments of Huxley is something hard to quantify. His nimble and lucid intelligence always contrives to keep him several paces ahead of the leaden-footed heresy hunters. His books are in print. *Brave New World* at least figures regularly on lists compiled to indicate the most popularly esteemed books of the twentieth century. His appeal is international – the *enfant terrible* of contemporary French writing, Michel Houellebecq, though seriously misinformed about some basic facts of Huxley's biography, makes a dialogue with the writer a feature of his novel, *Les Particules élémentaires* (1998).[29] Huxley scholars are few in number when compared to the Fordist masses at work in the Lawrence, Woolf, and Joyce industries. But Huxley is clearly still read, and still popular, and, although I have written a biography not a critical study of his novels, I hope to show in this fresh life that he may be speaking to our current condition in more interesting and thought-provoking ways than has recently been allowed.

Notes

1   *New York Herald Tribune*, 12 October, 1952
2   *Aldous Huxley: A Memorial Volume* edited by Julian Huxley (1966) [henceforward: *Mem. Vol.*] p148
3   *Aldous Huxley: A Biography* by Sybille Bedford. [henceforward *SB*] Volume 2 (1974), p280
4   *Letters of Aldous Huxley* edited by Grover Smith (1969) [henceforward *L.*] p357
5   *L.*361. See also *L.*390: 'my besetting sin . . . an avoidance of emotion'
6   *Harper's Magazine*, November 1944, p519

7   *Mem. Vol.* p35
8   *Mem. Vol.* pp33 and 153 respectively
9   Cyril Connolly, *Picture Post*, 6 November 1948, p21
10 *SB2*, p122
11 Christopher Isherwood, Interview with David King Dunaway, 2 June 1985. Huntington Library Oral History Transcripts [henceforward HL]
12 Frank Swinnerton, *The Georgian Literary Scene* (1935), p458
13 *The Diary of Virginia Woolf*, (1977–84) ed Anne Olivier Bell and Andrew McNeillie, Vol 1, 17 October 1917, Vol 3, I July 1926, *The Letters of Virginia Woolf*, ed Nigel Nicolson and Joanne Trautmann, (1975–80), Vol 4, 28 January 1931 respectively
14 *SB1*, p233
15 *The Letters of D.H. Lawrence*, ed James T. Boulton and Lindeth Vasey, Vol 5 (1989), p569, 31 October 1926. Frieda Lawrence to Montague Weekley
16 Sewell Stokes, *Hear The Lions Roar* (1931), p206
17 Harry Ransom Humanities Research Centre, Austin, Texas [henceforward HRC], Mary Hutchinson unpublished profiles of Aldous and Maria Huxley (undated)
18 Anita Loos, *Mem. Vol.*, p89
19 HRC, Mary Hutchinson Profiles
20 *Sound Portraits* (NY), July 1949. Text of sleeve note in University of California at Los Angeles (UCLA) Huxley archive
21 Gerald Heard, 'The Poignant Prophet', *The Kenyon Review* (1965), p51
22 *Mem. Vol.*, p137
23 *Mem. Vol.*, p86
24 Francis Huxley, 'Preface' to *Aldous Huxley Recollected* (1995) edited by David King Dunaway, pv
25 AH lecture at Santa Barbara, quoted in Laura Archera Huxley, *This Timeless Moment* (1969), p21
26 *Two or Three Graces* (1926), p88
27 See Nicholas Murray, *A Life of Matthew Arnold* (1996) p301. Arnold wrote to Huxley: 'I never doubted that the formula included science.'
28 HRC Letter to Lady Sandwich from AH, 17 April 1955
29 Michel Houellebecq, *Les Particules élémentaires* (1998, Paris). Houellebecq seems to think that Leonard Huxley was a scientist, not a classics master and literary journalist, and that Huxley in California was an associate of Alan Ginsberg. But see the chapter, 'Julian et Aldous', pp193–201

II

Grandpater

On 26 July 1894, Aldous Leonard Huxley was 'born into the rain' of the Surrey countryside at Godalming. This was the leafy English county where his free man, John, the 'Savage of Surrey', in *Brave New World* claimed his 'right to be unhappy' in a hermitage very precisely located 'between Puttenham and Elstead'. In 1925, in an essay on the appeal of country life, he recalled that: 'The Surrey I knew as a boy was full of wildernesses. To-day Hindhead is hardly distinguishable from the Elephant and Castle.'[1] In his later essay 'The Olive Tree' – that marvellous prose hymn to the Mediterranean spirit – he recalled 'the old elm trees' that were the backdrop to his Surrey childhood: 'I spent a good part of my boyhood under their ponderous shade.'[2] In his 1923 novel *Antic Hay*, the hero, Theodore Gumbril, 'began talking with erudition about the flora of West Surrey: where you could find butterfly orchis and green man and the bee, the wood where there was actually wild columbine growing, the best location for butcher's broom, the outcrops of clay where you get wild daffodils. All this odd knowledge came sprouting up into his mind from some underground source of memory.'[3] In the same novel, Lypiatt asks Myra to recall 'the fine grey sand on which the heather of Puttenham Common grows. And the flagstaff and the inscription marking the place where Queen Victoria stood to look at the view. And the enormous sloping meadows round Compton [the eventual burial place of Huxley's ashes] and the thick, dark woods.' Huxley was to live almost all of his adult life outside England, but the memory of that green Home Counties Arcadia – before the creeping suburbanisation of the twentieth century had changed it for good – never left him.

Not that his reminiscences were always so fond. In 1930 he told a correspondent: 'I sometimes wonder . . . whether it isn't perhaps rather bad for one to have been born and brought up a bourgeois in tolerably easy circumstances – with baths, fresh air, plenty of space, privacy and the other luxuries of bourgeois existence. The result is that any diminution of that treasure of space and time which money can buy – leisure and room to be alone in – seems an appalling hardship: and the actual physical contact with members of one's own species fills one with dismay and horror. The Marxian philosophy of life is not exclusively true: but, my word, it goes a good way . . .'[4] Huxley's acute self-awareness left him in no doubt about the strengths and weaknesses of his relatively privileged background. Travelling through India in 1925, Huxley mused on the traditional English reverence for parliamentary democracy – noting that it was in fact 'government by oligarchs for the people and with the people's occasional advice' – and wondered whether his freedom to indulge in such easy speculation was not due to the fact that, 'I was born in the upper-middle, governing class of an independent, rich, and exceedingly powerful nation. Born an Indian or brought up in the slums of London, I should hardly be able to achieve so philosophical a suspense of judgement.'[5]

Whether Leonard Huxley, then a modestly-paid Classics master at nearby Charterhouse school, would have placed himself so firmly in the company of the rich and powerful when his third son Aldous was delivered on 26 July 1894, is doubtful. Leonard was the son of the scientist Thomas Henry Huxley, and would later achieve greater prominence as a literary journalist and deputy editor of the *Cornhill*. His wife, Julia, was the daughter of Thomas Arnold, who was brother of the poet and critic Matthew Arnold, and Julia's sister was the novelist Mary Augusta ('Mrs Humphry') Ward. Julia Arnold was one of the first women to attend Somerville College, Oxford, graduating in 1882 with a First in English. She met Leonard in 1880 while he was an undergraduate at Balliol but had to wait some years until they could afford to marry.

At the time of Aldous's birth, the Huxleys had lived for a year in a comfortable, neo-Gothic, Victorian house called Laleham (Laleham-on-Thames had been Matthew Arnold's birthplace) at Godalming with an acre of garden including a tennis lawn, a rose-garden, and a rockery. On the top floor was a nursery with a rocking horse the size of a pony that could take four small boys at once. 'I remember the nursery with a fine rocking horse and a screen covered with coloured pictures or fragments of pictures cut from magazines and catalogues – a fascinating mosaic of unrelated faces, scenes, objects, co-existing in a surréaliste confusion,'[6] he recalled in 1960. Though Aldous's relationship with his father was to become strained, particularly after Leonard's second marriage in 1912, his early childhood was a happy one. He adored his mother and his father seems to have had some of the playful facetiousness of the Victorian paterfamilias. But was there anything of Leonard in the portrait of Mr Barnack in *Time Must Have A Stop?*

> that was one of the most disquieting things about his
> father: you never knew from his expression what he was
> feeling or thinking. He would look at you straight and
> unwaveringly, his grey eyes brightly blank, as though you
> were a perfect stranger. The first intimation of his state of
> mind always came verbally, in that loud, authoritative,
> barrister's voice of his, in those measured phrases, so
> carefully chosen, so beautifully articulated. There would
> be silence, or perhaps talk of matters indifferent; and
> then suddenly, out of the blue of his impassivity, a
> pronouncement, as though from Sinai.[7]

Aldous as a small child was looked after by a German governess from Königsberg, Fräulein Ella Salkowski, whom he later employed to look after his own young son, Matthew. There was a seven year gap between Aldous and his eldest brother, Julian, who was himself to have a very distinguished public career as a scientist and as the first Director-General of UNESCO. The next eldest son, five years older than Aldous, was Trevenen (the name shared by Matthew Arnold's son 'Budge', whose boyhood death so devastated the poet; there was Cornish ancestry in the Arnolds). Five years younger than Aldous was his only sister, Margaret, who hardly seems to figure in accounts of his life. It is possible that her unconventional life style – she would live with another woman, Christabel Mumford, on the south coast where they ran a school together – was the source of some disapproval by the Huxleys.

In his autobiography, published in 1970, Sir Julian Huxley recalled his father as 'a kindly man, full of almost boyish fun'.[8] But there is evidence, as has already been hinted, that Aldous was less enamoured of his father, whom he respected less and less as he grew into maturity. In part this was because of an inability, even as a small boy, to find himself able to pay his father sufficient respect. His cousin Gervas thought Leonard Huxley was 'silly. He wasn't the kind of father one looked up to, or went to when one was in trouble . . . I think it was this lack of respect that troubled Aldous and marred his relationship with his father.'[9] It appears that his behaviour towards the young girl pupils at the school his wife would open in 1910 was not always what it should have been,[10] and his rapid remarriage to a much younger woman after his first wife's death did not help the relationship. For Aldous, then, his strongest feelings were reserved for his mother, whom he adored. Julian describes her: 'She wore pince-nez, had great charm and a tremendous sense of humour – I remember the way she used to throw back her head and explode with laughter when amused – but could pass from gay to grave when the mood took her . . . Her steady gaze was truth-compelling, but full of love, even when she had to reprimand us.' Julian also recalled her 'sense of fun, her gay participation in simple games, her enjoyment of acting, her infectious vitality and love of life'.

Unfortunately, Aldous left no direct reminiscence of his mother, though traces can be detected in some of his novels – most notably *Antic Hay* – where, it must be admitted, the contrasting type of the awful 'greedy, possessive mother'[11] also abounds, a type destined to recur again and again throughout his fiction. The family as an institution gets a bad press in Aldous Huxley's novels but the reasons are not to be sought in his very early experiences at Laleham. When he came to experiment with drugs in the 1950s he reported that he was seeking to retrieve some unspecified childhood memory, which may relate to this time, but it is more likely that it centred on the trauma of his mother's early death. In a curious 1962 letter to a Californian music teacher whom he had met at Berkeley, which discussed the notion of a 'psycho-analytic ballet', Huxley suggested that such a production should deal with 'memories of traumatic events in childhood – punishments, humiliations, an attempted rape.'[12] One critic, noticing a prevalent sado-masochistic theme in Huxley's fiction, speculated whether 'it might perhaps originate from some curious experience in his own childhood'.[13] There is no evidence to confirm or deny such a hypothesis.

As a young child, Aldous was very pretty (as a photograph of him, aged five in curls and page boy costume, pensively examining the camera from a cane-seated leather armchair, makes clear). He had an enormous head which earned him the unkind nickname of 'Ogie', short for 'Ogre', and it was soon apparent to everyone that, as a young second cousin, Jill Greenwood, told Sybille Bedford, 'everybody knew that Aldous was different'.[14] He was fond of drawing and of childhood games, though rather delicate. The future satirist showed himself in a sally recorded by Julian. They both attended a neighbouring governess whose deafness caused Aldous to observe, of governesses in general, 'Deaf and dumb they may be, but contradict they must.' Another story told by Julian is of the young boy being asked by his godmother what he was thinking about, as he gazed pensively out of the window. The small boy replied solemnly, and monosyllabically: 'Skin.'[15] He told a friend in 1959: 'One of my early recollections is being taken to church in Godalming and disgracing myself by vomiting during the sermon – a precocious expression, no doubt, of anti-clericalism.' He also remembered the Muffin Man, 'ringing a dinner bell, like the character in *The Hunting of the Snark*. He had a long white beard and wore a flat topped military cap, on which he carried a large tray, on which, under a white cloth, were the freshly made muffins and crumpets . . . And once a steam roller came and rolled the road outside our gate – a truly glorious object with a spinning fly-wheel and a tall chimney. It exhaled a deliciously thrilling smell of hot oil, and on the front end of the boiler was a golden unicorn.'[16] Aldous's education began at a nearby day-school for infants called St Bruno's in 1899. That Christmas, staying at his Aunt Mary's (Mrs Humphry Ward) house, Stocks, at Tring, he wrote a letter to his teacher, Miss Noon, informing her that he had received six presents, and thanking her for 'my cannon'.[17] The following year he attended with his broth-ers, cousins, aunts and uncles the Christmas Pantomime at Drury Lane. The enormous family party, which had arrived by carriage, occupied the dress circle. The show lasted for four hours and Dan Leno and Herbert Campbell were the star comedians. The scene is fic-tionalised in *Antic Hay*:

> All the little cousins, the uncles and aunts on both sides
> of the family, dozens and dozens of them – every year
> they filled the best part of a row in the dress circle at
> Drury Lane. And buns were stickily passed from hand to
> hand, chocolates circulated; the grown-ups drank tea.
> And the pantomime went on and on, glory after glory,
> under the shining arch of the stage . . . And there was
> Dan Leno, inimitable Dan Leno, dead now as poor
> Yorick, no more than a mere skull like anybody's skull.
> And his mother, he remembered, used to laugh at him
> sometimes till the tears ran down her cheeks. She used to
> enjoy things thoroughly, with a whole heart.[18]

Aldous and his cousin Gervas were delighted and a long-lasting fond-ness for music hall was cemented.

By 1900, Julian was already at Eton, and required on that account by his mother to offer his top hat to six-year-old Aldous to be sick in as they stood waiting at the Natural History Museum for the Prince of Wales to unveil a statue of their grandfather. Even a six-year-old is impressed when a grandfather is cast in stone or bronze, and no Huxley was ever allowed to forget the awesome precedent of the great forebear. In an interview which took place in 1985, Julian's wife, Juliette Huxley, referred to the 'burden' that was imposed on Huxleys to succeed at all costs, to win the prizes and scholarships (which they generally did), to live up to the example of 'Gran-Pater'. The pressure on Julian was intense: 'Julian suffered from that. Very much . . . There is something really devastating about having a grandfather (grand-*pater* as they called him) who was a god in the family. These children grew up with that atmosphere: "Worthy of Grand-Pater – right! You must be worthy of grand-pater."'[19]

The old man died in June 1895, less than a year after Aldous's birth but his influence never went away. Because of the high intellectual achievements of the Huxleys they are sometimes represented as a formidably long-standing intellectual aristocracy. In fact, the dynasty was founded by Thomas Henry Huxley, son of a provincial savings bank manager, who had only two years of formal education. He was the type of the formidable Victorian autodidact, never more so than in the descriptions we read of him shipping aboard the HMS *Rattlesnake* in the 1820s as an assistant surgeon, and producing in his cramped, waterlogged cabin, the carefully drawn and noted biological observations that, after many setbacks, would be published and lead to his eventual triumph as one of the leading scientists, controversialists, and communicators of the nineteenth century. As he worked away, with only hope to sustain him, cockroaches feasted on the edition of Dante he was teaching himself to read with the help of an Italian dictionary. That example of courage, tenacity, and undeflectable intellectual ambition was a powerful legacy to his descendants.[20] Aldous paid tribute to him in the Huxley Memorial Lecture, which he delivered in 1932, in significant terms, praising his 'astonishingly lucid' style. Huxley – who had little sympathy with linguistic experiment of the kind practised by literary artists such as James Joyce – always preferred that touchstone of clarity, however deeply erudite and wide his range of allusion might be. 'Truth was more important to him,' he said of his grandfather, 'than personal triumph, and he relied more on forceful clarity to convince his readers than the brilliant and exciting ambiguities of propagandist eloquence.' Underlining the point, Huxley added: 'one of the major defects of nineteenth century literature . . .

was its inordinate literariness, its habit of verbal dressing-up and play-ing stylistic charades'. Thomas Henry countered this tendency by a 'passion for veracity'.[21]

If one of the central questions about Aldous Huxley is whether he was primarily a literary artist or primarily a thinker, a propagator of ideas, the polarities he sets up here are extremely interesting, and continued to exercise him throughout his career, surfacing in late works like *Literature and Science*, published in the year of his death. Whether there was something, as it is popularly expressed, 'in the Huxley genes', that helped to crystallise this glittering concentration of talent – a matter perhaps for the socio-biologists – or whether, as I am inclined to think, it was more a combination of naturally occurring gifts nurtured by precedent and example, a certain prevailing expec-tation that one would enhance the performance, not detract from it, the Huxley inheritance was an ever-present reality – though rarely spoken of by Huxley himself in his published work or unpublished correspondence. Yet, at the same time, in his youth Huxley was icon-oclastic towards the nineteenth century worthies. He once admitted to Julian that he had avoided reading them at Oxford: 'I somehow escaped that normal course in youth, that plowing through the Victorian Great and being reminded all the time that they are great.'[22] Even in his late fifties, he refused to be pious about them. His Californian friend, Grace Hubble, recorded in her diary an evening party in 1953 attended by Osbert and Edith Sitwell and Huxley where Aldous was pouring scorn on 'the Monstrous Victorians, who become increasingly alien and unnatural. More and more they seem like the characters in *Alice in Wonderland* and *Through the Looking Glass*.'[23] The McPhail dynasty in *Island*, or the Poulshots in *Time Must Have A Stop* ('An absolutely sterling goodness, but limited by an impenetra-ble ignorance of the end and purpose of existence'[24]), stand for a certain kind of heavy English *bourgeois* rectitude and dull propriety, with its roots in the Victorian and Edwardian drawing-room, that the gadfly satirist of the 1920s – who was never wholly submerged in the later *gravitas* – had no difficulty in holding up to ridicule.

In 1901, Julia Huxley, drawing on her own and her husband's slen-der capital and loans from the bank, founded a girls' school near

Godalming called Prior's Field. The family abandoned Laleham and went to live at Prior's Field, two miles away, set in twenty-five acres of land. The previous year, Leonard Huxley had published a biography of his father, *Life and Letters of Thomas Huxley*, whose success enabled him to end his fifteen year career as a schoolmaster and enter the literary world as reader and literary adviser for the publishing firm Smith, Elder and assistant editor of the *Cornhill Magazine*. The school opened on 23 January 1902 with seven pupils: one girl boarder, five day girls, and seven-year-old Aldous. Julia Huxley, a Miss English, and a Mademoiselle Bonnet were the staff. The school grew quickly and just as quickly it became clear that it was a very different sort of school from the prevailing norm. It was freer, more civilised, less regimented and attracted the daughters of some very eminent intellectuals and writers such as Gilbert Murray, Maurice Hewlett, and Conan Doyle – the Huxley and Arnold names no doubt being persuasive. One pupil, the writer Enid Bagnold, described it in her autobiography, however, as 'above all a literary school, they didn't lay stress on mathematics,' which is a little surprising. She recalled her first interview with the headmistress: 'A chintzy room, modern with William Morris – a slender lady with a beautifully-shaped small head. Kind, yes, but away and above my understanding. Each time before she spoke she seemed to reflect.'[25] By the time Enid Bagnold arrived in 1903, Aldous had moved to a nearby prep school, Hillside, but he had Sunday lunch with the girls. Enid had been told that she was supposed to make an effort and talk, so she breezily asked the boy who sat 'silent, rather green, inscrutable, antagonistic' next to her what he had done today. There was no answer. Growing embarrassed, she asked again, a little louder: 'What did you do today, Aldous?' The terse reply came back: 'I heard you the first time.' Forty years later, Enid Bagnold met Huxley at a tea party in Chelsea given by Ethel Sands. 'You were very frightening, Aldous,' she reminded him. 'He gave me a very sweet smile. "I'm frightening still".'

Julia Huxley read aloud to the girls in the evening in her 'silvery, even voice' and did the same, Julian recalls, for her own children, 'first nursery rhymes and fairy stories, then a little history and poetry'. She was 'the pivot of our family life' and used to organise picnic lunches in the Surrey countryside, and charades and round games. As far as the pupils of Prior's Field were concerned, Enid Bagnold wrote, Julia Huxley was also the essential pivot: 'the wonder went out of the school with Mrs Huxley'.[26]

In the autumn of 1903 Aldous was sent away from this happy Eden to the unpleasant rigours of an English preparatory boarding school. Hillside School, run by Gidley Robinson, was not far away but it was, certainly for the first couple of years, quite awful. The only consolation was the presence of his cousin Gervas Huxley (who would later marry the writer, Elspeth Grant). Another friend was Lewis Gielgud, brother of the actor, Sir John Gielgud. Gervas was older than Aldous by three months and has left a very detailed picture of their schoolboy horrors, which lasted five years. 'All I can remember of my arrival at Hillside,' Gervas wrote nearly seventy years later, 'is entering a large classroom full of boys and sitting on a wooden bench beside my cousin Aldous – also a new boy – who was weeping copiously at leaving home.'[27] The school had around fifty pupils aged between eight and fourteen years and the headmaster was 'old and definitely past his best'. The science master, Mr Jacques ('Jacko') was unmercifully ragged by the boys, the music teacher, Mr Macintosh was 'a bespectacled old buffoon', while the two Miss Noons from Godalming 'supposedly taught drawing'. Matron, 'Ma' James, was 'an irascible, ill-educated old woman, whose favourite phrase was "stop your imperence [sic] or I'll report you".' Bullying was rife and allowed to go on unchecked. Aldous and Gervas and the other newcomers would be lined up at one end of the large classroom and peppered with hard little paper pellets fired from catapults. They were then asked if they were 'mushrooms' or 'pears' (circumcised or uncircumcised) and made to fight each other on that basis for the amusement of the seniors. They were also made to run the gauntlet of flicked wet towels, were beaten with slippers or hair-brushes, or had cold water poured into their beds. In addition there was no privacy to read a book. Fortunately, Huxley Major and Huxley Minor (Aldous), were big for their age and stuck together. At the end of each week, after being marched down the hill, in stiff Eton collars and little black Eton jackets, to Farncombe Church, and after another execrable lunch, they

were allowed to walk over to Prior's Field. 'The home-like atmosphere of Prior's Field was a glorious change from Hillside, as was the
excellent tea we enjoyed,' Gervas recalls. Then it was back to the dor-
mitories of twelve beds each, the cold bath every morning and the
once a week hot bath. The teaching was uninspired and consisted of
learning dates by rote and memorising third-rate poems. There was
no encouragement of the boys to read or to learn for themselves. The
school had no library and no place or designated time for reading.
Gervas thought that the school, Bulstrode, in *Eyeless in Gaza* was a
thinly-disguised Hillside and that the schoolboy characters were versions of his and Aldous's schoolfellows. Quite how an inspired
educator such as Julia Huxley could have subjected her young son to
this brutally philistine routine is a mystery. After two years, however,
things began to change. In the autumn of 1905, a new headmaster,
Jimmy Douglas, arrived and, for the first time, a proper teacher called
Hugh Parr 'who really enjoyed encouraging the adolescent mind, particularly in anything relating to literature and art'. He refused to bully
or mock his charges and: 'the whole atmosphere of the school
changed'. There were concerts and Shakespeare plays were performed.
Aldous was said to have moved the old ladies in the audience to tears
in his role as Antonio in *The Merchant of Venice*. Even the food
improved. Encouraged by Hugh Parr – who in little over a decade was
to die in the First World War trenches – to read books and poetry,
Aldous and Lewis Gielgud became joint editors of a literary magazine
called the *Doddite* and Aldous contributed a poem called *Sea Horses*
and a short story he illustrated himself. Aldous and Gervas now
shared a double cubicle and one of their pastimes was sailing little
boats with matchstick masts and paper sails along a gutter which ran
outside the top of the windows. Huxley later fictionalised this pastime
in *Eyeless in Gaza*.

Aldous was frequently ill as a child and missed some of his lessons
but he seems to have developed a way of remaining immune to the
worst experiences of the school. In an earlier, and much less bleak,
account of their schooldays Gervas said that Aldous 'possessed the key
to an inviolable inner fortress of his own, into which he could and did
withdraw from the trials and miseries of school existence'.[28] He was

witty and joined in the schoolboy jokes, even if 'we somehow felt that Aldous moved on a different plane from the rest of us'. And there were also holidays in the Lakes, and the Swiss mountains, during these years where Aldous developed still further his love of natural scenery and wild flowers.

Many years later, writing about the problems of education, and the shortcomings he perceived – not just in the Edwardian upper-middle class English fee-paying schools he had known, but in all school education – Huxley wrote:

> Looking back over my own years of schooling, I can see
> the enormous deficiencies of a system which could do
> nothing better for my body than Swedish drill and
> compulsory football, nothing better for my character
> than prizes, punishments, sermons and pep-talks, and
> nothing better for my soul than a hymn before bed-time,
> to the accompaniment of the harmonium. Like everyone
> else, I am functioning at only a fraction of my potential.[29]

In his book on defective vision, *The Art of Seeing* (1943), Huxley (who incidentally remained firmly opposed to the more permissive kinds of education where children are encouraged to do as they please and learn what they want) complained that children were often 'bored and sometimes frightened, because they dislike sitting cooped up for long hours, reading and listening to stuff which seems to them largely nonsensical, and compelled to perform tasks which they find, not only difficult, but pointless. Further, the spirit of competition and the dread of blame or ridicule foster, in many childish minds, a chronic anxiety, which adversely affects every part of the organism, not excluding the eyes and the mental functions associated with seeing.'[30]

Aldous remained at Hillside until June, 1908. Clever and already a remarkable presence, he was destined for a very bright academic career, following in Julian's footsteps at Eton. But tragedy would very soon strike the family.

Notes

1 *Along the Road* (1925), 'The Country', p57
2 *The Olive Tree* (1936), 'The Olive Tree', p294
3 *Antic Hay* (1923), p184; p273
4 *L.*334 28 November 1930
5 *Jesting Pilate* (1926), p137
6 *L.*883
7 *Time Must Have A Stop* (1944), pp32–3
8 Sir Julian Huxley, *Memories 1* (1970) Chapter 1
9 *SB*1 p14.
10 Sybille Bedford in conversation with the author
11 *Time Must Have A Stop* (1944), p192
12 *L.*935
13 Philip Thody, *Aldous Huxley* (1973), p111
14 *SB*1 p3
15 Julian Huxley, *Mem. Vol.*, p21
16 *L.*872
17 *L.*23
18 *Antic Hay*, p221
19 HL, Oral History Transcripts. Interview between Juliette Huxley and David King Dunaway, 5 July 1985
20 See *The Huxleys* (1968), Ronald W. Clark and Adrian Desmond's two-volume life: *Huxley: The Devil's Disciple* (1994); *Huxley: Evolution's High Priest* (1997)
21 *Thomas Henry Huxley As A Man Of Letters* (1932). Reprinted in *The Olive Tree* (1936)
22 *L.*146
23 HL, Hubble Diary, 30 January 1953
24 *Time Must Have A Stop*, p273
25 *Enid Bagnold's Autobiography* (1969) p25ff
26 See *SB*1 5–11 for many comments by former pupils on Julia Huxley's special qualities
27 Gervas Huxley, *Both Hands: An Autobiography* (1970), p32
28 *Mem. Vol.*, p57
29 'The Education of an Amphibian', *Adonis and the Alphabet* (1956), p37
30 *The Art of Seeing* (1943), p106

III

Damage

Aldous arrived at Eton in September 1908 as one of the school's academic elite, the seventy King's Scholars, who lived in College, the original core of the ancient school, with its black oak benches carved deeply with the initials of young Etonians across the centuries. In Huxley's first letters from Eton the same jauntily facetious, precocious-schoolboy tone he had perfected towards the end of his time at Hillside (where he had been head of school that summer) is on display. 'I notice you say "term" instead of "half" the only and obvious expression,'[1] he primly reprimanded Huxley Major, a mere Rugbeian, who was unaware that at Eton three halves make a whole. Aldous was being initiated into the rituals of fagging, Homer and Virgil, and as a Colleger was installed in the Lower Fifth. Huxley would always be a dandy in dress and he lost no time in telling Gervas: 'I look so chic in tail coats mouldy collars and white ties.' He added that he had been whipped only twice '(1) in a general working off of the whole of college for hiding a letter and (2) for forgetting to take VI form cheese out of Hall'. Lewis Gielgud, he added, was beginning more and more to resemble a turnip. Aldous's letters to Julian were bright and clever, with sometimes a sense that he was trying to impress the elder brother, now at Balliol, whose triumph in reading out his prize-winning Newdigate Poem at Oxford, the younger had witnessed during the summer.

Aldous seems to have settled in well and towards the end of November, he was looking forward to Julian and his other elder brother, Trev, coming to Eton to watch the annual wall game on St Andrew's Day, Monday 30 November. In the event, they did not come because, on the Sunday, with terrible swiftness, Julia Huxley died of an inoperable cancer after a very short illness. She had been diagnosed only four months previously and was forty-five years old. Julian came back from Oxford to her bedside: 'Never shall I forget how wasted she looked,' he recalled later, 'nor the terrible cry she gave: "Why do I have to die, and so young!"'[2] Her sister, Mrs Humphry Ward, that night brought Margaret and Aldous – 'poor little fellow'[3] – home to her house, Stocks, at Tring in Hertfordshire. The funeral took place the next day at Compton, in the Watts Memorial Chapel designed by the wife of the portrait painter, George Frederic Watts. Surveying the rich *art nouveau* and Celtic decoration of the tiny chapel, the boys would have read the gilt legend that ran around the walls: 'But the souls of the righteous are in the hand of God, their hope is full of immortality.' Julia is buried in a grave close to the chapel wall beneath a broad-branched beech tree. Leonard was later buried with her, and Aldous's ashes, too, would one day, with his wife's, be laid to rest there in the same grave, sadly neglected now, and giving no clue about the famous author whose remains are buried there. On the day of Julia Huxley's funeral the girls from the school were in attendance. The previous night they had listened to a poem by Leonard Huxley, written to express his feelings about his late wife, which at least one girl, Enid Bagnold, found not true to her spirit. Aldous, sobbing, was comforted by Joan Collier. Julian described his younger, fourteen-year old brother as standing 'in stony misery' at the grave side. Mrs Humphry Ward's daughter, Dorothy, recalled: 'The little Eton boy very sensitive and brooding and white, and feels it deeply – and dumbly.'[4] Margaret, Aldous's nine-year-old younger sister, recalled the aftershock of this event which seemed to presage the end of the school and residence at Prior's Field: 'I lost my mother, my home, my school, living in the country and my governess all at one blow.'[5] Julia

Huxley's managing partner, Mrs Burton-Brown, emerged to carry on
with the school – she would be succeeded in turn as headmistress by
her daughter Beatrice – but for pupils like Enid Bagnold its magic was
over. The damage inflicted on the sensitive schoolboy – the first of
three powerful blows during his time at Eton and immediately afterwards – is self-evident. At such an age and with such a sensibility, an
early event of this kind, the discovery that the ground beneath is not
always firm and sure, can have a permanent effect. In *Grey Eminence*
(1941) Huxley wrote of another historical character's loss of a parent
at the age of ten: 'There remained with him, latent at ordinary times
but always ready to come to the surface, a haunting sense of the
vanity, the transience, the hopeless precariousness of all merely
human happiness.'[6] When Huxley later wrote of the isolation and
grief of Anthony Beavis when his mother dies during his schooldays
in *Eyeless in Gaza* (1936) 'he was drawing on his own bitter experience,' thought Gervas.[7] 'I am sure that this meaningless catastrophe
was the main cause of the protective cynical skin in which he clothed
himself and his novels in the twenties,' judged Julian. A later friend,
Dennis Gabor, would write: 'to the last he remained suspicious of the
scars left by the emotional ties of the family'.[8] In both *Brave New
World* and its counterpart, the 'good Utopia' of *Island*, the nature of
motherhood and the role of the family is an important theme, and
one informed by Huxley's complicated feelings about the matter
reaching back to his childhood experiences. On her deathbed, Julia
wrote Aldous a letter which he kept with him for the rest of his life
and in which she enjoined: 'Judge not too much and love more.'[9] The
immediate consequence of Julia Huxley's death was another expulsion
from the Surrey arcadia for Aldous. Leonard moved, in July 1909, to
what Julian called 'a gloomy London house in Westbourne Square,
away from our beloved Surrey'. Aldous shared Julian's dislike of the
Bayswater house at 27, Westbourne Square and tended to spend his
holidays at Stocks or with Gervas's parents, Dr Henry and Sophy
Huxley, in nearby Porchester Terrace.

But meanwhile, Aldous remained at Eton, fagging for his first year
in College, and generally avoiding, as he had done at Hillside, any
attempts at bullying by virtue of his distinctive manner. 'From the

word go,' Lord Justice Harman recalled, 'he was clearly going to be a superior being. He possessed a kind of effortless aristocratic approach to his work.'[10] The syllabus was mostly Latin and Greek (the subjects Huxley himself would teach when he was briefly a schoolmaster at Eton after Oxford, English literature not forming part of the syllabus at Eton until the 1960s). There was a little modern history and a little French. But the main effort was in classics. Huxley recalled: 'Actually, the education at Eton was uncommonly good at that time . . . There were a few very good teachers . . . We used to spend the whole of every Tuesday from 7 in the summer and 7.30 in winter till 10.30 at night composing Latin verses – we were given a piece of Tennyson or something and were told to turn it into elegaics or hexameters or Alcaics or Sapphics, and if you were a little further advanced Greek iambics – which was a sort of immense jig-saw puzzle game'.[11] These mellow reflections from an interview given at the end of his life should be placed against a sharper view from his essay 'Doodles in the Dictionary' from *Adonis and the Alphabet* (1956) where the very same above exercise was described as 'the exhausting and preposterous task of translating thirty or forty lines of English poetry into Latin, or on great occasions, Greek verses. For those who were most successful in producing pastiches of Ovid or Horace or Euripides, there were hand-some prizes. I still have a Matthew Arnold in crimson morocco, a Shelley in half-calf, to testify to my one-time prowess in these odd fields of endeavour. Today I could no more write a copy of Greek iambics, or even Latin hexameters, than I could fly. All I can remem-ber of these once indispensable arts is the intense boredom by which the practice of them was accompanied.'[12] At the same time, however, Huxley believed that 'the pupil in a progressive school lives in a fool's paradise' for the evident reason that: 'As a preparation for life, not as it ought to be, but as it actually is, the horrors of Greek grammar and the systematic idiocy of Latin Verse were perfectly appropriate.' Huxley, who was generally on the 'progressive' side of such questions, was nonetheless firmly of the view that the right to self-expression had done 'enormous mischief in the sphere of education'.[13] At Eton, where a new King's Scholar or 'K.S.' would begin in the original stalls or cubicles of College, Huxley soon graduated to a room of his own where he read voraciously. Here was 'the brilliant boy two years ahead of his contemporaries in book-learning' who figures in the unfinished autobiographial novel which Laura Archera Huxley excerpts in her memoir, *This Timeless Moment* (1969).[14] He also began to paint. This was a lifelong pleasure and recalls the skilled draughtsmanship of his grandfather, though Huxley claimed that he came from an aesthetically constricted family background. 'I was brought up in the strait and narrow way of Ruskinism,' he confessed in a passage in *Beyond the Mexique Bay* (1934) – this being the Ruskin who, for the high-minded English *bourgeois*, 'persuasively rationalised this ethico-religious preference [for the Oxford Movement] in terms of aesthetics' – and 'so strict was my conditioning that it was not till I was at least twenty and had come under the influence of a newer school that I could perceive the smallest beauty in Saint Paul's cathedral.'[15] In the company of the Eton aesthetes he read Pater and Wilde but he was also passionately interested in science in general and biology in particular. His biology master M. H. Hill kept a cage of lemurs in his garden and Huxley, whose house tutor and 'division' (form) 'beak' (master), was A.W. Whitworth, thought Hill one of the best masters in the school. In an essay in *Adonis and the Alphabet* (1956), written when he was an enthusiast for 'non-verbal education' and thus prone to criticise his own traditional education, he nonetheless recalled with pleasure how 'I collected butterflies and kept their young in glass jars on the window sill of my cubicle at school'.[16] Huxley's ambition at this time was to be a doctor not a writer – though his later friend Gerald Heard claimed that his wish also was to be a painter.[17]

Whether or not Huxley would have managed the necessary qualities to be a general practitioner – the bedside manner, the professional demeanour – events were soon to determine the issue. Quite apart from his appetite for highly unorthodox and fringe medicine throughout a life dominated by poor health, his principal interest in medicine was scientific, like his grandfather who admitted that he was drawn to medicine not as a career of healing but for the study of 'the mechanical engineering of living machines'.[18]

One Sunday afternoon in the winter of 1911 (the dates surrounding this episode are frustratingly vague), Dr Henry Huxley was coming back from a visit in the country when he decided to call in to see his precocious sixteen-year-old nephew, Aldous, at Eton during the Easter Half. He found the boy with an enormous compress on a very badly inflamed eye and immediately expressed his dismay to Matron, Gertrude Ward. Matron, in spite of her title, was not medically qualified and acted more in the role of a substitute mother for the boys, looking after their domestic needs. She had assumed that Aldous was suffering from a stye or the condition known as pink-eye. Dr Huxley announced that it was far more serious and said that he was taking him there and then to consult an eye specialist in London.[19] The explanation for the infection that has usually been proffered was that it came from dust – on the playing field or out on an OTC exercise (as a member of the OTC Huxley had stood guard on the route of Edward VII's funeral procession to Windsor, 'keeping the rabble back with the butt end of my rifle'[20]) – aggravated because of illness and being generally run-down. The two years since his mother's death at the end of 1909 had not been happy ones for Aldous who had frequently been isolated and left to his own devices. The boys were worked very hard at Eton and the diet may well have been unsatisfactory, all contributing to vulnerability to an infection that today would be cleared up quickly by a course of antibiotics. The cause of infection was diagnosed, after attempts by Henry Huxley and others to treat it, by the leading eye surgeon, Ernest Clarke, in December 1911, as *staphylococcus aureus*. The infection inflamed the cornea very badly – the condition is known as *keratitis punctata* – and, in spite of weekly injections at the Institute for Tropical Medicine in London, opacities in the cornea left when the inflammation subsided grossly impaired the teenager's sight. He was effectively blind and would remain so for at least a year, possibly as long as eighteen months – certainly from early 1911 to the middle of 1912. The vagueness is to do with the absence of records but also because the near-blindness on either side of the acute period affected his ability to read and write. A letter to his cousin Joan Collier in July 1911 says, briefly (though always a very concise writer, this is Huxley's shortest ever letter) and rather poignantly: 'Scuse bad writing which same I cant see'.[21] Looking back on this time, in an interview conducted in the United States in 1957, he recalled:

It happened when I was about sixteen and a half, and I
got this attack of *keratitis* which left one eye about nine-
tenths blind and affected the other quite badly. I was
unable to do any reading for nearly two years. I had to
leave school and I had to have private tutors. I learned to
read Braille and even Braille music, which is very
difficult. And then, I was able, after about two years, to
read with a rather powerful magnifying glass and went
through university on that basis.[22]

A voracious reader, a painter, a delighted explorer of the natural
world, Huxley suddenly found that all these pleasures had been
ripped away to be replaced by a darkness that must have seemed to
him to have a connection to the occluded life of the affections he was
living at this time. It was a catastrophe which he always believed was
the most important single determining event in his early life. In that
same interview, he went on to explain that this dousing of the light at
a crucial point in his adolescent development cut him off from sports
and 'a great many ordinary kinds of outlets for social communication
with people of my own age; and it did stimulate a tendency which I
think I have by temperament, a tendency towards solitude and what
may be contemplation, so that in a sense it confirmed things'. It also
meant that he missed another powerful experience shared by his contemporaries: participation in the First World War – 'and so I no doubt
may owe my life to it'.

In a short book written in 1943 called *The Art of Seeing*, in which
Huxley tried to popularise the doctrines of Dr William Bates who
challenged conventional ophthalmology by proposing exercises for
the eye instead of simply prescribing lenses, he gave a very precise
account of his condition:

At sixteen, I had a violent attack of *keratitis punctata*,
which left me (after eighteen months of near-blindness,
during which I had to depend on Braille for my reading
and a guide for my walking) with one eye just capable of
light perception, and the other with enough vision to

permit of my detecting the two-hundred-foot letter on
the Snellen Chart at ten feet. My inability to see was
mainly due to the presence of opacities in the cornea; but
this condition was complicated by hyperopia and
astigmatism.[23]

Medical records no longer exist but, in the view of a present-day
consultant ophthalmologist, who was shown Huxley's account, the
injections at the Institute for Tropical Medicine would possibly have
contained heavy metals, arsenic or other borates, boric acid, or bis-
muth with presumed antibacterial activity.[24] Other injections
favoured by ophthalmologists at the time included arsenicals,
atropine, eserine, iodine of various kinds, and cocaine topically and in
ointments but possibly even injected for pain.[25] *Keratitis punctata* is
classified into *superficialis* and *profunda*, the former the result of infection and leaving small grey dots in the cornea. One form of *keratitis
(interstialis)* is caused by measles or congenital syphilis and results in
complete corneal opacity for months and usually leaves considerable
corneal scarring. This seems very close to the condition described by
Huxley. It is reported that he had mumps at school, whose effects
would have been the same as measles. But in addition to the infection,
Huxley almost certainly had pre-existing eye problems to which the
illness added. His hyperopia – long-sightedness – would require
strong glasses for reading and long-sightedness can predispose to
amblyopia or lazy eye. Photographs of Huxley in his youth were taken
carefully to avoid showing this, and some may even have been
retouched, but at least one shows distinct abnormality in the eye.
'One eye resembles a blue smear,' the author Robert Payne noted in
1948.[26] And Virginia Woolf recalled: 'There was a look of sightlessness
in his eyes which reminded one of the blind seer.'[27] Corneal scarring
does tend to become thinner and less opaque as time passes and this
may account for the marked visual improvement Huxley claimed
after 1939 when he discovered the Bates method – though there
remain conflicting accounts of his visual capacity. It is worth noting
above how Huxley draws short of saying he was totally blind at sixteen, but the impairment of vision cannot have fallen far short of

total blindness. It is a topic to which it will be necessary to return frequently, since visual impairment was a constant in his life. Sometimes,
one feels, the problem was overstated. At others, his sight may have
been far more impaired than it was claimed at a particular moment.
Accounts sometimes clash. In short, the question posed by
Christopher Isherwood needs regularly to be put: 'How much did he
actually see?'[28]

In 1931 Huxley wrote to Clive Bell, after hearing from Jean Cocteau
that Bell was having eye problems. He advised him to learn Braille: 'It
takes a very short time – I think I was only three or four weeks before
I could read with reasonable facility and speed – and makes an astonishing difference ... Everything has its compensations and I
remember with pleasure the volupté of reading Braille in bed, in the
dark and with one's book and one's hands snugly under the bed-
clothes.'[29] Realising that a medical or scientific career was now out of
the question, Huxley turned to the idea of writing which, he told the
interviewers mentioned above, was 'a very important event in my
life'. He began by writing 'bad verses' and then even 'wrote an entire
novel which I never read because I couldn't see what I had written'.
This 80,000 word novel – written on a typewriter – is now lost, but
Huxley described it in an interview in 1961 as 'a rather bitter novel
about a young man and his relationship to two different kinds of
women'.[30] By means of Braille Huxley read a great deal (including
Macaulay) and also taught himself to play the piano by touch. He displayed enormous courage at this time in ways that recall the
determination in isolation of his grandfather Thomas Henry Huxley,
persevering in his scientific work throughout the years before his
fame. Even when he began to recover some sight during 1912 it was
hard. 'In looking back I am always amazed at the amount of reading
I did with a small, powerful magnifying glass,' he said in 1957. Without
a trace of self-pity he threw himself into the task of coping. He rose
above the disability but he never minimised the importance of the
experience in his life. Until his death he was preoccupied with the
relationship of mind and body, with the way in which the body often
hampered and constrained the mind – but also how mind needed to
discover the right sort of relationship with the body. 'How senseless

psychological and moral judgements really are apart from physiological judgements!' he exclaimed to his lifelong friend Naomi Mitchison
in 1933. 'And of course I am also to a considerable extent a function of
defective eyesight. *Keratitis punctata* shaped and shapes me; and I in
turn made and make use of it.'[31] In an essay in *Music at Night*, he
wrote: 'Men make use of their illnesses at least as much as they are
made use of by them.'[32] His phenomenally retentive memory, for
example, was almost certainly shaped by the need to retain information and to minimise the difficulty of frequent referring-back to
books and sources of information. Naomi, years later, recalled his use
of Braille music and his playing, even after his sight had begun to
return as an undergraduate, at her parents' home in Oxford: 'What I
remember most is his long hands on the piano and his half-blind
face reaching forward into the music. I only listened, but he was
immersed.'[33]

   The immediate consequence for Aldous of the blindness was the
end of his schooldays at Eton. For those dark months he was passed
around to relatives and friends – Aunt Mary at Stocks, the Selwyns
(relatives of Julia) at Hindhead, Naomi's parents (the Haldanes) at
Oxford, Gervas's parents, and then, as things began to improve, to
Marburg in Germany to learn German and to Oxford, with his
brother, Trevenen, from April to June 1913. He was taught by private
tutors, one of whom was Sir George Clark, the historian. Clark
taught him English history while staying with the Huxleys in
Bayswater as an undergraduate in September 1911. When Aldous
required a book, Clark would lead him round the corner to the
Braille lending library at Whiteley's department store. He also
attended some lectures at London University given by W.P. Ker.
Towards the end of November, 1911, Leonard Huxley, who had paid a
tutor's fee and £4 to Eton in order to keep Aldous's place in College
open across the summer, accepted that he was now unlikely to return
(though he retained an option of applying for a vacancy in May
1912). 'His eyesight is improving,' he told the Bursar on 24 November,
'but I see little prospect of his gaining sufficient advantage from a
renewal of his work at school. It is a great disappointment.'[34] If
Aldous's eyesight really was 'improving' as early as November 1911 it

may be that the period of actual blindness was less than a year in duration. Huxley himself was inconsistent, reporting anything from nearly two to three years as the period of blindness. In some very telegraphic, unpublished biographical notes prepared for his German translator, Herbert Herlitschka, in 1929, he wrote: 'Education interrupted for three years by an infection of the eyes which left me for some time nearly blind . . . I was much alone & thrown on my own resources.'[35] The shorter period is more likely to be accurate if we are referring to total blindness, but it is also true to say that for most of 1911, 1912, and 1913, Huxley's education was indeed 'interrupted' until October 1913 when he passed (with the aid of a magnifying glass) the entrance to Balliol College, Oxford.

In February 1912, Leonard Huxley remarried after three years of being alone. His new wife, Rosalind, was thirty years younger – younger even than Julian and Trev – and the difficulties of this arrangement can be imagined. The announcement seems to have been abrupt and, on Rosalind's side, these young intellectuals must have been a rather intimidating prospect. She was fond of them, however, and took good care of Aldous, allowing him to use the piano which her grandfather had given her as a wedding present. 'She really did try,' said Sybille Bedford.[36] He was soon off, in May, to Germany where he stayed with a Professor Kayser, a geologist, and continued with his music. On his return he spent part of the summer with Gervas and Lewis Gielgud. At Christmas, in spite of his limited vision, Aldous went skiing in Montana in Switzerland with his uncle, John Collier, and the other two members of the threesome, Gervas and Lewis. In January 1913 he went on a walking tour with Trev on the South Downs and during spring and early summer stayed with Trev at Oxford at his digs in the Banbury Road. In May, the two brothers and Lewis Gielgud were rehearsing a play at the Oxford home of the parents of its author, Naomi Haldane (later Lady Mitchison), brother of the scientist J.B.S. Haldane. Naomi Mitchison describes this summer of 1913 as 'a strawberry and gooseberry summer . . . We were always having picnics up the Cherwell, making fires and boiling kettles; we were always laughing and scrapping . . .'[37] Later, staying in their home, Aldous would persuade Mrs

Haldane that Naomi's education demanded that she be allowed to read hitherto banned books such as *Tom Jones* and *Madame Bovary*. He also introduced her to music and art: 'He knew an amazing amount about all the arts and took them seriously in a way that was tremendously encouraging to me in our somewhat anti-art Oxford home.' The nineteen-year-old on the threshold of Oxford – tall, precocious, learned, contemptuous of the bourgeois codes of his class in relation to 'shocking' art, pleasure-seeking but with a firm underlying moral sense, is the Huxley of the twenties emerging from its chrysalis.

It was in the summer of 1913, just before he went to Grenoble, that an incident occurred which is described, with her characteristic sensitivity and tact, by Sybille Bedford, who derived her account from conversations with Gervas – the only possible source.[38] That summer, Aldous found himself alone in his father's house in Westbourne Terrace. He decided to go out for a stroll during which he picked up a girl whom he assumed to be an au pair on her evening off. He took her back to the house and made love to her on the sofa, telling Gervas later that he had been surprised by her boldness of approach and eagerness – young men of that class and epoch assuming that these were prerogatives of the male. This was Huxley's sexual initiation and what Sybille Bedford calls his being 'extremely susceptible to pretty women' ensured that it was the beginning of a very active sexual career.

In July Aldous stayed in Grenoble, learning French – which he would always speak and write effortlessly. He visited, like his great uncle, Matthew Arnold, the monastery of the Grande Chartreuse. From La Tronche he reported to his father on the butterflies 'shining like new minted coins'[39] – his eyesight clearly functioning again and his alert attentiveness to the beauty of nature undimmed. On his return there was a brief stay in Yorkshire in September with his two firm friends. And then Oxford.

Trev, with whom Aldous had spent the earlier part of the summer, was aged twenty-three and in his last term at Balliol. He seems to have been the most likeable and charming of the three Huxley brothers. He is transformed fictionally into Brian Foxe in *Eyeless in Gaza*

(1936), who has the same stammer and the same scrupulous con-science: '"But if you d-don't st-tick to your p-principles . . ." he hesitated . . . "well, where are you?" he concluded despairingly.'[40] To anticipate the narrative slightly, what happened to him in August 1914, when Aldous had completed his first year at Oxford, was the third major blow of Aldous's youth, following the death of his mother and the loss of his sight, the three events constituting an undoubted impairment. These events injected a greater bitterness into his early writing than might otherwise have been there (though it would be over-determinist to ignore the contribution of his free-ranging intel-ligence, his immersion in literary precedents, his wider political and social awareness, his sensitivity to the historical moment). Trev was a worrier, which caused him to overwork and tire himself and in con-sequence he secured that summer only a second in Greats. Huxleys were meant to garner firsts. Trev stayed on at Oxford for a further year of postgraduate study, but his hypersensitive nature, the confusion within him between inherited high ideals and the normal sensual feelings of a young man, came to a head when he fell in love with a young woman who was not, according to the upper middle class codes his family lived by, 'suitable'. She has never been identified by name but she was said by Julian to be 'an attractive and intelligent' young housemaid who worked at the family home. Trev was secretly trying to educate her by taking her out to plays, concerts, and lectures but the affair was, they both realised, doomed. She eventually handed in her notice. Knowing the hoplesseness of the liaison, and tortured by his whole condition – he had also failed to pass the Civil Service examinations – Trev fell into a serious mental breakdown. The 'black melancholy' that had cursed his grandfather and which would afflict throughout life his elder brother Julian (though not the more equable Aldous) struck. He was sent, on specialist advice, to a Surrey nursing home, the Hermitage at Reigate, the same that had taken Julian the year before. Though instructions had been given that he was not to be allowed out of anyone's sight, Trev set out on Saturday morning, 15 August 1914, for a walk on the downs. When he failed to return the police were called. There was a search. Eight days later, on Sunday 23 August, Trev was found in a nearby wood. He had hanged himself from a tree. A letter from the housemaid was in his pocket and it was left to the parlourmaid, Sarah, to explain what it all meant. The family – particularly the younger members like Margaret who had treated Trev as 'the hub of the family wheel'[41] and Aldous – was devastated by the loss and the awful circumstances of the delay in finding the body. Aldous wrote to Gervas:

> There is – apart from the sheer grief of the loss – an
> added pain in the cynicism of the situation. It is just the
> highest and best in Trev – his ideals – which have driven
> him to his death – while there are thousands, who shelter
> their weakness from the same fate by a cynical,
> unidealistic outlook on life. Trev was not strong, but he
> had the courage to face life with ideals – and his ideals
> were too much for him.[42]

Julian later wrote: 'Trev's suicide was one of the most ghastly things that could have happened. He was brilliant, good-looking, athletic, especially as a mountaineer, wrote good poetry, and was very popular.'[43]

This event would cast a shadow across the middle of Aldous's Oxford career. But when he went up to Balliol in the autumn of 1913, his sight more or less restored, he threw himself into that brief pre-War moment of excitement and intellectual discovery with all the energy and enthusiasm at his disposal.

Notes

1 *L*.29
2 Julian Huxley, *Memories 1* (1970) p64
3 Letter from Mrs Humphry Ward's daughter, Dorothy Ward, to her friend, Miss Jewett, 13 December 1908. Quoted *SB*1.24
4 *Ibid*.
5 Margaret Huxley, letter to Sybille Bedford, October 1969. Quoted in *SB*1.25
6 *Grey Eminence* (1941), p21

7   *Mem. Vol.*, p59
8   *Mem. Vol.*, p69
9   Quoted by Sybille Bedford addressing P.E.N. meeting 'In Honour of Aldous Huxley', 15 November 1978. Tape in National Sound Archive
10 Quoted in *SB*1.28
11 Recorded interview with John Chandos July 1961. Quoted by *SB*1.29
12 'Doodles in the Dictionary', *Adonis and the Alphabet* (1956), p240
13 *Music at Night* (1931), p67
14 Laura Archera Huxley, *This Timeless Moment* (1968), p212–38
15 *Beyond the Mexique Bay* (1934), p124
16 *Adonis and the Alphabet*, p79
17 Gerald Heard, 'The Poignant Prophet', *Kenyon Review*, p52 'As a boy he was determined to become an artist.'
18 R. W. Clark, *The Huxleys* (1968), p11
19 HL, Oral History Transcripts. Interview between David King Dunaway and Juliette Huxley, 5 July 1985
20 *L*.36
21 *L*.39
22 Interview in Hollywood with students of Los Angeles School of Journalism, 18 December 1957. Text in UCLA Huxley Collection
23 *The Art of Seeing* (1943), pvi
24 I am greatly indebted for this information to Mr John Deutsch FRCS, FRCOphth, Consultant Ophthalmologist, Victoria Eye Hospital, Hereford
25 Mercurial inunctions were used as well as 'subconjunctival injections of plain water, saline solutions, chloride or cyanide of mercury' – *Aids to Ophthalmology* (1919)
26 Robert Payne, 'Aldous Huxley,' in *Now More Than Ever: Proceedings of the Aldous Huxley Centenary Symposium, Munster* (1995, Frankfurt), p5. From the Payne papers, State University of New York at Stonybrook
27 *Mem. Vol.*, p36
28 *Mem. Vol.*, p156
29 *L*.344–5
30 Interview with John Chandos, July 1961. Quoted in *SB*1.35
31 *L*.372–3
32 *Music at Night*, p37
33 *Mem. Vol.*, p52
34 Eton College MS, Letter from Leonard Huxley to Bursar, 24 November 1911
35 Reading MS. Unpublished note in Herlitschka file
36 SB in conversation with the author
37 *Mem. Vol.*, p51

38   *SB*1.57
39   *L*.52
40   *Eyeless in Gaza* (1936). Chapter 36
41   Quoted by *SB*1.47
42   *L*.61
43   *Memories* 1, p96

IV

Oxford

Aldous arrived at Balliol in October 1913 for the beginning of the Michaelmas term. 'Behold me established in the little alcove of my room, with a fine view of Balliol Chapel in the foreground and some bluer sky than usual,'[1] he announced brightly to his father, on Sunday 12 October. Constant confusions between the two Huxleys, Gervas and himself, dogged the first few days. Another inconvenience was having rooms opposite the Chapel, as he confided to his young friend, Jelly D'Aranyi, the concert violinist: 'one is made unhappy on Sundays by the noise of people singing hymns'.[2] Clearly, neither Chapel nor the 'awful noise' of the hymn-singers which 'rather gets on my nerves' would appeal to the grandson of the man who invented the word 'agnostic'. Huxley had also to face some examinations on the first day he arrived, which depressed him a little, but his chief anxiety was that he had been 'very dull and grumpy' at his last meeting with Jelly, adding 'perhaps I always am, I don't know'. Huxley's early encounters with women – to judge from the apologies and explanations in his youthful correspondence – appear to have been prone to gaucheness and the regretted *faux pas*. The normal moodiness and self-regard of the adolescent no doubt also played their part. Huxley's natural reluctance to engage in some of the more boisterous forms of social life, he realised, had to be overcome if the pursuit of women were to be assured of success. The following month, having attended a dance at the Haldanes, he resolved to improve his dancing technique 'or otherwise everyone suffers'.[3]

But it was his intellectual performance, rather than his conduct on the dance floor, which pre-occupied Huxley in the first months at Oxford. In spite of still impaired vision – almost no sight in one eye and limited performance with the other – Huxley threw himself into his reading. He would later tell an interviewer that he marvelled at his ability to read, sometimes for eight hours a day, at Balliol by means of a magnifying glass.[4] He loved the Bodleian and the opportunity to plunge into original texts. He was attending the lectures of Walter Raleigh – his tutor was R.J.E. Tiddy of Trinity – and reading Chaucer, Anglo-Saxon literature, and some Greek philosophers. He found Dryden and his contemporaries 'most exciting' and the latter's verse satire *Absalom and Achitophel* (1681), together with the responses it engendered, wholly absorbed him as he discovered in Bodley 'the most fascinating volume' of original satires. 'It gives one a queer new sensation, seeing all these absurd old books,' he told his father, 'as one somehow always pictures past ages as producing about ten classical works by one or two great names and nothing much else, whereas the trash must have been quite as plentiful in comparison, if not more so, than it is now.'[5] Huxley, all his life an ardent seeker-out of the best, and of the 'classical works', developed a very early disinclination to waste his time and his eyesight on trash. The sense one derives, from a reading of these first letters from Oxford, is of a delighted exploration of the English literary tradition that would form the foundation of the wide and easy allusiveness of the later essays. English Literature was still a relatively new subject at Oxford and Huxley was one of the first wave of beneficiaries of the new discipline. To his fellow undergraduates, Huxley seemed so much farther ahead and to have read so much – modern French poetry, for example – in spite of his handicap. He quickly became the centre of Balliol's literary intellectual set, as Gervas later explained:

> All freshmen had rooms in College and Aldous's 'sitter' soon became the rendezvous of the first-year

contemporaries who formed our set . . . Instinctively
Aldous's contemporaries must have recognised the
originality and distinction of his mind with its catholic
tastes and its curiosity about all things and all men. They
were drawn to him, too, by his unassuming friendliness,
his complete lack of any pretensions and the gaiety that
his company always engendered.[6]

Huxley attended the Balliol Sunday evening concerts as a matter of
course but he was also interested in the new jazz music that was arriving from America. 'He had an old upright piano in his "sitter" and on
it he entertained us by strumming the accompaniments to our singing
of such popular numbers as "The Wedding Glide", and "He'd have to
get under, get out and get under his little machine"', Gervas recalled.
Politics, however, seem not to have engaged the smart Balliol intellectual set. 'Most of us embraced a mild and indifferent Toryism and
joined the Union, though I only remember Aldous and I attending one
debate,' wrote Gervas. They were all 'wholly free' of the urge for political change which a minority at Oxford was working for and which
Huxley himself in later decades would put at the centre of his writing:

Looking back it seems extraordinary that we should have
shown such a complete lack of concern with the current
issues that were so deeply affecting our country and the
world, issues such as Irish Home Rule and the Ulster
rebellion and constitutional crisis, women's suffrage, the
Balkan Wars and their threat to the peace of Europe or
Anglo-German Colonial and Naval rivalry.[7]

As their first undergraduate year drew to a close in the summer of
1914 such political innocence no doubt quickly vanished. Huxley in
fact applied to join the Oxford Socialist Society, and in spite of
Gervas's witness, there is little evidence of any 'Toryism' of a mild or
strong variety in Huxley, though it is more than likely that he held the
usual prejudices of his class. In particular, casually anti-Semitic
remarks seem to have been endemic at the time in this layer of English

society. The Secretary of the Socialist Society was R. Palme Dutt, a Balliol contemporary, who enrolled Huxley – some time between 1914 and 1916 – as a full member. This involved making a declaration of socialist faith – or at any rate signing what was known as 'The Basis' (originally the old Fabian Basis) affirming acceptance of the principles of socialism:

> I recall the picture of him scrutinising most precisely, with the aid of the magnifying glass he used to aid his eyesight, the small print of the Basis, and then declaring his satisfaction and signing, but adding that he did not want to be 'an economic type of Socialist', since he hated economics, and supported Socialism for the same reasons as Oscar Wilde had done.[8]

The allusion is to Oscar Wilde's *The Soul of Man under Socialism* (1891), a significant one since Huxley's mature preference was for a politics of decentralisation and of small self-governing communities very similar to the classic libertarian anarchist tradition. That tendency is also present in what many have seen as the serious political vision which underpins the playful surface paradoxes of Wilde's essay. The alternative socialist tradition of statism and democratic centralism was one that was wholly unsympathetic for Huxley and in later years he was to prove equally forthright in his opposition both to communism and to fascism. At this stage, however, he was primarily an aesthete and it was the arts group of the Socialist Society which mostly engaged him. With Tommy Earp (later an art critic for the *Daily Telegraph*) and Grattan Esmonde (subsequently a Sinn Fein MP) and others, the group, in February 1916, launched a magazine called the *Palatine Review*, where Huxley's first writing appeared. Naomi Mitchison remembered: 'He was of course in Oxford politics, including the University Co-Op Shop, which had been started on highly ideological grounds, with a room above for discussions.' The socialist writer G.D.H. Cole was one of the members of the Co-Op as was Tommy Earp who had a pair of pyjamas made out of Liberty's silk by the Co-Operative dressmaker.

Quite soon, during that first year at Oxford, Aldous and Gervas began to visit Cherwell, the home of Professor and Mrs Haldane in the Banbury Road where open house was kept for friends of their son, Jack ('JBS') and daughter Naomi. Naomi thought that Lord Edward Tantamount in *Point Counter Point* might have been suggested by her father. The civilised and lively atmosphere of Cherwell was a welcome relief from undergaduate irritations such as the 'infernally stupid'[9] Pass Moderations which Aldous completed in February 1914 and Holy Scripture ('Divvers') which he passed at the second attempt in December of that year. He was still enjoying his reading and was bored only by the lesser poets of the eighteenth century: 'It is melancholy work ploughing thro' the "elegancies" and "just thoughts" in which they all abound,'[10] he complained to his father. Staying briefly in the summer at Hadspen House, home of the Hobhouse family at Castle Cary, in Somerset, he formed the idea of writing a poem for the Newdigate Prize – his great uncle and his brother Julian had both won it – which he had learned was on the theme of Glastonbury. He would eventually write the poem, but its cynical tone and a reference to the Kaiser as 'Sweet William with his homely cottage smell', was too much for the examiners.[11] During the summer, he and his friends had sought relief from the monasticism of the all-male colleges, which in those days, according to Gervas, did not fraternise with the women's colleges, in the company of Naomi and her friends. In the Haldanes' long garden running down to the Cher, in the summer term of 1914, only weeks before war was declared, plays were performed. One was written by Naomi 'about an imaginary country, Saunes Bairos, in the Andes under a vaguely Mayan culture'.[12] Another consisted of excerpts from Gilbert Murray's translation of Aristophanes' *Frogs*. Aldous and Gervas had parts, the former was Charon and the latter his slave. Lewis Gielgud, who was a nephew of Ellen Terry, doubled as Dionysus and stage manager. Naomi later recalled how the end of that summer and the outbreak of war (days before Trev killed himself) 'was for me and many another the end of the old life and the beginning of the personal evil and loss which we were going to experience'. At the end of term, Aldous visited relatives in Scotland then returned to his father's house at Westbourne Terrace from where he sent to Jelly D'Aranyi a book that had belonged to Trev. 'With all his books here,' Aldous told her, 'all the traces of him left in the character of our room, still fresh – it is hard sometimes to believe that he isn't just away and coming back in a day or two, to live the old life – sitting with his book and pipe in front of the fire in the evenings.'[13]

In October 1914, Aldous returned to a different Oxford, no longer in college but lodging now with the Haldanes at Cherwell. 'Oxford in wartime still managed a certain amount of gaiety,' according to Naomi, 'but the colleges were emptying.' Aldous played the piano while she danced and 'asked me what being in love was like'. He was trying to find the answer to that question with Jelly, whom he had seen briefly in the summer in London and to whom he confessed, 'I'm not good at expressing my feelings – Still, they are there.' He said he would try to 'grub up' some poems to show her at their next meeting 'but I warn you that I am not a poet – except perhaps in a certain didactically flippant manner, particularly irritating to the high-minded.' He added, 'I am destined to write some long work of satiric and philosophic tendencies – poetry only doubtfully – but quite entertaining.'[14] Julian and Aldous had both fallen under the spell of Jelly, whom Julian recalled playing at a Balliol Sunday evening concert: 'She was then only sixteen, a lovely creature with hair hanging down her back,'[15] Julian recalled. Aldous continued to write to her during the new term, starting one letter late one Tuesday night:

> You ought to see Balliol now – it's too curious. There are
> only about 60 undergraduates up and the whole of the
> front quad is filled with soldiers: there are 250 of them
> there, sleeping four or five in a room – a lot in my old
> room: I'm only hoping they won't smash my pictures and
> spoil my books . . . Most of my time now is spent in
> reading the most dreadful stuff for my work – Anglo-
> Saxon, the language of my ancestors a thousand years
> ago – you have no idea how extremely difficult it is and
> most of it fearfully dull . . . The abominable clock on the
> mantlepiece has ticked away into Wednesday morning
> and it was Tuesday night when I started. One day older!

How very unpleasant. I do most desperately want to be
always young. The only advantage of age, as far as I can
see, is that one's ideas begin to settle down: one's mind
becomes tidy instead of one great changing muddle as it
is when one is young. But I don't think it makes it worth
while being old.[16]

I do most desperately want to be always young. Aldous had suffered
so much already. His friends were starting to go off to war. The old,
who had manufactured this war, were not estimable. (Though his
first reactions to the war were conventionally patriotic.[17]) He would
one day write a book about a man who wanted to be always young
and who, like Swift's Struldbugs in *Gulliver's Travels*, discovered what
a horror being kept perpetually alive can be. But he was young and
ardent, and something of the candour that his friends cherished in
him – the obverse of what an outsider might see as bumptious arrogance – is visible in this letter (one of the several hundred that have
never been published before). Cherwell was far preferable to an empty
Balliol, but as he pointed out to Jelly, 'One has so few friends left to
one these days, when everyone has gone off to the wars, that those
who are left, are still more precious than they were before.'[18] To Jelly,
he unbuttoned himself more than in his brightly facetious letters to
his father or to Julian (letters to whom always seemed designed, just
a little, to impress the elder brother). He was clearly lonely, and confessed, 'One always feels so queer in the middle of the night, dreadfully
melancholy, and fierce, and sentimental, and bored.'

Literature, like friendship, was one of the necessary consolations
and he was discovering Baudelaire: 'Wonderful stuff French poetry –
I once tried to write some myself, without much success, as you might
imagine.' But he was conscious of his isolation and wanted to do
something for the war effort, perhaps working in some kind of non-
combative capacity. But the same cause – his defective eyesight –
seemed at first to rule out both. Gervas thought that 1914 was a worse
blow in many ways than having to leave Eton in consequence of his
blindness because the friendships from which he was now cut off
were profounder ones than those he had made with his schoolboy

chums. 'I have always felt that this second isolation must have been an even greater blow to Aldous than the first,'[19] he wrote. 'It was a forlorn and deserted Balliol, haunted by the ghosts of his friends, to which Aldous went back that October.' The two young men had been very close and now, in khaki, Gervas – Huxley Major to Huxley Minor – was not to see his cousin until the end of the war, except for a chance meeting at Paddington Station that Christmas (and a brief glimpse while on sick leave in June 1915 which seems to have slipped Gervas's memory). Gervas was on his way to Grimsby to join his regiment bound for Flanders. They did some Christmas shopping, then Aldous saw him off at King's Cross. 'I well remember how reassuring was his familiar presence in those hours of uncertain expectation, and how deeply comforting it was to know that, whatever the Fates might have in store, his friendship would always be with me.'

By the start of 1915, Aldous was very well settled in to life at Cherwell, in his large room next to the schoolroom where he played the piano and read continuously. He shared French conversation sessions with the Haldanes and a French speaker, Yvette Chapelain, who had been stranded in Oxford since before the war. Aldous was now reading mediaeval writers like Lydgate and Occleve whom he found 'terrible people'[20]. His historical imagination was only really kindled by the seventeenth century and after – though he adored Chaucer. He had become secretary of Walter Raleigh's essay society but the essays were read mostly to American undergraduates for most of his fellows, including Gervas and Jack Haldane, had gone off to what Huxley gloomily predicted would be 'a Thirty Years War'. It seemed that he and 'Sligger' Urquhart, the don, were 'the only two possible people left alive in Oxford'. He sent his poem on Glastonbury to Julian for his inspection, describing it as 'an experiment in realism'.[21] He added that his motto was now: 'Realism, in art and letters, in everything, except life.' Mediaeval miracle plays, Hardy's 'turgid' The Dynasts, had to be got through, not to mention 'the quiet life of Anglo-Saxon lectures amid a crowd of painful young women'. There is a bumptious, undergraduate tone in these letters from Oxford and plenty of self-confident, callow judgements: 'with the exception of Shakespeare's best – all Elizabethan tragedy is melodrama'.[22] But there were also more thoughtful observations where the essential Huxley decency came through. He told Leonard Huxley in April that: 'This hustling of aliens is rather damnable – mob-law.'[23] He felt the Government was taking 'repressive action' against foreigners simply to appease popular opinion: 'soon we shall be reduced to writing Hymns of Hate'. Huxley hated English xenophobia but at such a moment it was clearly flourishing. He turned to French poetry, especially 'the modern men' like Mallarmé 'who never says what he means, whose syntax is extremely peculiar and who prints his works without any punctuation except full-stops'.[24] A writer who always said what he meant and who had little passion for literary experimenters in his own tongue, Huxley nonetheless remained a lifelong admirer of Mallarmé. He also read Proust's *A la recherche du temps perdu* when it first started to appear in 1913. But literary discovery could not obscure the reality of war. Kitchener's armies were on the move 'so that I shall have a lot more friends out at the front – which I don't like – friends matter more than anything, when one is young,'[25] he told Jelly.

Throughout the hot summer of 1915, and from holiday at Connel Ferry, Argyll in Scotland, Aldous continued to write to Jelly. From a 'hot and stuffy' Oxford in June, and in his best undergraduate manner, he told her: 'When all my friends are dead I shall become a hermit, and live in a cave – and perhaps you will come occasionally and feed me with buns thro' the bars of my gate. It would be a charming life!'[26] He was walking with a limp just now, having short-sightedly walked into a bowl of nitric acid left outside the laboratory by one of the assistants of Professor Haldane (from whom Aldous was deriving much scientific knowledge). He left Oxford planning to return in September to read for the Stanhope Prize on the theme of 'The Development of Satire from Restoration to Revolution'. He told his father that the raw material was in Bodley – 'a huge corpus of ribald anonymity'.[27] There is once again a relaxed, flippant tone in these letters to his Edwardian pater which suggests that the relationship may not have been as difficult as some, like Gervas, insisted. He enjoyed the holiday at Connel Ferry. The beauty of the Scottish landscape and its calm, he told Jelly, 'all helps to mellow the thought, that one's friends are being killed, into a quiet kind of resigned sadness'.[28]

Huxley did not leave it there, however, and began to display to Jelly a new dimension of his mind. For the first time, we see the beginnings of that other Huxley, the unitive intelligence that would seek the kinds of large, universal truth he eventually explored in *The Perennial Philosophy* (1946):

> One does feel tremendously, when one is in this beautiful
> country, that one is part of a larger soul, which embraces
> everything . . . It looks as though the amount of good
> and evil were about the same in the world. I think the
> good will probably win in the end – though not
> necessarily, unless the most persistent and tremendous
> efforts are made . . . But I'm not a pessimist, and I think
> it will be all right. I think we shall ultimately work all the
> disorder into a single principle, which will be an
> Absolute – but which at present exists only potentially
> and at the nature of which we can only very dimly
> guess.[29]

Those who would chide Huxley, after the mid-1930s, for allowing the cynical satirist to give place to the idealist and the intellectual and moral seeker, ignore the fact that his mind was always disposed in a certain fashion, seeking organic unity, and trying to discover essential meanings in the world of surface phenomena. To Jelly, he quickly declared: 'This is rather rambling!' but it was a pointer. He closed the letter with a sonnet in French which he had just written, entitled 'Sentimalité d'un Soir d'Été'. Back in London, a month later, he had recovered his flippancy in time for his twenty-first birthday and was able to inform Jelly: 'Well, I'm twenty-one today – grown up – what a good opportunity to be sentimental about the days of my youth!'[30]

Taking stock of his youth, he might reflect that he had written a few stories, a few poems in English and French and a few translations. His poetry was clearly influenced by the French symbolists he was reading with rapture at the time – Mallarmé, Rimbaud, Laforgue, Baudelaire – and though these poems might strike us now as mannered and clotted with literary effects, they were helping to make his name in

Oxford. The first poem to be published was 'Home-Sickness – From the Town' in the annual *Oxford Poetry* for 1915.[31] Its general style and mood can be caught in the opening lines: 'Frou-Frouery and faint patchouli smells,/And debile virgins talking Keats.' Huxley's comment to Julian on Laforgue – 'he is interesting and amusing and intensely young, which is all that matters'[32] – gives some insight into his poetics at this time. But he also claimed to be writing 'an immense didactic poem' – a rather un-Laforgueian project. He described, in addition, 'a little poem on the habits of the MOLE' (which would be published in the first issue of *The Palatine Review* in February 1916) and regretted that his Newdigate poem had been dismissed by the Oxford judges – who in fact decided that year not to award the prize to anyone. The Oxford Professor of Poetry, Sir Herbert Warren, observed that 'there was one Byronic production; amused us very much, but we did not know whether it was meant to be serious'. Huxley protested to Julian, mockingly: 'as if it wasn't manifest that the thing was positively EARNEST!' His terms of praise for John Donne were characteristic: 'intense intellectuality, intense passion, concealed and restrained, intense sadness'.[33] Fulke-Greville also possessed 'intense intellectuality' – a Huxley *desideratum* – and it was he who would later provide the epigraph to *Point Counter Point*. Already, Huxley the lover of clarity and light was aware that it was that very intellectuality that could render a poet like Fulke-Greville 'obscure'.

In October 1915, Huxley returned to Oxford for his final year. Naomi had scarlet fever so Cherwell was out of the question. Aldous moved back into Balliol, an experience that was deeply moving as he began to contemplate the casualty lists of his former friends. He tried to explain his feelings to Jelly:

> This war impresses on me more than ever the fact that
> friendship, love, whatever you like to call it is the only
> reality. When one is young and one's mind is in a
> perpetual state of change and chaos it seems to remain as
> the one stable and reliable thing. It simply is truth in the
> highest form we can attain to. You never knew my
> mother – I wish you had because she was a very

> wonderful woman: Trev was most like her. I have just
> been reading what she wrote to me just before she died.
> The last words of her letter were 'Don't be too critical of
> other people and "love much".' – and I have come to see
> more and more how wise that advice was. It's a warning
> against a rather conceited and selfish fault of my own
> and it's a whole philosophy of life.[34]

Once again, unbuttoning himself to someone close to him, Huxley reveals a tenderness and a deep moral sense that run counter to the image of him prevalent in the twenties as a ruthless, amoral writer concerned only to shock. A few weeks after writing these words, he was complaining about the suppression of D.H. Lawrence's *The Rainbow* – 'It is always the serious books that get sat on'.[35] Such comments are an index of his refusal to compromise on intellectual values, to trim his sails for the benefit of those whose morality was worn on the sleeve.

Within weeks of taking up residence at Balliol, Huxley was to receive an invitation into a world where such attitudes would receive automatic acceptance. An entry in the visitor's book at Garsington Manor in Oxfordshire on 29 November 1915 shows the name of Huxley alongside Philip Heseltine and others. It was his first visit, and the beginning of a new and wider circle of acquaintance that included novelists, poets, painters, philosophers who had made or were in the process of making their mark in the world. For a young man who was now an aspiring writer – albeit with no clear view about whether he wished to be a poet or a novelist but certain only of his ambition – this was a peculiarly exciting milieu. He seized the opportunities it offered with both hands.

Notes

1   *L*.54
2   HRC, Letter to Jelly D'Aranyi, undated
3   *L*.55

4 James Lansdale Hodson, *No Phantoms Here* (1932), p257
5 *L.*56
6 Gervas Huxley, *Both Hands*, pp68–9
7 *Ibid.*, p70
8 Reading, Letter from R. Palme Dutt to Sybille Bedford, 28 May 1968
9 *L.*57
10 *L.*58
11 See Julian Huxley, *Memories 1*, p62
12 Naomi Mitchison, *Small Talk: Memories of an Edwardian Childhood* (1973), p44
13 HRC, Letter from AH to Jelly D'Aranyi undated but probably September 1914
14 HRC. Letter to Jelly from Cherwell, undated but probably October 1914
15 *Memories 1*, p60
16 HRC, Letter to Jelly, written from Cherwell, undated but probably October 1914
17 See, for example, *L.*62: 'What news today! It's splendid.'
18 *L.*63
19 *Mem. Vol.*, p61
20 *L.*64
21 *L.*66
22 *L.*67
23 *L.*69
24 *L.*67
25 HRC, Letter to Jelly D'Aranyi from Balliol undated but probably April 1915 (see *L.*69)
26 HRC, Letter to Jelly D'Aranyi from Cherwell 5 June 1915
27 *L.*71
28 *L.*73
29 *L.*73
30 *L.*74
31 Never reprinted by Huxley it is quoted in full in SB1.55–6
32 *L.*81
33 *L.*81
34 *L.*83
35 *L.*85

V

Garsington

Garsington Manor in Oxfordshire, a legendary site in early twentieth century English literary and artistic life, was the home, from 1915 to 1927, of Philip and Lady Ottoline Morrell. Ottoline was the half sister of the sixth Duke of Portland and Philip was Liberal MP for Burnley in Lancashire. They were not excessively rich by the standards of the day but the Bohemianism over which Ottoline presided was very definitely of the salon not the garret. A great deal – perhaps too much – has been written about Garsington. Its posthumous reputation has tended to rise and fall in line with that of Bloomsbury which supplied it with many of its characters and anecdotes. It is nonetheless worth quoting the judgement of David Garnett as being representative of those who came to enjoy Ottoline's hospitality but without losing their critical faculty. (One has some sympathy in fact for a woman who was repayed so unkindly for the hospitality she lavished; as well as Huxley's effort in caricature in *Crome Yellow*, she was Hermione in Lawrence's *Women in Love*, Lady Septuagesima Goodley in Osbert Sitwell's *Triple Fugue* (1921), and appeared also in Gilbert Cannan's *Pugs and Peacocks* (1921).) 'Though in no way an artist,' Garnett observed, 'she was an original character who managed by strength of will to escape from the conventionality of her upbringing, without losing her position in Society . . .

Spiritually her best quality was generosity: her worst, meanness and
the love of power. The good and evil in her waged frequent warfare.'[1] Virginia Woolf observed bitchily that: 'She had a great gift for
drawing people under. Even Middleton Murry, it is said, was pulled
down by her among the vegetables of Garsington.'[2] A more sympathetic observer, Lord David Cecil, observed 'she seemed built on the
Elizabethan scale with Elizabethan grandeur, imagination, and passion'. Moreover, 'though she had been born into the great world, she
had left it early and during the First War had lived in open opposition to it'.[3] This hints at the special flavour of Garsington, at its sense
of being at once privileged and anti-Establishment in its political
and social sympathies. In contrast to other artistic patronesses –
such as Sybil Colefax, whose visitors' book would also soon record
Huxley's name, and who was accused of merely collecting celebrities –
Ottoline Morrell exercised shrewd discrimination in her choice of
guests and had an eye for originality, including emergent originality.
It is not known how she 'discovered' Huxley, who at that stage had
merely a reputation as a brilliant undergraduate and an incipient
poet, but, six months after finally moving in to the Manor in May
(there had been delays with a sitting tenant), she invited Huxley to
join the party at the end of November. She chose to introduce him at
lunch as the grandson of Thomas Henry Huxley. Almost immediately, this encounter at Garsington resulted in a meeting with D.H.
Lawrence. Both men were impressed with each other and a friendship was formed that lasted until Lawrence's death in 1930 (he died in
the arms of Huxley's wife). Huxley's account of that first Sunday at
Garsington was up to the standards of acerbity normally adhered to
by Ottoline's guests. He told his father (who was to prove too
straight-laced to appreciate the freedom of the Garsington atmosphere):

> I had an amusing day on Sunday – going out to
> Garsington for luncheon to the Philip Morrells, who have
> bought the lovely Elizabethan manor there. Lady
> Ottoline, Philip's wife, is a quite incredible creature – arty
> beyond the dreams of avarice and a patroness of

literature and the modernities. She is intelligent, but her
affectation is overwhelming. Her husband, the MP, is a
conceited ass, very amiable, but quite a buffoon.[4]

Huxley was sharpening the tools that would be used to create *Crome
Yellow* six years later. He was not alone in his judgement of Philip.
David Garnett recalled that Morrell, 'posing as a farmer, exhibited
precisely the kind of humbug which the Victorian novelists, such as
Surtees and Thackeray, loved to make the subject of their good-
tempered fun . . . He was addicted to double-breasted waistcoats.'
He was also addicted to cutting the hair of the numerous young
women at Garsington in the prevailing page-boy fashion started at
the Slade, and trying his chances with them. Everyone was
enchanted with the manor house itself. 'It was noble, even grand, yet
it was the very reverse of ostentatious,' thought Garnett. Ottoline
had transformed the rooms, 'stamping her personality ruthlessly
everywhere . . . The oak panelling had been painted a dark peacock
blue-green; the bare and sombre dignity of Elizabethan wood and
stone had been overwhelmed with an almost oriental magnificence.'
The triumph was 'the Red room' where everyone gathered around
the fire in the evenings. In her diary of that first summer of 1915,
overshadowed by the war, Ottoline wrote: 'I should like to make
this place into a harbour, a refuge in the storm, where those who
haven't been swept away could come and renew themselves and go
forth strengthened.'[5] This sounds as if it were Lady Ottoline's war
effort. For the next few years, Huxley would be a regular visitor and
would meet here Lawrence, Bertrand Russell, Mark Gertler,
Katherine Mansfield, Middleton Murry, Lytton Strachey, Desmond
McCarthy, Virginia Woolf, Clive Bell, Dorothy Brett, Dorothy
Carrington, Mary Hutchinson, Gerald Shove, and countless others –
a roll-call of Bloomsbury's most celebrated names. So frequent were
his visits that the staff referred to one particular guest room as 'Mr
Huxley's room'. He was in no doubt that he had been one of those
renewed and strengthened in Ottoline's sanctuary, and was dis-
mayed at the later rift caused by her (understandable) anger at the
way she was portrayed as Mrs Wimbush in *Crome Yellow* (the house

in that novel, of course bore no architectural similarity whatsoever to Garsington).

She herself recalled her impression of Huxley on that first visit in November 1915:

> A very thin, very tall, delicate young man, with a very
> beautiful serious face arrived, dressed in a corduroy coat
> and cut breeches and stockings [he had bicycled over
> from Oxford]. His eyesight was very bad, which made
> him stoop in order to view things closely. He was rather
> silent and aloof, and I felt as he sat during the afternoon
> that he was rather bored, for we happened to be alone
> that Sunday.

Her reaction was characteristic of the way many people responded to Huxley. His silence and reserve – 'he was very shy',[6] according to Sybille Bedford – could be unsettling, especially when it was suddenly broken by some brilliant observation or unexpected flow of talk. Clever people are often mistrusted and Huxley, seeing other people imperfectly, impossibly tall, impatient of silly small talk, must often have been taken to be 'aloof'. Lytton Strachey – who might have been thought to have found in Huxley a kindred spirit in the sport of urbane mockery – complained to Ottoline that he was 'too Oxfordy' and 'frivolous'.[7] Katherine Mansfield found him too much of an innocent and mocked him behind his back, making fun of his famous conversational tic – '*incredible*'. Years later, in an interview, Huxley would say of Bloomsbury that in spite of the aesthetic education he received at the hands of Roger Fry: 'It was a rather limited world in a certain sense, but it was a very brilliant one.'[8] One of its limitations, in terms of humane sympathy, was its fondness for cruel gossip.

Another witness at that first lunch was the young and beautiful Swiss governess, Juliette Baillot, who had been appointed – after an interview with the Morrells conducted in the first-class waiting room on Oxford station – to look after their daughter who was christened Julian. In her memoir, *Leaves from the Tulip Tree* (1986) Juliette recalled the brilliant young man (whose elder brother, Julian, she would eventually marry) dismounting from his bicycle:

> His six-foot-two [actually it was six-foot-four-and-a-half] seemed even taller because of the slenderness of his body and his slight stoop. Under the thick brown hair his wide face was pale, with full lips and blue eyes which had an inwards look until one realised that he was totally blind in one eye and not seeing fully with the other . . . On this first occasion he was mostly silent but when he spoke, the mellow quality of his voice and the quality of what he said was surprising. The unusual beauty of his face, unselfconscious, with its elusive gaze (best said in French *un regard intérieur*), a slightly detached serenity – not shy, but self-contained, and added to this strange name, Aldous, made a memorable impression.[9]

Not long after this, Juliette took Julian to tea with the brilliant young man in his rooms at Balliol – where Ottoline herself would be entertained on another occasion, finding Aldous and his aesthetic undergraduate companions 'so soft and effeminate, elegant with gentle, affected movements and voices'.[10] Juliette remembered: 'He entertained us with delicious lemon tea and crumpets, speaking impeccable French, as well as reciting Lewis Carroll, *Struwelpeter, Max und Moritz*, all the cherished bits and pieces which had nourished his childhood. Half-teasing, half-serious, he treated us with a special courtesy.'

The meeting with Lawrence took place on 10 December 1915. At Lady Ottoline's suggestion, Lawrence had written to Huxley on 7 December asking him to come over to his house at Byron Villas, Vale of Health in Hampstead. 'Lady Ottoline Morrell wrote to me, that we ought to know each other,'[11] Lawrence explained. Lawrence was planning to go to Florida to found a community – 'a sort of unanimist colony'[12] as Huxley put it to Julian. Huxley always recalled vividly that 'wintry afternoon'[13] in Hampstead: 'Before tea was over he asked me if I would join the colony, and though I was an intellectually cautious young man, not at all inclined to enthusiasms, though Lawrence had startled and embarrassed me with sincerities of a kind to which my upbringing had not accustomed me, I answered yes.' The terms in which Huxley describes this encounter – the reference to the different expectations raised by his upbringing – hint at the nature of this unusual relationship between the cerebrotonic, the rational man, and the passionate, visceral, anti-scientific, novelist. It ought not to have worked but it did. Lawrence wrote to Ottoline after their first meeting: 'I liked Huxley very much. He will come to Florida.'[14] But the project never materialised – just as well, since Huxley had two more terms at Oxford to complete and would anyway have found it difficult to leave the country in wartime for such a venture. Ottoline had been anxious about the meeting she had engineered. 'I think he was puzzled and rather overcome, and perhaps scared, at Lawrence's quick and immediate approach, brushing away all preliminaries – vetting him, in fact, putting him under his X-ray.'[15] She also feared that Huxley was not quite the right candidate for such a utopian experiment. 'I felt how miserable Aldous, with his fastidious reserve, his delicate and perhaps over-intellectual temperament, would be if he went.' Huxley, however, reassured her. 'One can't help being very much impressed by him,' he told her, again revealing a kind of shame about his inability to respond, because of the nature of his background and education, to this quite exceptional, nakedly exposed spirit:

> There is something almost alarming about his sincerity and seriousness – something that makes one feel oneself to be the most shameful dilettante, persifleur, waster and all the rest. Not but what I think he's wrong. All that he condemns as mere dilettantism and literary flippancy – and the force of his sincerity carries one temporarily with him – all this is something much more than an excrementitious by-product of real life. It all comes back again to the question we were talking about the other day – the enrichment of emotion by intellect. And so too with Lawrence: I'm inclined to think that he would find a

life unenriched by the subtler amenities of intellect rather
sterile.[16]

Touched by a force of sincerity and passion in Lawrence that was
absent from the Bloomsbury 'persifleurs' like Strachey who gathered
round in the Red room, Huxley wasn't quite ready to forswear the
supremacy of the sceptical intellect. His continuing refusal to do so,
throughout his relationship with Lawrence, is what gives it its special
piquancy – visible in the twists and turns of his essay on Lawrence
which stands as an introduction to the selection of letters he edited.
That would come later. For now, he concluded to Ottoline: 'But I
think there's a lot in his theory of the world being in a destructive,
autumnal period.'

In the new year of 1916, Huxley's visits to Garsington became more
frequent. It was the perfect ambient for him intellectually: civilised,
witty, and daring. In addition, exposure to painters and to writers on
art like Roger Fry played a formative role in his aesthetic education.
Though some of the guests at Garsington were pacifists and conscientious objectors (Philip Morrell, in the House of Commons, had
spoken out against the war), Huxley was not at this stage of their
number and, early in 1916, he submitted himself – rather hopelessly in
view of his curtailed vision – to the army recruiting office. One
Thursday morning in January he went before a major to be sworn in
or 'attested' for service but, having taken one look at the blinking
poet, the major refused to go any further, 'saying it was the most
abject folly to go thro' all the farce with someone so almost certainly
unfit'.[17] A doctor examined Huxley, pronouncing him 'totally unfit –
class 1 category A', and he was sent back to Oxford. Instead of the
trenches, he spent the first days of the new term in the stuffy, over-
heated atmosphere of the Bodleian Library, swotting for the Stanhope
Prize. Huxley's special subject for 1916 was Milton, whom he was
forced to swallow with 'a nauseous diet of Anglo-Saxon'.[18] Academic
work was interspersed with visits to Garsington where Huxley at last
made the acquaintance of 'the strange creature Lytton Strachey . . . a
long-haired and bearded individual very like a Russian in appearance and very entertaining'.[19] He told Naomi Haldane about the 'japes

and harmless practical jokes'[20] that went on at these weekend parties at Garsington. In February, he attended her wedding to Dick Mitchison at the Oxford Registry Office. 'Pity it's not to be ecclesiastical,' he told her, 'I would have made such an excellent page.' She later recalled: 'In the gaps between slaughters we were being teenagers with our own delights and problems, and embarassments and importances and giggles and glimpses of overwhelming beauty and excitement.' There was also the cinema, another American import, like jazz, which Huxley was very interested by – though in the next decade he would sound a very different note. Huxley saw the film version of *Jane Eyre* after which he said he wanted to see *Birth of a Nation* which was 'said to mark quite a new epoch in cinematographic art'.[21]

Huxley was leading an increasingly social existence at this time, dining at All Souls', lunching with all the most important and interesting people in Oxford, and beginning to make himself known as a writer. The Socialist Society's new *Palatine Review* was just about to be launched and Huxley was touting for subscriptions at three-and-six for six issues. He hoped that Julian, now in an academic post in Texas, would help to recruit subscribers in the USA. H.W. Massingham of *The Nation* saw the first issue of the *Review* with Huxley's poem, 'Mole', in it and asked him to submit some poems to him. But it was not all dazzle and self-indulgent enjoyment. One day in February, Huxley went to listen to the Oxford tribunal which dealt with appeals against conscription and was appalled at the callousness and at the injustices done. His report of the experience to his father shows the humane side of Huxley, angered by the 'petty tyrannies and the wholesale attempts to cheat men into the army',[22] and by the rough treatment of conscientious objectors. Not so 'disgustingly hectored' as they were in London, Huxley still felt that 'the tribunals are far from treating them with the respect to which they are entitled both by the Act and by ordinary good feeling'. He concluded: 'The whole thing enormously decreases popular sympathy with the war.' He was also appalled by the xenophobia of the popular media like the *Daily Express* with their nicknames for foreigners and their whipping up of crude emotions. 'This sentimental honeymoon of hate has gone on long enough,' he told his father, 'it is time we settled down to thinking reasonably about each other.'[23] He was also sympathetic to the case of an undergraduate of St John's College, J.A. Kaufmann, a German Jew who had anglicised his name to Kaye, and who had been harangued by members of the tribunal after he applied for exemption on the grounds of conscientious objection to war and being an international socialist. Huxley's moral engagement with public issues and his essentially humane stance were growing. He still wanted to do something for the war effort (even as he was repelled by the war's reverberations in civil life, the erosion of civil liberty and the threat of 'collapse of English civilisation'[24] from militarisation). One possibility was to work for one of the Government departments. He had toyed over the winter with volunteering for work in the Foreign Press department of the War Office but, as he explained to Julian, the twelve to fourteen hour days would have been 'quite beyond my ocular abilities to stand the strain'.[25] The longer the war went on, the more he came to detest it, telling his brother: 'At the beginning I shd. have liked very much to fight: but now, if I could (having seen all the results), I think I'd be a conscientious objector, or nearly so. But I shudder to think what England will be like afterwards – barely habitable.'

Meanwhile, of course, there was Garsington as a refuge and a visible incarnation of the civilisation being fought for. 'The Morrell household is among the most delightful I know: always interesting people there and v. good talk: I go over from Oxford often to see them.' And not just the Morrells. 'I saw the amiable Barbara Hiles there the other day – very entertaining, and gipsy-esque with short hair and gold earrings.' Huxley had not, however, allowed the charms of Barbara Hiles to blot out those of Jelly d'Aranyi. The latter remained a very special confidante, to whom he unburdened himself more intimately than with anyone else at this stage of his life. After a brief visit at Easter to Stocks, followed by a walking holiday with Tommy Earp, business manager of the *Palatine Review*, in the Cotswolds – to Chipping Campden and Snow's Hill – Huxley returned to Oxford in May to work for his finals. He worked so hard, he told Jelly, 'that I feel I could almost shoot myself in the evenings out of sheer boredom'.[26] To assuage that boredom he had taken to going for long walks at night on his own 'miles and miles by the river till I get more cheerful again. Even if one wants to feel depressed one can't after an hour in the wind and the moonlight. So then I sing like a crow – symphonies and old French songs and things – and think of nice things and come back quite happy – and tonight I've done some work: but it's late and I'm falling to sleep in spite of strong coffee.' In another letter in the same month, he told Jelly that sometimes 'one despairs about things with this vampire of a war draining the life and soul out of the world'.[27] Already, he was beginning to think about his future beyond Finals. He might go to America to visit Julian – who will of course have changed. 'But I myself am so different from what I was two years ago. This is the period of one's life, I think, when one passes most rapidly from stage to stage of one's development. In many ways Julian is like me: but in certain points very different.' Jelly, too, was told how wonderful was Ottoline Morrell: 'I feel in her house most completely "at home" in a more congenial atmosphere than almost anywhere else.' And certainly more so than in his father's house at 27 Westbourne Square.

The most obvious career for Huxley would be teaching, preferably at Oxford, but his father recommended trying a temporary post at a public school, an idea which Huxley agreed was sensible, 'though I would not propose to adopt it permanently'.[28] But first the hurdle of Schools had to be surmounted, one which, he told Leonard, was 'more tiring than any labour I have ever undertaken. Not only is the mental strain great, but the physical strain on the eyes – even using a type-writer – is very considerable: and I stagger out of the papers feeling as if I had been bruised all over after an acute attack of influenza.'[29] By the middle of June, however, it was all over. His first good academic news of the summer was winning the Stanhope essay prize which gave him £20 to spend on some of the best modern scholarly editions of his favourite authors – Chaucer, Donne, Beaumont and Fletcher (though he told Julian he would have preferred the hard cash). But the pressure to find employment remained insistent. At the end of June he left the 'malarial dampness' of Oxford and went to London to investigate possible 'ways of escaping the work-house'.[30] The Oxford Appointments Committee said it would circulate his details to various headmasters but he decided to make his own approaches to Eton. It was to be, as he facetiously set out the options to Julian, either '(a) To disseminate mendacity in our great Modern Press. (b) To disseminate mendacity in our Great Modern Public Schools.'[31] Of the two he preferred the latter, interspersed with 'bouts of mild journalismus'. The imminent publication of his first book of poems, though more important than anything else, would have little bearing on the matter of earning a living. Nor, for that matter would the news, which arrived on 2 July, that he had been one of only two people to win a First in English – he shared this honour with a young woman from Somerville, M.D Niven. He was delighted to read in a list in the Sunday papers 'the most wonderful version of my name, viz ALDORES HUXLEY – which is most gloriously Spanish'.[32]

Almost immediately, Huxley was offered a temporary job by the headmaster of Repton School, Geoffrey Fisher – later Archbishop of Canterbury. His predecessor – though this was not actually stated – had been sacked and Huxley found himself teaching Latin to the Lower Fourth and English and History to other forms. Although this was a stop-gap, lasting only to the end of the summer term, it seemed to him a very poor use of his brilliant First. He had just visited Eton, and hoped to get a post there, but the same problem – public schools at that time did not teach English literature so he would have to teach classics – would recur. He also went for interview to Rugby, where he was worried that the school was 'traditionally ill-behaved and violent' and thus not suitable for a short-sighted aesthete like himself.[33] The school in turn was worried that 'I should not be able to see well enough to supervise the boys'. He boasted to Ottoline: 'No less than 6 Headmasters have implored me to consider their claims for next term.' A university job, however, would be preferable and he wondered if W.P. Ker would know of a place in London University or elsewhere. He was experiencing the familiar rude transition from the intellectual and other pleasures of undergraduate life to the brutal realities of the world of work. 'It's a wrench going down from Oxford: the place becomes as personal as an old house,'[34] he told his old headmaster, Gidley Robinson (apparently bearing him no grudge now for the prep-school bullying). It was also very lonely in digs, a far cry from the gregarious vitality of Garsington and Oxford which he had last tasted in the week before going to Repton. Then he had taken 'Oxford's most charming undergraduate (female)'[35] to a theatre, and found himself staying in the same house as her, acting charades in the middle of Bagley Wood with her and their friends 'like children' and sleeping on top of a haystack under a tarpaulin.

At Repton there was a fellow master he had known at Oxford called Victor Gollancz but little other company. He fired off letters to all his friends. Frances Petersen was told that the masters were all 'Calibans',[36] that the whole experience was 'bloody', and asked to send a two ounce packet of tobacco from the University Co-op; the poet Robert Nicholls heard that 'it is really quite fun simulating the possession of knowledge';[37] and Jelly, in a letter written on a piece of paper torn out of a school exercise book, was informed, 'I don't think I shall become a schoolmaster unless I can help it.'[38] He begged her to write, because 'letters are pleasant here as I am rather lonely and gloomy at times, not knowing anyone here'. He struggled to deal with the continuing reports of fatalities and, in his remarks to Jelly, gave some hint of the sort of post-war mood that would develop amongst him and his friends:

> Already quite a number of our friends have been killed in
> our offensive and I fear many more will go before it's
> over. What I feel about it is that the thing one must not
> do is look back. Certainly one way that people survive
> after they are dead is in the society to which they
> belonged and particularly in their friends. To look back is
> a kind of betrayal of the life entrusted to one: one must
> go forward. The best way of remembering them is not by
> dwelling on the past but the future.[38]

To Ottoline, whom he had failed to get over to see before leaving for Repton because his bicycle – 'my poor Rosinante' – suffered mechanical failure, he offered up the social comedy of Repton: the headmaster, Fisher, ('a hearty parson'[39]) with whom he had tea on arrival, in the company of a selection of 'local ladies – all definitely low-comedy in type – red-nosed spinsters who bridled and mopped and mowed and asked one "whether London was full" . . . oh these old masters! They speak with pride of having been here forty years: there is one who has a disease of going to sleep on all occasions, and another who is a dipsomaniac, and another who is indubitably possessed by the devil, and another whose sole knowledge of the classics consists in the 15th book of the Iliad, nothing other than which will he teach – is in fact incapable of teaching anything but it: he has been here since the Crimean War.' This is the world – and the critical view of it – that would reappear in Huxley's early novels.

By the summer, he would be back at Garsington. It was there that an event occurred which he reported to Julian on 2 July, just before leaving for Repton: 'I have at last discovered a nice Belgian: wonders will never cease.'[40] He had made one of the most important discoveries of his life.

Notes

1 David Garnett, *The Flowers of the Forest: Being Volume Two of the Golden Echo* (1955), p37
2 Virginia Woolf, *Moments of Being* (1976), p206
3 Lord David Cecil, 'Introduction' to *Lady Ottoline's Album* (1976) edited by Carolyn G. Heilbrun
4 *L*.86
5 *Ottoline at Garsington: Memoirs of Lady Ottoline Morrell, 1915–1918* (1974) edited by Robert Gathorne-Hardy, p35
6 SB in conversation with the author
7 *Ottoline at Garsington*, p199
8 Interview in *West Wind*, Fall, 1959. UCLA Huxley Collection
9 Juliette Huxley, *Leaves from the Tulip Tree* (1986; 1987 ed., pp54–5)
10 *Ottoline at Garsington*, p93
11 *Letters of D. H. Lawrence*, Vol 2, p467
12 *L*.88
13 'D.H. Lawrence', in *The Olive Tree*, p231 [reprinted from the Introduction to the Letters of Lawrence]
14 *Letters* Vol 2, p483
15 *Ottoline at Garsington*, p79

16 HRC, Letter from AH to Ottoline from Westbourne Terrace. Undated but clearly after 10 December 1916
17 *L.*89
18 *L.*90
19 *L.*89
20 Naomi Mitchison, *Small Talk*, p115
21 *L.*95
22 *L.*92
23 *L.*93
24 *L.*94
25 *L.*97
26 HRC, Letter to Jelly d'Aranyi, undated but probably May 1916
27 HRC, Letter to Jelly d'Aranyi from Balliol, 5 May 1916
28 *L.*99
29 *L.*100
30 *L.*103
31 *L.*104
32 HRC, Letter to Ottoline, August 1916
33 HRC, Letter to Ottoline Morrell from Repton, undated but probably early July 1916
34 HRC, Letter to G. Gidley Robinson from Repton, 12 July 1916
35 *L.*107
36 *L.*106
37 *L.*107
38 HRC, Letter to Jelly d'Aranyi from Repton, 17 July 1916
39 HRC, Letter to Ottoline Morrell from Repton, undated but probably July 1916
40 *L.*105

VI

Maria

The 'incomparable'[1] Maria Nys, to whom Huxley would propose marriage on a rug on the lawn at Garsington some time in the late summer or early autumn of 1916, was born in the Flanders town of Courtrai on 10 September 1898 in a prosperous bourgeois mansion on the Boulevard Van den Peereboom. Her father, Norbert Nys, owned a clothing factory and his wife, Marguerite Baltus, whose brother George Baltus was a painter and Professor of Fine Art at Glasgow University, had four daughters of whom Maria – nicknamed Yaya, her first childish attempt to mouth her name, though later her familiar name would be the Italian Coccola or 'little berry' – was the eldest. Shortly after Maria's birth, the family moved to Bellem, a small village on the canal between Ghent and Bruges, where Norbert – backed by substantial inherited capital – opened another clothing factory which would eventually end in ruin. As a child, Maria had a delicate bone structure – *comme un oiseau*,[2] her sister Suzanne wrote in an unpublished family memoir – and a curvature of the spine which caused her to be sent away to stay with her grand-mother at St Trond so that she could receive treatment from a renowned doctor at Liège. Marguerite Nys was a devout Catholic who christened her daughter after the Virgin to honour the fact that she had failed, at her first daughter's birth, to complete the last of three promised pilgrimages to the shrine at Montaigu. Educated by nuns of the Sacred Heart order in a convent at Liège, Maria's handwriting remained profoundly illegible – as a result, she claimed, of the example set her by the nun who taught her handwriting and whose hands were crippled and twisted with arthritis. Maria took ballet lessons and lessons in horse-riding, and was a clever and studious girl. The happy, privileged existence which Maria and her three sisters, Jeanne, Suzanne and Rose, enjoyed in Bellem – *dans un petit paradis*, in Suzanne's words – was shattered by the outbreak of the First World War. Suzanne's *campagne plate et poétique des Flandres* was about to be transformed into a war zone.

Marguerite and her daughters fled to England, embarking at Ostend on a beautiful sunny day, bound for a pension run by the sister of a Courtrai friend, located in Grosvenor Square in London. Marguerite had letters of recommendation for friends of Uncle George Baltus in London, and one of these, Lady Ottoline Morrell, invited Maria, whom she had met in London, to come to stay. Suzanne Nys, in her memoir, speaks sharply of Ottoline. The strikingly beautiful sixteen-year-old with her enormous blue eyes – passionate, intelligent, a little highly strung, a little disoriented at being cast out of her solid bourgeois home in Belgium – was wholly overcome and smitten by Ottoline – *subjugée et follement éprise* in Suzanne's words. Suzanne was not the only one to be concerned at the way Ottoline handled this naive young woman. D.H. Lawrence was outraged at an incident that took place in April 1915 at Garsington. Details are vague, but it seems that Maria, despairing at being left out of some activity, or feeling slighted, or perhaps anxious that she was going to be sent away (according to Suzanne she did in fact spend some time lodging in the home of the painter Roger Fry), swallowed some cleaning fluid. A doctor was called in the night and her life was saved but it is likely that permament damage was done to her internal organs. From being a little plump she was ever afterwards as thin as a rake – though one wonders whether, given the circumstances, a diagnosis of *anorexia nervosa* – not then an acknowledged illness and never mentioned before in connection with Maria – might be plausible. Lawrence was angry that Ottoline had, in his view, allowed her love of power to dominate in her relationship with Maria. 'We were shocked about Maria: it really is rather horrible,' he wrote to Ottoline on 23 April 1915. 'I'm not sure whether you aren't really more wicked than I had at first thought you. I think you can't help torturing a bit.'[3] He said it was as if she 'with a strong, old-developed *will* had enveloped the girl, in this will, so that she lived under the dominance of your will . . . So that when she says it was because she couldn't bear being left, that she took the poison, it is a great deal true. Also she feels quite bewildered and chaotic . . . Why must you use your *will* so much, why can't you let things be, without always grasping and trying to know and to dominate.' Then, as if conscious that he was on his high horse, Lawrence conceded: 'I'm too much like this myself.' He thought that the answer lay partly in class, in the patrician habits of domination Ottoline had acquired through her upbringing: 'I suppose it is breeding.' Lawrence and Maria would always be deeply fond of each other.

Ottoline herself, in her journals, put her side of the story of Maria, although she is silent on the poisoning incident, and on Maria's love for her, and treats her more as a rather vexing problem, in what is ultimately a partial and misleading account. She wrote that Maria had come to Garsington when she was 'hardly more than a child, her hair in ringlets and her stout legs in ginger coloured boots and stockings',[4] but soon developed into 'an attractive young woman'. She claimed: 'It was very difficult to induce Maria to work at anything, and I was unhappy to feel that she for whose welfare I had become responsible was spending her life in idleness.' It was for this reason that Ottoline resolved to badger the reluctant authorities at Newnham College, Cambridge to take Maria as an undergraduate, thinking that it would complete her education, force her to associate with other girls (reports from Cambridge suggest that this did happen, with Maria playing early morning hockey with her companions) and make her a little more independent of 'Auntie'. Ottoline had taken Maria's education in hand from the start, and the earliest letter from the young girl to her, in December 1914, before Garsington, presumably after a stay with her in London, Maria (still writing in French) thanked her hostess profusely and said that there was a library in the house in which she was writing the letter: 'I am sure that I will do what you told me: read, read, read' (*beacoup beaucoup lire*).[5] Maria had also received some ballet lessons (including some from Nijinsky) but her delicate physique did not allow her to pursue this as a career. It was in autumn 1915 that she started at Newnham, residing at Peile Hall. Maria's first letters to Ottoline from Cambridge, which have never before been published, convey movingly a young girl's passionate uncertainties and tentative yearnings and confusions. Still grappling with her second language, English, she bravely encountered the *Logic* of James Mill and reported to Suzanne that the work was 'terribly difficult, especially the logic'[6] but Cambridge was nonetheless 'very gay and exciting'. The tone of the letters to Ottoline is different. Maria is clearly overwhelmed by the older woman and fearful of doing and saying the wrong thing, anxious to follow her guidance. She addresses her in these early letters as 'Dearest Auntie', indicative of the protective element in the relationship. 'I really know I am a silly person but I don't think I will be silly always because I will listen to you as much as I can,'[7] she blurted out in a letter from Newnham. In another she confessed: 'I did an awful thing – Mr [Bertrand] Russell told me to remember him to Miss Stephen [Virginia Stephen, later Woolf] and I was quite convinced it was to Miss Fletcher until I did do it . . . It seems such an awful thing to do and I feel I ought to apologise to somebody.'[8] Adolescent gaucherie and self-consciousness, however, were accompanied by other, stronger, feelings: 'I cannot bear it, do so long to come back to you . . . Life is miserable here . . . I am so lonely and I only want to be with you because I love you so much. I love you so much more [than] I thought I did and I must be with you again I do so want you – dearest dearest Ottoline.'[9]

Maria's passion for Ottoline continued throughout 1915 and 1916, after the meeting with Aldous, whom they would occasionally discuss in the later letters. Maria's bisexuality had never been acknowledged by the Huxley family and friends (though her sisters were fully aware of it) until very recently when, in response to the rumour that a book was being written by a Belgian author, Stan Lauryssens,[10] which would apparently allege that the Huxley marriage was a marriage of convenience (if a true report, a preposterous reading of the facts), Sybille

Bedford told a London newspaper: 'Maria was bisexual and she did
have a series of short-term passionate relationships with other people
while she was married to Aldous . . . They were sophisticated people
who were not afraid to experiment.'[11] Huxley's son, Matthew, in conversation with me,[12] expressed bafflement at the suggestion about his
mother's sexuality, which had been discussed in David King
Dunaway's *Huxley in Hollywood* (1989). Huxley's second wife, Laura
Huxley, told me[13] that she simply didn't know whether or not Maria
was bisexual. The love for Ottoline was described by Maria herself in
a letter to Edward Sackville-West published thirty years ago[14]: 'In spite
of the agonies of those young loves it was my greatest . . . I loved her
dearly and am haunted by many thoughts,' she wrote after learning of
Ottoline's death in 1938. Perhaps the following letter – written by the
eighteen-year-old Maria on 24 January 1917, after she had fallen in love
with Aldous, though separated from him now in Florence – can, in its
naked feeling and passionate declaration, stand as the last word on
this intense love affair and its co-existence with the equally devoted
love for Aldous that was starting to flower at the same time:

> My loved, it is not life without you it is not possible
> without you – just nothing, nothing and I long to be with
> you and love you for ever and ever – for you know I love
> you – so much more and more I want to be over all to
> you – because I am not without you – my love for you is
> so great – it is everything . . . I am dark and full of all
> longings that are you – nothing but you matters . . . now
> all is black and grimm [*sic*] because you are not here to
> give all light to my sight . . . I want you and these nights
> are eternal and dark – and the days are haunted dreams
> with people trying to take you away from me . . . You and
> always you. I want to kiss you forever . . . I want to feel
> you . . . My loved, loved – all to you.
> Maria.[15]

The first recorded glimpse of Maria at Garsington, more than a
year before she met Aldous, is provided by Juliette Baillot, the

governess and future wife of Julian. To Juliette, Maria was more worldly and, in spite of her conventional Flemish Catholic upbringing, far more ready to embrace the Garsington/Bloomsbury ethic of personal freedom than Juliette herself, whose Swiss Calvinism had not wholly deserted her. In May 1915, arriving for the first time at the Manor, Juliette was ushered through to the Red room where she found Ottoline in a painter's overall. A younger girl was on the top of a ladder, painting the grooves of the panelling with a thin, gold line. This was Maria: 'She was small, rather plump, but lovely beyond words, with large blue-green eyes matching an Egyptian scarab ring on her long finger, a delicate slightly aquiline profile and a small pointed chin under a full mouth. Her hair, cut short by Philip Morrell (the fashion was just beginning with Slade students), hung like a dark helmet. She had the vulnerable and defenceless look of a child with a mature body.'[16] Descriptions of Maria abound, all stressing the fullness and sensuousness of her beauty, her 'serene Latin sensuality'[17] in Sybille Bedford's phrase. For Mary Hutchinson, there was a 'Persian' quality to her allure: 'Her eyes were almond-shaped and very beautiful, her expression languid, her nature innocent, sensual, uncomplicated, her heart warm and loyal. Her hair was dark. She always seemed to be sweetly scented, oiled and voluptuous.'[18] Sybille Bedford, in her autobiographical novel, *Jigsaw* (1989), describes 'her face of a young El Greco saint'[19] and Edith Sitwell noted her 'beautiful eyes like those of a Siamese cat'.[20] Anita Loos, meeting her much later, saw her as 'a lovely brunette no taller than five feet, with wavy hair, pointed oval face, and big blue-green eyes'.[21]

But what made Maria extraordinary – and justifies her prominence in biographies of her husband – is the role she played throughout Huxley's life, a role which will be highlighted again and again in the following pages. She devoted herself wholly to him – even declaring once: 'It would be wrong of me to die before Aldous.'[22] Because of his poor eyesight, she read to him, endlessly, even if the material bored her beyond belief. She drove him thousands of miles around Europe and the United States – putting her profession as 'chauffeur' in hotel registers. She typed his books and was his secretary and housekeeper. She held off visitors who might interrupt his writing. She supplied him with plots and insights into the human beings he did not always understand. 'She was his eyes and ears for what was going on in the human world,' wrote Sybille Bedford in *Jigsaw*, 'for his books, she would explain, any odds and ends came in useful.' She was intelligent and literate but had also a taste for the wilder shores. According to Anita Loos, 'she lived a life of pure fantasy. She studied palmistry, believed in the stars, and even in the crystal-gazers of Hollywood Boulevard.'[23] And all the time, Anita Loos recalled, 'her unconventional reactions amused Aldous as well as amazed him'.

This was the 'nice Belgian'[24] whom Huxley met on 2 July 1916 (though he had reported to Jelly at the end of the summer term that he had been prevented from speaking to Ottoline at a recent meeting because 'there were some horrid Belgians at tea, who talked incessantly about themselves'[25] – possibly Maria's mother and her daughters). His visits to Garsington increased with such frequency in 1916 that it seemed as though he was becoming a permanent part of the household. In August, finally rid of his temporary post at Repton, that is exactly what happened. He asked Philip Morrell if he might come and work on the farm and thus, from August until April 1917, he lived permanently at Garsington, working on the land alongside formal conscientious objectors like Gerald Shove whom Huxley nicknamed 'Chabbelow'. Ottoline recalled: 'We both liked him very much and were very pleased to have him and gave him a charming, quiet room.'[26] Huxley himself found it a welcome diversion from 'the hollowness of existence ... a hollowness, which I find peculiarly reverberant when I come to regard my future prospects'.[27] Two photographs from Ottoline's album[28] show the two sides of Huxley at this Garsington period. In the first he is deep in a winged armchair, his nose in a book held close to his eyes. In the second he is dressed as a haymaker – the most impossibly *chic* haymaker Garsington Manor had probably ever seen. Huxley was always a smart and stylish dresser. 'Wearing straw-coloured jodhpurs and pale stockings, with a dark-brown corduroy jacket, he looked absent-mindedly but absurdly romantic and beautiful,[29]' Juliette remembered. Woodcutting, in a house that depended exclusively on logs for fuel, was a useful activity and he threw himself into sawing fallen trees and splitting them with wedges. His work on the farm was light, but he enjoyed it – chasing escaped pigs, or rescuing the large black boar from the pond – but, above all, he enjoyed, after the intellectual desert of Repton, the stimulating company.

Within days of arriving at Garsington in August he was telling Frances Petersen how he had spent most of the night 'talking with intelligent people'[30] and sleeping out on the roof in the company of 'an artistic young woman in short hair and purple pyjamas' – this was Dorothy Carrington – and being woken at dawn by screaming peacocks on the roof. He had found what he was to go on finding throughout his life – a small but exquisite circle of intelligent friends who stimulated him and who in turn were stimulated by him. 'I keep a little cache of friends there,' he told Julian, 'and, after all, friendship is the one thing that makes life supremely worth living.'[31] Friends were essential: 'I am utterly stranded and wretched without them.' He was reluctant to tear himself away for a few weeks at Prior's Field, staying with his father and stepmother who were spending the summer there and whom he had not seen for four months – they offered a 'boring' prospect. But this short break from Garsington – he would be back around the end of September – enabled him to make a few acquaintances in London such as E. S. P. Haynes, 'England's most strenuous struggler for freedom of divorce',[32] with whom he lunched for three hours on lobsters, 'washing them down with huge quantities of Chablis and talking of liberty and sex and the decadence of the Huns in loud resonant voices'. But all the time the need to face up to his future nagged at him. 'I don't know what I am going to do for a profession,' he complained to Frances, 'I cannot even play the clarionette outside public houses.' Writing was what he wanted to do most and his first book of poems, *The Burning Wheel*, was almost due – though the excitement of the arrival of proofs was offset by the idiocy of *The Nation* which had just published three of his poems under the name of his father. He told Julian that the volume, 'a tomelet of fifty pages', made him 'heartily sick' as he read the proofs now – perhaps only four of the poems were any good. He had larger ambitions than a slim volume of soon-to-be-forgotten verse. 'But what we want is

men who can write prose . . . No young men write anything but journalism and verse. A sad fact.'

Huxley was conscious that he was at a crucial juncture in his life.
The academic world was quickly receding. He had been told by his
Oxford tutor that there was no chance of an Oxford post. No obvious
career beckoned. He couldn't make a living from verse and he hadn't
yet made a name for himself with fiction. The only temporary
prospect was helping the elderly Irish widow of a French nobleman –
he referred to this unidentified woman as 'the baronne' – with com-
piling her memoirs. With a deliberate swagger and exaggeration –
the tone he often adopted with his elder brother – Huxley summed up
the case at the start of September 1916:

> Well, Oxford is over. Crowned with the artificial roses of
> academic distinction, I stagger, magnificently drunk with
> youthful conceit, into the symposium, not of
> philosophers, but of apes and wolves and swine . . . No
> more of the sheltered, the academic life . . . the life,
> which, I believe, when led by a man of high and
> independent spirit, is the fullest and best of lives, though
> one of the most bedraggled and wretched as led by the
> ordinary crew of bovine intellectuals. I should like to go
> on for ever learning. I lust for knowledge, as well
> theoretic as empirical. Comparing small things to great, I
> think I am rather like the incomparable John Donne.[33]

To Ottoline he wrote from Prior's Field: 'I have never felt less master
of my fate.'[34] Much as he was to enjoy the next seven or eight months
at Garsington (he playfully offered to write Ottoline a mock-Augustan
poem called *The Pleasures of Garsington*, quoting a sample couplet[35]),
he knew that it was only an interlude and that schoolmastering was
the most likely outcome for an indigent poet. Meanwhile, he was
reading, with a magnifying glass maybe, but voraciously: *War and
Peace* ('the greatest book'[36]), *Les Liaisons Dangereuses* ('superb'[37]),
Montesquieu's *Lettres Persanes*, Dante's *Inferno* ('with difficulty and a
literal translation'[38]) the poems of Edgar Allan Poe, and Stendhal's

Chartreuse de Parme which Ottoline had lent him. He told her, in terms that give some insight into his aesthetic principles at this time, that the latter book was wonderfully restrained in its manner: 'There is no romantic devilling of the incidents, no highlights, no cooking of the evidence by the author. The facts just move with their own impetus and weight: mixing metaphors. They are self-luminous, shining from within, not lit by the writer.'[39]

In September, Huxley's first book was published. 'I was amused by the *Times* review of me – pleasantly offensive,'[40] he told his father when the first review of *The Burning Wheel* appeared. The slim, fifty-one page book had been published by Basil Blackwell in the series 'Adventurers All', which the jacket described as 'A Series of Young Poets Unknown to Fame'. Huxley's fellow poets in the series, Frank Betts, Sherard Vines and S. Reid-Hayman, were destined to continue to enjoy that status, perhaps because Blackwell's sales pitch was rather unimpassioned. 'The object of this Series is to remove from the work of young poets the reproach of insolvency,' the common preface began. A publisher's advertisement in the book quoted *The Observer* to the effect that: 'The get up of this series is very attractive. Type, paper, and the shape of the pages are all good, and the poems are printed with a nice regard for margins.' *The Observer* was silent on the actual merits of the poems that positioned themselves so prettily between those margins.

Huxley's poem, 'Mole', which had already appeared in *The Nation*, began the volume. Like most of these poems the diction is a little old-fashioned and 'poetic' and the impression is more of immense literary sophistication than of striking poetic originality. Metrically they are very regular, rhyme abounds. Huxley, though he shared his friend Eliot's fondness for the French Symbolist poets and, in 'The Walk', offers his own miniature *Waste Land*, was not a devotee of *vers libre*. Yet they are serious poems about perception, moments of vision. The vocabulary is rich and recondite – 'nympholept', 'amphisbaena' – and there are gestures of impatience towards the 'sordid strife of the arena' which sound a little precious, as does the title of that poem, 'The Ideal Found Wanting'. Occasionally, an image arrests: the poet sees, through 'a tunnelled arch', in one poem, 'the chestnut gleam/Of horses in a lamplit steam'. And there are several love poems, including 'Sonnet', which has the lines: 'Souls have been drowned between heart's beat and beat,/And trapped and tangled in a woman's hair', and 'Sentimental Summer' in which: 'Your voice sounds near across my memories,/And answering fingers brush against my own.'

It was during this summer, 1916, on a rug on the lawn at Garsington, that Aldous proposed to Maria, giving her a scarab ring, but the event must have been kept secret because it does not surface in any of his letters to family and friends (the first mention of her in the published letters is not until December when she is merely a name in a list of charades players). Ottoline, who probably knew about everything in her domain, was aware of the relationship, which was slow to develop on Maria's side (she took advice from the painter Dorothy Brett, who encouraged her to pursue it). It was a courtship which suffered from a long interruption from the end of 1916 to April 1919 when neither saw the other because Maria had gone abroad. Maria completed a year at Newnham then suddenly, in October 1916, Ottoline received a letter from the head of Newnham telling her that Maria had 'absconded and had gone to London to an unknown address'.[41] Ottoline blamed Brett for this and her fondness for inciting people to revolt against authority – in this case the authority of Ottoline. But Ottoline in her memoirs does not mention a letter she had received from Maria at Newnham on 16 October telling her that she was being sent down for academic failure: 'I never expected it – that is – to be sent down . . . instead of preparing myself to life I should have to begin life at once and go abroad . . . Brett and I have had a talk about it . . . I am certain I could find a job that would bring me enough money to get a room in London . . . And I must seriously begin my writing. Don't you think this is the only thing to do – and the best. You are not cross are you. You know I did my best.'[42] Ottoline clearly resented Brett's involvement (was there also some part of sexual jealousy here?) and saw her as leading Maria off the straight path. The letter is also interesting for its reference to Maria's ambition to write, an ambition which never surfaced again.

Worried that living alone in London was not a good idea for
Maria, Ottoline tried to persuade Brett to take her in to the Ark, a
house in Gower Street where Brett, Carrington and others were
living. Instead, Brett arranged for Maria to get some work at the
India Office, with the aid of a friend called Boris Anrep, the Military
Secretary of the Russian Government in England, and a painter and
sculptor in his own right. Ottoline realised that Aldous also was
getting rather concerned about Maria: 'My anxiety I found was
shared by Aldous, who was already more or less in love with her. In
October he had written to me about himself as having developed a
kind of doggy devotion for that rather absurd and very charming figure
Maria' [this sounds like Aldous's phrasing but the letter is lost].'[43]
Huxley arranged to have lunch with Maria 'in a small bun-house
off Holborn filled with earnest-looking women – all I am sure
readers at the Museum'.[44] Boris Anrep was clearly considered a rather
unsuitable person to have charge of an innocent young woman. In
the crowded coffee-house Huxley and Maria rather startled the
earnest bluestockings when they 'began (in that clear bell-like
voice of the *enfant terrible* that one somehow always adopts
when discussing in public the tetchier, more scabrous subjects of
life) to examine the probability of Maria being seduced by Anrep.'
The probability, however, was not great because by now Maria
was seen to have acquired 'a great deal of sense'. She was also 'very
happy' but that happiness, if it depended on being with Aldous, was
threatened now by her mother's decision to move the family to
Florence, and to summon Maria to rejoin them.

Throughout the autumn of 1916, Aldous had journeyed from
Garsington to London as often as he could to see Maria, who was surviving by giving French lessons. Their love blossomed in these last
months of 1916 but it was to face a severe test because he would not
see Maria again from December 1916 to April 1919. His social life
during that period was an often dizzying whirl. Maria herself discovered new friends and experiences in Italy. They were both young and
fond of pleasure. They could easily have drifted apart but their love
survived the separation. At the time, Huxley did not know how long
he would be cut off from Maria. He told Lewis Gielgud the bad news

on New Year's Day 1917: 'The worst, my dear Lewis, has not lost the
opportunity of happening. It rarely does. Poor Maria is being hustled
out remorselessly to her ghoulish mother in Florence . . . It is
altogether painful . . . I find the imminence of separation briny
enough and the thing itself will doubtless be worse. And then for
how long? It's the indefiniteness that is so distressing.'[45] Huxley had
a premonition – based no doubt in part on the fact of the war – that
he would have to wait a long time before seeing Maria again. The
letter shows how deeply he felt for her but to one of his closest male
friends, Lewis Gielgud, who knew as much as anyone about his private life, he hinted at continuing confusions. Playfully he invited
Gielgud to reflect on a number of propositions about life, the first
two of which were: 'The incomprehensibility of women and their
unlikeness to anything one had expected. The question whether
passion is necessary to love, or whether it gambols like a faun around
the shrine, unconnected and irresponsible.' Years later, in a letter to
her son, Matthew, Maria disclosed some of her feelings both about
Garsington and about Aldous:

> And why did I who was so horrified by those
> Garsington men (and women) I who was so squashed
> by the English and terrified of them, why did I let
> Aldous approach me . . .? Why, because, though I was
> not then in love with Aldous, even though he was in
> love with me, we could see all the underlying
> possibilities which are really facts. He could sense, shall
> we say, instead of see, that in spite of all he had been
> told, I was a steady one, and I could sense that I would
> be entirely devoted to his service for the rest of our
> lives. In fact we were fated to each other.[46]

Maria's feelings about marriage to Aldous will be examined in
more detail later. It is, however, worth noting here, not just Maria's
mature reflections on Garsington and her revulsion from it in retrospect, but the revelation that love was more ardent at first on Huxley's
side than on hers. This was the view also of Ottoline. In the last weeks

of 1916, when she returned from Harrogate where she had been recuperating from an illness, she had what she called 'long and anxious talks'[47] with Huxley about Maria and her future. 'I found that he was very much in love with her,' she wrote, 'but of course it was impossible for him to think of marrying then. He was not as yet earning anything and she was so absurdly young – but I was doubtful how deep or serious his feelings for her were.' She claimed that the summer before he had been very much in love with Carrington. 'Carrington, however, had many admirers, and fluttered from one to another, whereas Maria sat still, silent and receptive, her pale magnolia face and beautiful dark eyes gazing out in pathetic appeal. Of what was she thinking? That was the magnet that attracted Aldous.' Ottoline was also unsure whether Maria was in love with Aldous 'and I was doubtful if they were suited to each other'. The fact that Maria was 'foreign' seems to have been a problem for Ottoline who felt that she 'had no understanding of English ways or traditions'. Juliette – herself a victim of this casual patrician racism – would later reproach Ottoline for failing to understand Maria and her sense of displacement.[48] Maria confessed to Juliette, many years later, that she had often been 'deeply unhappy' at Garsington 'being teased by Ottoline for being plump, whilst also suffering from a complete lack of money'. Maria once walked all the way back from Richmond to her London digs because she had no money for the train fare.

Huxley, however, did not share the xenophobia of the English upper middle class. His worry was simply that Maria might not really love him. In the early months of 1917, when she was clearly very happy in Italy and careless about writing to him, these doubts made him very sad and melancholy in his room at Garsington next door to Mark Gertler, who 'used to tell us how he was kept awake half the night by Aldous, who sat without his clothes on his bed, his long legs drawn up under his chin, wondering and meditating aloud on the vast problems of love'. Ottoline claimed to have spent hours with Aldous trying to comfort him by talking about Maria. Juliette, too, recalled how she found herself one evening, gazing into the log fire, alone with him: 'Aldous was staring into the fire, and suddenly blurted out his feelings, the awfulness of separation and the misery of uncertainty.'[49] At that time, she noted, 'Aldous mooned about the place, silent and bottled-up.'

Meanwhile there was consolation in the fact that his slim volume had got him noticed – the editor of the *Times Literary Supplement* asked him to send some suggestions, on a postcard, of books he wanted to review and the *Morning Post* in a review of the annual *Oxford Poetry* for 1916 had singled him out for praise. But the fact remained that Huxley was jobless, having missed a clerical post in Munitions, and having apparently been rejected by Eton and with only a possibility of a post at Charterhouse, the school where his father had taught. He thus ended 1916 in some gloom about his prospects.

And Maria was gone. He would not see her again for two and a half years.

Notes

1   Sybille Bedford, Introduction to 1999 Penguin Edition of *Jigsaw* (1989)
2   Suzanne Nys, *Mémoires*, unpublished typescript (78pp), Musée de la Littérature, Royal Library, Brussels, in uncatalogued collection of Nys family papers
3   *The Letters of D.H. Lawrence*, Vol 2, edited by George J. Zytaruk and James T. Boulton, pp325–6
4   *Ottoline at Garsington: Memoirs of Lady Ottoline Morrell, 1915–18* (1974) edited by Robert Gathorne-Hardy, pp201–4
5   HRC, Letter from Maria Nys to Ottoline Morrell, 2 December 1914. Author's translation
6   Royal Library of Belgium (RL) Letter from Maria Nys to Suzanne Nys, November 1915. Author's translation
7   HRC, Letter from Maria Nys to Ottoline Morrell from Newnham, no date but probably autumn 1915. Maria almost never dated her letters at this time
8   HRC, Letter from Maria Nys to Ottoline Morrell from Newnham. No date but probably autumn 1915
9   HRC, Letter from Maria Nys to Ottoline Morrell, undated, no location but probably 1915
10 In conversation with me in Brussels, Lauryssens insisted that the argument of his book had been mis-represented by the *Sunday Telegraph*
11 Sybille Bedford, quoted in the *Sunday Telegraph*, 7 May, 2000

12 Matthew Huxley in conversation with the author, Washington DC, 14 April 2000
13 Laura Archera Huxley in conversation with the author, Los Angeles, 31 March 2000
14 *SB*1.359
15 HRC, Letter from Maria to Ottoline Morrell, 24 Jan 1917
16 Juliette Huxley, *Mem. Vol.*, p39. See also *Leaves from the Tulip Tree*, p32
17 *SB*1.136
18 HRC, Typescript profiles by Mary Hutchinson of Aldous and Maria Huxley.
19 Sybille Bedford, *Jigsaw*, p288
20 John Lehmann, *A Nest of Tigers: Edith, Osbert and Sacheverell Sitwell in their Times* (1968), pp68–9
21 Anita Loos, *Fate Keeps on Happening* (1984) edited by Ray Pierre Corsini
22 *SB*2.166
23 *Mem. Vol.*, p90
24 The 'nice Belgian' is not actually identified but I have made the assumption that Maria was the only Garsington habitué at this time who would match such a description
25 HRC, Letter to Jelly d'Aranyi from Oxford, undated but probably June 1916
26 *Ottoline at Garsington*, p124
27 *L.*109
28 *Lady Ottoline's Album* (1976) edited by Carolyn G. Heilbrun reproduces these and many other portraits of Garsington guests
29 *Mem. Vol.*, p40
30 *L.*109
31 *L.*112
32 *L.*110
33 *L.*112
34 HRC, Letter to Ottoline Morrell, undated but probably late summer 1916
35 HRC, Letter to Ottoline Morrell, from Prior's Field, undated but probably September 1916
36 *L.*116
37 HRC, Letter to Ottoline Morrell, from Prior's Field, undated but probably September 1916
38 *Ibid.*
39 HRC, Letter to Ottoline Morrell from Tring, undated but probably summer, 1916
40 *L.*116
41 *Ottoline at Garsington*, p201

42   HRC, Letter from Maria Nys to Ottoline Morrell, 16 October 1916
43   *Ottoline at Garsington*, p202
44   HRC, Letter to Ottoline Morrell from 27 Westbourne Square, undated
     but probably October 1916
45   *L*.119
46   Quoted in *SB*2.135. Whereabouts of MS unknown
47   *Ottoline at Garsington*, p203
48   *Leaves from The Tulip Tree*, p45
49   *Mem. Vol.*, p42

VII

Whizzing

After Maria had gone with her family to Florence in October, Aldous continued at Garsington, 'hewing wood, like Caliban',[1] for the remainder of 1916. During the autumn, he sent regular bulletins to Ottoline who was in Harrogate for her health. These contained reports on his reading (Conrad's *Chance*, and *War and Peace*, which, he thought, ought to be 'much longer, like the *Encyclopaedia Britannica*, so that one could go on reading it for a little every day the whole of one's life'[2]) and laments for the fact that all his friends were getting married. 'For the last three days,' he protested in October, 'special couriers seem to have arrived almost hourly to announce to me the engagement of almost every friend I ever had, of all the women I ever fell in love with ... Everything, however, is a little made up for by the dazzling beauty of my new breeches. I feel like the young Rostov, when he arrived in Moscow wearing riding-breeches of a brilliant blue.' Try as he might, however, to appear flippant and amused, Huxley's position was becoming untenable. His literary ambition and his desire to earn enough to be able to marry Maria were incompatible with a life of chopping wood and reading Russian novels. He was, it is true, making some effort with his own writing, planning a historical novel with a seventeenth century setting, but he was finding the execution difficult. 'I have not sufficient skill to conceive a number of characters and their relations at a single birth,' he confessed. Psychology was equally difficult for the aspiring novelist: 'the more I try to understand psychology the more mysterious does it become to me . . . particularly women, who seem to me . . . most of them . . . too utterly inexplicable.'

All this amused Ottoline, as did the poems he sent her, which expressed similar hesitations and bafflements before the presence of the opposite sex. She told Aldous, in another of those zoological similes his friends loved to deploy, that he was 'like a giraffe looking down on us poor human beings and enjoying the spectacle of our little futile lives'.[3] In search of work, Huxley went to Oxford to see Professor Walter Raleigh, Robert Nicholl Smith, and his old tutor, R.J.E. Tiddy – 'the three most important nobs in the English School'[4] – but they offered little comfort. Raleigh told him that a university job was unlikely because of wartime economies, and because the influx of young women into the English School made older men seem more proper as tutors. Raleigh recommended reviewing instead. 'My father is sufficiently acquainted with the immortal Strachey to exercise a little nepotistic pressure in that direction,' Huxley told Ottoline. He had scant respect, however, for the trade of book reviewer: 'The art of reviewing appears to consist in variations of the formula, "This book is on the one hand good and on the other and at the same time bad."'[5] The excursion to Oxford nonetheless had its compensations, in the shape of a meeting with Lewis Gielgud and friends at which 'we scintillated pleasantly over two bottles of burgundy'. Huxley was doing a good deal of scintillating at this time and trips to London took him to Fitzrovia and the rather elevated Bohemianism of the Eiffel Tower Restaurant. It was here that he met for the first time Evan Morgan (Viscount Tredegar, the prototype of Ivor Lombard in *Crome Yellow*), Lady Constance Stuart Richardson, Iris Tree, Nancy Cunard, and, in Ottoline's words, 'the tall, charming, unselfish dissolute Marie Beerbohm, of whom he was really very fond'.[6] Huxley was greatly attracted to such female free spirits. Frances Petersen, an Oxford friend, he once described – in significant terms – as 'a clever and amusing creature, whose greatest gift is an amazing light-hearted irresponsibility, which entirely cuts her free from the trammels of quotidian life'.[7] It was to Frances Petersen that he confessed at the start of 1917: 'I am becoming a third class tragic-comedian these days.'[8] Dorothy Carrington was another attraction. She made 'a very good drawing of Jonah seated on the whale's kidney' for a Christmas card for 1917, which reproduced Huxley's poem, 'Jonah'. Fifty copies of the poem were printed, but he lacked the funds to have Carrington's drawing included.[9]

Huxley, therefore, began 1917 facing the choices he had long ago identified as the inescapable ones: hack reviewing or schoolmastering. The war ensured that he could briefly defer the reckoning, for a clerical job came up at the Air Board, starting in April. Maria, meanwhile, was in Florence. She told Ottoline in February: 'I wish you could pack up Aldous for this part of the world – because there would be somebody to be with and enjoy everything with – I care for A so much . . . Think what fun it would be if instead of going to America that silly boy invented a reason to come here – it is wonderful and he would love me.'[10] Huxley – no doubt influenced by the precedent of Julian – was toying with the idea of work in America in the wake of his disappointing meeting with the Oxford nobs. An American school appears to have offered him a job and he made some efforts to get the necessary visa, but in the end it fell through. Aldous and Maria's love letters to each other – preserved in a tin trunk that survived all their travels together – were destroyed in the fire that swept Huxley's Hollywood home in 1961. There must have been many of these letters in this period of separation in the years 1917 and 1918.

Maria left Florence in June for the Tuscan coast at Forte dei Marmi (a location that will be described in more detail later) with Costanza da Fasola, whose Florentine family owned a villa at Forte. Costanza was twenty-three and engaged to be married to Luigino Franchetti, 'who does not love her . . . she knows she will be unhappy . . . What can I tell her . . . It is like someone running to an abyss he sees but runs to it all the same.'[11] Maria also had time to reflect on the desirability or otherwise of her own marriage. Writing to Ottoline from Forte, in a letter declaring her love for the older woman, Maria reported in detail on her summer idyll with the beautiful Costanza, and also managed – in this amatory whirl – to talk about Aldous too.

Madame Nys had tried to block the trip to Forte but 'now they are used to it at home and we live as if no-one but us two exists'.[12] The two young women, with the villa to themselves, went out in a sailing-boat and enjoyed swimming together, pouring scorn on the restrictive bathing-caps worn by the other swimmers. 'In the daytime when one gets far enough out we bathe without our clothes – it is too lovely.' Maria enclosed two snapshots of herself and Costanza posing naked on the top of the stone wall of the villa grounds. Poor Aldous, meanwhile, was commuting to a dreary clerical job in the Strand from his father's house at 16 Bracknell Gardens, Hampstead, made wretched at the fewness of Maria's letters to him from Italy. 'I have been hoping each day that there'd be a letter from Maria – but nothing. It makes me so absurdly miserable,' he complained to Ottoline.[13] Maria responded – in the same letter that enclosed the picture of the two water nymphs – that the last letter she had received from Aldous was 'not at all nice, grumpy and reproachfull [sic]. He is such a queer creature – But he has been sending me wonderful poems – Only he is so – I don't know what to say – perhaps merely tired.' Those 'wonderful poems' would include the contents of the second volume he was preparing for Blackwell the following summer, *The Defeat of Youth* (1918). The title sequence of twenty-two sonnets has a troubled youthful persona asking: 'or is she pedestalled above the touch/Of his desire . . .?', 'And ever more she haunts him, early and late,/As pitilessly as an old remorse', 'An island-point, measureless gulfs apart/From other lives, from the old happiness'. In a poem, 'Winter Dream' the poet writes: 'I am all alone, dreaming she would come and kiss me.' These youthful fears may have been justified – if a slightly coquettish letter to Ottoline is taken at face value. It appears to disclose that Maria had received a letter from another male admirer who was working as a typist in the Board of Agriculture. She was thrilled at the sensation of receiving it. 'I wonder what Aldous thinks? Because he never seems to me very much to understand. I write long letters to him of course, *friendly letters.* I suppose he shows them to you – I shall love it when he comes to Italy but he *must be* a friend. I have not behaved badly to him? Aldous is one of those people who cannot be roused – anyway by me – I must not become vain.'[14] All this worried

Ottoline, who appeared to warn Maria about playing with Aldous's affections, provoking immediate remorse and a promise to be 'more serious . . . But I am certain about Aldous – I care for him very much – more now – I think I always did really – only sometimes I care for no-one – and can't bear him – Don't let me miserable Auntie – because my feelings for him are real and strong.'[15] A little later, Maria was more emphatic: 'He really is wonderful – and so very clever. I sometimes just sit down and wonder why and how he ever managed to care for me because he really does love me. Are you not sure of it? Do say you are. After all I am so stupid and ignorant – and so young – but then I love him – and so much – I think it is being far away from people that gives me this feeling – though I always knew I was not worth people moving their little finger for me – though they did move it.'[16]

Aldous, however, was not wholly miserable in London, and was discovering diversions of his own. His social life was flourishing and his range of acquaintance quickly expanding. He was also writing reviews for the *New Statesman and Nation*, having been introduced to its literary editor J. C. Squire earlier in the year. He contributed three introductory essays to Thomas Ward's *The English Poets* (1918), on John Davidson, Ernest Dowson, and Richard Middleton. None of this, however, amounted to enough to live on and, in desperation, on 31 March, he inserted an advertisement in the personal column of *The Times* which read: 'YOUNG MAN, 22 (rejected), Public School and Oxford, First-class Honours, desires LITERARY, SECRETARIAL, or other Work.' He received many offers but contrived to get himself pushed by friends towards a dreary post in the Naval Law Department of the Admiralty at £2 for a fifty-four hour week. Just in time, a slightly better post turned up at the Air Board, which he held from April to July 1917. After the 'imbecility' of the Dardanelles campaign, Huxley had concluded 'it's not pleasant to think of lives thrown away by the sheer folly of the politicians,'[17] but he still felt the need to do some war work. As early as February he had worked for the Food Office on a trial basis, complaining to Ottoline: 'Here all is sugar, sugar . . . sugar everywhere.'[18] At last he was ready to bid farewell to Garsington. On ministry-embossed foolscap (evidently he was not

overworked), he drew up a most eloquent letter of thanks to the
Morrells, describing his stay with them as 'the happiest time in my
life'.[19] It had been a period, he went on, 'when I have been conscious
of the best and most fruitful development of myself'. He had learnt so
much from both of them, he said, 'that I feel I shall never be able to
compute the full amount of your giving . . . and I have been able to
return you nothing, I fear, unless a very deep devotion counts at all in
the balance against all your gifts of inspiration, almost of creation.' In
view of the later rift, when Ottoline saw not 'deep devotion' but cruel
caricature of herself in Huxley's first novel, *Crome Yellow*, the force of
feeling behind this outburst of gratitude is the more striking. In drawing up the Garsington account, he did not omit to mention that it was
at the Morrells' that he had met Maria and received from her 'a great
and violent emotional self-discovery'. That depth of feeling for Maria
had been attested to on another occasion when he told Ottoline he
had had no sleep one night 'owing to the excitement of a letter from
Maria'.[20]

Departure from Garsington, and arrival at his desk at Room 549 at
the Air Board in the Strand, where he dealt with 'all subjects from
timber to chemicals, electric lamps to wire ropes',[21] relegating most of
them to 'a sort of dustbin to wait', marked Huxley's final entry into the
world of serious work. Although he was not yet living wholly by his
pen, he would never again be allowed that aristocratic leisure he had
enjoyed at Garsington. Small wonder that his expressions of gratitude
were so heartfelt. During this period he was living at his father's
house in Bracknell Gardens in 'a most pleasant room, looking on the
garden' and, in spite of the banalities of clerical work, was throwing
himself with decent vigour into the social life of the capital. Katherine
('Ka') Cox, who had been romantically entangled with Rupert Brooke,
was a theatre companion one night after which he had 'a very pleasant little tête à tête conversation . . . about Things in General and the
fallacies of Bloomsburyism in particular'.[22] He dined with Carrington
and friends, including Virginia Woolf, who afterwards reported to
Vanessa Bell this first meeting with Huxley in April 1917, describing
him as 'a most singular speckly eyed young man . . . who owing to Ka,
has got put into a government office. I warned him of what might

happen to his soul; however, he spends his time translating French poetry.'[23] Huxley was immersed in Laforgue at this time and, a few weeks later, dined with T.S. Eliot at his London flat: 'Eliot in good form all considered, and he showed me his latest verses [this was the year of *Prufrock and Other Observations*] – very odd indeed: he is experimenting in a new genre, philosophical obscenity rather like Laforgue . . . very good: some in English, some in the most astonishingly erudite French.'[24] After their erudite chat, the two poets moved off to Omega – the Bloomsbury artists' studios and workshops – where Huxley spent the evening chatting to yet another young woman whom he referred to only as 'the Flashing Beauty'. In contrast to the mournful, moping presence evoked by Maria's letters, Huxley was in fact being sucked into an extraordinary social whirl. In June, the same month that Maria spent in Forte with Costanza, he reported breathlessly to Ottoline:

What a life! I have been ceaselessly whizzing. On Sunday I assist the Head of the Department in sending a lunatic guest to the local asylum. I lunch now frequently with Evan [Morgan] at the Savoy and with [Middleton] Murry at the A.B.C. Evan has become quite a feature in my life now: he is constantly ringing me up, coming to see me, asking me to meals, and so forth. I like him, I think, quite a lot, tho' he is the most fearfully spoilt child. Then I whizz round to Mr Mills, then fly to Putney to stay the night with an unknown admirer of my works. Then I rush to meet yet another figure – the editrix of *Wheels*, Miss Edith Sitwell, who is passionately anxious for me to contribute to her horrible production. The Wheelites take themselves seriously: I never believed it possible! I sit in the Isola Bella, naively drinking in the flattery of the ridiculous Sitwell, in dart Carrington and Barbara [Hiles?], borrow half-a-crown from me and whirl out again . . . What a life! Then an evening with Vernon Lee – each trying to get his or her word in edgeways. Then again at Eliot's, where I meet Mrs E for the first time and

perceive that it is almost entirely a sexual nexus between
Eliot and her: one sees it in the way he looks at her – she's
an incarnate provocation – like a character in Anatole
France. What a queer thing it is. This whizzing is a mere
mania, a sort of intoxicant, exciting and begetting
oblivion. I shall be glad when it stops.[25]

At least one of the riders on this whirling carousel, Edith Sitwell,
saw things a little differently. In her autobiography, Edith Sitwell
recalled that lunch at the Isola Bella in Frith Street, Soho, 'in a dream-
like golden day in June', and described Huxley as one of her first
friends in London. They would meet again many years later in the
United States and she would have been shocked by that cruel epithet,
'ridiculous'. Recalling Huxley in his prime in London during the First
World War (the brutal backdrop to all this gaiety) she pictured him as
'extremely tall . . . full lips and a rather ripe, full but not at all loud
voice. His hair was of the brown, living colour of the earth on garden
beds. As a young man, though he was always friendly, his silences
seemed to stretch for miles, extinguishing life, when they occurred, as
a snuffer extinguishes a candle. On the other hand, he was (when
uninterrupted) one of the most accomplished talkers I have ever
known, and his monologues on every conceivable subject were astonishingly floriated variations of an amazing brilliance, and,
occasionally, of a most deliberate absurdity.'[26] Another literary
acquaintance of this period was Katherine Mansfield who re-inforced
Huxley's bulletin to Ottoline with another, telling her that he had
called with 'more news in half an hour than I have heard for months.
At present he seems to be a great social success and incredible things
happen to him *at least* every evening. He spoke of the Isola Bella as
though it were the rendezvous of Love and High Adventure . . . I felt
my mind flutter over Aldous as if he were the London Mail. There was
a paragraph about simply everybody.'[27] He was also at a party thrown
by Mary Hutchinson – who would play a significant role in his private
life in the subsequent decade – but confessed to some social failures.
He couldn't get on with Siegfried Sassoon and Robert Graves. This
puzzled him and he tried to explain himself to Ottoline: 'the sense of

being out of contact and not knowing how to get into it, which is most baffling. I am afraid I'm rather bad at approaching people – the result of a habit, I think, of laziness and arrogance.'[28]

At the end of July, the job at the Air Board came to an end and with it his stay in London, the termination marked by 'the most prodigious orgy with Evan – a birthday party of at least 25 people, all of them ultimately drunk'.[29] Marie Beerbohm and Nina Hamnett attracted Aldous's attention. Evan, he told Juliette, was 'very salutary in stirring up my contemplative lethargy' but at the same time, after all this socialising, drinking, and party going: 'Coming back to books again is a pleasure.'[30] Before he left London he had lunch with Carrington at the Isola Bella, apologising to her (as he was so often to do to his young women) for an access of 'melodramatic melancholy'[31] in the small hours at their friend Mills's party. He told her that he was going to see the Headmaster of Eton about a job and was cheered by the prospect of freedom from clerking. After London he went to stay with the Haldanes at Oxford where another 'charming and talented creature', Yvette Chapelain, was on hand to give him Italian lessons – 'so that I hope to learn Italian quite without tears'.[32] Maria, meanwhile, sounded depressed in her letters because her father's factory had been destroyed in the latest offensive. The family fortunes would never recover after the war.

During the summer of 1917, between jobs in Oxford, staying at the Haldanes' and at the Petersens', Huxley had been doing some writing. He submitted a collection of poems to John Murray but was told 'to wait, polish and so forth. How trying one's elders are, to be sure.'[33] He planned now to prepare 'a largish book' including prose poems, some of which had been accepted by Eliot for *The Egoist*. He also was contributing to *Wheels*. He mocked the Sitwells, for the benefit of Julian, calling them 'Shufflebottom . . . each of them larger and whiter than the other'. Although he admitted to liking Edith he patronisingly described them as 'dear solid people who have suddenly discovered intellect and begin to get drunk on it'.

Meanwhile, the interview with the Headmaster of Eton had been successful. Rather suddenly, he felt, Huxley found himself installed there on 18 September. The distance from London entailed a certain lessening in the frenetic pace of his social life but that could only be to the benefit of his writing. He was conscious, as young writers always are, that the clock was ticking. 'It's one's duty to stay young as long as possible,'[34] he told Jelly d'Aranyi. The imperative to get published was growing stronger. But would the life of a schoolmaster be a help or a hindrance?

Notes

1   *Ottoline at Garsington*, p158. Letter from AH, October 1916
2   *Ibid.*
3   *Ibid.*, p197
4   HRC, Letter to Ottoline Morrell, from Garsington, undated but probably autumn 1916
5   HRC, Letter to Ottoline Morrell, undated but probably October 1916
6   *Ottoline at Garsington*, p200
7   HRC, Letter to Ottoline Morrell, undated but probably October 1916
8   *L.*120
9   Stanford, Letter from AH to Jake Zeitlin, 20 June 1942
10 HRC, Letter from Maria Nys to Ottoline Morrell, 1 February 1917
11 HRC, Letter from Maria Nys to Ottoline Morrell, 26 January 1917
12 HRC, Letter from Maria Nys to Ottoline Morrell, 30 June 1917
13 HRC, Letter from AH to Ottoline Morrell, 28 February 1917
14 HRC, Letter from Maria Nys to Ottoline Morrell, 11 February 1917
15 HRC, Letter from Maria Nys to Ottoline Morrell, 7 March 1917
16 HRC, Letter from Maria Nys to Ottoline Morrell, 10 May 1917
17 *L.*122
18 HRC, Letter to Ottoline Morrell, undated, but probably February 1917
19 HRC, Letter to Philip and Ottoline Morrell, undated from Air Board, probably April 1917
20 HRC, Letter to Ottoline Morrell, 23 April 1917
21 HRC, Letter to Ottoline Morrell, no date but probably April 1917, written on Air Board notepaper
22 HRC, Letter to Ottoline Morrell, 10 May 1917
23 *Letters of Virginia Woolf*, Vol 2, 26 April 1917, p150
24 HRC, Letter to Ottoline Morrell, 2 June 1917
25 HRC, Letter to Ottoline Morrell, 21 June 1917
26 Edith Sitwell, *Taken Care Of: an autobiography* (1965), p89
27 *The Collected Letters of Katherine Mansfield* (1984) edited by Vincent

O'Sullivan and Margaret Scott. Vol 1: 1903–1917. Letter to Ottoline Morrell, 3 July 1917

28 HRC, Letter to Ottoline Morrell, undated but probably early summer 1917.

29 HRC, Letter to Ottoline Morrell, 19 July 1917

30 *L.*128

31 HRC, note on scrap paper to Carrington undated but from 16 Bracknell Gardens

32 HRC, Letter to Ottoline Morrell, 19 July 1917

33 *L.*131

34 HRC, Letter to Jelly d'Aranyi, undated but probably September 1917

VIII

Eton

Huxley arrived at Eton on 18 September 1917 to take up residence at lodgings, still in use by the College today, called The Old Christopher, a former inn. A week into his new life he described himself, 'perched solitary in my high room that looks one way upon the Southern buttresses of the chapel, golden with this autumn sunshine, and on the other side, right over the roofs to the castle [Windsor] gigantic on its hill'.[1] He had arrived not without some misgivings towards his new position, which were promptly shared with Lewis Gielgud. Being a teacher had its pleasant side, he wrote to his friend, but also its 'tediousness'.[2] Nonetheless, the pupils were turning out to be 'very nice fellows' who treated him 'all being considered, wonderfully well . . . though I wish I could see them more penetratingly'. He had rather put his finger on the problem. The schoolboy will always be anxious to try what he can get away with and a master so palpably short-sighted is an unignorable gift. It was said that card games were played at the back of Huxley's classes and no doubt much escaped his notice, including boys playing truant through the simple expedient of getting their names called by others because the 'beak' could not see the identity of the boy who was calling out. The opening pages of *Antic Hay* (1923) in which 'Theodore Gumbril Junior, B.A. Oxon.', sits in his oaken stall on the north side of the School Chapel, thinking satirical thoughts, capture Huxley's attitude towards the life of the English public school. The new master shared his lodgings with a clergyman called Bevan, who was addicted to substantial meals and was in no sense an adequate intellectual companion for the brilliant young man. 'Sometimes I feel most intolerably lonely,' Huxley confessed to Gielgud, because, though nice enough, the teachers were 'so remote, so alien'. The truth was plain enough: 'On the whole I am fairly happy, but I have decided that God never intended me to do any regular work.' This recalls *Antic Hay*: 'Work, thought Gumbril, work. Lord, how passionately he disliked work!' Huxley was bumping slowly down to earth and wondering, perhaps, if he were really as clever as he had been led to believe. To his old confidante, Jelly, he confessed that 'I am just a mildly clever fool, educated from the earliest age to be "blasé": for in England one isn't supposed to be refined, unless one is blasé and cynical!'[3] At the heart of the English upper middle class's training ground for its young, Huxley was witnessing the patrician affectation of indifference to things of the mind: 'And the affectation becomes almost natural after a few years of it at that age. It's a peculiar national habit.' It was a national habit against which Huxley would strive for the rest of his life.

Hearing at last from Maria 'after a long period of silence',[4] he learned that she was back in Florence and planning to study German at the university. 'How I wish I could go on with my education instead of imparting what I have got to others, who don't in the least want it,' he exclaimed. 'It is absurd to teach when one wants to learn.' One of the problems was that Eton did not actually teach English literature – the subject in which Huxley had won a brilliant First – and he was compelled to teach classics. English literature was considered an accomplishment that should be acquired incidentally and, as has already been pointed out, it was not in fact part of the formal curriculum at Eton until the 1960s. Some of Huxley's former pupils, such as Sir Steven Runciman, have been kind to him in retrospect. 'I was, I suppose, in my second year in College at Eton when we were told that we were to be taught by this remarkable young writer. We Collegers were little intellectual snobs, and we were much impressed ... the name already had a glamour.'[5] Runciman remembered that the boys were not as badly-behaved and cruel as they might have been – for the simple reason that Huxley seemed quite unaware of their behaviour. Runciman recalled the physical impression left by the new teacher: 'that long, thin body, with a face that was far younger than most of our masters' and yet seemed somehow ageless, and, usually hidden by an infinite variety of spectacles, eyes that were almost sightless, and yet almost uncomfortably observant. He stood there, looking something of a martyr but at the same time extraordinarily distinguished.' Runciman considered that Huxley was not 'a good teacher in the narrower sense of the word' – a verdict with which Huxley would have agreed – but he was 'an educator in a wider sense. He showed us a glimpse of the fascination to be found in an unhampered intellectual approach to things.' There was a feeling that his voice was a little affected 'but soon some of us were trying to copy it'. And the words pronounced by that voice were most striking. The brighter boys seized on the new and recondite vocabulary they were encountering, as well as the example Huxley set of verbal precision and exact definition. Huxley was never a fuzzy or vague writer, even when he chose to deal with imponderable, abstract matter. It is clear that he made some effort to bridge the gap between his high intellectualism and the needs of young adolescent boys, recognising his practical shortcomings for the task in hand. He expressed it well to Ottoline: 'I find that I am not cut out for a teacher of boys; or rather I find that all my knowledge, such as it is, is quite of the wrong sort; remote, vague, facts inextricably mixed up with appreciations and opinions; I am setting to work to tabulate and compress.'[6]

Some of the especially favoured boys received extra literary sessions in Huxley's rooms and he was delighted to report that, 'a young poet has been discovered in the shape of Ld. David Cecil, a very charming frail boy of fifteen or so with quite remarkable talent'. Decades later, Cecil recalled how different Huxley was from the general conservative run of masters in the matter of dress: 'I remember seeing him walking out towards Arches, with a prim plain, tweed-clad cleric called Bevan, dressed in delicate dove-grey, a black sombrero hat, & round his neck a flowing scarf of flame-coloured silk which contrasted with his white countenance and wavy dark hair, which he grew much longer than was common in those days.'[7] Huxley enjoyed mocking Bevan – 'a thick square parson' who liked his regular meals: 'We always dress for dinner, sitting tête à tête in our black coats, attended by one of our not inconsiderable seraglio of domestics.'[8] He mocked, too, with the eye of Gumbril, the rituals of this 'comical place ... a real Nightmare Abbey of incongruous characters', rituals that were still the same as the ones he had endured as a boy at the school: 'It is so long since I was there; but it is all just the same, the bored, critical boys going through the appropriate gestures with the mechanical skill of long habit, the parson intoning through his Eustachian tubes ... All exactly the same, except for a few prayers couched in the most horrible imitation-seventeenth-century language about the War ... It is all so familiar, yet seeing it again, one has such a shock of amazement: can it really be, in this, the so-called twentieth century?'

Huxley regularly escaped to London, to dine with his young women or to converse at their lodgings with T.S. Eliot and Bertrand Russell. One evening in October he found this gloomy pair philosophising over a dying fire. Russell observed how much good it would do to exterminate the whole human race. 'I told him he was a little Sunbeam in the House; we all felt much better.'[9] Virginia Woolf spotted Huxley at *An Exhibition of Works Representative of the New Movement in Art,* curated by Roger Fry at the Mansard Gallery at Heal's: 'Aldous Huxley was there – infinitely long & lean, with one opaque white eye. A nice youth. We walked up & down a gallery discussing his Aunt, Mrs Humphry Ward.'[10] He even managed a visit to Garsington in November, where Woolf saw him again 'toying with great round disks of ivory & green marble – the draughts of Garsington' in the company of Brett and Evan Morgan ('a little red absurdity').[11] Eliot's influence on Huxley's poetry – though the former said he disliked it and was later to advise him to concentrate on prose – was considerable. They had similar tastes, and bits and pieces of Eliot's aesthetic were finding their way into Huxley's observations about poetry. Later, Huxley would disapprove of Eliot's criticism, which he found unconvincing in its mode of argument. Reporting to his father the news that Blackwell was to publish a second volume of poems by him, Huxley declared: 'I find that more and more I am unsatisfied with what is merely personal in poetry.'[12] *The Defeat of Youth* when it appeared, however, would contain much personal matter. Reading the new *Oxford Book of Mystical Verse*, he concluded that it contained 'a lot of tosh'.[13] Mocking his own efforts in the annual *Oxford Poetry* just published – a translation of Mallarmé's *L'Aprés midi d'un faune* – he observed: 'I am like the aged Swift looking back on the work of my youth: "What genius I had then!" is all I can exclaim.'[14]

Huxley's last expedition of 1918 was to a poetry reading at the home of the society patroness, Sybil Colefax. Taking part with mixed feelings, Huxley was joined by Eliot, Robert Graves, Siegfried Sassoon, Robert Nichols, and the Sitwells. The event, in aid of charity, and attended by 'a large expensive audience of the BEST PEOPLE',[15] was chaired by Edmund Gosse. Robert Ross stage managed the whole affair which Huxley found rather frightful: 'Eliot and I were the only people who had any dignity.' The best part of the event was the dinner afterwards at the Sitwells – whom Huxley was still calling the Shufflebottoms. He got tight with Mary Hutchinson, Montague Shearman, and Lalla Vandervelde, wife of the Belgian socialist, Emile Vandervelde. Then out into the cold night and back to the 'hole' of Eton by train. Huxley at this time was sleeping very badly, possibly from the strain of the teaching, but very probably because his health was never very good – Virginia Woolf had noted his pallor. 'I live in state of continual exhaustion,' he complained in December, 'and really haven't felt in any way well or alive during the last two months except on the occasions I have been away from Eton.'[16] He had just been rejected for the third time by the army medical authorities and was being tempted by the possibility of a trip, all expenses paid, to chaperone Evan Morgan on a trip abroad for six months, which would have been a salutary change from London's winter fogs. This came to nothing because, even with his medical discharges, there would have been a problem getting a wartime passport. Lady Tredegar was worried about Evan's dissolute lifestyle and, thought, as Huxley put it, 'that my respectable middle-aged temperament would act as a slight brake to Evan's whirligig habits'.[17] Lady Tredegar had reason to be concerned. The next day, Huxley was at the studio of a painter called

McEvoy where the artist was 'spasmodically trying to paint a nude study from a very lovely little model with red hair . . . Evan and the model became increasingly affectionate.' He and Evan later lunched with Carrington: 'We all three went whirling round London in a taxi.' In spite of this lively social life, he had not forgotten Maria. Just before Christmas, Aldous had 'a happy letter from Maria' which hinted at 'the possibility of seeing her again'.[18] Her letters kept on coming throughout the following year, which greatly cheered him (though he was unaware of Maria's letters to Ottoline describing her and Costanza's flirtations with Luigino Franchetti at the Villa Fasola in Florence. In one of these, Maria wrote: 'I have had such longings and desires for you and more so since the other day I came across a lady perfumed so as you were and it brought back such endless thoughts and past things,'[19] and in another she enclosed a poem of her own in French where a perfume 'Me rapportant l'éternelle obsession de vous'[20]).

The new year of 1918 was enlivened at Eton by a new project into which Huxley threw himself with great eagerness. Encouraged by a young aristocratic pupil called De La Warr, who had introduced Huxley in the previous November to the Labour politician George Lansbury, a man he had found 'extremely interesting, very tolerant, not bitter like so many of these labour men',[21] Huxley helped to launch the Eton Political Society, relishing the prospect of causing a little debate in 'the home of all that is least revolutionary'.[22] The piquancy of the young Earl De La Warr – 'a passionate socialist'[23] – being the instrument of this piece of mild 'eminently respectable' subversion rather appealed to Huxley. The inaugural meeting of the Society had taken place on 8 December 1917, with William Temple, the Bishop of Oxford, and George Lansbury as speakers, and was reported in the first issue of *The Eton Review*, which appeared in March 1918, priced one shilling. There were articles by Lord Haldane and by George Bernard Shaw, and two poems by David Cecil (who also reviewed the latest Georgian Poetry anthology, noting 'the numberless young poets whom this War has caused to spring up in a night, like so many mushrooms'). The anonymous Editorial bore the unmistakeable signs of Huxley's influence if not his actual pen. It revealed that Repton – where Huxley had taught briefly in 1916 – had provided the inspiration for the *Review* in its publication *The Public School Looks at the World*. 'The War has stimulated precocity. The boy of nineteen is launched into the world as a full-blown soldier,' it began, justifying the bringing of boys into contact with politics, but its real aim was to 'persuade people to think'. One can hear Huxley saying: 'There is nothing more wearisome than thinking, no task which human beings, old and young, will make such efforts to avoid. They will do anything rather than think . . .' There was also a report of George Lansbury's speech at the inaugural meeting in which he said that 'his only connection with Eton was that he lived within a few minutes walk of the Eton Mission at Hackney Wick . . . He went on to remind the Society of their advantages in education and upbringing, and of their great privileges – none of which the vast majority of boys possessed.' Shaw took the opportunity to mock the Eton school uniform, 'the Penguin costume, which makes a drive through Windsor so mirthful'. The *Review* lasted for six issues, until 1920, a year after Huxley had left. On 16 June 1918, one issue reported, a Mr Mansbridge of the Workers' Educational Association appealed to his audience to 'take greater interest in all matters connected with the working classes'. He offered 'illustrations of the passion for education of a great many [working people]'. The 'policeman who learnt phrases of Greek classics by heart during his perambulations; and above all the porter who waved his wooden leg at the Professor of Economics, provided much food for thought'. Eton's progressive elite occasionally forgot itself, as when Issue 4 noted that: 'An ignorant and superstitious age believed in the infallibility of the Pope; now we believe in the infallibility of the people.'

Whether from the diversion of the Political Society or from some other cause, Huxley's health and spirits improved in the new year. The work was 'less beastly' and he began to enjoy going over essays with individual boys. 'The time goes whizzing past at such a rate that one is hardly conscious of anything more than the rapid flickering of alternate night and day – which is a grand thing in war-time.'[24] The jaunts to London continued. He spent weekends with the Sitwells meeting Arthur Waley and many other literary figures. With Osbert Sitwell he visited the studio of the Vorticist painter Atkinson:

'Atkinson and I got on wonderfully well, drinking champagne at lunch and talking about the *zeitgeist* and the great currents of thought of the age – quite meaningless, but extremely impressive.'[25] He was at the private view in May of Gaudier-Brzeska's pictures, 'which seemed to me too lovely',[26] and at that event he saw 'almost everybody' in the avant-garde literary and painterly sets: 'the glorious company of Sitwells, the noble army of poets, including Graves and Davies and Eliot' as well as Mary Hutchinson, Mark Gertler, and Atkinson. The following day he was off to the Eiffel Tower restaurant in Soho (haunt of the Imagist poets including Ezra Pound) where he found Gerald and Trevegond Shove. Pound would also have been at the Gaudier-Brzeska show and Huxley's failure to mention him points to the limits of Huxley's appetite for the avant-garde. He was mixing in progressive circles and, through his friendship with Eliot (who, unlike Pound, moved easily between the world of Garsington and that of the Eiffel Tower poets), was aware of the new modernist currents in English poetry and prose. Initially, he admired Joyce's *Ulysses*, encountering it as early as November 1918 when he told Julian: 'Among the quite moderns I sip the brilliant *Ulysses* of James Joyce; it has, to be sure, a slight flavour of excrements, but is none the worse for that.'[27] The two writers would later meet in Paris but mutual admiration did not flower. Huxley was contributing at this time to J. C. Squire's *London Mercury*, a paper pugnaciously hostile to the avant-garde and to literary experimentation – which it branded 'stunts'.[28] The paper also lambasted two other periodicals to which Huxley contributed: *Wheels*, and Chaman Lall's quarterly *Coterie*. Huxley was actually a member of the editorial committee of *Coterie* with Eliot, Richard Aldington, Wyndham Lewis and others and had encountered at first hand some of the leading exponents of Dada in Paris. His open mind led him to explore this work but his natural sympathies were not with the extreme avant-garde. Moreover, his own poetic practice was quite at odds with the principles of the dominant movement in London at the time, Imagism. Its programme, drawn up by Pound in 'A Few Don'ts By An Imagiste', ('Go in fear of abstractions . . . Use no superfluous word, no adjective, which does not reveal something.etc.') was certainly not adhered to by the poet of *The Defeat of Youth*. Huxley would go on to identify himself as a 'highbrow'. He stood on the creative, risk-taking side of the fault line which opened up in English culture in the early twentieth century and which plagues it a century later. Frank Stuart Flint, the Imagist, rebuked Squire for being 'provincial' and 'illiterate' and observed at the start of 1917: 'This is a curious phenomenon that our most liberal papers politically are our most reactionary papers in literature.'[29]

After the private views and the literary encounters in Soho, Huxley went on to a party 'just up the river' at Frank Schuster's where Robert Nichols, the poet, was living. Enid Bagnold and many others were at the party, which reminded the schoolmaster that there was another way to live, the way of literary success: 'the talk was perpetually turning on the size of editions, royalties from publishers, splendid reviews'. Virginia Woolf noticed him at the 17 Club in London: 'One room was very crowded, & silent; at the end of the other Aldous Huxley & a young woman in grey velvet [Carrington? Naomi Mitchison? Jelly d'Aranyi? Juliette Baillot? Mary Hutchinson? Dorothy Brett? Frances Petersen? Katherine Mansfield?] held what should have been a private conversation. A. has a deliberate & rather dandified way of speaking . . . They were discussing Evan Morgan & his affairs of the heart I think.'[30]

The possible incompatibility of the round of pleasure (quite apart from his professional duties) with the discipline of serious writing seems to have forced itself onto Huxley's attention during 1918. He told Jelly in May that he was 'engaged in rapidly becoming a typical schoolmaster . . . Meanwhile one writes a little – moderately well. And that is almost all.'[31] More tellingly, he confessed to Ottoline during the summer break that 'the hecticness and frivolity of social life tends to get on my nerves – tho' I love it while it goes on. However, I am, I find, fundamentally too earnest and too bourgeois in outlook to be able to plunge into it wholeheartedly: it seems such an expense of spirit in a waste of pure folly and not worth while for more than a very little time.'[32] Such dawnings did not prevent him writing to old friends like Carrington letters intended, as he put it, 'to provoke reprisals'[33] when he was lonely. Maria, too, was concerned about the set he was in. Back in Forte for the summer again, she exchanged letters with Ottoline (who had been receiving constant bulletins from Aldous) in which they expressed their common anxiety that he might be in danger of, as Maria put it, giving himself 'entirely up to those flighty people'.[34] Maria told Aldous – and he replied rather stiffly to her in response to the rebuke – that he should avoid being 'eaten up and swallowed by the Englishness of England and get too tightly grasped in that clasping . . . but keep himself fresh for the whole world and new people and longings'. Maria, who reiterated with emphasis that '*I am devoted to him*,' had never been fond of Bloomsbury and its brittle cynicism but seemed now to think that it was also insular and that Huxley deserved better. She was also acutely aware of the passage of time. She told Ottoline that she had been the age now reached by her younger sister, Suzanne, when she first came to Garsington 'and now I am twenty – Barbara [Hiles] and Carrington's age at that time – It's a nightmare'.[35] Aldous himself had told Jelly that – apart from 'another horrid little book coming out' his life consisted in: 'Wasting time for the most part, and wondering what is going to happen in the horrible uncertainty of the future.'[36] Aldous and Maria needed each other. But they would not be married for a further twelve months.

The 'horrid little book' was Huxley's second – he would eventually write over fifty books – and it was another volume of poems. *The Defeat of Youth*, like his first volume of poems, was published by the Oxford bookseller, Blackwell, in a series called 'Initiates', a term designed to distinguish it from 'Adventurers All: a series of Young Poets Unknown to Fame' in which the last volume, *The Burning Wheel*, had appeared. Huxley had now progressed to the status of initiate in 'A Series of Poetry by Proved Hands' in boards at three shillings. The title poem consisted of twenty-two sonnets which explore the theme of youth learning the lessons of experience ('for love is infinite discontent/With the poor lonely life of transient things') and preparing to face reality ('Truth is brought to birth/Not in some vacant heaven: its beauty springs/From the dear bosom of material earth'). They are poems haunted by feelings of transience and uncertainty and by deep ambivalence towards the object of his love. 'I give you all; would that I might give more,' declares the poet at one point. At another he is tortured by lust and the 'sickening heart-beat of desire'. In spite of 'his high love for her', he entertains confused and sometimes hostile feelings: 'the hatred turns/To a fierce lust for her, more cruel than hate'. In spite of Huxley's official allegiance to Eliot's doctrine of impersonality, there is more of him, one feels, in these poems than there is of Eliot in Prufrock. It would have needed clairvoyance, however, to have seen the pointedness of: 'Naked you bask upon a south-sea shore/ . . . 'Twill please you awhile to kiss your latest lover'. Formally the poems occasionally waver into an old-fash-ioned poetic diction but more frequently display the positive influence of the modern French poets in which Huxley was immersed. He had told Juliette of his bicycle rides out into Windsor Forest to sit under the oak trees 'and peruse the works of the French romantics'.[37] There are fine translations of Mallarmé and Rimbaud. The whole is rescued from a certain precious literariness by a self-mocking wryness. In 'The Life Theoretic', for instance, with its: 'But I who think about books and such/I crumble to impotent dust before the struggling,/And the women palsy me with fear.' In another poem, he suggests: 'I am a harp of twittering strings,/An elegant instrument, but infinitely second-hand.' Did he fear that his poetry was too deriv-ative and dependent on its literary models? There was perhaps some justice in the view of the anonymous reviewer in the *Times Literary Supplement* who observed that he was 'better equipped with the vocabulary of a poet than with the inspiration of a poet'.[38] That reviewer turns out to have been Virginia Woolf.

The harp of twittering strings and the marking of schoolboy essays did not bring any nearer the prospect of marriage. Huxley's family seem to have been in two minds about Maria, hinting at some insta-bility of character or excessively romantic temperament. Aldous found himself having to defend her to Julian. He conceded both that she had ('hideous expression') – the 'artistic temperament to the high-est degree'[39] and that 'aestheticism is a dangerous thing'. He was trying to encourage her to focus her mind on 'some fixed intellectual occu-pation' and argued that, given her youth (she was nineteen) she had done remarkably well. 'I only wish I was with her, for I think I could be of help to her in growing up.' Which is rather the view she had of him. More than this, she would 'help me out of the curiously unpleasant slough of uncertainty in which one seems to wallow so hopelessly these days'. While waiting to be united with Maria, he continued to write the poems that would form his collection, *Leda*, and a play. Huxley's belief that writing a play was the route to fortune has its origin here and the delusion would stay with him for the rest of his life. Plays, he told Julian, 'are the only literary essays out of which a lot of money can be made, and I am determined to make writing pay'.[40] The play seems to have ended up as a short story ('Happily Ever After'), being 'wholly undramatic', but Huxley had some interesting thoughts on how the theatre might find a future, through reducing its dependence on realism and multiplying the number of scenes. Unfortunately he did not act on these insights and was in practice a very conventional playwright, wholly uninterested in the dramatic innovations of his era. He was beginning to write more stories and initiating the move to prose. He would always regret not having been able to sustain his poetic vocation but Eliot was almost certainly right in his view that his talent was for prose.

These personal and literary explorations were conducted against the background of war, the aftermath of which Huxley was pessimistic about: 'I dread the inevitable acceleration of American world domination which will be the result of it all . . . We shall all be colonized; Europe will no longer be Europe.'[41] One of the few diversions 'which brighten the general darkness is the Russian ballet, which is pure beauty, like a glimpse into another world'.[42] He was part of a crowd which went to the performance in September – 'almost everybody in London was there' – and afterwards he met André Gide: 'who looks like a baboon with the voice, manners and education of Bloomsbury in French'. Huxley was with the Sitwells at the Coliseum for the opening night of *Scheherazade* when news of the German surrender came through. They all went to the Eiffel Tower to celebrate. Music and art were rapidly developing interests at this time and after a stay with Roger Fry, who taught him so much about art, he praised him for being: 'So susceptible to new ideas, so much interested in things, so disliking the old – it is wonderful.'[43] The terms of praise are significant. Nonetheless, it was a sense of inadequate knowledge of art (not just a wish for more lucrative employment on which to marry) that led him to decline an offer from Fry to edit the *Burlington Magazine*. Julian held out the remote possibility of a job on *The Manchester Guardian*. 'What I want more than anything really is to get a year with nothing to do except write ... I cannot write properly in the midst of the perpetual distraction here, and besides, I am always much too tired.'[44] It was writing that possessed him now: 'I never feel I am performing a really *moral* action, except when I am writing. Then and only then one is not wasting time.'[45] But money, the pre-condition of marriage, would not go away. 'It haunts me sometimes, the horror of it.'[46]

As 1918 drew to a close, the Armistice signed, Aldous could think only of seeing Maria again. There seemed some prospect of catching her in Paris at Christmas: 'It will be an extraordinary and unbelievable thing to see her again. After two years it seems scarcely credible that she has a real physical existence or that one would ever see her again. I want to get married as soon as may be and start some kind of reasonable life: I only hope these damned material difficulties won't make it impossible.'[47] In the event he was cheated of this opportunity, for the Nys family chose Naples instead. It had also occurred to him that Italy could be a place where one could live cheaply and write. But another three months stood between him and his goal of seeing Maria, and marriage. His days as a schoolmaster were now numbered.

Notes

1 HRC, Letter to Ottoline Morrell, 24 September 1917
2 *L.*133
3 HRC, Letter to Jelly d'Aranyi, undated but probably September 1917
4 HRC, Letter to Ottoline Morrell, 4 October 1917
5 *Mem. Vol.*, p27
6 *Ottoline at Garsington*, p208 Letter of 24 September 1917
7 Eton College Library, Letter from Lord David Cecil to Tim Russell, 24 January 1980
8 HRC, Letter to Ottoline Morrell, 24 September 1917
9 HRC, Letter to Ottoline Morrell, 8 October 1917

10   *The Diaries of Virginia Woolf*, Vol 1, pp61–2, 17 October 1917
11   *Ibid.*, p78 19 November 1917
12   *L*.137
13   *L*.139
14   *L*.138
15   *L*.141
16   HRC, Letter to Ottoline Morrell, 8 December 1917
17   *Ibid.*
18   *Ibid.*
19   HRC, Letter from Maria Nys to Ottoline Morrell, 13 January 1918
20   HRC, Letter from Maria Nys to Ottoline Morrell, 16 January 1918
21   *L*.136
22   *Ibid.*
23   *L*.137
24   HRC, Letter to Ottoline Morrell, 11 February 1918
25   HRC, Letter to Ottoline Morrell, 19 March 1918
26   HRC, Letter to Ottoline Morrell, 19 May 1918
27   *L*.170
28   See Alan Young, *Dada and After: Extremist Modernism and English Literature* (1981), p39
29   F.S. Flint, letter to J.C. Squire, 29 January 1917. Reprinted in Peter Jones (ed), *Imagist Poetry* (1972), pp143–4
30   *The Diaries of Virginia Woolf*, Vol 1, p125. 9 March 1918
31   HRC, Letter to Jelly d'Aranyi, 24 May 1918
32   HRC, Letter to Ottoline Morrell, 31 July 1918
33   HRC, Letter to Dorothy Carrington, 6 October 1918
34   HRC, Letter from Maria Nys to Ottoline Morrell, 28 June 1918
35   HRC, Letter from Maria Nys to Ottoline Morrell, 18 August 1918
36   HRC, Letter to Jelly d'Aranyi, 6 June 1918
37   *L*.151
38   Donald Watt (ed), *Aldous Huxley: the critical heritage* (1975), p39. Hereafter, Watt
39   *L*.154
40   *L*.157
41   *L*.160
42   *L*.163
43   *L*.167
44   *L*.168
45   *L*.171
46   *L*.173
47   HRC, Letter to Ottoline Morrell, 28 November 1918

IX

Marriage

Huxley returned to Eton for what would be his final 'half' at the start of 1919, determined to push forward to a new start in his writing career and to marry. He had spent Christmas at Garsington and Eton was 'rather a relief, in a way, after the tearing restlessness of London. Quiet and regularity – I find these indispensable to doing work.'[1] In the wider world peace was being celebrated noisily by the Northcliffe newspapers and the loud patriotism of *The Times*. Like many progressive English intellectuals of the time, Huxley was not wholly euphoric, though relieved at the end of the slaughter. At the end of November he had urged Brett to 'vote Labour, our only hope',[2] but his private agenda dominated. 'The prospects of the universe seem to me dim and dismal to a degree,'[3] he told Julian. He went to Oxford again to see if he could get an academic post but Raleigh was even more discouraging this time than last, offering only the vague possibility of an introduction to a job at a provincial university. America again surfaced as a possibility, its additional attraction being that it would be 'the only place where revolution will not break out'. Totally preoccupied with creating space to write, Huxley did not want to find himself embroiled in political upheavals or revolution which interfered with 'the free exercise of the mind – and after all, that freedom is the only thing in the world worth having and the people who can use it properly are the only ones worthy of the least respect'.[4] His aim was frankly stated: 'What I want to do is to marry and settle down to write.' Juliette – who would marry Julian in March – remembered Aldous just before the start of term, at his father's house in Bracknell Gardens, Hampstead 'desperately looking for some suitable job to enable him to marry Maria. He hardly spoke – deep in one of his curious abstractions, seemingly unapproachable.'[5] He was reading Stendhal, Flaubert, nothing much contemporary, and writing a long short story, 'The Farcical History of Richard Greenow', which would open his first prose work, *Limbo* in 1920. He was also working on the poem, 'Leda'. In January he sent Brett a copy of the first part 'for you to read and select the indecent passages from for illustration',[6] having earlier sent her his own nude sketches – which do show real talent for drawing. The news of Julian's engagement was shared facetiously with Ottoline: 'It makes me laugh rather, but I expect it will do very well: What a clean sweep the Huxley family has made of Garsington – all but Brett; and who will sweep her? She will require a 40 horse power vacuum cleaner.'[7] Aldous was best man at Julian's wedding on 29 March and Juliette remembered him, in his best suit, bringing their luggage to Paddington. As the train pulled out 'the curtain fell on an empty stage with Aldous terribly alone, desperate, numb and lost.'[8]

In April, however, Huxley's luck changed. After toying with the idea of a poorly-paid lectureship at the Sorbonne, he was suddenly offered a job on the editorial staff of *The Athenaeum*, the paper edited by John Middleton Murry. He handed in his notice at Eton. He estimated that he needed £500 a year to marry on, plus a further £100 from miscellaneous reviewing and literary journalism. He asked (rather uncomfortably) his father for some money from the income which Leonard Huxley was receiving from Prior's Field, adding: 'I hope I shall do something not unworthy of all you have given me.'[9] The path was clear, and as soon as the Easter holidays came he dashed across to Belgium to see Maria for the first time in two years and three months. He reported back to his father from St Trond on this sudden immersion into a stolid, bourgeois element so utterly in contrast to Garsington and the higher Bohemia to which he was accustomed, that it was 'a rather oddly un-English life. A quiet Balzacian Ville de Province, where nothing happens and where everybody who is anybody is everybody else's relation.' He added manfully: 'I think they are fairly reassured by my appearance.'[10] Already, Huxley had an inkling that 'Mère' – Maria's mother, Marguerite Nys – might become demanding, but he would eventually come to show quite a degree of interest in this family so utterly different from his own. Perhaps the most striking observation to his father was the simple declaration: 'I am very happy.'

Suddenly everything was moving very quickly and the paralysis was broken. Before the marriage on 10 July, however, there were various matters to be resolved, practical and emotional. On Maria's side, these had been voiced at the beginning of the year in a long, deeply felt letter to Ottoline from her parents' house at 19 Grand Place, St Trond. Never before cited, this letter reveals the extraordinary delicacy of Maria's moral sense, and the profoundly complex reasons for her decision to marry Aldous.[11] Beginning with the disclosure that her parents were 'entirely ruined' after the war and as a consequence of business failure (Aldous had been assuming that she would have at least some money to bring to the marriage) she asked Ottoline, the only person 'who . . . can talk objectively to me', whether 'if I accept poverty without dread is it fair though and just to burden him with a wife he must keep? For I shall abandon everything rather than tie his hands or be a charge'. She was in love with Aldous. She wanted him. But she could not bear the thought that she might be standing in the way of his talent. Her sister Suzanne, years later, recalled an episode from Maria's childhood when she was walking with her mother along the Bruges-Ghent canal. Spying a family of bargees on the tow-path, pulling together on the rope, young and old together, Maria, taking her mother's hand, solemnly promised: 'Plus tard, je tirerai ton bateau.'[12] That childish piety of the convent girl was transformed in maturity into an ethic of dedication, of 'sacrifice'.[13] Maria went on: 'I would anything rather than force A for my sake to give up some of his own time and travels to earn money.' Something had to be done – 'it is killing me to wait . . . and which is more *he* cannot go on waiting for me'. She wanted to get a job herself to free him for 'that work in which

I have so much faith and confidence and in which I longed to help him'. Or should she take what appeared to be Julian's advice and forget him? 'If it is my whole happiness which depends on it, it is nothing in comparison with Aldous's because a whole work of creation depends on him and on his life . . . which so little can alter and I won't be the cause of that little.' Maria pleaded with Ottoline to be 'cruel if it is necessary'. She told her that she had written to Aldous telling him that he must feel free to abandon the marriage. But it is clear that this was not what she truly wanted. 'I can hardly bear life,' Maria protested. She wanted to come and see Aldous and Ottoline and talk it over but the family would not spend their scarce funds on allowing her to make the journey. 'You must know how much my love for A has grown during these two years – how much my life has been only part of his and how all I did was only in view of when we would be together – to be up to him – to be able to help him – and now there is the menace of my being taken from him . . . Auntie, I quite quite rely on you to help me.' Those who have argued that the Huxleys' was a marriage of convenience must explain away this letter. It was followed by another, several months later, when the crisis was over, and with the marriage due to take place in a month. Maria's doubts were not wholly silenced. Hoping that Ottoline would not feel displaced in her affections now that marriage was imminent ('You could never know how much you are to me always and very much above anyone else'[14]), Maria confessed that she was 'full of fear – and of the responsibility I take in binding his life to mine – and then – you must not find it silly because it makes one miserable I so fear that after a time he cannot help falling in love with another woman clever and beautiful – for he will not know I am absolutely worth nothing – till then. And I believe I will love him always which would be worse for him . . . Why he should be in love with me I cannot understand but even less why he still is after two years – Do you think he *knows* me? He certainly always has a very close insight into other people which astonishes me.'

Many years later, in a letter to her son, Matthew, Maria would ask: 'Why, why in the world did Aldous choose me of the many prettier, wittier, richer etc young girls? Why in the world did he come back to fetch me after two long years of running around with more of those pretty and amusing ones of his own world? Knowing all the time by my letters that he could never teach me to write poetry or remember what I read in a book, or spel [*sic*] or anything he did set value on.'[15] That phrase 'ones of his own world' hints at Maria's sense of being regarded as an outsider, a theme on which she expanded: 'And why did I who was horrified by those Garsington men (and women) I who was so squashed by the English and terrified of them, why did I let Aldous approach me . . .?' The answer she gave was that 'because, though I was not then in love with Aldous, even though he was in love with me, we could see all the underlying possibilities which are really facts. He could sense, shall we say, instead of see, that in spite of all he had been told, I was a steady one, and I could sense that I would be entirely devoted to his service for the rest of our lives. In fact we were fated to each other.' And so, in spite of the inevitable ups and downs, 'we still stuck it out. Nothing is always perfect for anybody. So Aldous had to put up with me and I had to put up with him, or rather we had to put up with the difficulties life with a big L, as it does everyone else, got us into. Why we managed is because, underneath, our psychological sensitiveness knew better.' Maria told Matthew that perhaps he had never realised 'the terribly difficult position of an upstart little refugee getting away with the prize of the artistic English world – and keeping her prize – and at the age of twenty and without any schooling except failures. I did not ever come down to their levels of malice or sex, but that does not mean that I ever rose to their heights of intelligence and brilliance.' The context of this confession is Maria's sending Matthew a pamphlet on 'E' therapy by A. L. Kitselman, something, she believed, that helped her and Aldous endure because it was something 'stronger and better than ourselves'.

One final element in this exceptional marriage was Maria's bisexuality – a fact that has taken a long time to be fully declared by her friends. How much did Aldous know of this before he married her? How did it affect him in his decision to marry her? These appear to be unanswerable questions. Those who might know the answers – and who have spoken relatively freely about Aldous's various affairs with other women – decline absolutely to speak of Maria's private life. All we have is the evidence of a long and happy marriage – notwith-standing Maria's hints above that the normal marital stresses and strains existed – that lasted for thirty-five years.

Notwithstanding the gravity of the letter to Ottoline, Maria was able to laugh at the idea of the unpractical Aldous 'worrying about furniture and such things' in his letters to her. He had been busy in June furnishing the tiny studio flat at 18 Hampstead Hill Gardens, NW3 where their married life would begin – with a pug and a kitten as a wedding present from Ottoline. Aldous, after staying briefly with his aunt, Mrs Humphry Ward, where he persuaded her to read Proust 'for the good of her soul',[16] moved in to prepare the flat in the middle of June. He then set off for Belgium for the wedding. 'I have been leading a very strenuous life, shopping, painting furniture etc',[17] he told his stepmother. It was not all domesticity, however, for he still found time to frequent his literary friends. Katherine Mansfield reported to Virginia Woolf on a discussion she had been having with friends on the topic of the eighteenth century. It was interrupted by the arrival of Huxley who 'lay upon the sofa, buried his head in a purple pillow and *groaned* over the "hor-rible qual-ity" of Smollet's coarseness'.[18] But this was an interlude in a furious programme of activity. Brett was recruited to paint the woodwork in the little sitting room 'a beautiful dove grey'. His cousin Marjorie (daughter of Dr Henry Huxley who had rescued his eyes) came in to hang wallpaper and there were deliveries from Heal's and a new carpet. He also bought 'a marvellous instrument for heating water – a little bar which you fasten to the light and dip into your water: it will boil a pint in about 5 minutes – very useful for shaving and the like, also for simple cooking, such as eggs and tea: much quicker than a spirit lamp.' This little device perfectly encapsulates the simple austerity of the Huxleys' first months of married domesticity. When they eventually moved into the flat in July after the wedding, Maria was amused by this new incarnation of Aldous the DIY expert, painting and sawing shelves: 'I never suspected him of being so handy.'[19]

Maria's father was ill so the only relatives present at the wedding at the Hotel de Ville at Bellem were Maria's mother, Marguerite Nys, and her sister Jeanne. No Huxleys came over, and indeed, Leonard Huxley had never set eyes on his son's bride except in a photographic snap which showed him that she was 'strikingly handsome . . . very clever and with the changeful variety of the artistic temperament'.[20] When Ottoline last met Leonard Huxley at Juliette's wedding she had remarked: 'You will think I keep a matrimonial agency at Garsington.' Maria had written to him in June, punctiliously declaring: 'I am so ready to love you and hope you will find in me a good wife to Aldous and a good daughter to you.'[21] The couple lost no time in getting back to London and establishing themselves. Book reviews and articles started to flow from Huxley's pen. Since November 1919 he had been writing reviews for J.C. Squire's new journal the *London Mercury* but this ceased when he joined the *Athenaeum* in April. Years later, when lecturing his son on the need to accept that the world of work was necessarily tedious, Huxley recalled 'the burdensomeness of the asininity of doing "shorter notices" of bad books on *The Athenaeum*.'[22] Also in April he became the drama critic of the *Westminster Gazette,* in which capacity he saw rather too many plays. He signed a £50 contract with Constable to do a book on Balzac by the end of 1920 for a series called 'Makers of the Nineteenth Century' – a commission that would turn into a millstone around his neck and never be completed. 'I am rather appalled at the prospect of having to read *all* Balzac!'[23] He was busy but it was a literary and a congenial business: 'It is a crowded sort of life, but I enjoy the work, and the whole atmosphere of the *Athenaeum* is so delightfully remote, in its purely literary preoccupations, from the horrors of the present that it is in a way restful work.'[24] The frequent loneliness and frustration of the last two years were now being banished by the excitements of the new life but, in a letter to Julian, Maria hinted that 'delightful and comfortable' as the flat was, and in spite of wondering if one more room could be acquired 'so as to enable us to remain here all our life' the future pattern of wandering was beginning to display its tentative outlines: 'I of course long to go to Italy – and Spain and all those wonderful places.'[25] The memory of those two years of Italy, and the easy civilised life she had enjoyed with the Fasolas, was competing with gas fires and egg-boilers and drizzling North London rain.

Huxley was still trying to find ways of escape from the pressing literary hack-work that was giving him a living but which was hardly conducive to the writing of his first book. In October 1919 he had told Ottoline Morrell that he was planning to take the examination for a fellowship of All Soul's on 22 October but nothing more is heard of this 'offest of off chances'.[26] Early in 1920 he had a brief holiday in Paris where he stayed with the young writer and poet, Drieu la Rochelle, whom he had met in Belgium, who became a good friend of both the Huxleys, and who would later, to Huxley's dismay, collaborate with the Nazis during the Second World War. He also saw 'a certain number of amusing people',[27] and had 'an entertaining time among the cubists of literature', telling his former pupil at Eton, Edward Sackville-West, that the Cirque Medrano he had seen at Paris was 'by far the finest circus in the world'.[28] The Dadaists, however, soon palled: 'Personally I don't like their theories or their practice. Their satire is healthy, but I see no point in destroying literature.'[29] Exciting as artistic London and Paris were, however, two inescapable facts presented themselves. The first was the need to write seriously – 'if you know of a cottage or small house in the country, anywhere, in charity tell me: for I must find one' he pleaded with Edward Sackville-West – and the second was Maria's pregnancy. She went into a nursing home in the middle of April. 'It was indeed strange to see her looking still such an immature child with a baby on its way,'[30] Ottoline Morrell noted in her journal. Matthew was born on 19 April with Maria having 'weathered the tempest safely and auspiciously'. Huxley told Arnold Bennett: 'These works of nature really do put works of art in the shade.'[31]

In January, Huxley's first fictional book, *Limbo,* had been published by Chatto and Windus. Chatto's reader, Frank Swinnerton, had immediately recognised the quality of Huxley's work and the firm would remain Huxley's English publisher for the rest of his life. The book consisted of six short stories and a short play. The stories were immediately striking in their elegance, satirical edge and boldness – readers had already encountered effeminacy, syphilis, homosexuality and auto-flagellation by page 12. There is plenty of sexual disgust in these stories – and they reflected Huxley's own jaundiced view of the literary life. The eponymous hero of the *Farcical History of Richard*

Greenow is a serious intellectual who impersonates a lady novelist to make his living. Success at the latter means that 'the fear of poverty need haunt him no more; no need to become a wage-slave, to sacrifice his intelligence to the needs of his belly' – an aspiration shared with Aldous Huxley. More unsettlingly, there is a fastidious distaste for ordinary humanity. Greenow has a glimpse of Glasgow: 'Was it possible that there should be human beings so numerous and so uniformly hideous? Small, deformed, sallow, they seemed malignantly ugly as if on purpose. The words they spoke were incomprehensible.' There is also a reference to 'a family of Jews, who were anxious to live down a deplorable name by a display of patriotism'. The portrait of Richard Greenow has much of Huxley in it: his intellectualism, his emotional reticence, his perception of the family as dysfunctional and frequently absurd. 'From childhood upwards, Dick had suffered from the intensity of his visceral reactions to emotion. Fear and shyness were apt to make him feel very sick . . .' Politically, 'Reason compelled him to believe in democracy, in internationalism, in revolution; morality demanded justice for the oppressed. But neither morality nor reason would ever bring him to take pleasure in the company of democrats or revolutionaries, or make him find the oppressed, individually, any less antipathetic.' When Dick does manual labour on a farm, like Huxley woodcutting at Garsington, he has a problem with his fellow-workers: 'Dick longed to become friendly with them. His chief trouble was that he did not know what to say.' In another story, 'Happily Ever After', a foreigner in Oxford observes his fellow-students 'with their comic public-school traditions and fabulous ignorance of the world'. The lineaments of Huxley the satirist are beginning to emerge: the undeceived anatomist of English upper middle class life (as the above quotations indicate, the working classes were not Huxley's field). The older generation, the clergy, the representatives of the establishment, are held up to ridicule. Guy Lambourne, a Huxleyan figure, is groping for some positive perspective: 'What the devil is right? I had meant to spend my life writing and thinking, trying to create something beautiful or discover something true. But oughtn't one, after all, if one survives, to give up everything else and try to make this hideous den of a world a little more habitable?' Underlying this story is a critique of the cerebral life: in the end it is the ordinary sensual man who gets the girl. In another story, 'The Bookshop', a character observes: 'This journalism . . . or call it rather this piddling quotidianism, is the curse of our age.' In another, 'The Death of Lully', someone else declares: 'Man has made a hell of this world.' In another anonymous review in the *Times Literary Supplement*, Virginia Woolf, under the heading 'Cleverness and Youth', conceded that the stories were 'all clever, amusing, and well-written' but asked for something more: that he be a little more positive and refrain from tilting at easy targets: 'we would admonish Mr Huxley to leave social satire alone, to delete the word "incredibly" from his pages, and to write about interesting things that he likes.'[32] Thanks to the New York publisher George Doran taking up Frank Swinnerton's recommendation to acquire the American rights, *Limbo* had a very enthusiastic reception in the United States. Herbert Gorman in the *New Republic* compared Huxley to Max Beerbohm and concluded that 'he is one of the finest writers of prose in England today'.[33] Huxley had very quickly progressed from a minor poet and miscellaneous reviewer to a writer attracting quite remarkable praise.

He was being widely noticed and, in June 1920, Michael Sadleir summed up the marvel: 'Here is a youth, reviewed seriously while still an undergraduate and now, a year or two later, enjoying the undeniable thrill of a first edition value, while booksellers compete for his large paper copies . . . Huxley has so far achieved little beyond a series of negations, but the little that is positive is of a kind to promise that in thirty years he will rank deservedly as an important and genuine artist. Already he is the most readable of his generation.' Sadleir concluded that there were at present 'several Huxleys – the artificer in words, the amateur of garbage, *pierrot lunaire*, the cynic in rag-time, the fastidious sensualist. For my part I believe only in the last, taking that to be the real Huxley and the rest prank, virtuosity, and, most of all, self-consciousness.'[34] What more could a young writer want than such enthusiastic, intelligent and perceptive praise? The answer is, of course, the opportunity to fulfil the welcomed promise through finding more time to write and Huxley's income was still too small to allow him, with a wife and a new baby, to cut free from literary journalism and concentrate solely on fiction.[35] With this praise ringing in his ears, he took a third job in addition to the editorial post on the *Athenaeum* and his role as a dramatic critic for the *Westminster Gazette*. For a few hours a day he worked at the Chelsea Book Club in Cheyne Walk run by Arundel del Ré.

There are brief glimpses of Huxley the literary journalist in May 1920, in a letter from Katherine Mansfield. She glimpses him at the offices of the *Athenaeum* 'wavering like a candle who expected to go out with the next open door'.[36] Virginia Woolf's diaries record another visit to the office. She noted that he had brought out a new volume of poems also, *Leda,* and asked sharply of the young literary lion: 'Will the public canonise him too?'[37] The volume of poems contained a much-quoted poem, 'Fifth Philosopher's Song', which was probably considered rather 'shocking' at the time: 'A million million spermato-zoa,/All of them alive:/Out of their cataclysm but one poor Noah/Dare hope to survive./And among that million minus one/Might have chanced to be/Shakespeare, another Newton, a new Donne -/But the One was Me.' Huxley bought a bicycle in order to cope with his constant voyagings around literary London which confirmed him 'as physically restless as continually and changingly active in mind'.[38] It was a ten mile round trip from Hampstead to Chelsea through two parks. 'We are well settled in now,' he told his father. In spite of the small space and the exiguous finances, there was a maid to look after the child, Matthew, 'who waxes and grows fat'.[39] Clinging to the notion that a stage hit would free him from this hectic schedule, he told Leonard: 'There is nothing but a commercial success that can free one from this deadly hustle. I shall go on producing plays till I can get one staged and successful. It is the only thing to do.'

The lively reception of *Limbo* in the United States may have encouraged Huxley to pursue a new contact there, the writer and critic H.L. Mencken. In January, he had written to Mencken expressing praise for the first series of *Préjudices* and declaring: 'I only wish we had a few more people in this country capable of producing anything as good &, at need, as destructive in the way of criticism.'[40] Mencken's fearless trenchancy of style and his refusal to tolerate the populist agenda appealed to Huxley and the critic in turn responded warmly to the gift of *Limbo*. Huxley began to bombard him with submissions for his journal *The Smart Set*, including work which had already appeared in England in *Coterie* and *Art and Letters*. He told Mencken in one letter: 'I have some more stories simmering on the hob which I shd like to send you when they are thoroughly cooked & finished.'[41] After Mencken had voiced some objection to Huxley's vocabulary in one of his stories, he responded: 'But you know the mentality of the smuthounds – I bless you for the gift of that enchanting word.'[42] Huxley's early work is characterised by a frank disregard of the taboos of those smuthounds. In his turn, Huxley tried to help Mencken by offering to persuade his boss at the *Athenaeum*, Middleton Murry, to take a piece by him on the American literary situation, adding: 'Things are pretty bad here, but I fancy they have not come to quite such a pass as with you.'[43] Huxley expressed the hope that Mencken would allow him, when he visited England, to 'arrange for the local menagerie to show its paces'. In these letters there is something of the tone of Huxley's letters to his elder brother Julian – an anxiety to impress – which in this case sometimes took the form of near-parody of Mencken's vigorous style. Huxley was more convincing when he was being his more unforced self.

In May 1920, Huxley's third book of poems, *Leda*, appeared. The title poem is written in fluent rhyming couplets and once again with a rather old-fashioned diction and syntax: 'Leda, the fairest of our mortal race.' It aims for an epic manner yet does not wholly escape the feeling of literary pastiche. Middleton Murry himself called it 'a conjuring trick played with the incidentals of poetry'.[44] His friend Eliot was at this time at work on *The Waste Land* and his indifference to Huxley's poetry ('I was unable to show any enthusiasm for his verse'[45]) is not really surprising. The themes of these poems are similar to the earlier volumes: 'the imbecile earnestness of lust', 'the pain and foolishness of love' etc etc. In 'The Ninth Philosopher's Song', the poet writes: 'But I, too rational by half,' as if he were aware that this was a verse that needed to alter the ratio of its cerebration to its imagining. *The Sunday Times* was repelled by its pose of sensuous disgust (derived perhaps from French models like Laforgue or Huysmans): 'Most of the lyrics are violently ugly, with a determination to shock and astonish, which is highly unpleasing.'[46] An important contrary view came from Harold Monro, founder of *Poetry Review* and the Poetry Bookshop. Huxley had been in correspondence with him, offering poems for publication, and Monro saw more in Huxley the poet than anyone else. 'Aldous Huxley is among the most promising of the youngest generation of contemporary poets,' he wrote in a new book, *Some Contemporary Poets* (1920). 'He has a brilliant intellect, rare force of imagination, command of language, subtle penetration, irony and style; and the progress of his style has been rapid from the beginning.'[47]

Huxley was now being noticed and conservative English opinion was beginning to wheel around its big guns. On 20 July, the *Daily Express* published an attack on 'The Asylum School' ridiculing the poetry of the Sitwells and 'the clever gibberish of Aldous Huxley'. Huxley told his father he was 'slightly irritated' by the attack and was 'preparing counterblasts'[48] but he must have thought better of it for the controversy was allowed to fizzle out. His energies were really needed for writing, and, after a brief visit with the family (he had reassured his atheist father that there was 'no question' of baptising the child) to Garsington where he met Eliot, Mark Gertler and others, he decided to sever his connection with the Chelsea Book Club (now under new ownership). While at Garsington he spoke to Philip Morrell about building a wooden house in the grounds where he could live and write in peace, but the idea was not taken further. In October, he resigned from the *Athenaeum* to take up a slightly more remunerative post on *House and Garden*. Published by 'the *Vogue* people'[49] (Condé Nast) the magazine was an instant success, in terms both of advertising and circulation, and Huxley took advantage of the publishers' buoyant mood to propose that he edit a paper of his own called *The Patrician*. 'I now see that the only possible papers are those with pictures: nothing else can hope to pay.' The first issue of *The Patrician*, the English version of *Vogue*, appeared in December 1919 and Huxley contributed to this and many other of the Condé Nast publications, although much of it was anonymous. He was good at advertising copy and learned some of the techniques he would parody in the hortatory jingles of *Brave New World*. He later recalled writing about interior decoration, fashion and beauty. He told an interviewer in 1930: 'I used to do brilliant articles in *House and Garden*, all about incinerators and how to put plaster on ceilings!'[50] From his offices in EC4, Huxley wrote to his friend, Mary Hutchinson: 'Would you allow us to send a man to take your Dufy-covered chair and sofa? At the same time, if you permit it, he might take a few views of the rooms for later use as specimens of "Good Interiors".'[51] Huxley would have plenty of such introductions to London's fashionable interiors but he had other ambitions and the job lasted less than six months. Amongst his non-journalistic activities was a speaking engagement at the Lyceum with T.S. Eliot in December at, in Eliot's words, 'a dinner of the Poetry Circle of a ladies' club'.[52] The speakers had all been assigned topics in advance and Eliot discovered in horror that his topic had been appropriated by someone else. Huxley seemed embarked on a long speech that might give him a chance to improvise something in advance but just at that point Aldous slumped forward on to the table: 'the room was close and airless, and Aldous had unwisely started to smoke a large cigar'. Three men carried him out of the room and Eliot – making his first ever after-dinner speech – was required to plug the gap, 'a baptism of fire'.

In December Huxley gave up the Hampstead flat, sent Maria and Matthew to Belgium for the winter, and went to stay with friends in Regent Square, Bloomsbury. Italy – and what was to some extent a dry run for a lifetime of willing exile (he would be back in October 1921 and would not leave permanently until May 1923) – was now only a few months away.

Notes

1   HRC, Letter to Ottoline Morrell, 22 January 1919
2   *L.*171
3   *L.*174
4   *L.*173
5   *Leaves from the Tulip Tree*, p70–1
6   HRC, Letter to Dorothy Brett, 17 January 1919
7   HRC, Letter to Ottoline Morrell, 22 January 1919

8 *Leaves*, p71
9 *L*.175
10 *L*.175
11 HRC, Letter from Maria Nys to Ottoline Morrell, 3 January 1919
12 RL, *Mémoires de Suzanne Nicolas Nys*, p3
13 SB, in conversation with the author
14 HRC, Letter from Maria Nys to Ottoline Morrell, 9 June, 1919
15 *SB*2.135. Letter from Maria Huxley to Matthew Huxley, 1952 (precise date not given)
16 HRC, Letter to Ottoline Morrell, 12 June 1919
17 *L*.177
18 *The Collected Letters of Katherine Mansfield*, Vol 2, p315: Letter to Virginia Woolf, 5 May 1919
19 *L*.178
20 HRC, Photocopy of letter from Leonard Huxley to Gidley Robinson, 8 June 1919
21 *L*.176
22 *L*.590
23 *L*.179
24 *L*.180
25 *L*.180
26 HRC, Letter to Ottoline Morrell, 3 October 1919
27 *L*.182
28 *L*.182
29 *L*.185
30 *Ottoline at Garsington*, p213
31 *L*.184
32 Virginia Woolf, *Times Literary Supplement*, 5 February 1920, p83. Also, Watt, pp41–2
33 Herbert S. Gorman, *The New Republic*, 13 October 1920. Watt, p43
34 Michael Sadleir, 'Aldous Huxley', *Voices*, June 1920, pp235–38
35 We will probably never know just how much Huxley wrote at this time because his contributions to publications like *The Nation, New Statesman, TLS* and others were often anonymous. But thanks to the outstanding bibliographical work of the Huxley scholar, David Bradshaw, much more is now known. See David Bradshaw, 'A New Bibliography of Aldous Huxley's Work and Its Reception, 1912–1937,' *Bulletin of Bibliography*, Vol 51, No 3, September 1994
36 Katherine Mansfield, *Selected Letters*, Letter to Sydney and Violet Schiff, 4 May 1920
37 *The Diaries of Virginia Woolf*, Vol 2, p44. 31 May 1920
38 *L*.186

39 *L*.187
40 New York Public Library, Letter to H.L. Mencken, 10 January 1920
41 NYPL, Letter to H.L. Mencken, 12 April 1920. For a quite different inter-
    pretation of Mencken and Huxley's response to him see David
    Bradshaw, 'Chroniclers of Folly: Huxley and H.L. Mencken 1920-26' in
    The Hidden Huxley: Contempt and Compassion for the Masses 1920–36.
    (1994). Bradshaw sees Mencken as 'a tireless foe of mass democracy'
    not, as I do, a tireless foe of the forcing by cultural producers of medi-
    ocrity onto a mass public
42 NYPL, Letter to H.L. Mencken, 26 May 1920
43 NYPL, Letter to H.L. Mencken, 13 November 1920
44 John Middleton Murry, *Athenaeum*, 28 May 1920. Watt, p51
45 *Mem. Vol.*, p30
46 *The Sunday Times*, 23 May 1920, Watt, p7
47 Harold Monro, *Some Contemporary Poets* (1920), p124–30
48 *L*.188
49 *L*.191
50 Louise Morgan, 'Aldous Huxley Who Wrote His First Novel in
    Darkness', *Everyman*, 25 September 1930, pp263–5
51 HRC, Letter to Mary Hutchinson, 'Monday', undated but probably
    autumn 1920
52 *Mem. Vol.*, p31

X

Italy

For the first few months of 1921, Huxley moved in with his old friends Tommy Earp and Russell Green, who had a flat at 21 Regent Square, Bloomsbury. Another member of this flat share was the South African writer, Roy Campbell, who recalled the experience in his autobiography, *Light on a Dark Horse* (1952). Campbell recorded that 'the great Mahatma of all misery, Aldous Huxley' was installed in the flat when he arrived. He poured scorn on his lack of rugged, outdoor *machismo*, this being Campbell's pronounced trademark: 'As a practical zoologist and botanist . . . I felt ill at ease with this pedant who leeringly gloated over his knowledge of how crayfish copulated (through their third pair of legs) but could never have caught or cooked one, let alone broken in a horse, thrown and branded a steer, flensed a whale, or slaughtered, cut, cured, and cooked anything at all.'[1] It is indeed hard to conceive of Huxley breaking in a wild horse, let alone flensing a whale, but few opportunities would have presented themselves, anyway, in London WC1. For Campbell: 'Huxley was always as lost and bewildered by the very scientific civilization of which he is one of the main prophets, as a wild African giraffe would be if it were suddenly to be dumped in the middle of Piccadilly or Broadway.' Campbell also remembered that Green and Huxley were frequently disturbed at their typewriters by the sound of dancing lessons being given at the flat upstairs. This could only have reinforced Huxley in his determination to find a proper ambient for writing.

He was now engaged in polishing up the 1200 word pieces he had been writing weekly for the *Athenaeum* over the past nine or ten months, under the pseudonym 'Autolycus', in the magazine's 'Marginalia' column. He wrote to Frank Swinnerton at Chatto, the man who had 'discovered' Huxley, to ask whether the firm would be interested in publishing a collection in the spring: 'They are literary & moderately erudite, but not pedantic, as I don't know enough to do the professor stunt with confidence!'[2] These were the essays that would eventually form the collection *On the Margin* (1923). To Mencken, in March just before he went to Italy, he complained that he had been doing no proper writing other than the 'quotidian journalism'[3] – reviews, literary articles and 'the most fantastic hackwork (happily well paid) for an American fungoid growth which has established itself here recently, called *House and Garden*'. This work was now coming to an end, mercifully, and he was engaged 'in burning my boats preparatory to starting in a week's time for Italy, where money looks four times as plentiful as it does here, and where . . . it is still possible to live fairly cheaply. There I shall spend the next few months writing to amuse myself and seeing if I can make the process pay. If so, good; if not, then back here to journalism.' Huxley mentioned Lawrence to Mencken, mocking both his alleged psychoanalysis and its effects on his writing, and the recent *Women in Love* with its cruel representation of 'an old friend of mine' Ottoline Morrell. In a few months time, Huxley would be doing the same to that old friend, although he always protested his innocence. 'What an odd thing it is in a man who has done such exceedingly good things,' he said of Lawrence's book. Clearly Huxley's early enthusiasm for Lawrence had cooled, but as the decade wore on it would be rekindled with the same intensity as before. Trying hard to parody his master, Huxley told Mencken: 'Mr Clutton Brock is now known to write his sermon-leaders in the *Times Literary Supplement* by means of automatic writing; he sits still and his pen disgorges the excrements of his brain at the rate of eighteen hundred words an hour. Result: vast salary for

Brock and ever increasing popularity and esteem.' Huxley was worn out by his current style of life and had told Mary Hutchinson: 'I find myself forced to adopt a misanthropical attitude out of sheer self-defence – because I simply can't afford to spend time seeing people'. Unlike these fluent hack-writers, 'it takes me 7 days out of the 7 to do what I have to do'.[4] Nonetheless, he made a lunchtime assignation with her as 'a short holiday' from this work. By the end of March he was so exhausted by overwork and the stress of trying to write in the intervals of paid work that he was seriously ill – so much so, in fact, that the London Life Association refused to insure him in his present condition. 'It is absurd and rather humiliating to be a Bad Life,' he told his father.[5]

At the end of March, however, he finally left for Italy. He rejoined Maria and Matthew at the Villa Minucci in the Via di Santa Margherita a Montici in Florence. Costanza's parents, the Fasolas, lived in the same street, at number 15, in a villa called Castel Montici – still standing today though divided into separate dwellings and with a fine view of the city below, San Miniato on its hill, and the tip of the Duomo glimpsed through a frame of olive trees – ' a sort of Oxford from Boar's Hill effect'[6] as Huxley put it rather unusually to his father (having stood in both places I can just about see his point). The Huxleys would later live at the Castel Montici themselves between 1923 and 1925. For now, they had three rooms at number 4 furnished 'somewhat hideously' and at a rent of 150 lire a month. Post war inflation in Italy was high but the Huxleys felt they could live on up to 2000 lire a month. Bread was rationed and there was no electricity at number 4 so they were dependent on oil lamps and candles. It was nonetheless a pleasant spot, just a few metres outside the city boundary, and with a tram which ran from the bottom of the hill to the centre of the city in twenty minutes. Huxley did nothing at first but eat and sleep which did him a lot of good. In addition to all the journalism and professional theatre-going, he had translated Remy de Gourmont's novel, *A Virgin Heart*, which was now issued by a New York publisher. It is small wonder that he felt tired. But Florence was not to prove his resting place. Cities always exhausted him, and it was getting very hot, with a long spell of scirocco. The English colony there – 'a sort of decayed provincial intelligentsia'[7] – was proving irk-some and the art of Florence, to Huxley's rather exiguous taste, was 'too tre- and quattrocento. There is too much Gothic in the architec-ture and too much primitive art in the galleries.' The result was a decision to go to Forte dei Marmi, no doubt at the suggestion of the Fasolas. He and Maria and Matthew settled there for the whole summer from May to September 1921. Just before leaving Florence he wrote to his new American agent, J. B. Pinker, hoping that the latter would help to place material in the USA. He gave Pinker a list of English editors 'with whom I am on friendly terms',[8] a list which included his father on the *Cornhill*, J. C. Squire on the *Mercury*, and Austin Harrison. In America he had already been published by *Century* and *The Smart Set*.

Forte – a place already familiar to Maria – is about twenty miles north of Pisa on the Tuscan coast, below Viareggio, 'the coast where Shelley was washed up, under the mountains of Carrara, where the marble comes from. It was an incredibly beautiful place then.'[9] Today it is a busy resort, its flat, sandy beach – which Lawrence said reminded him of Skegness – crowded in summer with bathers and decked with bright beach huts. Though less developed when Huxley arrived at the end of May, 1921, contemporary photographs show plentiful families on the beach, sheltering under white canvas sun-umbrellas. The little jetty, now purely used for pleasure purposes, was used then to load blocks of marble, brought down on a railway line, to waiting ships. Huxley was fascinated by the 'enormous white oxen with long horns and melancholy black eyes,'[10] which were used to drag the slabs of marble. It was here that Huxley wrote that very English novel, *Crome Yellow*, in the summer months, from June to August. He wrote to Frank Swinnerton at Chatto: 'This is a good place: Mediterranean bathing at one's front door & large mountains entirely constructed of Carrara marble at one's back. The natives sup-port themselves by carving angels for tombstones, which they then export by the thousands to the U.S.A.'[11] For those three months, he established a very regular routine – apart from the setback of an attack of ophthalmia in the middle of July – which he described for the benefit of his father:

The day's programme here is simple and unvarying.
Work in the morning till twelve or half past, then a
bathe, then lunch, then a rest till four; then tea and a
little more work, till about half past five or six, when one
goes out for a walk till dinner time; then reading or work
till bed . . . One has all one's meals out of doors, wears a
shirt, flannel trousers and a pair of sandals and remains a
long time in the water without getting cold.[12]

In short, it would be 'perfect if we can solve the servant problem'.

Throughout the summer, at 29 Viale Morin, a shady street set back
from the beach, opposite the Villa Fasola, Huxley worked for five or
six hours a day on what he was now describing as 'my Peacockian
novel' – inspired by the short, witty 'novel of ideas' of Thomas Love
Peacock (1785–1866), whose sparkling prose and light satiric touch
were the perfect model for the young Huxley. Good progress was
being made by the middle of July when he wrote to Swinnerton in
London proposing a title, *Crome Yellow*, 'pleasingly meaningless
except in so far as the Peacockian house [Peacock's novels were invariably set in country houses where the characters have been assembled
in order to be put through their conversational paces] in which the
scene is laid is called Crome . . . The book, as I hope you realise, will
be fairly short: for the Peacockian novel is not a form that can go to
great lengths. About 50,000 words, I think it will work out. I can see a
smallish book of rather pleasant form – with perhaps a crome yellow
binding to carry out the hint of the title [a suggestion that was taken
up by Chatto].'[13] On 28 July, barely two months after starting, Huxley
mailed off the first 30,000 words with the promise that another
20,000 would follow in ten days or a fortnight. His typewriter, 'the
sole stay and comfort of my life',[14] had broken down at the revision
stage – the first draft seems to have taken about eight weeks – and
Huxley was worried that the rough script with handwritten additions
would be illegible.

By the end of August the book was off his hands and the reward
was a trip to Rome where he met Ottoline and Philip Morrell.
Ottoline claimed that they had come there because Maria wanted to

get work as a movie star (the careers of ballerina and novelist having been tried and abandoned in the past).[15] Huxley fell in love with Rome, telling Mencken that it was 'certainly the place where I shall come to spend my old age and if possible, large portions of the rest of my existence. Architecture, sculpture and painting give me, I find, as much pleasure as music.'[16] To Mencken he confessed that he had written *Crome* because 'I lack the courage and the patience to sit down and turn out eighty thousand words of Realismus. Life seems too short for that.' He inquired whether Mencken knew of any editor in the USA 'sufficiently *ramollite* [soft-witted] to offer me large sums for writing articles – word pictures I believe they call them – about Italy and art and all that sort of thing?' He explained that he would soon have to return to England to deal with the lease of the Hampstead flat and might have to stay: 'It depends whether I can lay hands on any cash without having to work for it journalising.' He made the same point to his father: 'The though of replunging into journalism appals me; I had been living for 2 years in a perpetual state of fatigue and I don't want to go back to it if I can help it.'[17] He estimated that he could live in Italy on £300 as opposed to £750 or £800 a year in England, and that the money would come from existing royalties, another £100 for *Crome*, short stories, and sub-letting the Hampstead flat. The only drawback to Italy seemed to be the political situation – they had just witnessed a band of seven hundred Tuscan fascists demonstrating against the Left in the course of which several people had been killed – 'a horrible and extraordinary episode'. It would be the rise of Fascism that would eventually drive the Huxleys from Italy at the end of the decade.

After the ecstasy of seeing Rome (undiminished by having had his pocket picked), Huxley returned to Forte with the idea of doing 'a gigantic Peacock'[18] suggested by the experience of the Sitwells' enormous castle at Montegufoni ('Here one has the essential Peacockian datum – a houseful of oddities.'). It is rather a pity that this idea wasn't pursued. 'I am giving Realismus a little holiday:' he told Julian. 'These descriptions of middle class homes are really too unspeakably boring. One must try and be readable.' One piece of very palpable realismus caught his eye in the newspapers, the case of Harold Greenwood, who had been acquitted at Carmarthen of poisoning his wife. This was the inspiration of a short story that had just appeared, thanks to Pinker, in *The English Review*, with the title, 'The Gioconda Smile'. What Huxley really wanted, however, was the chance to live a little, to travel and to explore, instead of this relentless hand-to-mouth existence of the writer striving to establish himself and keep afloat. The child had come too soon, so he had to go on earning, but as he explained to Julian: 'What I should like now more than anything is a year or two of quiet devoted simply to seeing places and things and people: to living, in fact. When one hasn't much vitality or physical energy, it is almost impossible to live and work at the same time. At least, I find it so. Life and work are always, for me, alternatives. Circumstances demand that I should work almost continuously, and I can't squeeze in enough living.' The next two years, however, would offer no respite of this kind. He was offered £750 a year by Condé Nast which was enough to make him return to London. As he explained to his father: 'The disadvantages of England are too much work and too little superfluous time or energy. The drawbacks of Italy are the absence of libraries and the lack of informed and intelligent society.'[19] The job with Condé Nast would last until May 1923 and there was a flat at 155 Westbourne Terrace in Paddington where they would stay until the end of 1922. The wanderer's life was being put on hold.

The Huxleys were back in London for the publication of *Crome Yellow* in November 1921. It was a striking debut and confirmed the twenty-seven-year-old's commanding position in the world of contemporary literary reputations. Several aspects of the book are worth noting. Scogan's description of the typical young man's novel, shows Huxley's awareness both of his own position and of the literary milieu he was entering – not without some misgivings and uncertainties: 'Little Percy, the hero, was never good at games, but he was always clever. He passes through the usual public school and the usual university and comes to London where he lives among the artists. He is bowed down with melancholy thought; he carries the whole weight of the universe on his shoulders. He writes a novel of dazzling brilliance; he dabbles delicately in Amour and disappears, at the end of the book, into the luminous Future.' Scogan's question: 'Why will you young men continue to write about things that are so entirely uninteresting as the mentality of adolescents and artists?' was one that Huxley would have been asking himself. His whole career was an attempt to frustrate the traditional expectations of the English novel, but the only solution he had come up with to date was to be clever and witty. There are hints of future directions, of *Brave New World*, for example, in Scogan's envisioning of The Rational State, and there is evidence that Huxley was not without self-knowledge. Jenny's notebook, which Denis accidentally discovers, contains a description that Huxley might have chosen to apply to himself: 'He liked to think of himself as a merciless vivisector probing into the palpitating entrails of his own soul.' The novels that would come throughout the nineteen-twenties and thirties, would contain much merciless vivisection of the life and the classes that Huxley knew.

The reviews of *Crome Yellow* immediately acknowledged its vivacity – it is certainly the brightest and wittiest of Huxley's books – and the fact that, as the anonymous *Times Literary Supplement* reviewer put it, 'Mr Huxley's personages are drawn with an extreme verve of crispness'.[20] There were some reservations about its bookishness, and consequent derivativeness ('he almost invites us to believe that the proper study of mankind is books') but the view of Lady Williams-Ellis in *The Spectator* (who described it cleverly as 'a Cubist Peacock'), that it was 'delightful', was the prevailing view. *The Nation* in New York felt that Huxley 'lives in a different world from that of D.H. Lawrence or James Joyce' – in other words that he was working inside a tradition rather than trying to revolutionise it. In *The Dial*, Raymond Mortimer worried that this 'desperately clever' book was too concerned to be iconoclastic and 'amusing' to be able to find time to be serious. He also made a far more pertinent criticism that would persist throughout Huxley's novel-writing career: 'I doubt if he is a story-writer at all. He does not care to concentrate, to dig.'[21] F. Scott Fitzgerald said simply: 'I find Huxley, after Beerbohm, the wittiest man now writing in English.'[22]

But those who knew Huxley and his milieu more closely had begun to notice another aspect of the book, its rather too uncomfortable drawing of portraits from life. Quite apart from the bicycling young man of letters 'enamoured with the beauty of words' encountered in its opening pages, who could not be anything other than a wry self-portrait, wasn't Jenny rather like Dorothy Brett? Ivor Lombard like Evan Morgan? Mary Bracegirdle like Dorothy Carrington? Gombauld like Mark Gertler? Scogan like Bertrand Russell (with shades of Mencken or Norman Douglas)? And, most worrying of all, was not Priscilla Wimbush, who presided over Crome, rather too obviously like Lady Ottoline Morrell at Garsington (an identification in no way lessened by the lack of architectural likeness to Garsington)? 'When I read in it the description of life at Garsington, all distorted, carica-tured and mocked at, I was horrified,' Ottoline declared. 'Here were scenes from the farm and the sayings of the farm labourers, which in real life were so witty and wise, made flat and artificial and quite denuded of their salty wisdom. Then there were pages and pages taken from a book of sermons by our rector, all mocked at and held up to derision. Long conversations which Aldous had had with Mark Gertler and Bertie Russell were here, but these were transposed and treated with contempt and ridicule, and portraits were put in sadly and cruelly distorted. Poor Asquith was depicted as a *ci-devant* Prime Minister, an old man feebly toddling across the lawn after any pretty girl. I was filled with dismay.'[23] She felt that Huxley had taken advan-tage of all the opportunities she had provided him with to meet these people 'and that not only had he himself behaved dishonourably but that he had involved me in his own dishonour'. She wrote immedi-ately to tell him so. He produced a long and pained reply, claiming to be dumbfounded that anyone could 'suppose this little marionette performance of mine was the picture of a real *milieu* . . . I ought to have laid the scene in China – nobody could have any doubt then that it was a marionette show . . . A caricature of myself in extreme youth is the only approach to a real person; the others are puppets.'[24] He claimed that he had neither the wish to represent real people, nor the capacity to do so, 'for I am not a realist, and don't take much interest in the problem of portraying real living people . . . the personages are just voices . . . They are puppets, devoid of all emotions, devoid indeed of most of the attributes of living humanity . . . it is absurd – and at the same time distressing and painful to a degree – that a long-cherished friendship should run the risk of being broken because the scene for a comedy of puppets [and now be begins to concede a little] has been laid in surroundings partly recognizable as real ... This incident is to me another proof of something I said in the book: we are all parallel straight lines destined to meet only at infinity. Real understanding is an impossibility.' Ottoline found the answer 'strangely disingenuous' – which it almost certainly was – and a breach opened up between them that was not healed for many years. She was still smarting from it the following summer when Virginia Woolf, who was staying at Garsington, went into 'her little green book room with the gilt pillars stuffed with pretty yellow books' to console Ottoline who claimed to be 'now indifferent to disillusionment', quoting from Aldous's letter and its expressed regret that 'mere marionettes' should have destroyed their friendship. 'But mere marionettes have destroyed it,' Woolf observed.[25]

Huxley remained on good terms with the other marionettes and, after his return from Italy, quickly re-inserted himself into London good society, as is instanced by an episode which took place just before Christmas 1921. Huxley, in a group which consisted of Lord Berners, the three Sitwells, William Walton, Augustine Rivers, and Alan Porter, the literary editor of *The Spectator*, and which called itself the representatives of 'The Poets of England', presented the soprano Luisa Tetrazzini with a chaplet of bay leaves at the Savoy. The Sitwells, with their gift for publicity, had ensured that press photographers and journalists were present.[26] Virginia Woolf's diaries show that he was dining around this time with Clive Bell, Mary Hutchinson, Maynard Keynes and herself. Huxley was certainly not being shunned as a result of his wicked satire.

Notes

1   Roy Campbell, *Light on A Dark Horse* (1952) p184ff.
2   Reading, Letter to Frank Swinnerton, 13 January 1921
3   NYPL, Letter to H.L. Mencken, 16 March 1921
4   HRC, Letter to Mary Hutchinson, 31 January 1921
5   *L.*194

6   *L*.194

7   *L*.197

8   HRC, Letter to J.B. Pinker, 16 May 1921

9   *Paris Review* interview, 1961, in *Writers at Work,* 2nd Series. (ed George Plimpton) (1963)

10 *L*.196

11 Reading, Letter to Frank Swinnerton, 20 June 1921

12 *L*.197

13 Reading, Letter to Frank Swinnerton, 9 July 1921

14 Reading, Letter to Frank Swinnerton, 28 July 1921

15 *Ottoline at Garsington*, p214

16 NYPL, Letter to H.L. Mencken, 8 September 1921

17 *L*.200

18 *L*.202

19 *L*.204

20 *Times Literary Supplement*, 10 November 1921. Watt, p58

21 Raymond Mortimer, *The Dial*, June 1922. Watt pp65–8. All other reviews quoted here in Watt, pp58–74

22 F Scott Fitzgerald, *St. Paul Daily News*, 26 February 1922. Watt, p72

23 *Ottoline at Garsington*, p215

24 HRC, Letter to Ottoline Morrell, 3 December 1921. An edited version of this letter is in *Ottoline at Garsington,* p216

25 *The Diaries of Virginia Woolf,* Vol 2, p180, 17 July 1922

26 See Mark Amory, *Lord Berners, the last eccentric* (1998), p74

XI

Entanglements

Huxley began his new office job at *Vogue* in January 1922 but by May he was writing to Norman Douglas: 'I moulder along in a pretty chronic state of boredom, and my dislike of work grows steadily towards a fanatical passion.'[1] He had already told Mencken that as soon as he could afford to do so he would 'flit off once more to some cheap Dago state'[2] to live cheaply and write. Meanwhile he was settled in the flat at Westbourne Terrace – three large rooms, including a study which the couple painted lemon yellow, and a basement infested with black beetles. In 1922 Maria invited her nineteen year old sister, Suzanne, to come to live with them. In a rather curious arrangement, Suzanne and Aldous shared a bedroom, separated by a screen, through which they would sometimes talk to each other at night. Suzanne accompanied him to musical concerts sometimes when he was required to write a notice, and she found him a fascinating companion, full of conversation on music, art, and literature, and with never a trace of condescension and never making her feel inferior in understanding. She noted that he was fond of 'les gens les plus simples' such as the daily, Mrs Jones. Maria tended to go to bed when Aldous and Suzanne were out at a concert – she slept in a separate room and in a third, the nanny, Bella, slept with Matthew ('Baby'). When Aldous and Suzanne returned, all three would take refuge in Maria's bed in the large cold room and read to each other. Huxley's eyesight was still very poor and when he offered, as he invariably did, to accompany guests part of the way home, Maria grew terribly anxious. So short-sighted was he that on more than one occasion he found himself embracing Suzanne who had been sitting in Maria's room, thinking she was his wife ('ce qui d'ailleurs ne lui était pas désagréable'). There was a perfect innocence about all this and Suzanne noted, from her vantage point of unique intimacy, that Maria – whom she always called 'Coccola', or 'little berry', the nickname she had acquired in Italy and which Aldous always used, lived with Aldous 'in perfect harmony'. Suzanne later recalled how fond Aldous was of a Siamese cat, which he allowed to climb on to his shoulder while he was writing.[3] There would be frequent dinner parties at Westbourne Terrace, for the Sitwells, Naomi Royde-Smith, Jack and Mary Hutchinson, Mark Gertler, and old friends of Aldous such as J. N. Sullivan and Tommy Earp. On evenings alone Maria and Aldous would sometimes wind up the gramophone and dance together, tangos and foxtrots, with Baby hanging on to what Suzanne called 'one of the long legs of Aldous'. He told Suzanne that the royalties from *Crome Yellow* were such that he would soon be able to abandon the reviewing and the journalism to concentrate solely on writing.

Aldous had been in discussions with his publishers since the return from Italy in the autumn about a new book (as well as talking of a translation of Flaubert's *Trois Contes*, which he declined on the grounds that 'to do the translation as well as it deserves to be done would be almost as much time as the writing of an original book'[4]). *Mortal Coils* was published in May. It contained 'The Giaconda Smile', Huxley's best-known short story about a man who poisons his wife (and who is writing a book entitled *The Effect of Diseases on Civilisation*). Huxley's morbid interest in human decay and debility is evident in much of his early work and though this is in part the traditional satirist's preoccupation, it has also something of the coldness of the vivisectionist. His sister-in-law, Juliette Huxley, was typical of many who found something faintly repugnant in early Huxley: 'Every time I read a new book of Aldous's I had a feeling of apprehension, because he peeled personalities to a painful surface sometimes. One

had the feeling that he was almost corrosive . . . There was something
vindictive in those early books.'[5] As usual, Huxley would have been
aware of this charge. As a character says in 'The Tillotson Banquet' –
actually the best story in the collection – 'What was the use of his own
youth and cleverness? He saw himself suddenly as a boy with a rattle
scaring birds – rattling his noisy cleverness . . .' Max Beerbohm, one of
Huxley's most famous admirers, wrote to praise the book. An even
more surprising one was Marcel Proust who, in the first volume of
'Sodome et Gomorrhe' in 1921 in *A La Recherche du Temps Perdu*
referred to; 'L'illustre Huxley (celui don't le neveu occupe actuelle-
ment une place prépondérante dans le monde de la littérature
anglaise) . . .' Huxley never quite understood how Proust had formed
this view (written even before *Crome*) of an eminence he certainly
didn't consider himself to possess at this time. Huxley thanked
Beerbohm for his comments and promised to call in on him at
Rapallo if, as he hoped, he was passing that way to Forte by train next
year. He hoped that an American success for *Crome* would enable
him 'to get away to Italy for a fairly long spell to write another on a
more grandiose scale and of a slightly solider texture'.[6] In July he was
complaining again to his father about the inroads of journalism into
'intelligent writing' and the 'necessary quiet thinking one must do in
order to write'.[7] At the end of May, Maria and Baby set off for Italy and
in June Aldous followed via Paris and Salzburg to join them at Venice
and Padua before settling for August and September at Forte. Then it
was back to London, to sit for a portrait by William Rothenstein and
listen to Paul Valéry lecturing at Lady Colefax's salon 'to a room full of
feathers and white gloves' according to Virginia Woolf, who sat with
Lytton Strachey, the pair taking 'a great dislike . . . to Aldous . . . in
spats and grey trousers'.[8] The following month she was dining with
him and Clive Bell and Mary Hutchinson and found Aldous 'very
long, puffy, fat-faced, white, with very thick hair & canary coloured
socks' and playing 'the raconteur; the young man of letters who
sees life'.[9]

   In one of the stories in *Mortal Coils*, Tillotson remarks in his
speech: 'The life of an artist is a hard one . . . It demands from him a
constant expense of spirit.' The echo of Shakespeare's famous sonnet

('expense of spirit in a waste of shame'), draws attention to another aspect of Huxley's life at this time. The pressure on him as a writer came not only from the dreary diurnal office work at Condé Nast's building at Rolls House, EC4, and from the theatre reviews and the music reviews he was starting to write for the *Westminster Gazette*, but from other claims on his energies. In her biography of Aldous Huxley, Sybille Bedford was frank about the way in which the Huxleys' marriage dispensed with conventional notions of fidelity: 'Maria took what I should call the aristocratic view of sex.'[10] She encouraged him in his affairs, helped him to pursue them and, it seems, may have – through her own attraction to beautiful women – been the means of introducing some of them to Aldous. 'Maria thought that he enjoyed such distractions, needed the change and his mind taken off his work. They amounted to very little, the distractions, and were either short or intermittent over the years. Aldous was never in the least involved.' Maria seems also to have taken responsibility for what Sybille Bedford calls 'the logistics' of these affairs since Aldous was disinclined to waste time on the intricacies of courtship. 'In a subtle way she prepared the ground, created opportunities, an atmosphere, stood in, as it were, for the courtship.' The contrast with Julian's similar pursuit of an 'open marriage' is painfully clear. Juliette suffered greatly from Julian's infidelities. What Sybille Bedford was unable to say so soon after Huxley's death, but has said equally frankly since, is that: 'Maria was bisexual and she did have a series of short-term, passionate relationships with other people while she was married to Aldous. But we are talking about one or two relationships . . . They were sophisticated people who were not afraid to experiment.'[11] Only the relationship with Maria and the intense, unhappy and unrequited relationship with Nancy Cunard were serious, Sybille Bedford maintained.

But there was a third relationship, with Mary Hutchinson, the writer and friend of Virginia Woolf and well-publicised mistress of Clive Bell (who was still alive when Sybille Bedford wrote her biography) which should perhaps be added to that list. Letters describing that relationship – which has never before been described – are now deposited in the Harry Ransom Humanities Research Center, at the University of Austin, Texas. There are also letters from Maria to Mary

Hutchinson, which indicate the complexity of this tripartite relationship which began some time towards the end of 1922, at precisely the same time that previous biographical accounts have emphasised the dominance of Nancy Cunard in Aldous's life. Disentangling these strands is not easy but in the case of Mary Hutchinson the evidence of the letters from both Maria and Aldous (none from Mary in return exist) is incontrovertible. In the case of Nancy Cunard it is wholly a matter of other people's recollections. There is not a scrap of documentary evidence. It has been assumed that the sudden departure of the Huxleys for Italy in July 1923 was the result of Maria's recognising that things had gone too far this time. Yet the relationship with Mary Hutchinson seems to have been, as it were, superimposed on the Nancy Cunard affair – if we assume that the latter began in the early autumn of 1922 and lasted until July 1923. The former certainly lasted well beyond this date. That two affairs could have been simultaneously carried on is of course wholly plausible but, at the very least, the situation was complicated. It can be argued that such inquiries are prurient or intrusive, and perhaps they are. But traces of these affairs are to be found in Huxley's novels. For that reason alone they are relevant. Huxley's view of human sexuality was complicated. Although he was unsympathetic to male homosexuality (in spite of having many close friends such as Gerald Heard, Edward Sackville-West or Christopher Isherwood who were homosexual) and therefore not wholly 'correct' by current standards, Huxley was certainly, from his youth, quite free from sexual inhibition. 'The incorrect sexual act,' he wrote in an essay in *Music at Night*, 'corresponds, in certain contemporary societies, to the expression of heretical opinions in Catholic and early Protestant Europe during the ages of faith.'[12] In his novel *After Many a Summer*, Mr Propter asks himself: 'What sort of sexual behaviour was normal? . . . there was not one type of human sexuality that could be called normal in the sense in which one could say there was a normality of vision or digestion . . . The different kinds of sexual behaviour could not be judged by referring them to an absolute natural norm. They could only be judged in reference to ultimate aims of each individual and the results observed in each case.'[13] But in a letter to J.B. Priestley in 1937 in which he discussed a book called *Sex and Culture* by J.D. Unwin, he observed that 'there does seem to exist a correlation between social energy and a degree of restraint'.[14] In other words, he seems to have been moving towards a critique of promiscuity – of the kind that features so markedly in his imagined societies, whether in *Brave New World* or *Island*. More than once he refers to the experience of 'alienation' in sexual activity – the 'alienating frenzies' of the 'Other World of sensuality' in *Island,* for example.[15] Quite free from the restraining hand of English Puritanism and Mrs Grundy, and from the notion that fidelity to one partner was a necessary ingredient in marriage, Huxley seems to have had nonetheless some reservations about the desirability of total sexual freedom, particularly when – as in his Utopian novels – sex is wholly divorced from procreation or any other social consequence.

Early in December, 1922, Huxley wrote from the offices of *Vogue* at Holborn to Mary Hutchinson, whom he had been seeing quite regularly at dinner parties with her husband Jack. Mary Hutchinson's name is to be found scattered throughout the voluminous reminiscences of Bloomsbury – mostly for her affair with Clive Bell – but also for her entanglement with others such as Virginia Woolf who seems to have enjoyed a complicated relationship with her. Woolf wrote in her diary in 1920: 'She might be one of those impulsive, affectionate, rather unfortunately concocted natures who are to me interesting, perpetually venturing out, rashly importunate, & then snubbed back again; aspiring; fastidious, vain & so on, but impelled by a kind of passion, for Clive, I suppose, which is sincere.'[16] Woolf, in other moods, contrived to suggest that Mary was a little predatory and manipulative, 'she is decorative, and hunts like a beast of prey, whatever it may be – a jewel, a toy . . . she is a crafty devil, Mary.'[17] But D.H. Lawrence told her husband St John Hutchinson in 1929 when he was staying with the Huxleys in Paris: 'Mary is one of the few women left on earth who really listens to a man – no men do – and it's quite stimulating.'[18] She was a writer – of one book, the aptly-named *Fugitive Pieces* (1927) – and had contributed, like Huxley, to the *Athenaeum* and *Vogue* – her essays in the latter appearing under the pseudonym of Polly Flinders. It is slight stuff, with a vein of higher coquetry ('We ladies are said to be frivolous . . . Certainly we are not useful . . .' etc.

etc.) and peppered with quotations from French poetry, and (rather too frequently) from Proust. The most vigorous passage in the whole book is her praise of Diaghalev for having breached the defensive wall of English philistinism with the thrilling modernisn of the Russian ballet. A reference by her to the 'fog of democratic dullness' sent up by the mass of ordinary people suggests that she was no stranger to the snobbish side of Bloomsbury. In spite of the notorious affair with Clive Bell, Mary had a bisexual side (faced with the intricacies of these Bloomsbury pairings – and this one is about to become more intricate – such labels as 'bisexual', 'lesbian', 'homosexual' seem clumsy and somehow inadequate to the task). She may also have had an affair with Vita Sackville-West. She allowed herself to be courted by Aldous because it was Maria she had in her sights: 'Of the two Huxleys – Maria and Aldous – Maria was the one I loved. Aldous was gentle, aloof, affectionate and even ardent sometimes, but it was Maria who attracted and charmed me. I always imagined she was "like a Persian". Her eyes were almond-shaped and very beautiful, her expression languid, her nature innocent, sensual, uncomplicated, her heart warm and loyal. Her hair was dark. She always seemed to be sweetly scented, oiled and voluptuous.'[19]

Huxley, as this first letter of 4 December 1922 shows, had been intimidated by this potent Siren: 'How much I enjoyed last Friday: I always used, in the past, to be so terribly shy and nervous of you. Why I hardly know – unless it was your air of impenetrable serenity that disquieted me. What are you really like?'[20] From the end of 1922, letters to Mary flowed steadily, and the two were involved for the rest of the decade at least, as was, gradually, Maria, a *ménage à trois* as it became, that seems to embody the popular idea of Bloomsbury sexual freedom. On the way back from a brief trip to Brussels in mid-December, Huxley scribbled another note to Mary in pencil, heading it 'In the Train' and asking: 'Mary, when shall I see you again? May it be soon? . . . My head turns a little when I think of you – still as enigmatic as ever, still somehow a little charming in your serenity.'[21] That this affair did not proceed entirely smoothly is clear from a telegram sent from Paddington a week later following a meeting at which some gaucherie on Huxley's part had evidently spoiled the evening: 'HAVE

RISEN EARLY TO BEG YOU FORGIVE A STUPIDITY THAT WAS
RATHER OFFENSIVE AND TO REQUEST AN OPPORTUNITY
NOT TO REPEAT IT.'[22] His next surviving letter to Mary, early in the
new year, again seems to indicate that this relationship had a prolonged and bumpy start.

Meanwhile, Huxley was planning his campaign of liberation from
journalism. Frank Swinnerton, of Chatto, later wrote that the journalistic discipline of these years had actually proved salutary in two
ways: it had given Huxley a training in the art of communicating
directly with a large audience which he would exploit to great effect in
his essays and non-fictional works; and it had knocked some of the
corners off him by giving a potentially remote intellectual a taste of
the real world of work.[23] That was almost certainly true, but the pressure – professional and personal – that was driving him towards a new
way of life was building up inexorably. Journalism was beginning to
disgust him because he was beginning to see how the new organs of
mass communication were sacrificing quality to profit. Huxley's
vigour of denunciation of these trends has caused some to see him
not as a hater of those who foisted bad art on the public but as a hater
of the mass audience which, willy-nilly, became the consumers of it.
This is a reprise of the argument sparked by his great-uncle, Matthew
Arnold, in the middle of the previous century. To these critics he is
guilty of 'contempt for mass society'. They would adduce as an example his remarks to Mencken at the close of 1922: 'The Press & now the
Wireless Telephone are doing wonders in the way of spreading darkness, vulgarity, fifteenth-rateness, folly, mental idleness, cant and
confusion, waste of energy: once can see the results at once. The gulf
between the populace & those engaged in any intelligent occupation
of whatever kind steadily widens. In twenty years time a man of science or a serious artist will need an interpreter in order to talk to a
cinema proprietor or a member of his audience.'[24] Huxley's unusually
colourful language here may reflect his own intellectual frustration at
this time or his desire to vie with Mencken's own vigorous mode of
expression.

In January 1923, the Huxleys moved house again from Westbourne
Terrace to 44 Princes Gardens SW7, a much more satisfactory address

in Kensington. On 8 January, Huxley signed a momentous agreement with his publishers. In exchange for a guaranteed income of £500 a year he would deliver two new works of fiction a year, one of which would be a full-length novel. He would retain his American rights and the prospect of renewal at the end of this three-year contract was strongly hinted at. This looked like the financial security he had sought and which would allow him at last to concentrate his energies on 'intelligent work'. But, as an internal Chatto memo had put it just before the meeting to agree the contract: 'How many works can he produce in one year?' Exactly. Was Huxley, in fact, exchanging one remorseless treadmill for another? No present-day writer would be offered such a contract, though it was not unheard of at that time. There is clear evidence over the next three years that the pressure of churning out two books a year was taking its toll, even for a writer who had already perfected the art of meeting regular deadlines. Moreover, although freed from the pressure of daily journalism – 'after April I shall be able to write what I want',[25] he told Suzanne – the pressure of his emotionally turbulent private life was rapidly filling the vacuum. The first typescript was due in July. 'For my sort of fever there is no specific quinine,' he told Mary three days before the contract was signed, 'Only, perhaps, work; I want to play – not a game but a new sort of music, a Mozartian relationship . . . I kiss your hands because I am not allowed to kiss your mouth.'[26] The relationship was still at a very early stage and not at all clandestine. He asked her and Jack to come to see a performance at a club called the Cave of Harmony, of his play, 'Happy Families', which had been published in *Limbo*, or, failing that, would she join him at a concert 'just to indicate how two people might know one another, lightly and profoundly . . .'[27] Mary was told to phone Maria to confirm the arrangements.

Maria was also aware of another woman in Aldous's life: Nancy Cunard. As has been indicated above, this is a very difficult relationship to pin down. There is no letter or note. No-one knows when it began or ended (probably late 1922 to May or June 1923, though they would have met earlier at the Eiffel Tower) and the sole sources are oral. One might even be inclined to dismiss it were it not for the powerful evidence of novels such as *Antic Hay* (1923) where Nancy

Cunard is transformed fictionally into Myra Viveash, the driven socialite, maimed by the death of her young lover in the War, as Nancy Cunard mourned her young lover, Peter Broughton-Adderley – whose name is on the war memorial at Eton. Nancy Cunard – whose image has been unforgettably caught in Cecil Beaton's photograph of 1930 – was by any measure extraordinary. Daughter of Sir Bache Cunard of the shipping company (that is, if she was not actually the daughter of George Moore by Lady (Emerald) Cunard) she was strong-willed, certain of herself, and, according to Harold Acton she had 'inspired half the poets and novelists of the twenties. They saw her as the Giaconda of the Age . . . She was slim to the point of evanescence . . . Her small head so gracefully poised might have been carved in crystal with green jade for eyes, and this crystalline quality made some people think she was cold to the core. But she felt passionately about injustice . . . [particularly for the African American].'[28] For David Garnett: 'She was very slim with a skin as white as bleached almonds, the bluest eyes one has ever seen and very fair hair. She was marvellous. The world she inhabited was that of the rich and smart and the gulf between us seemed unbridgeable . . . She was always certain that what she saw was the truth and there was no room for doubt.' For Mary Hutchinson: 'Her character I am sure must be described as deeply disturbed and violent, subject to fierce angers, fierce indignations, fierce enthusiasms.' Iris Tree recalled 'the delicate dance of her walk through London streets'. William Carlos Williams, the poet, called her 'that tall, blond spike of a woman' and Raymond Mortimer noted 'the mixture of delicacy and steel in her build . . . Never in her life, I believe, was she frightened of anything.' Virginia Woolf saw a 'little anxious flibbertigibbet with the startled honest eyes, & all the green stones hung about her'.[29] In short, she was a striking, powerfully emotional and passionate rebel. In Allanah Harper's words: 'There was no middle way for Nancy.' Was this the sort of woman who would want to attach herself to Aldous Huxley?

Maria talked about this affair to Sybille Bedford – who describes it, and Nancy, in important detail.[30] It was unlike any of Aldous's other affairs in its intensity, which was hopeless because Nancy had no interest in Aldous, preferring less sensitive, less 'cerebrotonic', and more aggressively virile, men. Some of the pain of this rejected address and thwarted desire is revisited in Walter and Lucy in *Point Counter Point* (1928). Nancy Cunard's fast life and sexual allure, her 'image', were the cause of his infatuation, one which proved too much for Maria, who, tolerant of sexual variety as she was, disliked the values and attitudes of Nancy Cunard's set and feared for Aldous. They had a brief holiday in Florence in April 1923 (passing back through Paris at the beginning of May), and were spotted on the ferry to Dieppe by Virginia Woolf, who darted out of view, afraid that her dowdy patrician Bohemianism would be shown up by the Huxleys' customary fashion-plate *chic*: 'I can't think it right to look precisely like an illustration to *Vogue*; and I daresay they thought the same t'other way round about us,'[31] she told Vanessa Bell. Huxley was always a very stylish dresser, fond of handmade suits from fashionable London tailors, and Maria was frequently stunning. Her son Matthew joked to me that he would generally have to walk several yards behind his mother for fear of detracting from the extraordinary elegant figure she cut in whatever she was wearing.[32] According to Sybille Bedford, 'Nancy and Aldous had a brief affair. Nancy gave in, out of affection, exasperation; after a few days discarded him.' His health suffered. Never a night owl or a drinker, his sojourns in the sorts of smoky night club frequented by Nancy and her set, were ruinous for him. He once spent a whole night pacing up and down outside her window. Things came to a head – and Sybille Bedford's account of what Maria told her directly is the most important piece of evidence we have (and will ever have) – when Maria confronted Aldous one night when he returned late to Princes Gardens and delivered an ultimatum. They would leave for Italy the next morning. She started to pack, with Aldous hovering around her. By first light she had finished. She tossed out of the window anything else left unpacked and they left for Victoria and the boat train to the Continent. It was the end of their period in England for at least a decade. That summer, at Forte, Aldous would write, furiously, the novel his contract demanded, and which his need dictated: *Antic Hay*.

Notes

1   *L.*206
2   NYPL, Letter to H.L. Mencken, 5 February 1922
3   RL, *Mémoires de Suzanne Nicolas Nys*, p38
4   Reading, letter to Chatto and Windus, 10 November 1921
5   HL, Oral History Transcripts, Juliette Huxley interview with David King Dunaway
6   *L.*206
7   *L.*209
8   *Letters of Virginia Woolf,* Vol 2, Letter to Ottoline Morrell, 1 November 1922
9   *Diaries of Virginia Woolf,* Vol 2, p216 3 December 1922
10 *SB*1.295
11 Sybille Bedford quoted in *The Sunday Telegraph*, 7 May 2000. See also Margot Peters, *May Sarton: a Biography* (1997) in which Sarton is quoted as saying to her biographer: 'Maria Huxley, you know, tamed women for Aldous. The young tigress, you know, she broke them in. Sybille what's her name who wrote about Aldous was both Aldous's and Maria's lover.' p394
12 *Music at Night* (1931), p108
13 *After Many A Summer* (1939), pp 228–9
14 L.430
15 *Island* (1962) p9
16 *The Diaries of Virginia Woolf*, Vol 2, p63 8 September 1920
17 *The Letters of Virginia Woolf*, Vol 4, p20. Letter to Vita Sackville-West 12 February 1929
18 *The Letters of D.H. Lawrence*, Vol 7, Letter to St John Hutchinson, 25 March 1929
19 HRC, Mary Hutchinson *Profiles* typescript. Mary's interest in Aldous as a means to Maria confirmed by SB in conversation with the author
20 HRC, Letter to Mary Hutchinson, 4 December 1922
21 HRC, Letter to Mary Hutchinson, 20 December 1922
22 HRC, Telegram to Mary Hutchinson, 28 December 1922
23 Frank Swinnerton, *The Georgian Literary Scene*, (1935)
24 NYPL, Letter to H.L. Mencken, undated but probably December 1922
25 RL, Letter to Suzanne Nys, 9 February 1923
26 HRC, Letter to Mary Hutchinson, 5 January 1923
27 HRC, Letter to Mary Hutchinson, 16 January 1923
28 Hugh Ford (ed) *Nancy Cunard: Brave Poet, Indomitable Rebel, 1896–65* (1968). All quotations on Nancy Cunard in this chapter from this source unless otherwise indicated

29 *The Diaries of Virginia Woolf*, Vol 2, p320, 1 November 1924
30 *SB*1.132–38
31 *The Letters of Virginia Woolf*, Vol 3, Letter to Vanessa Bell, 1 April 1923
32 Matthew Huxley in conversation with the author

XII

Disgust

'When one looks back at the twenties,' George Orwell wrote in 1940, 'nothing is queerer than the way in which every important event in Europe escaped the notice of the English intelligentsia.'[1] He noted a *pessimism of outlook* in the post-war writers such as Huxley, and concluded, 'they are able to "see through" most of the things that their predecessors had fought for. All of them are temperamentally hostile to the notion of "progress"; it is felt that progress not only doesn't happen, but *ought not* to happen.' The result was that there was 'no attention to the urgent problems of the moment'. Frank Swinnerton had made a similar point a few years earlier, on the basis of actually knowing Huxley directly (which Orwell did not). Swinnerton saw the work of these writers as 'a direct outcome of the mood of dissatisfaction, even despair, by which honest thoughtful young people were seized as they saw the consequences of four years of slaughter . . . They all feel that the world is a revolting place, and a hopeless place . . . they are all in a condition of gloom and disapproval regarding the world into which they have been flung. It is a world in a mess . . . The air is full of criticism and bad words.' Huxley in particular, in his early work of the 1920s, 'seemed without hope, and therefore without philosophy, without anything but horror at the futility of things'.[2] Swinnerton (presciently, as it turned out) believed that Huxley would find a way out of this impasse, but Orwell was largely right in his verdict on the decade. Until his political awakening in the mid-1930s, Huxley was concerned more with private ends than public means – symbolised by the sexual *ronde*. The story of his 1920s is a story with much of the outer world of English domestic politics (he travelled a great deal of course) removed. The *fascisti* who bothered him from time to time in Italy tended to be seen rather as comic opera buffoons than as the stormtroopers of a sinister ideology. His main reason for being there was, at last, to write fiction and nothing else.

'Most of my time is taken up doing fiction,' he told Mencken. 'I am contracted to produce a certain wad of it each year. I find it more interesting and more profitable than miscellaneous journalism. It also enables me to live here: which I prefer to London, finding on the whole that the pleasiveness [*sic*] of the prospect makes up for the vileness of man in these regions.'3 He had earlier made a similar point to his old friend the poet Robert Nichols (who, incidentally, had also fallen under the spell of Nancy Cunard at one time, writing her a clutch of sonnets). Nichols was told that the famous departure 'in rather a hurry' was a consequence of Maria's health and a desire to escape 'the odious tumult of London'.4 At the start of July they were giving themselves a break at Siena, watching the Palio, and glorying in the escape from drudgery. 'I am now cutting myself off almost completely from regular journalism,' he told Nichols, though he said he would still be doing the odd piece for *Vanity Fair* in the United States. They proposed to settle 'more or less permanently – as far as any arrangement with us is ever permanent' in Italy and had already taken a lease on the Castel Montici in Florence with which they were already familiar. 'There I shall settle down to grind out two yearly books of fiction for Chatto's [*sic*] and any other things I can manage. The life, I think, ought to be agreeable, and one's money goes nearly twice as far as in London. I shall come back to civilisation a few months every year to find out what is going on.'

One thing that was going on was the publication, in May, of a collection of essays, *On the Margin*. This was Huxley's first collection of essays – a genre in which he excelled – and all had first appeared above the pseudonym Autolycus in the *Athenaeum*, or in *The Westminster Gazette, The London Mercury* and *Vanity Fair* (New York). They are sparkling and irreverent. In an essay on the Shelley centenary (which allows him a pen portrait of the Tuscan coast at Forte) he mocks the fusty English approach to honouring the dead and suggests that the dreary establishment take a leaf out of the Italians' book: 'In this dim land of ours we are accustomed to pay too much respect to fictitious values; we worship invisibilities and in our enjoyment of the immediate life we are restrained by imaginary inhibitions. We think too much of the past, of metaphysics, of tradition, of the ideal future, of decorum and good form; too little of life and the glittering noisy moment.' The collection also launches some characteristic Huxley themes which would be elaborated in the years ahead – such as the critique of what we would now call 'the leisure society'. 'Like every man of good sense and good feeling, I abominate work,' he observes in an essay, which, if it appeared today, would send a shiver of horror through the young upwardly mobile professional. He attacked the 'stale balderdash' and the 'tepid bath of nonsense' coming out of Hollywood and argued that the Press exists merely to provide 'distraction' not thought. Even sport had now become a vicarious experience, watched not participated in. This is the frame of reference in which some of the ideas of *Brave New World* were developed a decade later. 'Self-poisoned in this fashion, civilization looks as though it might easily decline into a kind of premature senility.' Huxley sympathised with the industrial proletariat, forced to perform unrewarding production line tasks, and then provided by the cultural industries in their leisure with 'distractions as mechanically stereotyped and demanding as little intelligence and initiative as does our work'. Huxley wanted the ordinary man and woman to have the opportunities for mental stimulation and imaginative and intellectual freedom which highly cultivated people like himself enjoyed. This is an argument that would once have won him active sympathy on the Left. Today it has resulted in his being branded an 'elitist'.

Many of the essays are very light (but occasionally deceptively so) but some begin to point to an incipient dissatisfaction with the frivolity that has been enjoined on him. In a telling essay on Lytton

Strachey (who held Huxley, perhaps as a result of a certain competi-
tiveness, in some reserve) he noted: 'One cannot imagine Mr Strachey
coping with Dostoevsky or with any of the other great explorers of the
soul.' For his part, Strachey described Huxley as 'a piece of seaweed'.[5]
Yet Huxley also praised Edward Lear, whose nonsense, he argued, was
no less than 'an assertion of man's spiritual freedom' and his work that
of 'a profound social philosopher'. The 'They' of the limericks embodied 'that eternal struggle between the genius or the eccentric and his
fellow-beings'. In these essays one sees elaborated Huxley's belief that
art for art's sake was a dead end and that writing must convey something other than its own self-delight in form and must have content,
and a moral basis. In his essay on Ben Jonson, he argues: 'His greatness is a greatness of character.' And, finally, it is impossible to read
these essays without a sense of regret that the essay form is now virtually defunct. A young writer today has only the brief and tightly
edited book review, or an ephemeral newspaper column, as an alternative to these freer, more talkative forms.

The Huxleys' first stop in Italy was Forte dei Marmi and the Villa
Fasola. In a letter to Pinker from Forte, Huxley again claimed that,
'My wife's health is making it essential for us to settle for most of the
time at any rate, out here in Italy.'[6] Though Maria plainly preferred to
live in Italy, with which she was in love, and though she was a little
thin and 'too light',[7] at this point, the real story of why they had left
London could not be told. 'Ever since I have been in Italy,' he told
Nichols, 'I have been so wildly busy tapping on this machine for my
living – a book to be finished by the beginning of August and hardly
ten words on paper before I started.' A series of letters to Mary
Hutchinson (with Nancy Cunard out of the way, this relationship
was free to develop) from an address at 65 Victoria Road, Kensington,
seem to indicate that Huxley must have returned to England in the
second half of July, no doubt to deal with business consequent on
their sudden departure in June. The letters show Huxley still in the
mode of anxious and aspiring suitor ('The misery of dashed antici-
pation: the cold, unhappy anger of the disappointed against the raiser
and the destroyer of charming hopes.'[8]). Writing to her in red ink –
the only kind he had to hand – he quips: 'Not my heart's blood,

Mary'[9] and goes on to regret that he is going away again. She does not reply, so he writes again the next day: 'I don't want to suffer at all any more . . . I want to laugh and exchange delightful sentiments, ideas and kisses. And meanwhile you are always no more than the rustle of a skirt disappearing round the corner: you are a perfume in the corridor and the discreet closing of a door. And one evening conceivably . . . you might feel that it was time, today, for an answer.'[10] He begs her to give him an answer and to follow him to Florence: 'There are so many pathways in the Italian landscape.' The Huxleys seem to have made another visit to London in October 1923 because they were among a group involved in another jape orchestrated by Lord Berners. This time they signed – along with the Sitwells, William Walton, Harold and Vita Nicolson, and Evan Morgan – a plaster cast of Psyche owned by Lord Berners which Ronald Firbank had had the temerity to criticise. After being signed it was put in a taxi with Berners' butler and delivered to Firbank's home.[11] Huxley's association with Berners and the Sitwells – who were not really 'Bloomsbury' at all – shows how wide his circle was and is reminder that, notwithstanding his close association with Garsington, he was to some degree at a tangent to the mainstream Bloomsbury of the Stracheys and Woolfs. The term 'Bloomsbury' used to convey a certain approach to private friendship and sexual ethics and an aesthetic, has nonetheless been used here for convenience. And he used it in this way himself.

At the beginning of September, *Antic Hay* was finished – 100,000 words written in two months – and the Huxleys moved to Castel Montici, in the Via di Santa Margherita a Montici in Florence, having visited Belgium in August, then Milan where they bought their first car, a four-seater Citroën. The six-bedroomed house was cold and ugly – they had a genius for choosing ugly houses – 'but the position is marvellous'.[12] There was a fine view, from a south-west facing terrace and from a room in the tower, of the city below. The argy-bargy with the proprietrix over a defective water pump finds its way into *Those Barren Leaves* (1925). The Huxleys were not enamoured of the English expatriate community in Florence and saw only Norman Douglas and occasional birds of passage. When the 'servant problem' had been sorted out, Matthew and Bella came on from

Forte and the boy took great pleasure in playing with the peasant children in the sun, riding on mules, and collecting frogs in a *vasca*. Life promised to be happy, the only shadow on the horizon being a letter from Constable just before Christmas asking what progress (none) he was making on the Balzac book which should have been delivered no later than December 1920. 'We should also be glad to know when we may expect the manuscript,'[13] the publishers asked firmly.

In November, Huxley's second full-length novel, *Antic Hay*, was published. It was longer and more substantial than its 'Peacockian' predecessor but written with the same satirical verve and dash. Too satirical, in fact, for the United States, where his publisher, Doran, found the book being reported by the censor to the New York District Attorney's office. In his autobiography, George Doran revealed that the DA had personally enjoyed the book, finding it 'fascinating and artistic',[14] but he feared that 'some parts of the book might be misconstrued into the pornographic'. A compromise was reached whereby Doran promised, in publicising the book, not to stress 'the pornographic aspect', nor to refer to the threatened seizure of the book as a tactic to boost sales. Eighty years on, it is hard to see what could have been considered pornographic in the book. In England, however, trouble would be caused by the Huxley family. Like Lady Ottoline Morrell, they thought they saw resemblances and did not like what they saw. The memorable opening scene in which 'Theodore Gumbril Junior, B.A. Oxon.' sits in his oak stall in what is pretty obviously modelled on Eton chapel, is a sprightly mockery of conventional religion as embodied by the Church of England chaplain intoning before the 'spread brass eagle', as well as giving some insight into Huxley's view of his time at Eton. Gumbril's father, 'an anti-clerical of the strict old school', sounds very much like Leonard Huxley, and Gumbril's mother, who died when he was a boy, is pretty unmistakably modelled on Julia Huxley. Gumbril's hatred both of what he was currently doing and of work in general is also very familiar and the comic business of his patent device of pneumatic trouser seats echoes his desire for a quick economic rescue from the drudgery of work.

Like most of the people with whom Huxley consorted, the characters of *Antic Hay* are aesthetes and literary types who have no knowledge of the commercial or industrial worlds. Gumbril's visit to a Leninist tailor who denounces the pursuit of political liberty as 'never a greater swindle 'atched in the 'ole of 'istory' reminds us also that working class characters were never to be Huxley's forte. This is a very *amusing* book, the satire frequently very clever, as when the literary journalist Mr Mercaptan denounces the patent small clothes as 'too Wellsian'. Huxley is trying to forge an appropriate style – rapid, dislocated and impressionistic at certain points – to capture the restlessness of the bright young things, notable amongst whom is Myra Viveash with, like Nancy Cunard, her desperate memory of the lover lost in the war, 'that deathbed on which her restless spirit for ever and wearily exerted itself'. There is satire on the art world – the aggressive earnestness of Lypiatt, whom some have taken as a portrait of Wyndham Lewis, and the art critic, Mr Mallard, who 'had an immense knowledge of art, and a sincere dislike of all that was beautiful'. There is also satire on the cult of 'The Complete Man' so created by donning a false beard, and on modern advertising, as well as self-directed mockery at the Huxley figure himself: 'Have I lied to myself. Have I acted and postured the Great Man to persuade myself that I am one?' But at the core of the book are the exposed wounds of Huxley's passionate entanglement with Nancy Cunard. '"What have I done to you?" Mrs Viveash asked, opening wide her pale-blue eyes." Gumbril replies, "Merely wrecked my existence". In Chapter 21, Gumbril and Myra take a trip around London seeing 'all that is most bestial and idiotic in contemporary life', a trip in which the lights of Piccadilly Circus 'give one temporarily the illusion of being cheerful . . . It's like the Last Ride Together.'

> Gumbril and Mrs Viveash leaned their elbows on the sill
> and looked out. Like time the river flowed, staunchlessly,
> as though from a wound in the world's side. For a long
> time they were silent. They looked out, without speaking,
> across the flow of time, at the stars, at the human symbol
> hanging miraculously in the moonlight . . .

'Tomorrow,' said Gumbril at last, meditatively.

'Tomorrow,' Mrs Viveash interrupted him, 'will be as awful as to-day.'

But it was the scene in which the death of Gumbril's mother is described that angered Leonard Huxley, who accused his son of 'botanising on your mother's grave'. Huxley's reply to his father is very solemn and firm and cold. He was prepared to make no concessions: 'I will only point out that it is a book written by a member of what I may call the war-generation for others of his kind; and that it is intended to reflect – fantastically, of course, but nonetheless faithfully – the life and opinions of an age which has seen the violent disruption of almost all the standards, conventions and values current in the previous epoch.'[15] Huxley stressed what he claimed was the book's 'artistic novelty', which consisted in its being 'a work in which all the ordinarily separated categories – tragic, comic, fantastic, realistic – are combined so to say chemically into a single entity, whose unfamiliar character makes it appear at first sight rather repulsive'. This is an important insight into Huxley's view of artistic innovation (it anticipates the musical analogy of *Point Counter Point* or the dislocated time scheme of *Eyeless in Gaza*). Huxley's critics sometimes accuse him of 'inorganic' structural innovations that are no more than shuffling the elements rather than making it new in more imaginatively revolutionary ways. There is some degree of truth in this (a scissors and paste quality in the flashbacks and fast forwards of *Eyeless* for example). But at the very least he was confronting the issues and seeking formal solutions to the problem of representing 'an age which has seen the violent disruption of almost all the standards, conventions and values current in the previous epoch'. Conservative England certainly got the message. It swung into action in the shape of James Douglas in the *Sunday Express*. His review was headed 'Ordure and Blasphemy' and declared: 'Mr Aldous Huxley is beyond question a diabolically clever young man . . . It is a witty novel, but its wit compels the reader to hold his nose' (a more temperate review in the *Times Literary Supplement* had already concluded that Huxley had in fact 'faced his disgust' and was likely to move on from it; the

Sunday Express, however, was not about to let him get away with it). 'The sixteenth chapter,' spluttered Douglas, 'is almost Ulyssean in its nauseous horror.' Fearing that imitators would be spawned, Douglas held up his hand: 'If *Antic Hay* escapes uncastigated and unpilloried the effect upon English fiction will be disastrous.' He called on the great British public to repudiate this filth: 'The great poets are as clean as the east wind . . . Mr Huxley is a blowfly.'[16]

Huxley – who always claimed never to read reviews of his work – was nonetheless aware of the attack but continued to work away steadily in Florence, preparing his next fictional collection, the stories in *Little Mexican,* which would be published in 1924. 'Life proceeds very calmly here and I manage to get a good deal of work done, together with a certain amount of reading,' he told his father. He added that he envied Balzac's legendary productivity. 'I find that eight hours of writing is my extreme limit.'[17] Although he was able to talk about Mussolini rather frivolously in a letter to Julian about the concept of leadership in the modern state ('A little more pure reason and he would be the philosopher king.'[18]) the growing strength of the fascists in Italy meant that he had less than eighteen months left in what, for now, was still proving a far better way of life than the one he had enjoyed in London.

Notes

1   George Orwell, 'Inside the Whale' (1940) in *The Collected Essays, Journalism and Letters of George Orwell, Volume 1: An Age Like This 1920–40*, p557
2   Frank Swinnerton, *The Georgian Literary Scene* (1935), pp453ff
3   NYPL, Letter to H.L. Mencken, 10 August 1923
4   L.215
5   Michael Holroyd, *Lytton Strachey* (1994 edition), p455
6   HRC, Letter to J.B. Pinker, 6 July 1923
7   L.219
8   HRC, Letter to Mary Hutchinson, 18 July 1923
9   HRC, Letter to Mary Hutchinson, 26 July 1923
10   HRC, Letter to Mary Hutchinson, 27 July 1923
11   Mark Amory, *Lord Berners, the last eccentric* (1998) p91

12 *L*.218
13 HRC, Letter from Constable and Co. to Aldous Huxley, 17 December 1923
14 George H. Doran, *Chronicles of Barabbas* (1935), p168
15 *L*.224
16 James Douglas, *Sunday Express*, 25 November 1923. Watt, pp80–3
17 *L*.221
18 *L*.223

XIII

Florence

The winter of 1923 to 1924 in Italy had been 'the worst in Italy since Dante's days',[1] Huxley told Charles Prentice, the new man at Chatto and Windus, the publishers with whom he would evolve a long and creative association that would also include Prentice's Chatto partner, Harold Raymond, and, later, Ian Parsons. Huxley enjoyed a unique relationship with Chatto, who published all his books (something of a marvel by today's publishing standards) and they in turn benefited from his name and from his extraordinary co-operativeness. He was the easiest of authors to deal with.[2] With the New Year, he resolved to put his literary house in order, telling Prentice that he had abandoned a projected long novel, because it needed more time, and that he was going to offer him in fulfilment of the contract a volume of short stories to be called either *Brief Candles* or *Little Mexican* – 'I leave the choice to you'. (In the event the former title was used for a later collection.) His offer to send some of the manuscript immediately 'so as to begin setting up' and the rest within four weeks indicates the sort of 'Fordist' production line Huxley had strapped himself to with this contract. To Eric Pinker – who fulfilled for Huxley some of the functions of the modern literary agent but was really only supposed to be helping to place material in US magazines – he asked for guidance on how to get out of the wretched Balzac contract,

signed when he was 'very young, very foolish and poor'.[3] Constable's
Michael Sadleir offered a few compromises – another literary biography, a set of dialogues – but in the end, after much discussion, Pinker
used his influence to get the agreement cancelled. This was a great
relief, for Huxley was 'desperately busy',[4] and had fallen deeply out of
love with Balzac, seeing him as little more than 'a sort of gigantic
film-scenario writer' (as Huxley himself would eventually become).
He finally got the MS of *Little Mexican* off to Chatto in February.
Immediately, the chassis of *Those Barren Leaves* was trundled out on
to the production line. But not before he began to think of a journey
to Tunisia, and through North Africa generally, by car, with a book in
mind as the outcome. The Huxleys had begun to develop a passion for
motoring – with Maria, an expert driver as she became, at the wheel,
for it was inconceivable that Aldous, with his eyesight, would drive a
car. In March they were up in the Apennines in the snow and motoring across Northern Italy, the first of several motor tours this year.
Then Maria went across to Belgium to see her sister Suzanne, married
to Joep Nicolas, a Dutch painter. The couple spent a part of their
honeymoon with the Huxleys in Florence in April.

With the new novel, Huxley was still interested in trying to escape
the tyranny of Realismus: 'The mere business of telling a story interests me less and less. I find it very difficult to understand the mentality
of a man like Bennett who can sit down and spin out an immense
realistic affair about life in Clerkenwell (his latest, *Riceyman Steps* is
that) . . . The only really and permanently absorbing things are attitudes towards life and the relation of man to the world.'[5] It was for this
reason that the Byron centenary left him cold. The poet lacked substance, in Huxley's view: 'More and more I find that I can only read
poets who have something to say, not those who make beauty in the
void.' This is the Huxley aesthetic *in nuce*. Increasingly, he would
become preoccupied with 'attitudes towards life and the relation of
man to the world' and seek forms – the discursive essay, the historical
biography, the critical anthology – that were primarily vehicles for
ideas, chosen for their functionality. He was frequently explicit about
this. 'By profession I am an essayist who sometimes writes novels and
biographies,' he told the *New York Herald Tribune* three decades later,

'an unsystematic cogitator whose books represent a series of attempts to discover and develop artistic methods for expressing the general in the particular, the abstract through the concrete, the broadly historical and the deeply metaphysical and mystical within the special case, the localized scene, the personal adventure.'[6] Possessed by the intellectual's infatuation with the abstract idea, Huxley seems to be denying, in passages such as this, the capacity, the inventive capability, of the fictional imagination.

In May the six stories of *Little Mexican* appeared, 'very smart, in what the poet would call "England's bloody red". I think it ought to amuse.'[7] The book was another opportunity to see in Huxley's practice the intellect at war with the novelist's imagination. Often in these stories one feels that there is too much authorial commentary and generalising, too little abandonment to the inventive flow of narrative. Not that these reflections are at all uninteresting. In the story 'Uncle Spencer' the sceptical and free-thinking Huxleyan narrator is awakened to the limits of 'the materialistic philosophy, the careless and unreflecting scepticism which were, in those days, the orthodoxy of every young man who thought himself intelligent' and is brought to the realisation: 'Now it is possible – it is, indeed, almost necessary – for a man of science to be also a mystic.' This is the first tentative sign of the emergence of the later Huxley, and the slow eclipse of the angry young sceptic of the immediate post-war period. Noticeable also, is the fact that only one of the stories is set in England. Up to now, Huxley's brilliant satires on English life had been written wholly in Tuscany. Now Italy itself, Belgium, and France entered into his books in their own right. In 'Young Archimedes' there is a lyrical description of what must have been the view from the Castel Montici: 'And looking across the nearest tributary valley that wound from below our crest down towards the Arno, looking over the low dark shoulder of hill on whose extreme promontory stood the towered church of San Miniato, one saw the huge dome airily hanging on its ribs of masonry, the square campanile, the sharp spire of Santa Croce, and the canopied tower of the Signoria, rising above the intricate maze of houses, distinct and brilliant, like small treasures carved out of precious stones.'

In June Huxley's adaptation of Frances Sheridan's play, *The Discovery*, was published and was due to be performed in the 300 Club in London, produced by Nigel Playfair. In a crisp and witty introduction, Huxley explained that in adapting it for the modern stage 'I did my best to identify with Mrs Sheridan, to think in her terms, to catch her turns of phrase. I fear, however, I have not been entirely successful.'[8] Given the premise, he probably had been successful. The Introduction was Huxley's second attempt. In the intervals of everything else in Florence, he had quickly knocked out for Prentice a preface, which, after consultation, he admitted was 'rather too off-handed'.[9] This is an understatement for it is a rather too frank and insouciant statement of the low creed of the freelance writer (we may sometimes think these thoughts but it is unwise to broadcast them). The scrapped introduction confessed that in the course of 'a strenuous career as a literary journalist'[10] Huxley had been required often to write at short notice 'about subjects concerning which I knew little or nothing at all'. At first he was nervous about being found out in this imposture but eventually: 'I found that an hour's reading in the London Library was enough to provide me with just the convincing little facts on any topic which only the erudite would be likely to know; I acquired the art of setting forth these scraps of information casually and with an air of professional ease, that was wholly convincing.' Journalism, he concluded, 'is not the best form of intellectual training for a young man', a remark reminiscent of one he would make towards the end of his life to a group of journalism students in Los Angeles: 'It's an awfully good field to get into, if you make sure that you get out of it.'[11] Huxley went on to make another confession, which would be repeated several times subsequently, that he took no interest in the books he had written: 'The writing of FINIS at the end of a manuscript should be the equivalent of burning it and when a book is published it is for the author as though it has been destroyed.' This was because he did not want to 'allow recollections of past states of mind to interfere with present thoughts' and to move on.

Chatto were no doubt wise to dissuade a writer from asking the public to take an interest in books in which the author professed to take none. Chatto were also at this time dealing with the continuing consequences of *Antic Hay*. Woken up by the *Sunday Express*, the moral guardians were on the march. The Bishop of London, in his capacity as chairman of the London Council of the Promotion of Public Morality, had requested Chatto either to withdraw the book or to expunge certain passages which would, in their present form, be injurious to 'women and girls . . . who constitute so large a proportion of the Readers of fiction'. Chatto replied politely that it would do no such thing, pointing out that it was a book 'of interest exclusively to intellectual people', as sales were making clear, and therefore was no threat to 'the large class of women and girls to which you refer' (who presumably did not form part of the class of 'intellectual people'.)[12] Huxley himself observed: 'As for these Moralists – they are a little late in the day, aren't they? The devilish work is done already.'[13] Shortly before leaving for Forte, where he would spend July and August finishing *Those Barren Leaves*, Huxley told Prentice what he planned to follow this novel: 'a portentous historical novel of which the disjected members of the germ have been weltering in my mind for years. It should be done in about 18 months or two years [his next novel would actually turn out to be *Point Counter Point* in 1928]'.[14] The contractual obligation for 1925 would be met, Huxley promised, by a collection of short stories in the spring and a 'light novel with mild detective interest' for the autumn. In fact 1925 and 1926 would see, apart from the novel, two travel books, a collection of essays, and a book of short stories. The novel, he reported from Forte at the Villa Fasola, was not going well: 'Meanwhile, this damned book of mine is still on my hands . . . I've had a lot of trouble getting the thing into shape, writing and re-writing whole chunks before they took their proper form and proportion. I'd rather like to begin the whole thing over again now, to redigest & polish. But time lacks.'[15] Still, there was the consolation of seeing the egregious James Douglas recanting with praise of *Little Mexican*. 'What a frothing swill-tub of a man!'

Those Barren Leaves, was not finished when the Huxleys, leaving Matthew at the Villa Fasola, set off again for the Alps, where he completed it along the road, at a place called Amberieu in Savoie. Then they drove on to Paris, staying a couple of nights with Lewis Gielgud, with Maria having established herself as an excellent chauffeuse: 'She drives our little Citroën with great vigour and skill and has taken us across the Alps and through France in a most dashing fashion.'[16] From Paris they crossed to London, staying at 258 King's Road in Chelsea, a flat lent to them by an old friend, Rachel Russell. One purpose of coming to London was to enable Huxley to consult some decent libraries – something he was unable to do in Italy. He caught up with friends such as T.S. Eliot and Osbert Sitwell who told him some gossip. Huxley's cousin, Arnold Ward, Mrs Humphry Ward's son, had drunkenly announced in the St James's Club that Huxley had disgraced his ancestors by writing *Antic Hay*. The Huxleys also met Mary Hutchinson, who had offered to put them up at her house in Upper Mall, Hammersmith, and who complained later to Maria that Aldous had had a depressing effect on her – perhaps through his mooning attentions. He wrote to her to apologise, complaining that he was an unsuccessful lover but still a hopeful one, adding in a post-script: 'If only you'd come to Italy.'[17] Then the Huxley cavalcade – the Citroën was performing well but they had their eyes on a new Lancia 'which is said to have all the qualities of the Alfa Romeo, which won the Grand Prix this year'[18] – moved on to Holland and Belgium, Paris, central and southern France, and finally back to Florence by the start of October. Just as Huxley's book plans were often torn up as soon as they were announced, so his domicile was always imper-manent. Back in Florence he tried to persuade Robert Nichols to live in Italy because it was so cheap: 'On the same income on which I just kept alive, uncomfortably, in London, I live in a large house, with 2 servants and a nurse, keep a small car, travel quite a lot and save money to boot. I am also far healthier, put on weight.'[19] His good health and spirits were reported to several friends. He fully intended to stay in Italy – but not Florence because of the 'frightful' English expats – and would come back to England – London or Oxford – only when Matthew needed to be educated (he was now four). Meanwhile he was 'incessantly busy' with his writing and pleased enough with *Those Barren Leaves*. 'The main theme is the undercutting of everything by a sort of despairing scepticism and then the undercutting of that by mysticism.' Prentice was pleased too. 'The book seems to come off alright,' Huxley told him. 'The characters are better done, I think, than in *Antic Hay*; & what was only implied there is made much more explicit in this book.'[20] Prentice was also informed that Huxley was at work on a volume of essays: 'The central theme will be travel: but I mean to make it the excuse for a variety of lucubrations. For a title I thought that *Along the Road* or *At the Road's Edge* or something like that, reminiscent of *On the Margin* would vaguely indicate the nature of the book.' The lucubrations, however, were the thing.

Towards the end of November, Maria wrote from Florence to Mary Hutchinson with whom she had been corresponding regularly. She was rather less enamoured than Aldous of the Castel Montici and letters over the previous year had complained of the ugliness of the house and its furnishings and the flow of visitors ('I have had little pleasure out of it; turned me into a taxidriver – meet them at the station . . . take them back with their luggage'[21]) many of whom she did not care for. There was Lady Colefax and Lord Berners in his gleaming Rolls-Royce, the trio of titled persons completed by Evan Morgan in his beautifully cut and bejewelled clothes – 'an 18th century figure come to life again'.[22] J. W. Sullivan was a much more sympathetic figure to them, full of serious ideas and interesting talk. But, notwithstanding the cold of a second winter, the beauty of the house's aspect made her talk of wanting to buy it. Maria's letter of 20 November 1924 reveals that the Huxley–Hutchinson relationship was more intricate than it hitherto might have appeared. A veiled reference to 'the Oxford beds' (had they visited Oxford in September when in England?) and 'the hours wondering when and where we will meet' is followed by the exclamation: 'Darling Mary, how often I think of our mysterious escapade and our last evening in your room, sweet memories, few but endless in their details . . .' Aldous is mentioned. 'He knows I am writing and pay you devoted court and wishes to be allowed to kiss your hand hoping you forgave him long ago for discovering his character not to be frivolous and naughty.' What had begun as a pursuit of Mary by Aldous was now clearly a complicated relationship between three people. Aldous and Maria never ceased to love each other. Maria and Mary loved each other. Aldous loved – or desired – Mary with a force that was not reciprocated.[23]

The Huxleys enjoyed a cold Christmas at the Castel Montici – Aldous writing a very brief children's story called *Noa* for Gabriella Fasola, Costanza's daughter, which he illustrated with his own water-colours – there are scenes of animals ascending the ark, and an elephant getting stuck, which are quite charming.[24] They had six months left in Florence.

In January 1925, Huxley finished *Along the Road* and *Those Barren Leaves* was published. It sold 8000 copies in the first year – which demonstrates that Huxley was becoming a novelist of some reputa-tion, with the discriminating reading public at least. Like the two previous novels it is satirical in intent and if anything the writing is crisper and brighter. The continuing influence of Peacock is there, but also perhaps something of Ronald Firbank and Norman Douglas. Plainly unrepentant about drawing from life, Mrs Lilian Aldwinkle, who makes an early appearance – 'one of those large, handsome, old-masterish women' – looks very much like Lady Ottoline Morrell once more. The same unsparing light is cast on all the characters, raising questions about Huxley's own frame of reference. For all his free-thinking modernity, his mind and morals were formed by a Victorian tradition of ethical high-mindedness. Whatever the sexual freedoms which we can see that he claimed in his personal life, there is, para-doxically, a deeply moral view – in what one might be tempted to call an old-fashioned sense – of the antic hay danced by these characters. And always ideas are as important as plot. Characters are always saying interesting things and mounting interesting arguments. Where a less sophisticated novelist would begin with a simple description of the English abroad, Huxley in this novel immediately focuses our attention on the nature of English Italophilia. Mrs Aldwinkle is cru-elly judged to have 'the thoughts and feelings of a generation that had grown up placidly in sheltered surroundings – or perhaps had not grown up at all'.

But it was not just the comfortable bourgeois who was being satirised. The complacent 'progressive' of the older generation also feels the lash. Mr Cardan is made to observe: 'I was brought up in the simple faith of nineteenth century materialism.' His conscience was appeased by a philanthropy which resulted in 'a quite superfluous number of white-tiled lavatories for our workers'. The younger generation, in the person of Calamy, lives, like Huxley, in a time governed by 'the sense that everything's perfectly provisional and temporary . . . it's all infinitely exhilarating.' There is perhaps something of Huxley in the self-assessment of the novelist, Mary Thriplow: 'They like my books because they're smart and unexpected and rather paradoxical and cynical and elegantly brutal. They don't see how serious it all is. They don't see the tragedy and the tenderness underneath. "You see," she explained, "I'm trying to do something new – a chemical compound of all the categories. Lightness and tragedy and loveliness and wit and fantasy and realism and irony and sentiment all combined."' Huxley's tussle with the rival claims of art and social commitment – seen at this stage in terms merely of the need for art to have some content – was steadily expanding. Francis Chelifer, observes: 'I have learned the art of writing well, which is the art of saying nothing elaborately.' He adds that the doctrine of art for art's sake is 'the last and silliest of the idols'. In a self-reflexive manner that is almost proto-post-modernist, Huxley is engaged in a running debate with himself about the nature of writing.

But the main sense of revulsion in this novel is at 'the horrors and squalors of civilised life', in Chelifer's words, which arise from 'men's lack of reason – from their failure to be completely and sapiently human'. Chelifer's job on the *Rabbit Fancier's Gazette* is a fairly obvious analogy with Huxley's stint on *House and Garden*. In a series of questions and answers Chelifer draws up to settle the matter of why on earth he is working in an office is included: 'In order that Jewish stockbrokers may exchange their Rovers for Armstrong-Siddeleys'. In each of the novels so far (and in private correspondence), there are similar references to Jews which, taken together, may not be as noxious as the much more pronounced anti-Semitism of his friend T.S. Eliot, but are nonetheless unsettling. The usual explanation is that this was an unthinking feature of the English upper middle class milieu in which Huxley grew up. But he was not supposed to be unthinking, rather he was 'sapiently human'. Another theme in the novel – which is essentially a series of satirical tableaux – is the state of contemporary culture. The word 'highbrow' was in vogue and Huxley was certainly entitled to that label. Like Francis Chelifer, he was aware of 'living in an age where the *Daily Mail* sells two million copies every morning' – and one where people were increasingly being manipulated by media and politicians. 'Personally, I have always the greatest suspicion of your perfectly hygienic and well-padded Utopias,' says Mr Cardan at one point, a view echoed by Chelifer 'in the Utopian state where everybody is well-off educated and leisured, everybody will be bored'. This was the line of argument that would run towards *Brave New World*. In this book, Huxley is clear what he is against, but less sure about what he is for. He is searching for an answer to the perennial question: how then must we live? In the closing section of the book, he appears to be taking the first tentative steps towards an acknowledgement of the mystical element in human experience. Calamy speculates: 'Perhaps if you spend long enough and your mind is the right sort of mind, perhaps you really do get, in some queer sort of way, beyond the limitations of ordinary existence. And you see that everything that seems real is in fact entirely illusory – *maya* in fact, the cosmic illusion. Behind it you catch a glimpse of reality.' Those who would later complain when Huxley the brilliant iconoclast became Huxley the sensitive humanist were perhaps not reading him carefully enough. His very freedom of thought and emancipation from convention meant that he was always searching. Calamy again: 'It takes a certain amount of intelligence and imagination to realize the extraordinary queerness and mysteriousness of the world in which we live.'

Critical reception of the novel seemed to suggest that, having branded Huxley the spokesman of his generation, critics were rather relying on him to lead that generation out of its post-war disillusion. It was still not clear, however, where the road would lead but in private he was sharing his thoughts. To Naomi Mitchison, who liked *Those Barren Leaves*, he confessed that he did not read much ethics 'if only because it is perfectly obvious to me that ethics are transcendental and that any attempts to rationalize them are hopeless'.[25] His mood after the book, he told her, was to feel 'jejune and shallow and off the point. And I've taken such enormous pains to get off it; that's the stupidity. All this fuss in the intellectual void . . . I wish I could afford to stop writing for a bit.' Robert Nichols had some criticisms and suggested that he read Goethe, which Huxley hadn't to date. 'But for me,' he told Nichols, 'the most vital problem is not the mental so much as the ethical and emotional. The fundamental problem is love and humility, which are the same thing . . . men are more solitary now than they were; all authority is gone; the tribe has disappeared and every at all conscious man stands alone . . . Some day I may find some sort of an answer. And then I might write a good book, or at any rate a mature book, not a queer sophisticatedly jejune book, like this last affair, like all the blooming lot, in fact.'[26] Was Huxley reaching the limits of satire and feeling that a more nourishing, more positive creative energy needed to be released instead of these scintillating patterns traced in the 'intellectual void'? A break from writing to allow a new direction to develop was hardly a possibility because of that inexorable contract. He had ruled out the American lecture circuit in spite of having had offers but had applied to Oxford for the Kahn travelling fellowship – which he considered he stood no chance of getting, and which would have resulted in visiting the Jesuit missions in Mexico and Goa to look at architecture. His reading was beginning to extend to books on paranormal states and faculties. He asked Julian if he thought there was anything in telepathy or 'eyeless sight'.[27] He was also reading Lawrence's *Kangaroo* and still in two minds about a writer he hadn't seen since Garsington: 'What an extraordinary man- such prodigious talent, with such hiatuses where judgement, sense of proportion, self-criticism should be!'[28] His descriptions of nature saved him: 'there has never been anything so vividly beautiful and true, so artistic in its unfailing grasp of the essential and significant things'.

In March and April the Huxleys went off on a trip to Tunisia which is described in *Along the Road*. They returned to a Florence 'colonized by English sodomites and middle-aged Lesbians'[29] and realised that they wanted to do a little more substantial travelling which would involve leaving Matthew with his grandmother at St Trond in Belgium. Most of Huxley's writing now was done with a typewriter but he told Mary Hutchinson that it 'isn't really suitable for intimate letters'.[30] He confessed to her: 'I am not imaginative . . . Personally I have lived so long and so exclusively in a private literary-intellectual world, that I am case-hardened and find the greatest difficulty in getting out, into contact with other forms of existence – forms of existence in many respects much more satisfactory than my own.' For a writer sometimes represented as arrogant, Huxley at this point in his life seemed extraordinarily self-aware and self-critical. Shortly before leaving for London via Belgium, a group of *fascisti* burst into the Castel Montici, ostensibly looking for someone, Professor Gaetano Salvemini of the University of Florence, a critic of the government but in fact wholly unknown to the Huxleys who harangued the policemen and threatened them with the British Ambassador. It was a disturbing incident, 'comic if it weren't tragic'.[31]

In London, amongst other business, Huxley made contact again with Mary Hutchinson. He tried to do some work in his club, the Athenaeum, but: 'Some of your scent, Mary, still clings about me; and when I move I suddenly catch little whiffs of it – and there's an end for the moment of any pursuit of the *mot juste*.'[32] He was distracted by the thought of Clive Bell enjoying her favours, admitting to feelings of jealousy 'that perhaps he is profiting by tendernesses and fires and meltings which he evoked and which by right are mine . . . Good night but not *too* good, Mary.' A month later, from Belgium, just before leaving for their long trip, Maria wrote to Mary: 'Aldous has just come into my bed & he smelt so strongly of you still that it made one giddy.'[33] They had not enjoyed the brief stay in St Trond. Maria's grandfather was grumpy and presided over 'gloomy breakfasts in silence' and her grandmother was a 'tyrant' bullying everyone and being 'beastly' to Maria's mother.[34] It was a relief to go. The Huxleys eventually set sail from Genoa on 15 September, leaving Matthew behind for their eleven month trip to India, South East Asia and the United States. 'Seeing that one practises a profession that does not tie one down, I feel that one ought to see as much of this planet as one can,'[35] he announced to his father.

Notes

1   Reading, Letter to Charles Prentice of Chatto and Windus, 11 January 1924
2   Ian Parsons, speaking at P.E.N. meeting in honour of Huxley, 15 November 1998. Tape in National Sound Archive (the tape of this event is a most useful biographical source)
3   *L.225*
4   *L.226*
5   *L.228*
6   *New York Herald Tribune*, 12 October 1952
7   Reading, Letter to Charles Prentice, 22 May 1924
8   Introduction to *The Discovery* by Frances Sheridan (1924), pvi
9   Reading, Letter to Charles Prentice, 1 April 1924
10 Reading, typescript of unpublished draft introduction to *The Discovery*
11 UCLA, Copy of interview by students of LA School of Journalism, 18 December 1957, in 'Library of Living Journalism'
12 Reading, Letters between both parties, April 1924
13 Reading, Letter to Charles Prentice, 9 May 1924
14 Reading, Letter to Charles Prentice, 22 May 1924
15 Reading, Letter to Harold Raymond, 9 August 1924
16 *L.232*
17 HRC, Letter to Mary Hutchinson, 23 September 1924
18 *L.239*
19 *L.234*
20 Reading, Letter to Charles Prentice, 26 October 1924
21 HRC, Letter from Maria Huxley to Mary Hutchinson, 5 October 1923
22 HRC, Letter from Maria Huxley to Mary Hutchinson, 7 January 1924
23 See unpublished thesis by Margaret Clare Ratcliff: *The Correspondence of Mary Hutchinson: A New Look at Bloomsbury, Eliot and Huxley* (May, 1991). PhD Dissertation, University of Austin. Copy in HRC
24 UCLA, Incomplete copy of *Noa* in the hand of Aldous Huxley
25 *L.242*
26 *L.245*
27 *L.241*
28 Reading, Letter to Charles Prentice, 18 February 1925
29 *L.246*
30 HRC, Letter to Mary Hutchinson, 9 May 1925
31 *L.249*
32 HRC, Letter to Mary Hutchinson, 22 July 1925
33 HRC, Letter from Maria Huxley to Mary Hutchinson, 28 August 1925
34 HRC, Letter from Maria Huxley to Mary Hutchinson, 1 August 1925
35 *L.251*

XIV

Sailing

The Huxleys set sail just as a new book was being published. *Along the Road*, subtitled *Notes and Essays of a Tourist*, began with an essay: 'Why Not Stay At Home?' which had appeared in January in *Vanity Fair*. It is a typical example of the sort of piece that Huxley could now turn out to order: lightly serious, witty, irreverent, able to make a worthwhile point without straining the capacities of the reader of the magazines in which most of the pieces in the book appeared. After noting that 'tourists are, in the main, a gloomy-looking tribe. I have seen much brighter faces at a funeral than in the Piazza of St Mark's' he goes on to suggest that people travel out of snobbery 'because the best people do it'. He admits that 'With me, travelling is frankly a vice,' and notes that both reading and travelling are popular 'because they are the most delightful of all the many substitutes for thought'. An unsympathetic reader of Huxley's travel writing might be inclined to endorse this judgement for the book of the travels on which he was about to embark, *Jesting Pilate*, although full of characteristic and stimulating lucubrations, was not always very profound in its sounding of other cultures. Earlier in the summer he had told Norman Douglas that he had been queasy at the sight of the Tunisian Arabs picking and packing dates: 'How tremendously European one feels when one has seen these devils in their native muck . . . In fifty years time, it seems to me, Europe can't fail to be wiped out by these monsters.'[1] He would later let slip an ambiguous remark that could be taken as describing the native Javanese as 'the local orang-outangs'[2] (though on the same occasion his remarks about the British colonial society in Malaya were equally unsparing). On the other hand, he announced before setting out that his intention was to test his very English assumption that the Indians were not able to govern themselves. He declared carefully: 'I shall be interested to see what conclusions a closer acquaintance will bring one to.'[3]

In *Along the Road*, he reveals a little about himself – 'my dislike of large dinner parties, soirées . . . I do not shine in large assemblies . . . I never move without a plentiful supply of optical glass . . . I like the country, enjoy solitude . . . I love the inner world as much as the outer . . . If I could be born again . . . I should desire to be a man of science etc.' The persona is relaxed, engaging, well-informed but wearing its considerable learning lightly, playfully paradoxical in the essayistic manner, sceptical about progress in art and the claims of the avant-garde, and unimpressed by trends in contemporary popular culture. In the essay, 'Views of Holland', he mocks the complacent rationalism of the Enlightenment, its 'noble and touching dreams, commendable inebriations!' which are no longer available to the modern mind: 'We have learnt that nothing is simple and rational except what we ourselves have invented; that God thinks neither in terms of Euclid nor of Riemann; that science has "explained" nothing; that the more we know the more fantastic the world becomes and the profounder the surrounding darkness . . . and that even in the twentieth century men behave as they did in the caves of Altimira and in the lake dwellings of Glastonbury.' In another pleasantly witty piece on what books one should take on a journey, Huxley talks about one of his most curious obsessions – with the *Encylopaedia Britannica*. 'I never pass a day away from home without taking a volume with me,' he confesses. 'It is the book of books. Turning over its pages, rummaging among the stores of fantastically varied facts which the hazards of alphabetical arrangement bring together, I wallow in my mental vice.' Bertrand Russell joked that one could predict Huxley's subjects of conversation provided that one knew which alphabetical section of the *Encylopaedia* he happened to be reading at the time. Huxley even constructed a special carrying-case for it on his journeys. It shows a particular side of Huxley – the fascinated accumulator of facts rather than opinions, the scientific inquirer in the Huxley family tradition. Later, when living in the United States, he would ask his publisher to arrange a subscription to *Nature*. No corresponding request was made for the *Times Literary Supplement*. He would show little interest in literary small talk and gossip, and was just as likely to be found reading a book about science or politics or society as a contemporary novel or book of verse. He became less and less 'literary' with the years. Just before he left he had been reading Burtt's *Foundations of Modern Science* noting that science, with its 'arbitrary assumptions' had 'Quite gratuitously . . . gone on to assume that all aspects of the world that can't be treated mathematically are illusory.'[4] Passionate as his belief in science was, Huxley never let it become an idol or a fetish and was always acutely aware of its limits.

The Huxleys shipped from Naples on the SS *Genova*, sending a facetious farewell postcard to Mary Hutchinson of a naked Venus from the Museo Nazionale in Naples, whose marble buttocks gave 'a Lytton-eye view . . . our last glimpse of Europe'.[5] Only days before, Maria had written to Mary: 'I so tremendously wish you were here that I almost expect you to come and so violently think of your lips and eyes that I feel my mouth searching for yours.'[6] On the day of departure, Huxley wrote to Mary: 'I have thought of you Mary, with each of your delicious organs . . . that you are beautiful and voluptuous . . . your body is round and slender like a white serpent's and that your hair is tied in a little pig tail it is a *détournement de mineure* [seduction of a minor, a phrase Huxley would use again in a later letter to Mary, as well as playing with the concepts of androgyny and hermaphroditism] – of how deliciously perverse a minor!' He noted that there were three beds in the cabin and that she should be occupying one of them – 'nature abhors a vacuum'.[7] Both the Huxleys seem to have existed in a permanent state of sexual desire for Mary throughout their ten month voyage, and the correspondence between all three is frank, open and passionate. The narrative of the voyage is woven here from these and other letters and the published diary of the journey, *Jesting Pilate* (1926).

Huxley's tone in the book is of the languidly amused rational man in the East – his later involvement with Californian gurus nowhere prefigured in his mid-1920s attitudes. He is dismissive of the 'wisdom of the East' but also curious, wishing to make an intellectual analysis of everything he sees. He also distances himself from his frivolous European shipmates, bent on merely 'having a Good Time' – a twenties obsession that he would continue to mock throughout the decade. 'We make contact with the Orient tomorrow morning,' he told Mary on 1 October. 'I think it might be amusing.'[8] Their first view of India was Bombay, whose architecture is judged 'appalling', and in the bookstall of the principal hotel, the Taj Mahal, Huxley noted one of his own novels. He was greatly impressed by the intellectual power and charm of Mrs Sarojini Naidu, the newly-elected President of the All-India Congress, to whom the Huxleys, as famous guests, were introduced. They also met the local intelligentsia 'the majority of them are frail little men, very gentle and underfed-looking . . . No wonder the British rule, if these are typical.'[9] No wonder if Indians took offence if this observation was typical.

After Bombay the Huxleys travelled, in two days and nights, by train to Lahore where they stayed with an old Oxford friend, Chaman Lall, a young barrister and politician with an English wife – 'very classy Brahmins'[10] – then on by train again to Rawalpindi and thence to Srinagar to a cool, elevated bungalow, owned by Lall, looking out over beautiful poplar trees at the blue hills, though Huxley was disappointed by the famous Mogul gardens there. He was reading a history of India and the EDW–EVA volume of the *Encyclopaedia Britannica*.[11] Before setting off, Huxley had arranged to syndicate some articles and had an offer from *The Times* to write some pieces. Settled in Srinagar for a month, he started to type, and suffered no mishap greater than being stung on the leg by a giant hornet. Mary wrote to say she had dug up an old Valentine's Day letter from him dated 1918, before his marriage. He replied with a very clear awareness of the gap between the sort of privileged, libertine life he and she led in England and the life of his Kashmiri neighbours: 'They make one realise how excessively odd and remote is the society of highbrows and immoralists which we generally frequent . . . One moves among them like a Martian.'[12] By mid-December, he was back in Lahore where it was clear that the open mind about Indian self-government he had boasted of was doing its work. He was revolted by the general run of English imperialist he met – 'stupid, uncultured, underbred, the complete and perfect cad'[13] – and even in the presence of the more decent representatives he was forced to confess to Lewis Gielgud that he understood Indian nationalistic aspirations: 'We really have no business here. And there is no doubt whatever that we are steadily making the country poorer and poorer.' In Kashmir he had observed the 'small and very corrupt despotism' and 'still more fascinating is the study of the relations existing between the English and the educated Indians . . . The cruelties, the humiliations, the pompous make-believes, the snobberies . . . Proust should have lived here for a few years.'[14]

The Huxleys travelled to Agra, Jaipur, Cawnpore, Peshawar, Amritsar, Benares, Lucknow, Delhi, and Calcutta. Amritsar sparked the reflection that the world had changed and that a humanitarian movement had been unleashed that would no longer tolerate human rights abuses: 'At any other period of the world's history than this, Dyer and Mussolini would have seemed the normal ones.' At Jaipur he was given an elephant to ride (which would have been a sight to relish, the tall Englishman in pith helmet, waistcoat and long, trousered legs – as one photograph of the journey shows him). At Cawnpore, he witnessed Gandhi and Nehru at the All India Congress. Gandhi was 'the little man in the *dhoti*, with the shawl over his naked shoulders; the emaciated little man with the shaved head, the large ears, the rather foxy features'. In private correspondence, Huxley was even ruder about Gandhi: 'half-naked, doing the holy man with an adoring young English woman [Miss Slade] in attendance, handing him his spectacles, adjusting his loincloth etc. – a most unsympathetic looking man with a foxy shopkeeper's face'.[15] Huxley was not wholly enamoured of Hindu 'spirituality', calling it 'the primal curse of India and the cause of all her misfortunes'. He went on: 'A little less spirituality, and the Indians would now be free – free from foreign

dominion and from the tyranny of their own prejudices and traditions.' It was wrong likewise to indict the materialism of the West: 'We
are not materialistic enough; that is the trouble. We do not interest
ourselves in a sufficiency of this marvellous world of ours . . . The
Other World – the world of metaphysics and religion – can never
possibly be as interesting as this world . . .' Hard to imagine the writer
of these words as the author of *The Perennial Philosophy* (1945). At
Christmas he wrote to Mary from Bombay: 'Middle age creeps on
apace. The only remedy is to live much, strongly and multifariously
while the thing lasts.'[16] She sent him a present of a diary and he
responded: 'May there be many engagements with you recorded on
those blue pages, and after the engagements there will be perhaps, certain little hieroglyphs and mysterious symbols like those which
Stendhal recorded in his diaries . . . the shorthand and indecipherable
record of longdrawn pleasures and delicate complicated feelings.'[17]
The Huxleys sent her a pair of transparent trousers made of flowered
black muslin from Delhi, an item of clothing that offered frequent
opportunities for saucy remarks in future letters exchanged between
all three.

In the New Year the Huxleys – especially Maria – became worried
about Matthew who had been reported as having trouble with his
lungs. They started to make arrangements to go to Switzerland on
their return or the mountains at Cortina d'Ampezzo in Italy. Huxley
was giving some thought to what would happen when they returned.
An attempt at doing a film script with Gielgud had failed as had
another proposal with Robert Nichols. The basic problem was his
unwillingness to work collaboratively in a studio: 'You depend on
Jews with money, on "art directors", on little bitches with curly hair
and teeth.'[18] But for now, they were anxious to get on and see Burma,
and Singapore and the islands of the Malay archipelago – 'I feel there
must be more in them than met the eye of Conrad,'[19] he wrote to the
Proust translator, Sydney Schiff, from Benares where they had witnessed an eclipse. His final wish for India 'as a lover of freedom and
of change, a hater of fixity and ready-made commandments, a
believer in individuals, and an infidel wherever groups, communities
and crowds are concerned' was that the ordinary Hindu would be

emancipated from the bonds of community life and 'develop his
own personal resources', with the British having relinquished their
control.

After the briefest passage through Burma, the Huxleys proceeded
along the Iriwaddy, where Aldous reported to Mary on St Valentine's
Day ('the anniversary of that first letter, dear Mary, I wrote to you –
how long ago – and from the banks of a very different river [pre-
sumably the Thames at Eton in 1918]') that the great pagoda at
Rangoon had been 'a sort of Sitwell's paradise'. He added that 'our
fellow-passengers are dim. A pair of earnest and Lesbian ladies of
unequal age are the most intellectual'.[20] Mary was given details, this
time by Maria, of a new diversion for Aldous. A Romanian aristocrat
living in Paris called Henrietta Sava-Goiu, who was on the boat,
began to excite Aldous's interest. 'I pointed out her attractions &
advised him to try his luck . . . It is odd that A should always be
attracted by self-advertising & loud women – this one is not bad
really – but stupid. I suppose it is the extreme that appeals to him
who is so reserved and *sensitif* . . . Her mouth legs & hands are
hideous, the rest plump and very pretty – like a fruit hard to bite on
though perfectly ripe – age 28 . . . not my type . . . but it seems he can
manage his own business this time – Poor Aldous – Of course I
should be jealous instead of finding him pathetic & loving him
more – but he is not like other men – don't you think he is *very* different – delicate & sensitive. As I now write to you he is in her room
where I left them – sleepy – after dinner – as before dinner they were
so entranced . . . that they heard no gong . . . or felt any hunger. I do
hope he will succeed.'[21] This is the only first-hand evidence we have of
the habit described by Sybille Bedford of Maria's encouragement of
Huxley's affairs. Aldous gave Mary his version of the fling with the
Princess: 'She was Tom's [T.S. Eliot] Princess Volupine in youth –
rather bitchy, but with ideals; a philosophising cock-teaser.'[22] The
charms of the Princess Volupine were not so encompassing that he
was unable to make plans for their return: 'So go to Paris in May and
receive us in your secret house – it sounds too romantic . . . How
much I look forward to it, Mary.' The Princess arranged to rejoin
them in Hong Kong, after their Malayan stay, in order to sail with

them to California. The *San Francisco Chronicle* of 5 May had a photograph of the Huxleys and the Princess under the heading: THEY LAND IN CALIFORNIA ON GLOBE-TROTTING TOUR. The two women are swathed in furs and capped in cloche hats. Huxley is dignified with stick and trenchcoat. Maria has scrawled across the cutting: 'The Princess'.

At the beginning of March the Huxleys arrived in Penang on the last day of the Chinese New Year celebrations. With another of those European comparisons with which he punctuated his travelogue, he decided: 'Penang has a certain Sicilian air.' After noting at the rice table the indulgence given to gluttony characteristic of the age – 'all the fury of the moralists is spent on other sins, especially lasciviousness' – they moved on to Singapore where they stayed in some splendour with the Governor and his wife, the Guillemards. 'One doesn't realise what an astonishing affair the British Empire is until one begins to wander about it,' he told Mary from Singapore. 'Everywhere Englishmen, playing tennis, eating porridge at 8.30 am, drinking whiskey at 6.0 in comfortable club-houses, dressing for dinner even in the jungle and to entertain the local orang-out-angs.'[23] Next, they made a quick trip to Java, the southern Philippines, then Manila, to catch a liner to San Francisco (stopping at Hong Kong where the Princess would rejoin the boat). From Singapore another steamy letter was despatched to Mary: 'In my memory you live Adamistically, in only your hair . . . tied up behind like a schoolgirl . . . Why aren't you here to lie naked under the mosquito nets . . . etc. etc.'[24] On arrival in Java, he could only 'gasp with admiration at the fabulous and entirely unbelievable beauty of the landscape'. Within hours of landing he had been interviewed by fourteen reporters which made him conclude: 'The literary man is invested, it seems to me, with a quite disproportionate aura of importance and significance . . . Art has filled the vacuum left by the decay of established religion.' The remark recalls Arnold's famous prediction that poetry would replace religion. The Huxleys visited Batavia, Garoet, Buitenzorg, Sarawak, Labuan, Kudat, Sandakan, and changed at Zamboanga to a ship for Manila bound via Hong Kong for San Francisco. There was a brief stop in Shanghai where he noted 'the *vitality* of Chinese civilisation' and in Japan which he does not seem to have taken to. On 5 May they arrived at San Francisco. More reporters were waiting on the quay to ask Huxley what he thought of the General Strike, which had been flourishing in his absence. 'I gave them my prejudices, which are Fabian and mildly labourite,' he wrote. An Oxford socialist (intimate of the Haldanes and a member of the University Co-Op), a freethinker and debunker, Huxley was unlikely to have taken the right wing side of this question but the reporters went away and twisted his words into an endorsement of the bosses. Huxley was annoyed at this: 'Such a paean in praise of capitalism and Mr Baldwin!' He complained: 'The reporters had made me respectable.'

In the ship's library in Malaya, Huxley had found a copy of a book important for the future author of *Brave New World*, Henry Ford's *My Life and Work*. His view of American civilisation in general, and Hollywood in particular, are what might be expected, in one sense, of an upper middle class literary Englishman in 1926. He was sniffy about the roaring materialism of the Jazz Age and about the products of Hollywood (notwithstanding earlier attempts to respond to the 'golden lures' of American syndication, and his tries at screenwriting). His tutor in some of these attitudes, H.L. Mencken, was the first to be contacted on Huxley's arrival. Writing from the SS *President Cleveland*, in San Francisco, Huxley told Mencken: 'I am entering the USA by the back door . . . from the Orient, where I have been spending some months to satisfy myself empirically that all this rigmarole of Light from the East etc is genuinely nonsense.'[25] Huxley was anxious to meet his hero at last and suggested to him that he should consider recording his latest volume of *Prejudices*, the fourth, on gramophone records: 'The majority of people in our modern world are not educated up to the point of understanding what they read in books. But they can understand a thing when it is spoken *viva voce*.' Huxley was later to predict that books would eventually be issued in recorded form, anticipating the phenomenon of the audio book, but his enthusiasm for recording is not difficult to understand. Much of his own reading was ingested orally – by Maria reading to him – and he was thus more ready than most to advocate non-print methods of publishing.

After San Francisco, the Huxleys moved on to Los Angeles – which gave Aldous an opportunity to inveigh again against the vice of 'having a Good Time'. He noted that 'thought is barred in this City of Dreadful Joy and conversation is unknown'. The next stage of the trip was Chicago, and from the train taking him there, Huxley wrote to Robert Nichols: 'Hollywood is altogether too antipodean to be lived in; it gives you no chance to escape.'[26] Taken with his earlier rejection of Eastern philosophy, this was the second piece of poor prophecy in a week, given the direction his life would actually take. Generally, however, Huxley was unusually prescient about the course of his own and his century's life. To Mary, however, he was more upbeat about America. At the end of the first week he declared to her: 'We have been in America 5 days and have already seen its two most remarkable natural phenomena – the Grand Canyon and Charlie Chaplin. Both very splendid, especially Charlie, who is, in conversation, like Mark Gertler at his best but more so and better. The most ravishing man.'[27] They spent the afternoon walking on the beach 'in the midst of crowds of exquisitely pretty flappers, dressed in bathing costumes so tight that every contour of the Mount of Venus and the Vale of Bliss was plainly visible'. The flappers, it goes without saying, were 'quite soulless' and Hollywood was 'quite unbelievable . . . Such roaring comedy, oddness, vitality, vulgarity'. Maria was not quite so enamoured. 'Nothing would induce me to live in this country, not even money,'[28] she confided to Mary.

Maria also announced with triumph: 'The fall of the Princess is imminent . . . now that in America we find that all little girls expose so brazenly their charms she loses most of her attraction.' She had, however, spent half the night in their compartment, reminding Maria at least of her preferred companion in such a situation: 'How we both longed for you.' Maria had more positive news of their plans. They would be returning to England in June 'and I hope you will think me very very sweet for Aldous is coming straight to England though if I had wanted it he would of course have come to Belgium . . . it will delight me to think of you through days and nights that I will only be able to imagine.' All three, however, were aware of the need to keep this extraordinary triangulation a secret. Urging Mary and Aldous to be very discreet, Maria counselled: 'I hope that both your reasons will make you guard a secret so well kept and on which depends the light-heartedness of all our future meetings and voyages.' Maria's plan was that Mary would meet them at Plymouth docks, enabling her to see Mary however briefly, before going on to Belgium to be reunited with Matthew. Aldous and Mary would avoid any waiting journalists and travel to London as Mr and Mrs Huxley: 'You will have him quite fresh and delightful before anyone else has had anything to do with him.'[29] But Mary must let no-one know about this plan in case Aldous was met by 'cumbersome people of his family'.

The Huxleys were in New York when all these plans were being drawn up and enjoying being tossed into New York literary society. Mencken was the most important to Huxley and they had their one and only meeting over lunch. Mencken ('very amusing and looks like Belloc or like a travelling salesman or farmer', in Maria's view) was a gentleman who preferred blondes and Maria instantly took a dislike to the 'vulgar and hideous' flapper he had with him 'who made wor-shipping eyes at A. I could see no excuse for her but A suggested that she probably is alright in bed. I suppose that is enough for some people.'[30] The Huxleys met several other 'nondescript celebrities' as well as 'a really charming one of the rather-vamp type who is coming to England and you must meet, though I do hope you will not let her make more than eyes at you. She is Elinor Wylie.' Even before arrival at New York, Huxley had written an unsolicited fan letter to Anita Loos, author of *Gentlemen Prefer Blondes* (1925). He told her he was 'enraptured by the book'[31] and had just enjoyed the play. One can imagine Huxley being captured by a book which opens with the hero-ine – having just been told by her gentlemen friend that if she put down all her thoughts it would make a book – saying: 'This almost made me smile as what it would really make would be a whole row of encyclopaediacs. I mean I seem to be thinking practically all of the time.' Loos and the Huxleys met in New York at her apartment for tea. 'On first meeting Aldous,' she later recalled, 'I was immediately struck by his physical beauty; he was a giant in height, with a figure that was a harmonious column for his magnificent head; the head of an angel drawn by William Blake.'[32] Anita Loos found Maria to be 'a lovely

brunette . . . as unusual in her way as Aldous was in his'. In a later
letter to Julian, Aldous described Anita Loos as 'ravishing. One would
like to keep her as a pet. She is the doyenne of Hollywood, having
started to write for the movies when she was seven. Now, at the age of,
I suppose, about twenty-eight [she was in fact thirty-five, a year older
than Huxley], she feels that she can retire with a good conscience . . .'[33]
In the space of a few weeks, Huxley had thus met two of the people –
Chaplin and Loos – who would form part of the small circle of friends
in which he moved from the late 1930s onwards in Hollywood.

The dizzying life of New York won Maria over at last to America: 'I
have enjoyed every minute of it . . . Aldous has cramp from auto-
graphing books.'[34] Journalists asked her whether Aldous was a
romantic lover – 'to which I cannot answer'. Mary also had a report
from Aldous: 'You have no idea how famous one is in America. It's
frightful. I long to be back in my own country. I don't like being a
prophet at all.'[35] He was amazed at the audience of forty-three million
for a radio talk he gave. He was keen now to make arrangements for
seeing Mary. From the Hotel Belmont in New York he issued instructions to her to find a small *garconnière* in London – 'one room wd be
enough provided it is a bedroom. I look forward to endless delights.'
Maria scribbled a postscript asking Mary to try and find a room: 'He
hopes he will need it constantly and so surely shall I when I come . . .
with kisses and caresses . . . Maria.'

Huxley's verdict on America was delivered from Chicago: 'The
thing which is happening in America is a revaluation of values, a radical alteration (for the worse) of established standards . . . This
falsification of the standard of values is a product, in our modern
world, of democracy, and has gone furthest in America.' Hollywood,
he had already noted in Java, had 'scattered broadcast over the brown
and black and yellow world a grotesquely garbled account of our civilization'. He had little enthusiasm for the American belief that: 'The
democratic hypothesis in its extreme and most popular form is that
all men are equal and that I am just as good as you are.' Finding one
of his novels available in Boston only under the counter 'as though it
were whiskey', he noted the strange co-existence of Puritanism and
wild hedonism in America. He had caught something of the raw

energy of the United States in the 1920s and *Jesting Pilate* concludes with a moving statement of his liberal faith in tolerance and the admission that he returns 'richer by much experience and poorer by many exploded convictions'.

Before his ship docked in Plymouth there was to be one final shipboard adventure on board the SS *Belgenland*. One night, Aldous and Maria were woken by the discovery of someone in their cabin. Maria leapt out of bed 'naked as a worm' and screaming at the intruder. The steward was called and it later transpired that it was all a mistake and that Lady Dorothy Mills, the writer and explorer, had mistaken their cabin for her own. Maria was badly shaken and felt that the incident – which seems to have been traumatic far beyond its essentially comic properties – had exposed some realisation of fear in both of them. She tried to explain to Mary that Aldous had not made light of their joint alarm because he knew 'that he *shakes* with terror is *sick* with terror – & could go mad with terror.'[36]

On 5 June, the *Belgenland* docked at Plymouth where Mary was meant to be waiting to embrace them both and whisk Aldous off to their secret *pied à terre*. In the event she was unable to be there and sent telegrams instead with instructions about how to locate the studio. After eleven months of separation from Matthew – in India she had been so anxious about his health she had wanted to return – Maria went straight to Belgium. Although all Aldous's comments at this time show love and solicitude for his six-year-old son, he nonetheless felt it more urgent to return immediately to London (where Mary would be waiting) and postpone the reunion until August.

Notes

1 *L*.250
2 HRC, Letter to Mary Hutchinson, 10 February 1926
3 *L*.253
4 *L*.253
5 HRC, Postcard to Mary Hutchinson, 16 September 1925
6 HRC, Letter from Maria Huxley to Mary Hutchinson, 7 September 1925

7   HRC, Letter to Mary Hutchinson, 15 September 1925

8   HRC, Postscript by Aldous Huxley in letter from Maria Huxley to Mary Hutchinson, 1 October 1925

9   *L*.253

10 *L*.256

11 HRC, Letter to Mary Hutchinson, 25 October 1925

12 HRC, Letter to Mary Hutchinson, 2 November 1925

13 L.261

14 BL, Letter to Sydney Schiff, 9 November 1925

15 HRC, Letter to Mary Hutchinson, 6 January 1926

16 HRC, Letter to Mary Hutchinson, 22 December 1925

17 HRC, Letter to Mary Hutchinson 21 January 1926

18 *L*.266

19 BL, Letter to Sydney Schiff, 14 January 1926

20 HRC, Letter to Mary Hutchinson, 14 February 1926

21 HRC, Letter from Maria Huxley to Mary Hutchinson, 8 March 1926

22 HRC, Letter to Mary Hutchinson, 22 February 1926

23 HRC, Letter to Mary Hutchinson, 10 March 1926. It is, of course, conceivable that the 'orang-outangs' are not meant literally and that the remark, instead of being a facetious comment on the fact that wild life is the only form of life likely to be impressed by dressing for dinner in the jungle, is intended to be a jocosely racist reference to the native population of Java

24 HRC, Letter to Mary Hutchinson, 19 March 1926

25 NYPL, Letter to H.L. Mencken, 5 May 1926

26 *L*.269

27 HRC, Letter to Mary Hutchinson, undated but possibly 10 May 1926

28 HRC, Letter from Maria Huxley to Mary Hutchinson, 13 May 1926

29 HRC, Letter from Maria Huxley to Mary Hutchinson, 16 May 1926

30 HRC, *Ibid*

31 *L*.269

32 *Mem. Vol.*, p89-90

33 *L*.272

34 HRC, Letter from Maria Huxley to Mary Hutchinson, 21 May 1926

35 HRC, Letter to Mary Hutchinson, 26 May 1926

36 HRC, Letter from Maria Huxley to Mary Hutchinson, undated, late May 1926

XV

Cortina

Aldous spent June in London, where Maria was intending to rejoin him in July. She sent Mary a note from Paris on 6 June on the way to her grandparents at St Trond congratulating her on having found a flat: 'How clever you are . . . Where is it? Is it nice? Will you write to me from there? I gave Aldous a little note for you – urging you to be careful. But I think you will be . . .'[1] A fortnight later, in St Trond, Maria recalled her meeting with Mary last August, just before she set sail: 'Never have I seen you more lovely, Mary & I remember with poignant tenderness your new beauty with closed eyes during last night . . . I could come to London . . . should I come? . . . Goodbye my precious Mary be happy and wild and gay and don't forget how I kissed you . . . Why don't you write to me? Does Aldous take up all your thoughts?'[2] There is no evidence that Maria did come and she may well have stayed in St Trond. Aldous was busy catching up with literary friends, making arrangements from his club, and dining, at the end of June, for example, with St John and Mary Hutchinson and Virginia Woolf. In July he went to Garsington, which displeased Maria, 'seeing that Philip has such unpleasant things to say about me'.[3] Robert Bridges was there, with the manuscripts of Gerard Manley Hopkins, which he had made arrangements to publish in 1918, and which would appear in a second edition in 1930 after

Bridges's death. Virginia Woolf sat on the lawn examining the MS 'with that gigantic grasshopper Aldous folded up in a chair close by'.[4]

A few days later Huxley wrote to Mary from an address at 4 Onslow Mews East. He was officially staying with his Aunt Ethel Collier – whose husband, John, painted Aldous's portrait at this time, exhibiting it in the 1927 Royal Academy Exhibition – at North House, 69 Eaton Avenue in Hampstead, after a brief stay with Julian, so this may have been the address of the studio. He said he would be waiting for her after her dinner with Osbert [Sitwell?]. 'The place is haunted, Mary, by your invisible but perfumed ghost. I embrace it, unsatisfyingly. May I hope tomorrow to caress something more than a disembodied memory?'[5] Several days later he was inviting her to lunch: 'a picnic in disorder and perhaps also in bed'.[6] Elinor Wylie, the writer he had met in New York, arrived in London and Aldous arranged for her to have supper with the Woolfs at their house in Tavistock Square. Virginia Woolf was unimpressed by Wylie, 'that arid desert', and wondered how it was that she had 'Francis Birrell, Aldous Huxley, at her feet, and she no better than a stark staring naked maypole?'[7] He was also trying to arrange a meeting in either London or Paris with Anita Loos and her husband. It was during this summer of 1926 that the first signs of uncertainty in the relationship with Mary began to emerge. He appears to have been in Cambridge at the end of the third week in July and arranged to meet her there 'but not for the last time, Mary . . . I can't bear the sound of the words . . . Let it be uncertain; let there be the possibility of repetitions. But in any case we will dine together.'[8] Perhaps the re-emergence of Huxley on the scene had reminded her of the difficulty of the relationship (mindful of Maria's cautions) and the consequences for her relationship with Clive Bell – which had been a constant throughout the period. It seems that she was trying to tell him of the need to call a halt.

Huxley's arrival in New York the previous month had coincided with the publication, on both sides of the Atlantic, of his latest collection of short stories, *Two or Three Graces*. His three-year contract with Chatto had expired in January. He had more or less fulfilled the contract – except that two rather than three novels had emerged, books of essays and travel having made up the shortfall. Chatto proposed a new three-year agreement which Huxley signed on 7 June, the day after he returned from America (this was perhaps his real reason for making haste to London). It stressed that at least one of the books each year should be a full-length novel but in the event only *Point Counter Point* in 1928 appeared between *Those Barren Leaves* in 1925 and *Brave New World* in 1932, though Huxley the essayist and travel writer was very active. The yearly advance, which formed the bedrock of his income and on which the superstructure of freelance income was raised, was increased from £500 to £650 – equivalent to a five-figure salary today.

Two or Three Graces, which immediately went into a second impression in its second month, contained four stories, with the title story – which may have been a novel that did not quite make its length – occupying the bulk of the volume. Once again the story is long on authorial commentary and short on plot, essayistic rather than dramatic, its themes being the generation gap, the endless round of human vanity, and the struggle of the young to find the right way of living. Very early on a rather Lawrentian character, Kingham ('a close-cut beard, redder than his hair') inveighs against the frivolity of modern life and the refusal of the young to look beyond pleasure-seeking: 'It's the war that did it . . . It's time to stop, it's time to do something. Can't you see that you can't go on like this? Can't you see?' The narrator is phlegmatic in contrast to Kingham, who 'loved to flounder in emotion – his own and other people's'. In his self-accusa-tion – 'I have always been too tender-hearted, insufficiently ruthless' – is there something of Huxley the intellectual faced with the impas-sioned ranters like Lawrence? Grace's discovery of the 'fashionable Olympus' of contemporary art and music and her enthusiastic pur-suit of 'all that was smartest and latest in the world of the spirit' shows Huxley's contempt for the fashionable aesthetes with whom he gen-erally mixed. He exposes the same tendency in morals. Entering a party in an artist's studio, the narrator overhears a young man saying: 'We're absolutely modern, we are. Anybody can have my wife, so far as I'm concerned. I don't care. She's free. And I'm free. That's what I call modern.' Huxley's readers – who would have of course no idea about his private life – would take it that he was condemning such attitudes and securely possessing the high ground of more or less conventional morality.

One reader of the new book was the ageing Thomas Hardy at Max Gate whom Virginia Woolf called on in July. Mrs Hardy asked her whether she knew Aldous Huxley. She and her husband had been reading the new book and found him 'very clever' though they immediately forgot what each story was about (recalling Huxley's plots is indeed a challenge). 'They've changed everything now,' Hardy said. 'We used to think there was a beginning a middle and an end. We believed in the Aristotelian theory. Now, one of those stories [presumably 'Half-Holiday'] came to an end with a woman going out of the room.'[9] Hardy chuckled. 'But he no longer reads novels,' Woolf concluded.

On Friday 6 August, Huxley set off for St Trond to collect Matthew from his grandparents. It had been decided, for the child's health, that they would go to live in Cortina d'Ampezzo in the Italian Dolomites. Huxley took with him 'about two hundredweights of gramophone records'[10] and, somewhere between Calais and Brussels on the train, began a letter to Mary recalling their snatched amours of recent weeks: 'A few brief hours, during which, however, we abolished duration and space, made one another free of paradise and eternity, unchained ecstasies and, touching bodies, moved through one another's minds like divine presences, apocalyptic gods. Epic and supernatural moments.' And in between these ecstasies (whose language, appearing in *Two or Three Graces*, would surely have been satirised) there were quieter moments together: 'One lives on so many planes, and fully delightfully on each; every human being has as many storeys as the Woolworth Building and shoots effortlessly and imperceptibly in spiritual elevators from floor to floor.' As the train rattled on through the Low Countries he sent her 'impalpable kisses of melancholy and loving remembrance'. Not merely was he saying farewell to Mary (the relationship now had probably peaked) but he was exchanging the buzz and excitement of artistic London for a cold chalet in the mountains. His last week had been hectic, starting with a lunch with T.S. Eliot 'who looked terribly grey-green, drank no less than five gins with his meal, told me he was going to join Vivien in her Paris nursing home to break himself of his addictions to tobacco and alcohol, and was eloquent about Parisian luncheons with resoundingly titled duchesses'. Then on Tuesday he lunched with Beverley Nichols 'that plump and rosy-bottomed ex-friend of Tommy's [Earp's]'. Nichols wanted to write a profile of him for the *Daily Sketch* and Huxley predicted it would be 'awful, no doubt; I adopt ostrich tactics towards these things and don't read them.'

Had Huxley done so he would have read, under the heading 'Aldous Huxley or A Very Cold Young Man', how: 'Quantities of Mr Aldous Huxley reclined on my sofa, spreading over the cushions, and stretching long tentacles on to the floor. I had never before realized the curious fluidity of his frame.'[11] Nichols wrote that Huxley's mind was like his body, 'cold, exceptionally fluid, wandering with equal facility into any channel of learning or experience' but he said that Huxley threw cold water over people, institutions, emotions, and affairs, not because he was disdainful 'but because he has an exceptionally high standard by which to judge them'. Huxley reportedly said to Nichols: 'As I grow older I become more and more highbrow.' He said it wasn't a pose but the result of these last two months in London where he had evidently been to many of those parties that are described so savagely in his fiction: 'One goes to a party, and, apart from receiving extravagant and nauseating compliments oneself, one hears the word 'divine' applied indiscriminately to ballets, operas, actresses, novelists, free verse – to anything that can possibly be labelled artistic.' Perhaps that chalet in the mountains beckoned after all. He told Nichols: 'The whole thing revolts me because it's soft, and softness is the end of everything.' Nichols's summing-up was that Huxley had no sentimentality and wrote with a pen 'filled with ink that has first been clarified and then frozen'.

This is an important sketch for it is the first draft of a view of Huxley whose outlines would slowly solidify. This is Huxley the cold-eyed, unsentimental highbrow, looking down on a world which disgusts him, and from which he expects – and offers back – a certain hostility: 'He gives one a sense, in his writings, of a little group of intelligentsia clinging unhappily together in a grossly hostile world.

Not merely unsympathetic, or lacking in understanding, but grossly, actively hostile.' This is caricature – though persistent enough to inform certain commentaries to the present day – and, like all caricature, to do its work it must contain at least a grain of truth. That was that, from Garsington onwards, Huxley had mixed in high cultural elites that saw themselves from time to time as hated and misunderstood by the public. It is not surprising that the public would occasionally repay the compliment.

Having frozen Nichols to the marrow, Huxley the same evening went to see D.H. Lawrence, who was over in England briefly, and whom he had not seen since that meeting in Hampstead in 1915. Huxley found him 'charming. So much quieter than he was – it's the approach of middle age, with success and the removal of the horrors of the war'. Lawrence was about to re-enter the lives of the Huxleys after a long absence. They would meet him shortly again in Florence and find him a neighbour in Cortina. On his side he found Huxley on this first encounter again 'no brisker than ever'.[12] The final event in this crowded week's social calendar was dinner at the Eiffel Tower with Anita Loos and her husband. Huxley was still enchanted by her: 'She is tiny, pretty in a charmingly ugly way, with enormous eyes, and has a drawling little voice in which she brings out very good and fruity comments on the universe.'

Arriving in Belgium Huxley found his young son 'very well and in uproarious spirits. He eats copiously and makes himself a great nuisance – healthy signs.'[13] He tried to do some work at 19 Grand Place but was soon thinking of Mary and anxiously making plans to meet in Paris, at the Hotel Bergère, on the way to Cortina. 'The atmosphere here is impregnated with the misery and horror of old age,' he wrote from Maria's grandparents' house 'at the heart of the patriarchal system'.[14] By contrast he was bursting with intellectual energy and desire for new knowledge: 'All knowledge, desperately, while it's possible to acquire it – while there are still internal secretions.' They were soon off to Florence to do battle with the Italian bureaucrats and retrieve their car, discovering that new rules meant Maria must return to take a second driving test. Huxley read Gide's *Les Faux Monnayeurs* for the first time, finding it 'the oddest book. You feel that it must have been such a relief to the man to confess, at last, openly, that he preferred boys to girls.'[15]

By the start of September they were finally at Cortina d'Ampezzo installed in the Villa Ino Colli. It was a nice house with 'a perfect aspect, teems with terraces and balconies on which it is possible to get every ray of sunlight that falls on Cortina between dawn and evening, has baths, a garage and central heating, is simply but very comfortably and sensibly furnished and costs something less than nine pounds a month'.[16] More to the point: 'Cortina seems already to have done Matthew a great deal of good. He is perceptibly more robust than he was, has a fine colour, and eats well.' Cortina was a wide saucer-shaped valley surrounded by enormous limestone crags, was sunny, and the air was 'extraordinarily keen and stimulating'. They would remain here until February 1927. Within a month, however, having started writing *Point Counter Point*, Huxley was complaining that it was a 'hideous' place – 'there is a finality about it that is hardly bearable'.[17] He described the novel to his father as 'ambitious, the aim of which will be to show a piece of life, not only from a good many individual points of view, but also under its various aspects such as scientific, emotional, economic, political, aesthetic etc . . . It will be difficult but interesting.'[18] Huxley's description of the novel's method makes it sound like a scientific anatomy of life rather than an imaginative portrait.

The hard work was making him seek distractions. He begged Mary to consider coming for Christmas to renew the sexual pleasures of the summer and 'invent new ones, perhaps, if there are any that we have still left untried'.[19] There would be skiing, a sport which Maria had discovered, having bought some scarlet skis and 'ravishing calliphygous breeches'. He elaborated on the book to Mary and its aim of showing man in all his aspects: 'Any human being is a mass of organized molecules, a physiology, a part of the social organism, believes himself to have an immortal soul and to be of cosmical importance, is a patch of colours that can be painted and can look at the world as patches of colour, can feel enormous emotions, can worship goods; every act he performs can be interpreted in terms of physics and chemistry, of psychology, morality, of economics; his life can be described in the style of the natural history textbook or in that of *Paradise Lost* . . . It remains to be seen whether I can manage it.' To some fiction editors such a proposal would start to ring alarm bells but the result, when it came, was not as fearfully abstract as this seemed to promise. Towards the end of October the Huxleys went to Florence to see the dentist and meet Lawrence, who was impressed by their 'grand new Italian car – 61,000 lire'.[20] He thought they were bored by Cortina already and he found Huxley 'triste: *un uomo finito*, to be sentimental and Italian'. Over the next few days Lawrence shared his reactions with several correspondents. He told Ada Clarke: 'They were very nice, very pleasant, but sad, as if life had nothing for them. Really people have no pep, they so easily go blank, and so young.' They offered him their old car but Lawrence saw no point in rushing around from place to place and declined their offer. Frieda Lawrence told Mabel Dodge Luhan that Aldous was 'such a weed . . . and she was one of Lady Ottoline's protégées and never got over it.' Lawrence claimed he was unmoved by the suggestion that he was the model for Kingham in the recent book: 'He never knew me, anyhow.'

Before leaving Florence again Huxley quickly finished off revising a dramatisation of *Antic Hay* which an American writer, a Miss Werner, had done and which he hoped would make their fortune. 'What fun if it comes off,'[21] he told Mary. When they got back from Florence to Cortina (having stopped off at Padua to see Pirandello's *Six Characters in Search of an Author* and to dine with the author) Maria was suddenly seized with a sense of the 'hideousness' of the Villa Ino Colli – the artificial flowers and imitation bronze pottery. 'Except our bedroom the place is a nightmare,'[22] she told Mary. A parcel arrived from Mary, delivered at a pleasant time around 7pm when Maria and Aldous liked to talk before their baths. Maria teased Aldous for smelling the red gloves she had sent and complaining that she had changed her scent. 'I like to imagine you here – in my bed under the eiderdown you know – or rather in what would be yours – a very wide one – Aldous would come up later,' she wrote to Mary in reply.[23] Mary now seemed to be looking for a flat for them again, because Aldous planned to visit England to do some research. Maria had received a long and friendly letter from Ottoline which suggested that relations were about to thaw out.

As the end of the year approached, Huxley worked harder and harder, tapping away 'furiously' at his typewriter in what Maria called his 'tower of ticking'.[24] After these sessions 'we go for delightfully intimate walks under grey woods – & at night when all places are uniformly passionate'. Maria had come up with a 'brainwave' for a movie scenario – the first of many – which Aldous had approved and which would enable them to come to London, they hoped. Huxley seems to have been looking for any excuse to stop work on the novel because he was 'bored to death . . . he was like a baby who comes down from his lessons on an unstudious day'. He was forced to write to Prentice at Chatto to say that it was unlikely to be done before next summer. 'This would leave a blank for the spring,'[25] he admitted, with the suggestion of a collection of poetry to plug the gap. *Jesting Pilate*, which had come out in October, was doing very well and had sold 3000 copies in the first two months. Another diversion from the book and from the absence of people at Cortina – Lawrence thought they were lonely – was a Christmas shopping trip to Venice. From there Huxley wrote to Mary recalling the 'unadulterated phantasy' of 'Onslow'[26] in the summer. Venice was 'fabulous' though marred by a performance in Italian of Shaw's *St Joan*, 'a pretty bad play . . . so hopelessly without passion or poetry'. Maria was flourishing in the Cortina atmosphere, 'puts on weight and flesh . . . She drives the new car with great dash and has so far touched only 105 kilometres in it; but hopes on better roads to do 120' – a speed which would feel like fifty in the old Citroën so smooth was the new machine, an Itala six cylinder two-litres.

Christmas Day was spent 'perched on an icy solitude, which would be intolerable if it didn't do us all, especially the little boy and Maria, so much good'.[27] For the first two months of 1927 the Huxleys stuck it out at Cortina: 'Day succeeds day; I work, read, meditate, slide a little on my skis when there is snow,'[28] he reported to Mary early in January. So far the relationship of the Huxleys and Mary Hutchinson had been a secret one, but a sense that all was not well with Mary was beginning to take hold of her friends. Early in February, Virginia Woolf had

dined with Clive Bell – who knew about Mary's bisexuality, which he
once referred to as her 'catholicity'. He confessed to Virginia that
things were not going well between himself and Mary. It had reached
such a pitch that, suddenly, in a theatre box he had blurted out to
Mary: 'I am wretched.' She told him the truth that she was, in Woolf's
words, 'slightly, but only slightly, in love with someone else.
Thereupon he practically went mad.'[29] Whether to resolve this or
because she had succumbed to constant pressure from the Huxleys to
come and see them, Mary finally came over to Italy in early March. All
three paid a visit to Lawrence in Florence where the latter found
Maria, whom he grew more and more fond of, nonetheless 'ambitious' for monetary success; 'if you've got nothing else in your life, I
suppose money and push make a life for you'[30] – an uncharacteristi-
cally cruel comment on Maria. 'Mary Hutchinson seems nice and
gentle,' he told Brett, 'very faded, poor dear – almost a little old
woman . . . They seem to me like people from a dead planet.' Perhaps
Aldous was exhausted by the strain of the book which, 60,000 words
on, seemed to be getting nowhere. 'The fact is,' he told Prentice, 'that
the book, which seemed in its infancy a kitten is turning out to be a
leopard cub . . . The thing increases, not merely in size, but in complexity and difficulty under my hands.'[31] Huxley's solution was to call
a halt for a while, go to England and do some more research for it, and
meet his obligation with an essay collection, *Proper Studies*. He was all
too conscious of the success of people like Arnold Bennett, who had
come to stay with them at Cortina and who never took less than 'two
bob the word' for an article. 'Like a cable to the USA. Magnificent!'
H.G. Wells, too, that 'horrid, vulgar little man',[32] was odiously successful, though Huxley did agree to dine with him when he got to
London to talk politics. He did, however, manage to sell two articles in
America 'for a thousand dollars apiece!'[33] Noticing the clarity of
Julian's recent essays, Aldous told him: 'I find the desire for lucidity
grows in me. Not simplification, but clean dissection and clear exposition of as much of the immeasurable complexity of things as one
can dig into.'[34] That is probably as good a statement of Huxley's
approach to prose style as one could find.

    After a brief stay in Florence the Huxleys started their journey back to London where they would spend the spring. But they had every intention of returning to their beloved Forte in June.

Notes

1   HRC, Letter from Maria Huxley to Mary Hutchinson, 6 June 1926
2   HRC, Letter from Maria Huxley to Mary Hutchinson, 20 June 1926
3   HRC, Letter from Maria Huxley to Mary Hutchinson, 24 June 1926
4   *The Diaries of Virginia Woolf*, Vol 3, p93. 1 July 1926
5   HRC, Letter to Mary Hutchinson, 8 July 1926
6   HRC, Letter to Mary Hutchinson, 12 July 1926
7   *The Letters of Virginia Woolf*, Vol 3, p280. Letter to Vita Sackville-West, 19 July 1926
8   HRC, Letter to Mary Hutchinson, 21 July 1926, 'Cambridge'
9   *The Diaries of Virginia Woolf*, Vol 3 25 July 1926
10 HRC, Letter to Mary Hutchinson, 6 August 1926, 'In the train between Calais and Brussels'
11 Beverley Nichols, reprinted in *Are They the Same at Home?* (1927), pp157–158
12 *The Letters of D.H. Lawrence*, Vol 5, p532. Letter to Giuseppe Oroli, 11 September 1926
13 *L.*271
14 HRC, Letter to Mary Hutchinson, undated but probably August 1926
15 HRC, Letter to Mary Hutchinson, 1 September 1926
16 *L.*273
17 HRC, Letter to Mary Hutchinson, 30 September 1926
18 *L.*275
19 HRC, Letter to Mary Hutchinson, undated in pencil, but probably October or November 1926
20 *The Letters of D.H. Lawrence*, Vol 5 p563. Letter to Martin Secker, 27 October 1926
21 HRC, Letter to Mary Hutchinson, 23 October 1926
22 HRC, Letter from Maria Huxley to Mary Hutchinson, 4 November 1926
23 HRC, Letter from Maria Huxley to Mary Hutchinson, 9 November 1926
24 HRC, Letter from Maria Huxley to Mary Hutchinson, 3 December 1926
25 Reading, Letter to Charles Prentice, Chatto, 9 November 1926
26 HRC, Letter to Mary Hutchinson, 20 December 1926
27 *L.*278

28 HRC, Letter to Mary Hutchinson, 13 January 1927
29 *The Letters of Virginia Woolf*, Vol 3. Letter to Vanessa Bell. 2 February 1927
30 *The Letters of D.H. Lawrence*, Vol 5, p650–1 Letter to Dorothy Brett, 8 March 1927
31 Reading, Letter to Charles Prentice, 15 March 1927
32 *L.*281
33 *L.*284
34 *L.*285

XVI

Counterpoint

The Huxleys had driven across Italy and France to London in the new car, with Aldous recovering from a bout of 'flu acquired in Florence. Immediately, from the studio in Onslow Mews, and from Aldous's desk in the Athenaeum where he wrote letters, they rekindled their social life. They met Mark Gertler and Samuel Koteliansky ('Kot'), the translator and friend of Lawrence, at the Restaurant Bienvenu in Greek Street, with Maria offering to sit for Gertler. Mary was a frequent visitor to the flat. Increasingly interested in what H. G. Wells had to say about politics, Huxley tried to meet him for lunch. An article of Wells's in the *Sunday Express* on 20 March entitled: 'Is Parliament Doomed?' on 'new experiments in government' made Huxley want to quiz him about the viability of proportional representation. Increasingly, progressive intellectuals were questioning the effectiveness of traditional democratic institutions at a time when fascism was on the rise in Europe. As economic conditions worsened in the late 1920s and 1930s, many were persuaded to explore ideas such as 'world government' or eugenics and other kinds of scientific social control. As historians such as Mark Mazower in *Dark Continent* (1998) have shown, the triumph of liberal democracy was far from a foregone conclusion in the middle years of the twentieth century. Quite apart from the assaults from the totalitarians of Left and Right, from fascism and militaristic nationalism, many supposed 'progressives' began to question the effectiveness of traditional parliamentary democracy and to give hospitality to some profoundly illiberal ideas. Huxley's renewed friendship with Wells, and his brief flirtation with eugenics, have been seen by some as evidence of his faltering commitment to democratic principles in the period leading up to his political awakening in the mid-1930s.[1] Someone like Huxley, who thought openly and freely about the problems of man and society, respecting no traditional boundaries or professional lines of intellectual demarcation, was bound to throw out from time to time ideas that cause a *frisson* of alarm to the present day academic sensibility, hedged about as it is with notions of what is or what is not correct utterance. But one would be hard put to pinpoint in Huxley's published work anything that would place him in the 'anti-democratic' camp where some have sought to corral him. On the contrary, as Europe moved towards 1939, his was a voice of sanity. And the message of *Brave New World* from 1932 still speaks to our present predicament. Looking back on the period, in *Brave New World Revisited* in 1959, Huxley stressed that the depression years seemed to many 'a nightmare of too little order' whereas 'a nightmare of total organization' seemed to characterise the post-war world. His political prescriptions reflected these contexts.

At the beginning of May, Maria's grandfather, the old patriarch who had cast a shadow over the young couple when they returned from their world trip, died at St Trond. This put paid to a trip to Paris to see Lewis Gielgud and the Huxleys immediately set off for Belgium. Coming from an English upper-middle class household of intellectual agnostics, Huxley was fascinated by the rituals of Flemish bourgeois Catholicism. 'The days leading up to the funeral, and the funeral itself,' he reported to Prentice, 'have been "Uncle Spencer" [the story from *Little Mexican*] to the nth degree, at once lugubrious and grotesque as these things can only be in a Belgian provincial town complete with family quarrels, black sheep and all the other adjuncts of patriarchal life.'[2] He told Lewis Gielgud that it was 'at once lugubrious and farcical – the real Balzacian comedy of a funeral in a little town . . . the poor old man's body in full evening dress; monks and sisters of charity padding about . . .'[3] His report to Mary showed that the death had given him a rather more profound lesson than these mocking comments suggest: 'The poor old man fading out painfully and finally dying amidst the rather noble and impressive pomp of Catholic ritual – candle in hand with a monk in brown habit praying at his side and pronouncing the general absolution. There is something very admirable about the way in which Catholicism turns what, by itself, is a merely physiological and painfully animal process – dying – into something of cosmic significance, a dignified and tragic act of the greatest importance.'[4]

After the funeral, and a period of sharing the mourning with the family, the Huxleys set off to Cortina, with Maria driving even faster than usual, to tie up their affairs there before moving on to Forte dei Marmi where they planned to stay 'more or less indefinitely'.[5] Given the restlessness of the Huxleys that was a rash prediction. They invited Lawrence to stay but he was initially reluctant, especially when Maria turned up at his villa in Florence with the Franchettis, Italian friends of the Huxleys. 'I *loathe* rich people,'[6] said Lawrence testily. He yielded, however, and commented afterwards: 'Forte dei Marmi was beastly, as a place: flat, dead sea, jelly fishy, and millions of villas. But the Huxleys were nice to us, and they have such a nice little lad.' The Huxleys did not find it 'beastly'. They were staying at the Villa Maietta, with a garden, a pergola draped with a vine, and the sound of Beethoven trios coming from the Lener string quartet who happened to be staying next door. All their old Italian friends came round, especially Costanza, now married and full of gossip. A new Italian servant, Rina Rontini, aged fifteen, arrived and became fond of her new employers, with whom she would stay for many years. The Huxleys were always good with servants. 'Our little house is comfortable,' Maria told Mary. 'At the very end of the village in a *pineta* and in front of it through the trees the sea. Small rooms. From Aldous's to mine a terrace, covered and cool, on which he works.'[7] Mary, it seemed, was still unhappy and having difficulties with Clive. Virginia Woolf wrote in her diary: 'The point of Clive's affair is that Mary is in love with another . . . Unless she will bed with him he is distracted. That she will not do; yet, for lack of him, is distracted herself. The love affair rather increases on her side. It is said to be for someone low in the world.'[8] This could be taken at face value or it could be Mary's way of inventing a story to cover the affair with the Huxleys – it would be understood in her milieu that 'someone low in the world' would not need to be identified.

Huxley liked Forte – the ambience, the friends, and as a place to work. *Crome Yellow, Antic Hay* and now, with difficulty, *Point Counter Point*, had been written there. Maria was typing out the draft of *Proper Studies*, the essay collection on which he had been working as a break from *Point Counter Point,* which was stalled. It was finally finished in July and despatched to Chatto. To Huxley's horror the MS went missing. He shared his fears with Harold Raymond at Chatto: 'What I really fear is that the Fascist Censors (who are always busy) have stopped the package, thinking so much MS suspicious – for they are in a blue funk of accounts unfavourable to the regime coming through.'[9] Fascism was a growing menace to this Tuscan seaside idyll. 'Italy is becoming so bloody as to be practically uninhabitable,' he complained to Mary. 'We are seriously thinking of moving to France. The Fascist efforts to civilise Italy result merely in the action of an interfering police which one would call Prussian if it weren't corrupt and inefficient as well as tyrannous.'[10] In the event the MS turned up, having languished for fourteen days in the Post Office at Florence.

With the book off his hands, Huxley was free to return to the novel – provided that he could find time from playing host to his summer visitors. Sullivan and Lewis Gielgud passed through, but the most striking of these guests were the Morrells – the wound now having healed. Maria – who was very wary of Philip in particular, reported to Mary that the Morrells had arrived 'in great style, with the car full of only unnecessary things and fantastically dressed'.[11] Aldous was 'tall and all in white, barefooted in sandals'. Maria put herself out to do everything the way it had been done at Garsington, only to receive the breezy comment from the duo that they *did* so enjoy the simple life. Aldous improved the tale in his account to Mary. Their two seater tourer was 'hung all over with strange luggage, like the White Knight's charger . . . Philip seems to be less mad, as age creeps on, but more imbecile – the mouth gapes continuously, the eyes and attention wander, there is a kind of involuntary detachment from reality . . . my hermitage has been disagreeably violated.'[12] Huxley seems to have been accepting that perhaps the affair with Mary was in decline: 'I live here the life of a meditative tree and all past activity seems a dream which has no probable prospect of being renewed. But perhaps it will renew itself? I hope so, Mary.'

As well as struggling to write the intractable novel, Huxley was reading with his usual voraciousness, *Don Quixote* – 'What a book! It couldn't be better' – and Cardinal Newman – 'very fine as a psychologist . . . And how well he wrote!'. But he confessed to Mary that Meredith did nothing for him 'so much literature to express so little substance'. For Huxley 'literature' was developing into a term of abuse. He had also been reading Pascal, Baudelaire, Bossuet's *Variations of the Protestant Religion* and, again, Burt's *Metaphysical Foundations of Modern Science*. 'I wish I could afford, like Flaubert, to spend four or five years over a book,' he told Julian. 'There might be a chance then of making it rather good.'[13] Instead he worked away, seven or eight hours a day, running out of time, with no question of meeting the January 1928 deadline. In spite of the pressure of work he still found time to write, for the August issue of *Harper's Magazine,* an essay on 'The Outlook for American Culture: Some reflections in a machine age'. It argued that 'The future of America is the future of the world.' And that everyone would follow the path America was blazing. Whilst he conceded that machinery had enabled a 'fuller life' in the material sense he doubted if culture had been promoted by it. Ever the uncompromising highbrow, he asked whether in spite of 'all our humanitarian and democratic prejudices' (which he shared) it was not true that many people did not want to be cultured. And the mass forms of entertainment being devised by Western consumer capitalism would not promote it either: 'All the resources of science are applied in order that imbecility may flourish and vulgarity cover the whole earth.' Machinery of this kind would standardise ideas globally and make people passive consumers – 'It removes man's incentive to amuse himself.'

Much of this can be seen, seventy-five years on, as good prophecy. Much of this went into *Brave New World.* But there is one disturbing passage about the 'revolt against political democracy' which Huxley sees as inevitable (though not in the form of a return to autocracy) as part of a process of giving power to 'intelligent and active oligarchies'. He goes on: 'The ideal state is one in which there is a material democracy controlled by a an aristocracy of the intellect . . . where those with the greatest talent rule.' These were dangerous ideas to be playing with at a time when totalitarianism was on the rise and do not represent Huxley's mature political position. Some will see them as sinister, others as a genuine attempt to deal with an issue that remains unresolved today: how does one reconcile the formidable power of global media and entertainment conglomerates, and the governments who appear to fawn upon them, with the need to nurture an intelligent culture that allows the individual citizen to possess the intellectual and imaginative space, the cultural space, in which to make its own choices and assert its own sense of value?

As the summer ended, Maria found it gloomy: 'Aldous goes on working with a regularity and a tap-tapping which seems increased by the waves. If the light goes out, which it does every five minutes, he taps in the dark and does not even stop to see if he wrote correctly . . . Aldous's writing is rather like Casanova's (pleasant and unpleasant things are revealed) enough to make it amusing.'[14] What *did* Maria think of his writing? Lawrence – with whom they were now very much involved, supporting him after a lung-trouble which they feared was caused by the salt water swallowed when he was bathing with them at Forte – later said that the death of the child in the book Aldous was writing on the terrace now was something she never forgave. But her loyalty was absolute. When he was not writing there were diversions. They went to Lucca to see the procession of the *Volto Santo* – 'very fine and impressive with a magnificent procession at dusk marching straight out of the fourteenth century'[15] – and to Florence to retrieve their winter possessions from Costanza's villa. The autumn weather could still be magnificent – 'the air like crystal, the colours wonderfully rich & bright'[16] – but the book was insistent. His first idea for a title was *Counterpoint*, but another recent book had been titled *God's Counterpoint* so he was trying to think of another but by the end of November he settled for the eventual title 'making it more specific – note against note'.[17] His real worry was that it would be too long: 'The thing has an unpleasant way of growing and developing in my hands – a habit which has necessitated frequent scrappings, rewritings and re-scrappings of earlier sections. I hope it won't do anything disturbingly new between now and January.' He told Mary: 'I wish I had another year to work at it. More time so matures and ripens every idea – not in the consciousness entirely, tho' to some extent even there; but mainly when one isn't specifically thinking of it – by entwining new experiences with old, by relating memories and knowledge to the idea so that it can grow and diversify itself.'[18]

Proper Studies was published in November. The book marked a step forward from the sort of essay collection he had previously put together. It evidenced a greater seriousness and some methodological ambition. It was a step towards the kind of book that *Ends and Means* (1937) would be. 'These essays,' he explained, 'represent an attempt on my part to methodize the confused notions, which I have derived from observation and reading, about a few of the more important aspects of social and individual life.' He also stated: 'The most important part of man can be studied without a special technique, and described in the language of common speech.' Today, with the growth of academic specialisation, that assertion would be harder to make. Huxley emerges in these essays a critic of the facile eighteenth century view of human nature as essentially rational, humane and good. He believed in reason, virtue and humanity but acknowledged that social institutions had to be fashioned with difficulty from Kant's 'crooked timber of humanity' not from a perfect blueprint. He also set out the names of his mentors such as the Italian sociologist Vilfred Pareto, whose massive and intimidating *Sociologica generale* had become something of a social theory bible to Huxley in the 1920s. He admitted that he preferred Jung to Freud and Adler who were merely 'monomaniacal'.

The essays are interesting in the light they shed on Huxley's emerging thought, its attempt to reconcile an inherited liberal humanism with the more recalcitrant facts of human nature. 'The greater part of the world's philosophy and theology is merely an

intellectual justification for the wishes and day-dreams of philosophers and theologians,' he opined in one essay, adding: 'the doctrine
of Original Sin is, scientifically, much truer than the doctrine of
natural reasonableness and virtue'. The limitations of the essay,
'The Idea of Equality', are that in spite of its witty, fluent, sceptical,
sensible manner, it is not actually *advocating* anything. In view of
the political instability and growing sense of crisis of the times perhaps some more positive thinking was required. Like most
concerned thinkers in the 1920s Huxley was groping for an answer
to the problem identified by Lorelei Lee in *Gentlemen Prefer
Blondes,* when she tells her rich philanthropist admirer Mr Spoffard:
'civilisation is not what it ought to be and we really ought to have
something else to take its place'. He returned to the argument of his
Harper's Magazine piece in an essay on 'Political Democracy' and,
referring to the fact that at the Brixton by-election on 27 June 1927
only fifty-three per cent voted (it would be fewer today!) he asked
again whether people were actually much interested in democracy
and repeated the desirability of a state 'ruled by the best of its
citizens'.

This was in part a desire to see the best ideas prevail, but in part,
one senses, it was a frankly admitted desire not to have to do the job
himself and to be allowed to get on with his own life: 'I myself lack
all capacity and ambition to govern.' In an essay on religion he
praised Catholicism, no doubt influenced by what he had seen in
Belgium and in Italy: 'Catholicism is probably the most realistic of
all Western religions. Its practice is based on a profound knowledge
of human nature in all its varieties and gradations.' Elsewhere he
attacks Proust (whom he read with admiration when he was first
published but whom he later came to devalue) for being 'a scientific
voluptuary of the emotions' who had no ambition to do more than
know himself: 'the idea of using his knowledge in order to make
himself better never seems to have occurred to him. There is a
strange moral poverty about his book.' For the person, like Huxley,
who wished to engage usefully with the world and find some sort of
unifying principle to inform right action, Proust's revelling in the
discontinuity of his own personality was impossible. An essay on

'Eugenics' is his first foray into the subject and concludes (after noting that 'It is quite possible . . . that they will learn to breed babies in bottles') that a world run by the perfect specimens might be a little unbearable: 'If the eugenists are in too much of an enthusiastic hurry to improve the race, they will only succeed in destroying it.'

One of the first readers of the book was Lawrence: 'I have read 70 pages, with a little astonishment that you are so serious and professorial. You are not your grandfather's *Enkel* [grandson] for nothing – that funny dry-mindedness and underneath social morality.'[19] The Huxleys went to Florence at Christmas to spend it with Lawrence and Frieda and, in what is perhaps the only extract from a 'spasmodically kept' diary by Huxley (presumably destroyed in the 1961 fire but the extract is printed in his introduction to his selection of Lawrence's letters) he described this event: 'Lunched and spent the p.m. with the Lawrences. DHL in admirable form, talking wonderfully. He is one of the few people I feel real respect and admiration for. Of most other eminent people I have met I feel that at any rate I belong in the same species as they do. But this man has something different and superior in kind, not degree.'[20]

Just before Christmas, the Huxleys had been thinking about their future. They had formed the plan of going to live in the English countryside. But this quickly gave way to another project, which Maria outlined to Mary: 'We are instead going to build an enchanting house here in the middle of a pine wood onto the sea. The house will be ready by next June . . . The house will be small but it will have room for you in the tower or on the ground floor facing the sea.'[21] The construction of the novel, however, was not so promising (though the house was never built) and by late January 1928, Huxley was offering Prentice the chance to reduce his advance for non-delivery. He was writing from a new address, not Cortina again as they had planned, but Les Diablerets in the Vaud in Switzerland. Julian and Juliette Huxley had taken the Chalet des Arolles, above Aigle, for the winter, where Aldous and Maria joined them. Juliette later recalled the long leisurely breakfasts, after which Maria sent Aldous off to grapple with the novel. There were visitors, such as Juliette's pretty cousin, a professional dancer, who attracted interest both from Maria and Aldous, who described her to Mary as 'a tremendous cock-teaser, who yet doesn't realise what she's doing'.[22]

But the main attraction was Lawrence whom they had invited to stay nearby. 'What an astonishing man! He does take the shine out of most other people. Such insight, such wit, such prodigious vitality and in spite of his sickness such humour.' Sybil Colefax was told that Lawrence made most other people seem 'half-dead by comparison'.[23] Mary's troubled love life, meanwhile, had been dissected by Lytton Strachey who advised Clive to play hard to get in order to drive Mary back to him. Virginia Woolf thought that Mary was 'very lonely and anxious to come back'.[24] Huxley told Mary he was reading E. M. Forster's *Aspects of the Novel*, based on Forster's 1927 Clark Lectures at Cambridge and just published. He found the book 'amusing but thin and rather tiresome, I thought, so spinsterishly giggly and sniggery and so terribly without guts and testicles – the untesticled quality showing up specially strongly in just those passages in which he expresses himself most decidedly on the side of the gutty books against the gutless, like H. James'. Lawrence was not initially enthused by Les Diablerets: 'Aldous, like a long, stalky bird, all stalk and claw, goes mildly skiing in the afternoon . . . Aldous and Maria mildly ski without much joy, and we trudge a while, then go home. There are very few people – practically all the chalets shut and snowed over . . . Aldous looks a rare shoot, as he's 6ft 4 and thin and half blind, and his skis are over seven feet long.'[25] Lawrence was frustrated by the long intellectual conversations: 'I must say I get tired of so much talk. What is the good of it! It is really much better to possess one's soul in patience.'[26] He was particularly enraged by the scientific talk of the two Huxley brothers, and their belief in the theories of evolution and what Julian called 'the possibility of mankind's genetic improvement'.[27] Lawrence believed that the solution to mankind's problems lay, not in science, but in greater freedom for the instinctive and intuitive life. But he was interested in one idea he had thrashed out with Aldous, that a group of authors should join together to publish their own books, calling themselves 'the authors publishing company'. His difficulties with publishers (Huxley had none) were no doubt behind this for it was the period of *Lady Chatterley's Lover,* which he was just about to deliver to the publisher – the manuscript typed by Maria, who did not always appreciate the obscene quality of the more robust English sexual terms, introducing them blithely into the general conversation.

These first three months of 1928, up in the snows, were idyllic. The winter sun was brilliant, though entering shadow a little prematurely because of the mountains. In the evenings Julian and Aldous took it in turns to read. *The Pickwick Papers* were got through in their entirety. During the day they skied and played with the children – Aldous and Julian built an igloo for them. Juliette, as a recreation from typing Julian's *The Science of Life,* embroidered an Adam and Eve, whose genitalia were finished off by Lawrence himself, who was very accomplished at all the domestic tasks.[28] The Huxleys were falling under the spell of Lawrence again and began to talk of going for six months to live on his ranch in New Mexico. In the event, the need to attend to Matthew's schooling took them back to London in March. Maria had written to Mary at the end of February about her 'violent desire for a kiss', but in the same breath mentioning Aldous: 'Do you remember how he can make your whole body quiver?'[29] Back in London they all made contact again at Onslow Mews. The novel was nearly done but Huxley was still wanting to tinker with the title, which he now decided 'doesn't really get all I want to express'.[30] He wanted to change it to *Diverse Laws*, a phrase from the Fulke Greville poem which would form the book's epigraph, but the American publishers insisted on the original title. He had complained to Lewis Gielgud that fiction was full of difficulties 'especially to one who, like myself, isn't really a born novelist but has large aspirations',[31] an unimprovable summing-up.

By the middle of May, the typescript finally off his hands, Huxley was free to continue catching up with friends and new acquaintances. He had already lunched with Noel Coward 'who seems much nicer and more intelligent when he's by himself than when he's being the brilliant young actor-dramatist in front of a crowd of people'.[32] He was reading Goethe's *Wilhelm Meister* which reminded him how much he detested Goethe: 'What an odious character! And as for saying he's a great writer – no, it won't do.' Matthew Arnold would have turned in his grave. He was grudgingly enjoying Yeats, whose magnificent volume *The Tower* (containing poems like 'Sailing to Byzantium', 'Meditations in Time of Civil War', and 'Among School Children') had just appeared: 'They have a strange power about them – underneath their superficial literariness and preciosity.' Apart from a contribution to *The Best Poems of 1926* ('Arabia Infelix') Huxley's life as a poet seemed over: 'Verse I find almost unwritable these days,'[33] he had confessed a year earlier.

In June the Huxleys crossed to Paris to stay with Lewis Gielgud and his wife in the Rue Decamps and to make arrangements to take their latest house, at Suresnes, north of the Bois de Boulogne at 3 Rue du Bac. They would keep this house, though typically not in continuous residence, until March 1930 when they moved to the South of France. Today the roar of traffic along the north bank of the Seine a few yards from the house – in a small complex of rather suburban-looking villas with tall pointed roofs known as Le Village Anglais and subject to a preservation order by the local *mairie* – makes it a less attractive spot than it would have been in 1928. The present owner – by her brass plate a psychotherapist – seemed mildly interested to learn in the Spring of 2000 that her home had once been lived in by the author of *Le Meilleur des Mondes*. One of Huxley's favourite novels was Flaubert's comprehensive indictment of bourgeois stupidity, *Bouvard and Pécuchet*. Suresnes was one of the destinations that marked the outer limits of the eponymous characters' Sunday walks in the early days of their friendship. At first, they seemed to like the house: 'The surroundings are really delightful – a tiny provincial town, enlivened by Sunday boating, with the river at the door and the Bois – where one can walk on weekdays for an hour and hardly see a soul – 3 minutes away.'[34] The Huxleys hardly had time to complete the arrangements before they were off to Forte for the summer. They would not return to Paris until October. The drove from Paris to Forte, taking in three days with Lawrence at Chexbres above Vervey. They were fined thirty francs for speeding in Switzerland, passed through the Simplon pass, and drove down to Milan along the new *autostrada*. They boasted of maintaining an average speed of fifty miles per hour all the way. At Forte, in temperatures of ninety-four degrees, which persuaded them to buy an electric fan, they settled in to 'a very tiny but charming little house back from the road and the sea in the pine woods'[35] – the Villa Il Cannetto. Huxley was reading Pascal – 'really one of the strangest and most interesting of men, and certainly, I think, the subtlest and profoundest intellect France ever produced' and awaiting the reaction to the new novel, which would be published in the autumn. It was his most substantial and ambitious novel so far and had cost him much pain and effort. But would he be seen to have succeeded?

Notes

1 See for example David Bradshaw, 'Open Conspirators: Huxley and H.G. Wells 1927-35', in *The Hidden Huxley* (1994)
2 Reading, Letter to Charles Prentice, 19 May 1927
3 L.286
4 HRC, Letter to Mary Hutchinson, 30 May 1927
5 Reading, Letter to Prentice, *Ibid*
6 *The Letters of D.H. Lawrence*, Vol 6, p77. Letter to Kot, 6 June 1927. All subsequent Lawrence quotations in this chapter from Vol 6
7 HRC, Letter from Maria Huxley to Mary Hutchinson, 29 June 1927
8 *The Diaries of Virginia Woolf*, Vol 3, p141. 23 June 1927
9 Reading, Letter to Harold Raymond, Chatto, 5 August 1927
10 HRC, Letter to Mary Hutchinson, 15 August 1927
11 HRC, Letter from Maria Huxley to Mary Hutchinson, 9 September 1927
12 HRC, Letter to Mary Hutchinson, 15 August 1927
13 L.291
14 HRC, Letter from Maria Huxley to Mary Hutchinson, 11 November 1927
15 HRC, Letter to Ottoline Morrell, 8 October 1927
16 Reading, Letter to Charles Prentice, 27 October 1927
17 Reading, Letter to Harold Raymond, Chatto, 24 November 1927
18 HRC, Letter to Mary Hutchinson, 5 December 1927
19 *Letters of DH Lawrence* (1932) edited by Aldous Huxley, p693. Letter to Huxley, December 1927
20 Introduction, *The Olive Tree*, p231
21 HRC, Letter from Maria Huxley to Mary Hutchinson, 9 December 1927
22 HRC, Letter to Mary Hutchinson, 10 February 1928

23 Bodleian, Letter to Sybil Colefax, 13 February 1928
24 *The Letters of Virginia Woolf,* Vol 3. Letter to Vanessa Bell, 29 January 1928
25 *The Letters of D.H. Lawrence,* Vol 6 p276. Letters first to Secker then to Brett, 27 January 1928; Letter to Ada Lawrence, 3 February
26 Lawrence to Max Mohr, 29 February 1928
27 Julian Huxley, *Memories 1,* p153
28 Juliette Huxley, *Leaves of the Tulip Tree,* p117
29 HRC, Letter from Maria Huxley to Mary Hutchinson, 23 February 1928
30 L.296
31 L.295
32 HRC, Letter to Mary Hutchinson, 26 April 1928
33 L.287
34 L.299
35 L.310

XVII

Suresnes

That long, penultimate summer at Forte was a welcome easing of the stress of composition of *Point Counter Point*. 'Here it is vegetative and solar,' Huxley announced to Mary. 'The sun does most of the living for one; one abandons oneself to its energy. In the intervals I do a little work.'[1] He was busy with the essays – he called them 'biographies', the vestige of an idea discussed with Lawrence at Cortina for a book on the world's great intellectual 'perverts' such as Wilde and Baudelaire – that would form *Do What You Will* the following autumn. 'The beach is crowded with flashing young Italian aristocrats, like very handsome young chauffeurs, and shapely young women. Pleasant to look at, but rather tedious; the sort of young women who ought only to exist in bed and naked, and with whom there should be no communication except a physical and nocturnal one. They ought to be trained to hibernate in the intervals of love-making.' *Lady Chatterley* had appeared and people kept writing to Maria indignantly 'as though she was the author. What a strange hatred for the truth most human beings have! Or rather not for the truth, because it doesn't exist, but for reality. A loathing and fear.' A month later, Mary was told the same story of sunny indolence – 'the grapes hang almost ripe from the pergolas, the figs have begun to burst with sweetness'.[2] They had been to see the Palio again at Siena

and taken 'one or two astonishing drives through the local mountains'. H was reading Renan ('remarkable') and Boccaccio. On 10
September it was Maria's thirtieth birthday. She asked Mary: 'Do
you remember yours & that first kiss?'[3] Mary was born in 1889 and
therefore her thirtieth birthday would have been in 1919. If these
words are taken at face value, the sexual relationship between Mary
and Maria would have begun at around the same time she and
Aldous were beginning their affair.

On 22 October, Lawrence exclaimed: 'I've begun Aldous's book,
what a fat book!'[4] He was right. The orange volume weighed in at one
and a half pounds and was 601 pages in length. It was a long way
from the elegant brevity of Crome. It was also weighty with expectation. Huxley had invested a great deal of emotional and intellectual
energy in the book. He had expounded, to anyone who would listen,
his theories of its composition: the attempt to reflect all the aspects of
human nature, balancing one view by another (the musical analogy of
counterpoint where competing voices forge complex harmony
explaining the title), exploring the human specimen from every angle
and with every scientific instrument in the laboratory. He had confessed himself not to be a born novelist yet claimed 'large aspirations'.
The only question for the reader would be: does it work? All the evidence was that they believed it did. It was a success in terms of sales
and brought in some welcome income. Critics were cautious. Cyril
Connolly, in an anonymous review in the New Statesman, thought it
'if not Mr Huxley's best book . . . certainly his most important'. The
anonymous TLS reviewer criticised it from the point of view of the
craft of fiction: 'It does not weld story and ideas into one: it cares little
about progression, proportion, climax and so forth. In spite of a few
masterly scenes and descriptions, the persons always come second to
the ideas.' Arnold Bennett in The Realist, said it contributed nothing
to the 'evolutionary development' of the novel and he objected to its
'destructiveness', its hostility towards its characters, and the fact that,
although at least three of the characters were writers, there was 'not a
single passage in which are broadly treated the repercussions of literature upon life or vice versa'.[5] Connolly noted the influence of the
Gide of the Faux Monnayeurs – a much-discussed influence on

Huxley – but Gide himself, his journal later recorded, after three abortive attempts to get beyond the first seventy pages, and finding not 'a single line somewhat firmly drawn, a single personal thought, emotion, or sensation, the slightest enticement for the heart or mind', gave up the struggle.[6]

The older generation of novelists were finding difficulty with Huxley's alienation effect and the robustness, indeed ruthlessness, of his satire. The younger generation probably found it more exciting and dangerous. The novel is a portrait of contemporary types (the literary and artistic types in the main whom Huxley knew) set against each other, each illuminating the other by contraries and comparisons, in order to express Huxley's overall view of society, a fictional equivalent of those big, comprehensive works like Pareto's sociology he loved to grapple with. Except that it dealt with quite a limited segment of contemporary society. The epigraph from Fulke Greville (1554–1628) – the poet of 'man's degeneration' – is from his verse drama *Mustapha*, published in 1609, a chorus of priests who sing of the 'wearisome condition of humanity', a condition of trying to live the Christian life yet being defeated by Nature. 'What meaneth Nature by these diverse laws?/Passion and Reason self-division cause.' The chorus ends in lines, not quoted by Huxley, which are the priests' lament: 'Yet when each of us in his own heart looks,/He finds the God there far unlike his books.' Secularised in the context of Huxley's novel this would mean that reason and the passions are at war and that life is 'unlike his books'. It is the argument of Huxley the essayist, trying to reconcile the intellectual and the ideal with the practical realities of society. In its sense of the illusory nature of the perfect society in the face of reality it is the argument of a man whose next novel would be *Brave New World*. In a way which the post-modernist novel has now made routine, the book signals a commentary on its own procedures at certain points. The novelist, Philip Quarles, is talking about the book he wants to write: 'the essence of the new way of looking at things is multiplicity. Multiplicity of eyes and multiplicity of aspects seen . . . there's the biologist, the chemist, the physicist, the historian. Each sees, professionally, a different aspect of the event, a different layer of reality. What I want to do is to look with all those eyes at once.' So what did Huxley see? The vanity of pleasure-seeking, intellectuals like Walter Bidlake who were 'frightened of the lower classes' and couldn't bridge the gap between art and life, the emotional immaturity of the rich aristocrat Lord Edward Tantamount ('a kind of child'), the glamorous fascist, Everard Webley, head of the British Freemen, who is brutally killed, the spectacle of dysfunctional marital relationships (due as often as not to the indifference of the male partner), the ranting Lawrence-like figure, Rampion, 'the cool indifferent flux of intellectual curiosity' of Philip Quarles, the novelist and the character nearest to embodying Huxley's pre-occupations, Spandrell's 'refinements of vice', the irrelevance of much modern art to life.

Even Huxley's critics conceded that there was powerful writing and striking scenes in the book. It is not hard to see how Huxley became a favourite with liberal intellectuals. He was bringing matter into the literary novel that was generally not found there, his intellectualising was always stimulating and provocative, and there was a sense of modernity and daring about his writing. As always, there were autobiographical connections. Philip and Elinor Quarles have much in common with the Huxleys. Philip, quite early in the novel, travelling as the Huxleys did through India, realises that he had not loved Elinor enough at the beginning of their marriage: 'For even at the beginning he had evaded her demands, he had refused to give himself completely to her. On her side she had offered everything. And he had taken, but without return. His soul, the intimacies of his being, he had always withheld.' Is this a kind of confession? Philip's game leg, analogous to Huxley's disability acquired in childhood, is explained to Elinor by his mother as something that should never have happened to someone of his nature. 'He was born far away, if you know what I mean. It was always too easy for him to dispense with people. He was too fond of shutting himself up inside his own private silence. But he might have learned to come out more, if that horrible accident hadn't happened. It raised an artificial barrier between him and the rest of the world . . . Intellectual contacts – those are the only ones he admits . . . Because he can hold his own there; because he can be certain of superiority.' And again, Elinor is seen as a go-between, telling the intellectual about the realities of ordinary life, 'the habits of the natives', something she does: 'Not only for her own sake, but for the sake of the novelist he might be, she wished he could break his habit of impersonality and learn to live with the intuitions and feelings and instincts as well as with the intellect. Heroically, she had even encouraged him in the velleities of passion for other women. It might do him good to have a few affairs.'

On 28 October 1928, a few days after H.G. Wells had sent 'a very nice note',[7] about the novel, Lawrence wrote with his reactions: 'I have read *Point Counter Point* with a heart sinking through my boot-soles and a rising admiration. I do think you've shown the truth, about you and your generation, with really fine courage. It seems to me it would take ten times the courage to write *P. Counter P.* that it took me to write *Lady C.* and if the public knew *what* it was reading, it would throw a hundred stones at you, to one at me . . . All I want to do to your Lucy is smack her across the mouth'. As to the character thought to represent Lawrence, 'your Rampion is the most boring character in the book – a gas-bag. Your attempt at intellectual sympathy! – It's all rather disgusting, and I feel like a badger that has its hole on Wimbledon Common and trying not to be caught.'[8] This was a common reaction to the book – that it was brave and put its finger on the contemporary pulse, but was not always wholly attractive. As Koteliansky told Virginia Woolf, 'it is typical of the age. It is a painful book, a horrid book, but it is that.'[9] Lawrence – whose friendship with the Huxleys, especially with Maria, was at its warmest at this time – didn't seem to mind Rampion and was pleased at the commercial success of the book. 'Do hope the book makes *real* money,' he told Maria. 'I'm glad you'll get money out of your *Counterpane* – sounds quite a lot – you'll be able to squirt around.'[10] Lawrence was reacting to erroneous reports that 80,000 copies had been sold in the United States. 'If that is so,' he told his friend, the Florentine publisher, Giuseppe Orioli, 'he will be very lordly and uppish, no answering for him.'[11] By December, 10,000 copies had been sold of the English edition. Throughout his life, Huxley's books sold more copies in Britain than in the United States. Privately, Lawrence had reservations. He demanded of Brett: 'Did you read Aldous's book? A bit cheap sensational I thought.'[12] Huxley himself was aware of such an objection. To an unsolicited correspondent, who was to keep on writing to him for many years from America, a Mrs Flora Strousse who wrote under the pseudonym of Floyd Starkey, he confessed facetiously: 'I have at last written rather a good, but also rather a frightful, novel.'[13]

The Huxleys were still settling in slowly to the house in the Rue du Bac, sorting out the central heating, painting and papering. Maria ensured that fabric designed by Dufy was used for the sofas and cushions. Armchairs specially made to accommodate Aldous's proportions were ordered from Maple's in London, and Maria's brother-in-law, René Moulaert, the painter offered his skills. He designed a dining-table with a reflective surface that allowed guests to catch the faintly unsettling image of themselves eating. Huxley's neighbour – a rather more popular French novelist – was so disconcerted by the praise of Huxley that appeared in *Les Nouvelles Littéraires*, that he took to turning his garden hose on the author of *Point Counter Point* when he came out into the pocket-handkerchief back garden.[14] The Huxleys were starting to enjoy Paris, however, and sampling some of its pleasures, which included a Lesbian bar featuring 'a wrestling match between two gigantic female athletes'. It occurred to Huxley that: 'The funniest feature of this town is the people who try to be wicked in supposed haunts of sin.'[15] He was not reading anything particularly interesting, he told Lawrence, having struggled with a 'tiresome' book by Virginia Woolf called *Orlando* 'which is so terribly literary and *fantaisiste* that nothing is left in it at all.' By contrast, a re-reading of *Our Mutual Friend* reminded him how much it was 'So painfully true to life.'[16] Huxley's aesthetic philosophy continued to prefer 'life' over the 'literary', a distinction he seemed confident in being able to make. He was now asked by Lawrence, who was in Bandol on the Côte d'Azur, to find out whether pirated editions of *Lady Chatterley* were on sale in Paris. They were, and Huxley, always interested in new communications technology, tried to recommend using the new technique of photo-setting to produce an edition to undercut the pirates, having bombarded Chatto with questions about the technical process. He went to see Sylvia Beach of the legendary bookshop Shakespeare and Company in Paris but in the end Lawrence found another Paris publisher, Edward Titus, to bring out an edition in May 1929. The Huxleys spent a 'nightmare' Christmas in Belgium with Maria's family. 'One can easily have too much of family life!'[17] he complained to Ottoline Morrell. Back in Paris at the start of the year, he told her that, whilst finding most French literary men impossibly 'dreary', he had been seeing a good deal of the young French poet, Drieu La Rochelle, and had had a meeting with Paul Valéry. Valéry told Huxley that an author shouldn't frequent other authors after the age of twenty-four – 'once formed, he can only find them uninteresting – as a class – that is to say: tho' of course there are always individual exceptions'.

In the wake of his triumph with *Point Counter Point,* Huxley was no doubt taking stock at the start of 1929. During a brief visit to London in January, he wrote from the Athenaeum to Flora Strousse, who had evidently asked him to give some account of himself: 'I have almost no ideas about myself and don't like having them . . . For "know thyself" was probably one of the stupidest pieces of advice ever given – that is to say, if it meant turning the self inside out by introspection . . . for the self only exists in relation to circumstances outside itself and introspection which distracts one from the outside world is a kind of suicide.'[18] It was bad enough exposing one's inner life to the public by endeavouring to 'commit hara-kiri every publishing season' without adding to the exposure by analysing oneself for the benefit of others. He did however produce a brief biographical note for his German translator, Herbert Herlitschka, which referred to his blindness – 'I was much alone & thrown on my own resources' – and which described his post war career in the following terms: 'Took to journalism in the intervals of which, whenever I had enough money to get away, I wrote my first books, mostly in Italy . . . Have now a house in the neighbourhood of Paris.'[19] In spite of its almost telegraphic brevity, the note importantly confirms that, for Huxley, journalism was the despised necessity and his object was always to 'get away' to write. The getting away was a necessary part of his creativity. In many respects a typical Englishman of his class and epoch, Huxley was also the type – more common in the early twentieth century than today when young writers seem to be more stay-at-home – of the willingly self-exiled. Like Lawrence Durrell who mocked his native land as 'Pudding Island', Huxley was one of those who functioned better abroad – not just because it was cheap and freer from stuffy convention – but because distance sharpened the pen.

On his way back to Paris, rattling across wintry south-east England in the train towards Dover, Huxley started to write to Mary – the almost feverish sexual passion for her which had been expressed in the letters of the middle of the decade seemingly now all spent: 'Farewell, sweet Mary; why do we live in this filthy climate? Too depressing. The sight of the landscape outside the train windows is really sickeningly dismal.'[20] He also described to her his dalliance with Beaverbrook who wanted him to write on contemporary literature for his newspapers. In a foretaste of the sort of aesthetico-ethical dilemma he would experience again in Hollywood, he told Mary: 'I so resent the pressure these swine put on one with their beastly money. At the same time it's almost a duty to milk them of as much of it as one can. So I remain torn between a desire to send him to the devil and a desire to haggle for the highest price.' Huxley decided in the end to refuse the devil's shilling, largely because the task would have been to plough through pages of contemporary writing, most of which he despised, telling Julian: '99.8% of the literary production of this age – as of all other ages, for that matter – is the purest cat's piss'.[21] The profession of literary journalism rests on the assumption that the opposite is true, however compelling the evidence to the contrary. That January in London Huxley signed his third agreement with Chatto for two novels in three years with three further books if possible. It was more realistic – previous targets never having been met – and, together with the royalties from *Point Counter Point*, his first big financial success, he was to be able to live comfortably through the first years of the next decade. He also met, at the home of the critic Raymond Mortimer, Gerald Heard – another fabulous talker and explorer of ideas who will be described more fully later, and who was a key intellectual companion of his American years. Heard later recalled how they stayed talking on this occasion until one in the morning, after all transport had ceased.

Nonetheless, Huxley accompanied Heard the three miles back to his flat and then set off for another couple of miles to his own lodging. He was always addicted to long night-time walks.

Once back in Paris, the Huxleys learned that Lawrence was not well and resolved to go and see him in the south of France at Bandol where he was staying at the Hotel Beau Rivage. They also wanted to press on to Florence to sell their Italian car. As it turned out, Lawrence seems to have been more concerned about the Huxleys' state of health. When they finally left on 1 February (having expressed much anger at the seizure by police of Lawrence's typescript of poems, *Pansies*, and of published copies of *Lady Chatterley's Lover* – an act that would be followed in June by the seizure of Lawrence's paintings from the Warren Gallery in London), Lawrence reported to Juliette: 'Aldous and Maria left this morning in the car – a lovely morning indeed, still and sunny. But they are neither of them very well – Aldous liverish and run down, Maria very thin and not sound, somehow. They worry me a bit. Aldous was in bed two days with his liver . . .'[22] Lawrence was grateful for Huxley's sympathy and his promise to get Mary's husband, Jack Hutchinson, to have a word about the seizure of the typescript of the poems with Oswald Mosley 'the Socialist with whom he is great friends'. After the Huxleys had gone, Lawrence wrote to Ottoline, repeating his concerns about their health and their general mood: 'I think the *Counter-Point* [sic] book sort of got between them – she found it hard to forgive the death of the child – which one can well understand. But as I say, there's more than one self to everybody, and the Aldous that writes those novels is only one little Aldous among others – probably much nicer – that don't write novels: I mean it's only one of his little selves that writes the book and makes the child die, it's not *all* himself. – No, I don't like his books: even if I admire a sort of desperate courage of repulsion and repudiation in them. But again, I feel only half a man writes the books – a sort of precocious adolescent. There is surely much more of a man in the actual Aldous.'[23] To Koteliansky, a couple of days later, he concluded: 'Aldous is really nicer – getting older and a bit more aware of other people's existence.'[24] Lawrence was convinced that the death of the child (which may have been suggested by the death of Naomi Mitchison's child from meningitis) was the cause of a certain difficulty in the relationship of Aldous and Maria in early 1929. Moreover, the love affair in the novel with Lucy Tantamount 'was Aldous's affair with Nancy Cunard – I think Maria hardly forgives it. And perhaps he's sorry he did it. But it has made them money, and Maria wants money – says so. Yes, she wants to buy a new car in Paris.'[25]

When the Huxleys reached Florence, via Genoa where the car's magneto froze, it was six inches deep in snow, fifteen degrees below zero, every water pipe frozen, and the Arno a solid mass of ice, as Huxley reported to Arnold Bennett.[26] It was not a good time to sell a car so they left it with a garage to sell and came back again by train via the Riviera where they encountered a seventy-miles-an-hour icy gale. In March, in Paris, they bought the famous red Bugatti (Enrico Bugatti apocryphally astonished that a woman should be driving one of his hand-built cars). It was the new 1929 touring model and came garlanded with praise from the AA engineers. It was the first materialistic fruit of the *Point Counter Point* success. It was a two-seater with dove-grey leather upholstery and a great box-like trunk at the back. It had been specially adapted for Aldous's long legs – which was hard luck on Matthew who had to squeeze into a sort of gap behind the two front seats. Seventy years later, in his apartment in Washington DC, Matthew's eyes lit up when he recalled for me the days at Sanary-sur-Mer (where the Huxleys went after Suresnes) when he would hear the roar of the Bugatti, his mother at the wheel, coming back along the coast road from Bandol to their home at La Gorguette. The car needed running in and the Huxleys gladly took the chance to drive all the way to Madrid (looking at the Prado) and on to London. They were thus spending very little time in the ugly house in Paris and Huxley did a great deal of his work on the move, setting up his typewriter without fuss in various hotel rooms. He was finishing off the essays for *Do What You Will.* Lawrence managed to stay with them briefly in March, attending a Paris salon with Aldous where they both met Daniel Halévy and Mauriac. At a lunch at Paul Morand's, Huxley met the American writer Glenway Wescott and found that he liked him very much: 'It would be pleasant to meet him again. Which is *not* the case with most of the literary men I meet in Paris!'[27] Lawrence later told Ottoline: 'They were very good to me, tended me so kindly. I am really very much attached to them, humanly. There is that other side of them, the sort of mental and nervous friction and destructiveness which I can't bear, but they leave that out with me. As I grow older I dread more and more that frictional nervousness which makes people always react *against* one another, in discord, instead of together in harmony.'[28] After the motoring trip to Spain they were in London again, meeting Mary again and Clive Bell, at Virginia Woolf's house at 52 Tavistock Square in Bloomsbury. When Huxley returned, he realised how little he desired to live in England. He told Flora Strousse that he felt 'very gloomy about my native land and very glad I don't have to spend all my time in it. I have reached a point where I value sunshine more than people, culture, arts, conversation. So I'm off to Italy for the summer.' Commiserating with Ms Strousse for having to go to Liverpool 'an odious town', he declared 'The Mediterranean is the centre of the world. Everything of which human beings can feel proud has come out of the Mediterranean . . . All that's beastly in human life comes from the North or West or the East . . . So *viva il Mediterraneo!* And down with Liverpool.'

And so the Huxleys set off for Forte dei Marmi for the last time, where they would be joined by Lawrence, now in his last months of life.

Notes

1 HRC, Letter to Mary Hutchinson, 2 August 1928
2 HRC, Letter to Mary Hutchinson, 1 September 1928
3 HRC, Letter from Maria Huxley to Mary Hutchinson, 10 September 1928
4 *Letters of D.H. Lawrence* (1932) edited by Aldous Huxley, 22 October 1928
5 For all these reviews see Watt, pp147–76
6 *The Journals of André Gide* (1949) trans Justin O'Brien, Vol III, pp154–5
7 L.303
8 *Letters of D.H. Lawrence*, ed Huxley, p757. Letter to Aldous Huxley, 28 October 1928

 9   *The Diaries of Virginia Woolf*, Vol 3, p217. 4 January 1929

10   *Letters of D.H. Lawrence*, ed Huxley, pp762 and 764. Letters to Maria
     Huxley 8 November 1928 and 5 December 1928

11   *The Letters of D.H. Lawrence*, Vol 7, p21. Letter to Giuseppe Orioli, 21
     November 1928

12   *Ibid*, p55. Letter to Dorothy Brett. 10 December 1928

13   *L.*302

14   See *SB*1. pp195–98 for a full description of the 'Cottage on the Seine'

15   *L.*305

16   *L.*305

17   HRC, Letter to Ottoline Morrell, 3 January 1929

18   *L.*306

19   Reading, Herlitschka correspondence, biographical note by Huxley. No
     date (1929)

20   HRC, Letter to Mary Hutchinson, 15 January 1929

21   *L.*307

22   *The Letters of D.H. Lawrence*, Vol 7, p160. Letter to Juliette Huxley, 1
     February 1920

23   *Ibid.*, Letter to Ottoline Morrell, 5 February 1929, p164

24   *Ibid.*, Letter to Samuel Koteliansky, 7 February 1929, p167

25   *Ibid.*, pp169–70. Letter to Earl and Achsah Brewster, 7 February 1929

26   Princeton, Letter to Arnold Bennett, 19 February 1929

27   UCLA, Letter to Eugene Saxton, 7 May 1929

28   *The Letters of D.H. Lawrence*, Vol 7, p234. Letter to Ottoline Morrell, 3
     April 1929

29   *L.*311

XVIII

Lawrence

Huxley's relationship with Lawrence fluctuated considerably, from the extraordinary initial impact of their first meeting, through a perceptible cooling off on Huxley's part in his respect for Lawrence's writing during the years when they were not in contact, to a renewed admiration during 1929, the last year of Lawrence's life. During this latter period Huxley's letters are strewn with references to Lawrence as a wholly exceptional human being, though he always remained a step short of hero-worship. He could never quite silence his doubts about the anti-intellectualism (though one seeks a better term for the cautions and reservations of that profoundly intuitive intelligence) and anti-scientism inherent in the Lawrentian philosophy. On his side, Lawrence had reservations ('No, I don't like his books') and disliked Huxley's inherited faith in science, and his discursive intellectualising – he would rage against all that 'talk'. This oscillation between extreme admiration and intellectual reserve on Huxley's part informs the essay on Lawrence, discussed later, and makes it an especially interesting document.

In June 1929 the Huxleys arrived in Forte dei Marmi where they would stay, off and on, until September, at the Villa Il Cannetto, in the Viale Morin. Just before he left, Huxley told Norman Douglas that he had found 'poor old England' to be 'sadly mouldy and dim' on his recent visit. The Italian sunshine beckoned. They went via Rome and were appalled at what was happening to it: 'for the Fascists, who have an Empire-complex and see themselves as Cato and Augustus . . . are busily engaged in pulling down all mediaeval and Renaissance Rome in order to dig up more and yet more antique rubbish heaps . . . so that in a few years time Rome will be one vast hole with broken pillars and bits of masonry in it, surrounded by hideous garden suburbs and international hotels.'[1] An early visitor to Forte was Lawrence – 'not better but quiet & happy which is one better than he was in Paris',[2] Maria thought. After staying with them in Paris he had gone to Mallorca for three months. After a brief spell in Forte he went to Florence, then Baden-Baden, and then, from October to February 1930, he was in Bandol before moving to Vence, where he died on 2 March. The Huxleys saw a great deal of the sick man during this period. At Forte in June, staying at the Pensione Giuliani in the Viale Morin, Lawrence went to the Huxleys next door at Il Cannetto for tea and met them on the beach. They seemed to him to be physically well and glad to have escaped from the Paris house they had come to hate. But Lawrence told his wife Frieda: 'Maria is still tangled up in a way I dislike extremely with Costanza.'[3] Lawrence's friend, Maria Chambers, was staying in Forte at the time and she asked Lawrence about these afternoon teas *chez* Huxley. 'Talk, talk, talk,' he said to her. 'Words, words, words! They kill the flow of life.'[4] Quoting to her a Spanish saying he had probably just picked up in Spain (*Moros en la costa y gatos en la azotea* – 'Moors on the coast and cats on the roof') Lawrence called the Huxleys 'The Moros' because they were always busying themselves around him and intruding too much, he felt. The Huxleys, however, probably thought they were being solicitous. They had to force him to see a doctor when he was with them in Paris. 'He doesn't *want* to know how ill he is,' Aldous complained to Julian. 'That is why he won't go to Doctors and homes . . . We have given up trying to persuade him to be reasonable.'[5]

Lawrence's endless shifting of place was a doomed attempt to find some spot where he might feel better, but his health was deteriorating steadily. 'How horrible this gradually approaching dissolution is,' Huxley told Robert Nichols. 'And in this case specially horrible,

because so unnecessary, the result simply of the man's strange obsti-
nacy against professional medicine.'[6] 'He never does anything from
morning till night, except sit about & talk a certain amount &, very
occasionally, glance at a book,'[7] he told Maria's sister Jeanne.
Meanwhile, though Lawrence might think the coast at Forte as flat as
Skegness, the Huxleys were enjoying trips to the Etruscan places at
Cerveteri and elsewhere and splashing in the sea in their new acqui-
sition, an inflatable rubber dinghy – 'A most entertaining toy.'[8] The
stay was interrupted in July when Huxley, who had experienced a
little jaundice in the spring, went for a week to the Italian spa of
Montecatini, in the Apuan Alps – 'the most grotesque vision imagi-
nable – all the obese, the bilious, the gluttonous, the constipated, the
red-nosed, the yellow-eyed, standing about in a pump-room that
looks like ancient Rome through the eyes of Alma Tadema'.[9] Huxley
was there with 'Pino' Orioli, Lawrence's bookseller and publisher
friend from Florence who later testified to Huxley's non-stop dis-
coursing at the spa with the laconic observation: 'Aldous he sit and
make remark.'[10] When Aldous returned from this cure, Maria was of
the opinion that he was 'limp as a sawdust doll'.[11] Huxley, however, was
taken with the Apuan mountains so they both went for a week in
August to explore the place from which the Carrara marble came.
Huxley took his paints with him to try to capture mountain sunsets.
Painting was always a love of Huxley's (though the only example in
any public place is a portrait of Gerald Heard which hangs in the
lobby of the Library at the University of California at Los Angeles and
his family disclaim any knowledge of the whereabouts of the paintings).
Maria once complained to Lawrence that she got cold posing for
Aldous in the nude at Forte.

In the autumn, the Huxleys returned to Suresnes and immediately
started to plan another trip, to Spain. 'They are always so restless and
unsatisfied,'[12] Lawrence thought. There was a chance of Huxley being
a delegate to a 'Congress of Unions for Intellectual Cooperation' at
Barcelona and another of joining his friend, Sullivan, on a tour of 'the
Great Men of Europe',[13] for a series of profiles in *The Observer* of
Einstein, Heisenberg etc. But first he made a quick visit to London on
his own at the end of September. He lunched with Clive Bell at the

Eiffel Tower and saw Mary Hutchinson. Maria, alone in Paris, because
she did not want to go, not having enjoyed her last visit for some
reason, found that Aldous was 'enchanted'[14] by London again. When
he came back they talked of going to live in Bandol to be near
Lawrence who was now installed there. Maria was anxious to get away
from the Rue du Bac – 'this odious place . . . it is neither town nor
country'.[15] Lawrence, however, told Elsa Jaffe, Frieda's sister, when he
learned of this plan: 'I rather hope they won't.'[16]

The trip to Spain by car was quite exhausting for Maria as driver
but they found it 'the strangest country in Europe'.[17] They began with
a week at Barcelona where they attended the conference of intellectuals – 'indescribably awful!'[18] – then drove to Tarragona, Valencia,
Alicante, Murcia, Almeria and Granada. They wandered through the
byways of Andalucia to Ronda, Jerez, San Fernando, Cadiz and back
through Jerez (where they were greatly impressed by the 1847 sherry
they drank), Seville, Cordoba, Madrid, Burgos, then back to France.
They had left it a little late and the weather towards the end was rather
cold. Lawrence was in receipt of postcards along the way. He was
intensely anti-car and felt that Maria must be exhausted by all that
driving. 'I don't think they *loved* Spain,' he told Pino Orioli, 'but
Aldous, no doubt, will write *articles* on it.'[19]

It was in Paris in 1929 that Huxley had his first encounter with the
talkies. In view of his later life as a would-be screenwriter in
Hollywood, the experience is amusing and is described in a piece
written for *Vanity Fair* in July (reprinted in *Do What You Will*, the
essay collection published in October). He admitted that it was a
little late in the day to be catching up with the talkies: 'But being
up-to-date and in the swim has ceased, so far as I am concerned, to be
a duty.' He describes how he entered 'that fetid hall on the Boulevard
des Italiens, where the latest and most frightful creation-saving device
for the production of standardized amusement had been installed'.
This phrase is immensely revealing and points forward to some of the
leading themes of *Brave New World*. For Huxley was not enamoured
of the new popular cultural forms. He believed that the new
entertainment industries had harnessed new technology to increase
their profits rather than to facilitate individual artistic creativity. The

tone is playful, self-mocking – Huxley the young fogey of thirty-five pretending to be unfashionable – and refers to the 'beneficent providence' which robbed him of proper eyesight 'so that at a distance of more than four or five yards I am blissfully unaware of the full horror of the average human countenance. At the cinema, however, there is no escape.' On the giant screen he saw everything and found it 'terrifying'. A jazz band was playing on screen and its melodies and sentimental lyrics expressed for him 'corruption'. The performance sounds like *The Jazz Singer*, the first talkie. This is all laid on a bit thick and the tone of the essay seems to allow that it is deliberately over-stated. 'Ours is a spiritual climate in which the immemorial decencies find it hard to flourish,' is a large conclusion to draw from a short movie in a smoky Paris cinema. Huxley had just told Julian: 'I've been reading little recently except the Great Authors and have come to the conclusion that it's really rather a waste of time to read anything else.'[20] The encounter on the Boulevard des Italiens was a case of the irresistible force of European high culture meeting the immoveable object of modern commercial popular entertainment.

The twelve essays of *Do What You Will* (the title from Blake's 'Do what you will, the world's a fiction/And is made up of contradiction') embody – in a lighter, fizzier form than *Proper Studies* with its professorial *gravitas* – Huxley's world view at the start of the thirties. It is a sceptical, humane outlook, rejecting monomaniac creeds of the kind which were just being unleashed on Europe: 'There can be no crucial experiments in history . . . History is not a science,' Huxley asserted. For the first time he launched his big idea about the need for right ends to choose right means – those ends destined to be cancelled out if the wrong means were chosen. The only workable ideal is 'not of superhumanness, but of perfected humanity'. This is a plea for humane realism not the tyrannous forcing of human beings into some pre-cast idealistic mould: 'Man is multifarious, inconsistent, self-contradictory'. In the essays on writers in this collection, such ideas are traced out in detail. Swift's misanthropy is 'profoundly silly' because it expresses 'a childish resentment against reality'. Wordsworth, too, forgetting that nature in the tropics is far from

beneficent to man, 'asks us to make the same falsification of immediate experience' and puts us in the 'snug metaphysical villa' of
simplistic philosophies. Huxley confesses that he has changed his view
to one that argues: 'Only by living discretely and inconsistently can we
preserve both the man and the citizen, both the intellectual and the
spontaneous animal being, alive within us.' Much of this shows the
influence of Lawrence who is referred to explicitly as offering a 'fruitful' contribution.

Abreast as usual of new intellectual developments, Huxley noticed
the *embourgeoisement* of the working class and wondered how capitalism would survive the end of the industrialised proletariat and the
inequalities which powered the capitalist machine. In the first signs of
a pessimism that would come into his political thinking over the next
few years, Huxley raised the spectre of 'a nihilist revolution', fuelled by
frustration at the mechanisation of every aspect of life, the eradication
of much that made human existence rich and various and vital. 'All
that we can hope is that it will not come in our time.' In the final long
essay on Pascal, Huxley set out his own preferred philosophy: '[My]
fundamental assumption is that life on this planet is valuable in itself,
without any reference to hypothetical higher worlds, eternities, future
existences . . . that the purpose of living is to live . . . Without contrast
and diversity life is inconceivable . . . [I] will have nothing to do with
a perfection that is annihilation.' This is Huxley's finest essay-collection to date (and a good starting-point for anyone seeking to explore
further this aspect of his talent). It also raises the issue of how far the
essayist was beginning to compete with the novelist.

Returned from Spain, the Huxleys spent Christmas at Suresnes.
Lawrence thought he noted some difficulty between Aldous and
Maria. She told Lawrence that she might come to see him at Bandol
alone in the New Year. 'Something seems to have gone wrong
between him and her, I don't know what.'[21] Sybille Bedford, however,
doubts there was any such difficulty,[22] and it must be remembered
that Lawrence was a dying man at this point. In December, Huxley
met James Joyce in Paris. It was not an eventful meeting, for there
was an aesthetic chasm between the two men. Huxley was reading
Dante at this time and observed: 'The art of producing infinite effects

HULTON GETTY

Huxley in his precocious youth enjoying the hospitality at Garsington and making the acquaintance of the leading writers of the day, such as T.S. Eliot, seen here with his first wife, Vivienne.

TOPHAM

MATTHEW HUXLEY COLLECTION

TOPHAM PICTURE POINT

Huxley's Garsington circle around 1916: Maria Nys who would soon become his wife; Dora Carrington (the model for Mary Bracegirdle in *Crome Yellow*); Katharine Mansfield Lytton Strachey who described Huxley as 'a piece of seaweed'.

Maria Huxley shortly after her marriage to Aldous in 1919; the Hampstead flat where she and Aldous spent the first months of married life.

NICHOLAS MURRAY

HULTON GETTY

Nancy Cunard, the model for Myra Viveash in *Antic Hay*, by whom Huxley was dazzled in the twenties and Edith Sitwell who, with her brother Osbert, remained lifelong friends.

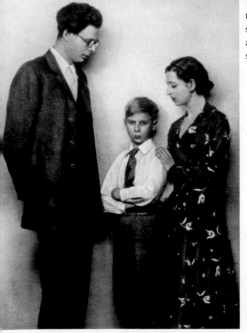

The Huxleys as a young family in the 1920s, Aldous, Maria and their son, Matthew. Firstly on the beach at Forte dei Marmi in Tuscany and secondly in London.

CAMERA PRESS

Cecil Beaton's image of the brilliant iconoclast of the 1920s tearing aside the veil of bourgeois respectability.

Huxley and D.H. Lawrence, a complex and surprising relationship of two very different sensibilities.

MATTHEW HUXLEY COLLECTION

Mary Hutchinson, writer, socialite, lover of Clive Bell, intimate of both Aldous and Maria Huxley in the 1920s.

NICHOLAS MURRAY

Huxley houses at Suresnes in Paris (1928–30)
and the Villa Huxley at La Gorguette,
Sanary-sur-Mer (1930–37) where the
legendary red Bugatti was first acquired.

MATTHEW HUXLEY COLLECTION

POPPERFOTO

Huxley in 1936 signing copies of *Eyeless in Gaza* and with his friend and mentor in the Peace Movement, Gerald Heard, in 1937 at Black Mountain College, North Carolina at the start of a lecture tour which turned into permanent residence in the USA. 'Let us hope we shall not have to scuttle when Mosley gets into power,' he had written in 1933. Mosley was the model for Webley and his Greenshirts in *Point Counter Point*.

POPPERFOTO

NICHOLAS MURRAY

The cabin in the woods at
Wrightwood, California, where the
Huxleys lived in the second half of
the 1940s.

Huxley at around this period.

HULTON GETTY

POPPERFOTO

HULTON GETTY

...uxley's small intimate circle of Hollywood friends included Harpo Marx, the Stravinskys, ...dwin Hubble the astronomer and the novelist Anita Loos. The circle also included ...nerwood, Garbo, Chaplin, Paulette Goddard and others.

Eileen Garrett, the medium whose parapsychology conference Huxley first attended in 1954 when his reputation as an intellectual explorer without boundaries was established.

A late picture of Maria not long before her death in 1955.

TOPHAM

Huxley not long after his marriage
to Laura Archera in 1956;
Mrs Huxley today at her home
in Hollywood.

TOPHAM

POPPERFOTO

Huxley at his typewriter in
Hollywood, 1958, the established and
well-coutured Englishman at the height
of his fame.

CAMERA PRESS

Huxley the intellectual and
Californian sage in expressive
and attentive moods.

HULTON GETTY

HULTON GETTY

Huxley at the end of his life already suffering from terminal cancer with his brother, Sir Julian Huxley, at his home in Hampstead.

And in his prime as a hopeful visionary.

CAMERA PRESS

CAMERA PRESS

with the minimum of obviously visible means has never been carried to such a height.'[23] The sheer prodigality of *Ulysses*, its exuberant delight in language for its own sake, its endless formal invention, would not recommend it to Huxley. He nonetheless told Mary that he had seen Joyce 'whom I found extraordinarily much pleasanter than *Ulysses* and the *Work in Progress* would lead one to expect, tho' I don't like either of those two books any the better in consequence.'[24] A month or two later, Huxley was telling Robert Nichols that he preferred Graham Greene's *The Man Within* to Virginia Woolf's *To the Lighthouse*.

The big event of the new year was the staging of *This Way to Paradise*, a stage version of *Point Counter Point* written by Campbell Dixon. It ran at Daly's Theatre in London from 30 January to 1 March 1930, directed by Leon Lion, and was the latest in a long-running series of attempts by Huxley to make his fortune with a stage success. He was still trying to do this on his deathbed. Lawrence gossiped that: 'Aldous seems to be enjoying himself, figuring among the actors and actresses and being *It*.'[25] Maria wrote to Lawrence that the play was awful but might bring them some money. The short run ensured that it would not. Huxley gave Lawrence a full report on the first night at which the actors were so nervous that they forgot their lines 'and ranted all those they could remember'.[26] He boasted: 'If I could have gone over the last scene, rewriting the whole thing, I could have made it quite prodigious, I believe.' Huxley learnt a great deal from this experience: 'learnt in the first place that actors are incredibly stupid and don't know their business . . . Lion was a bit of a disaster. So bottomlessly commonplace . . . Actors being what they are, the producing of a play is like the performing of a quartet on instruments made of packing cases and string.'[27] The licence for the play had been held up temporarily because Huxley refused to allow the doctoring of the text at the request of the Lord Chamberlain. This functionary had found a reference to impotence unacceptable. Lord Cromer was in fact fairly liberal-minded for the time and pointed out wearily that he was due to meet the Bishop of London and his Purity Committee the following day. In the end, he came and enjoyed the opening night.[28] The text was published with a preface by Huxley in which he confessed – in terms that would become familiar in his later screenwriting career – that the collaborative procedures of the theatre were hard for a writer used to composing in solitude: 'To someone who has been accustomed to working in an art where all the responsibilities are personal and in which success or failure depend exclusively on himself, nothing is more curious than his first experience of an art where creation is multiple, an affair of cooperation and interpretation.'[29] Huxley appears to have received an offer at this time to write for the cinema which tempted him with its largesse but Maria – in spite of having been accused by Lawrence of having too much regard for money – was hesitant, telling Mary, 'money is not worth certain things. If one has enough to live on comfortably why slave for more!'[30] The offer must have fallen through or been declined because Huxley announced around the same time: 'I am writing a play of my own now; which is quite fun.'[31] This was *The World of Light* which would be produced the following March.

On return to Paris the Huxleys made active moves to find a house in the vicinity of Bandol where Lawrence was now entering a sanatorium at Vence near Grasse. They saw Lawrence at the end of February and he was still worried about them: 'Queer – something gone out of them – they'll have to be left now to the world – finished, in some spiritual way.'[32] This was the last letter Lawrence wrote, for he died on 2 March, ten days after the Huxleys had arrived. 'We were with poor Lawrence when he died – a very painful thing to see an indomitable spirit finally broken and put out,' he told the translator, Sydney Schiff. 'The disease had made terrible ravages since we last saw him in the summer, and our visits to him . . . were sad affairs.'[33] Maria wrote a brief account of the death in a letter in 1943: 'Lawrence grasped my two wrists with his hands and said, "Maria, Maria, don't let me die." But he was more peaceful a little later . . . He told me he saw himself, his head, just there, next to me, and that he knew he would die.'[34] Maria held him in her arms. He died at 10.15pm. She was utterly devastated by the death for she had been inordinately fond of Lawrence. The Huxleys stayed in the south of France after the funeral because they had partly come to look for a house. From Bandol, where they were staying at the Hotel Beau Rivage, whose proprietor gave them some advice about the local property scene, they found one, at La Gorguette, a rocky promontory above the beach between Bandol and Sanary-sur-Mer. It was to be their home – once again one must add the phrase 'on and off', for the restless couple could never stay too long in one place – for most of the next seven years.

Notes

1   HRC, Letter to Mary Hutchinson, 6 August 1929
2   HRC, Letter from Maria Huxley to Mary Hutchinson, 26 June 1929
3   *The Letters of D.H. Lawrence*, Vol 7 p346, Letter to Frieda Lawrence, 24 June 1929
4   Maria Chambers, 'Afternoons in Italy with D.H. Lawrence', *Texas Quarterly*, 1964
5   *L*.314
6   *L*.315
7   Royal Library Brussels (RL), Letter to Jeanne Neveux, 16 July 1929
8   *L*.315
9   *L*.316
10 Quoted by Richard Aldington, *Pinorman* (1954), p68
11 HRC, Letter from Maria Huxley to Mary Hutchinson, 28 July 1929
12 *The Letters of D.H. Lawrence*, Vol 7, Letter to Ada Lawrence, 17 October 1929
13 HRC, Letter to Mary Hutchinson, 30 September 1929
14 HRC, Letter from Maria Huxley to Mary Hutchinson, 3 October 1929
15 *Ibid*
16 *The Letters of D.H. Lawrence*, Vol 7, p510 Letter to Else Jaffe 4 October 1929
17 *L*.319
18 Reading, Letter to Charles Prentice, 5 November 1929
19 *Letters of D.H. Lawrence*, Vol 7, Letter to Pino Orioli, 13 November 1929
20 *L*.318
21 *The Letters of D.H. Lawrence*, Vol 7, p600, Letter to Pino Orioli 18 December 1929
22 SB in conversation with the author
23 *L*.322
24 HRC, Letter to Mary Hutchinson, 21 December 1929
25 *The Letters of D.H. Lawrence*, Vol 7, p630, Letter to Pino Orioli, 30 January 1930

26 *L*.328
27 BL, Letter to Sydney Schiff, 28 March 1930
28 See Leon Lion, *The Surprise of My Life* (1948) p198
29 *This Way to Paradise* (1930) by Campbell Dixon. 'Preface' by Aldous Huxley
30 HRC, Letter from Maria Huxley to Mary Hutchinson, 17 February 1930
31 *L*.329
32 *The Letters of D.H. Lawrence*, Vol 7, p653 Letter to Earl Brewster, 27 February
33 BL, Letter to Sydney Schiff, 28 March 1930
34 Quoted in *SB*1.224; see also *Ibid* a long letter from Robert Nichols describing the day after the death

XIX

Sanary

From the gracious Hotel Beau Rivage at Bandol, a week after the death of Lawrence, Maria wrote to Mary to describe the new house they had bought: 'It is nothing that I wanted except the position – in the country & at two minutes for good bathing. For the rest it is only comic & charming. Aldous wants to call it Villa Pécuchet – so you guess more or less what it is – hideous of course and we should have to fiddle with it – but it has a large vineyard, infinite water & we can come for Easter already as the furniture – the Pécuchet furniture – goes with it.'[1] The reference here is to Flaubert's novel, *Bouvard et Pécuchet* (1881) whose eponymous heroes buy a house in provincial France which they proceed to improve and manage – with comic results. The owner – 'a short fat man of 55' from Marseille – and his wife were 'charming' and proud of their bourgeois comforts – a bathroom in the cellar and a W.C. on every floor, a conservatory on three sides of the house, and 4000 square metres of land containing olive trees, figs, and a large eucalyptus maimed by last winter's frost. Maria thought that it would be a pleasant place for walks as well as bathing but presciently realised that the suburbanisation of the coast would proceed apace: 'The coast is so over built with awful people . . . that I don't know how long we really shall be safe.' Huxley told Sydney Schiff it was 'a ridiculous little house . . . but easily transformable'.[2] They commissioned builders to make alterations, and an enthusiastic mason is said to have painted on the gateposts, VILLA HULEY [sic], in preparation for the return of his clients.

In those first weeks of settling in and disorder the Huxleys had a visit from Roy Campbell and his wife, who arrived with the daughter of the family with whom they were staying, Sybille von Schoenebeck, who, as Sybille Bedford, would provide a vivid description of the Huxley's home at Sanary, and her first meeting with Huxley, in her biography.[3] The Campbells brought with them 'a rush of vitality & adventurousness' in contrast to another couple – Cyril Connolly and his wife – who had lost no time in beating a path to the Huxleys' door. Maria's first impressions of the Connollys hint at the strains of this relationship – essentially to do with her fear that the boozy, good-living Connollys would intrude upon Aldous's vital and to some degree ascetic solitude. Jean Connolly referred to Maria as 'the watch-dog'. Maria told Mary that they had squabbled with the Connollys: 'I believe they dislike me very much but . . . they keep seeing us . . . for the sake of Aldous though he does not like them any better. Connolly was very hurt – because . . . I called him by his surname & on top of that asked him whether he was Catholic – which gave rise to a litany of his pedigree.'[4] Cyril Connolly – a hugely influential critic who had come to Sanary to hero-worship Huxley – would later refer in his novel, *The Rock Pool* (1936), to 'the competent intellectual vulgarity of Aldous Huxley' and in *Enemies of Promise* (1938) would characterise him as the type of 'the Oxford boy, the miserable young man on the flying trapeze' who later became 'a moralist and a puritan'. In the same book he said of Huxley: 'He is a defaulting financier of the written word, and nobody since Chesterton has so squandered his gifts.' But in 1930 Connolly was all admiration.

He had first met Huxley in Paris in the autumn of 1929 at Sylvia Beach's bookshop and moved to Sanary, to a house called Les Lauriers Roses, in 1930. 'All along the coast from Huxley Point and Castle Wharton [Edith Wharton was at Hyères] to Cape Maugham, little colonies of angry giants had settled themselves,' he would write in *The Rock Pool*. Writing much later, in the 1960s, Connolly confessed that he became 'on terms of profound ambivalence'[5] with the Huxleys and

the admiration that had brought him to Sanary 'curdled'. He describes
a lunch with the Huxleys at Edith Wharton's grand chateau at which
they felt slighted and at which the conversation is described in terms
of a tennis match with game set and match awarded to the Huxleys
who next time were invited without the Connollys. The problem
seems to have been that Connolly, in a sense, reminded Huxley too
much of his former self. He was the dazzlingly clever, urbane, young
man of letters, with the social panache and lightly-worn learning of
the Eton and Balliol man. Huxley, at thirty-eight, was beginning his
long trek away from 'literature' towards social and moral concerns.
The fluttering brilliance of Connolly – his unabashed hedonism and
aestheticism – was something the older man wanted to move on from.
As Connolly wrestled with the enemies of promise, Huxley appeared
to vault over their heads and to rebuke the younger man with his
astonishing productivity. Having once confessed that '"Aldous!" that
unique Christian name has reverberated throughout my life . . . I settled in Sanary to be near him and one of my happiest moments was
when his red Bugatti first swung into the drive,' Connolly eventually
concluded: 'The Huxleys have added ten years to my life.'[6]

The Huxleys continued to see the Connollys throughout the spring
and summer of 1930 and Huxley did admit to Mary that they were
'amusing' – 'he like a highly-educated, Eton-and-Balliol street arab,
she a perfect specimen of the hard-boiled young rich American girl'.[7]
As late as the end of October Maria was reporting that they were
seeing them still 'fairly often' even if they were 'unpleasant people
with suddenly spots of niceness – like an unpleasant child has
moments which make him touching. With Cyril I quarrelled – often –
but now they must have made up their minds that as we are the only
neighbours they had better keep in our good graces & as a result are
so deferential to me that I must laugh all the time'.[8] There is something about the way this is put that inclines one to some sympathy
with the Connollys.

In May, Aldous went to London to deal with the editing of
Lawrence's letters, which he had been invited to compile. He left the
Sanary house in the hands of the builders. 'Aldous Huxley is over
here, buzzing about his letters,'[9] Virginia Woolf told Brett. Frieda

Lawrence had originally accepted Huxley's idea of a memorial volume interspersed with letters but eventually he settled on an edition of the letters for which he refused to accept payment or royalties. He also declined a proposal from T.S. Eliot to write a book on Lawrence the poet. In the 'whirl of spirit-expending activity'[10] which had consumed him in March, Huxley had dashed to England for three days to sign the sheets of a special limited edition of his new book of stories, *Brief Candles*, which was being issued by the Fountain Press in New York. Back in London in May he could see the book published by Chatto. It consisted of three short stories and a longer one, 'After the Fireworks', that approached novella length. The themes of *Do What You Will* interestingly recur in these stories – there was always cross-fertilisation between Huxley's fictional imagination and his intellectual preoccupations. 'The Claxtons' is an attack on puritanical self-righteousness – 'how beautifully the Claxtons lived, how spiritually!' – echoing the warnings about the coercive nature of the idealistic programme in the essays. In 'After the Fireworks', Miles Fanning – yet another writer – declares 'a writer can't influence people' and inveighs against the 'illiterate idealist' who is no more than 'A Higher Thinker with nothing to think about but his – or more often, I'm afraid, *her* – beastly little personal feelings and sensations.' The social comedy of these stories is moving towards a clearer indictment of thinking in a moral vacuum, of mere aestheticism. In the same month, Huxley wrote a piece for the *Evening Standard* called 'Babies – State Property', which discussed the crisis in the family brought about both by individuals increasingly wanting to assert their rights and freedoms and by the standardisation imposed by modern democracy. He noted how in Soviet Russia the family was under attack as a locus of individual autonomy from the State and therefore: 'The State-paid professional educator is to take the place of the parents.'[11] One thinks, inescapably of course, of *Brave New World*. There is a curiously clinical tone to this writing. Huxley is observing what he sees as the decline of the family, and analysing its causes, but it appears to the reader that he is not himself greatly engaged.

Although Huxley always claimed never to read any reviews of his work (or even to cast another glance over his own work once it had

been published) he did see the reviews of *Brief Candles* and was disappointed. 'The *mot d'ordre* at the moment is that all literature must
be eminently public-schooly, with touches of Barrie-esque whimsi-
cality to relieve the gentlemanly tedium. If one's works don't resemble
those of Mr Priestley, then one's damned.'[12] Although having read
'nothing lately except historical and philosophical works' Huxley was
greatly impressed by his first reading of Kafka's *The Castle* in Edwin
and Willa Muir's translation. 'One would need to have a very special
sort of mind to write it; it's something one couldn't do oneself. I
think it's a fascinating book . . . In a work of art, a truth is always a
beauty-truth; and a beauty-truth is a mystical entity, a two-in-one; the
truth is quite inseparable from its companion, so that you can only
state in the most general terms what its nature is.' This is a line of
aesthetic thinking that one might have wished Huxley to pursue
more vigorously but he was set on another path. Reading so little
contemporary literature, however, his enthusiasm for Kafka as he
prepared to write *Brave New World* is worth noting.

The brief stay in London hunting down Lawrence letters (in the
spaces of which he was trying to finish his play) made him reflect on
his ambivalent feelings towards Lawrence's writing. 'What a queer
devil he was! The queerer, the more I think of him and know about
him. So many charming and beautiful things in him, such a lot too
that wasn't sympathetic.'[13] Towards the end of the month, Huxley
returned to Sanary via Suresnes. From the Rue du Bac, he wrote to
Mary about a new 'spy-glass' he had acquired to improve his vision
and which enabled him to see Calais for the first time: 'It's melancholy
how much one misses by seeing badly – but perhaps one's also spared
a good many horrors! Only the horrors are probably paid for by the
loneliness, with a bit to spare on the credit side, perhaps. With my little
spy-glass I felt suddenly like a convalescent rediscovering the world
after an illness and finding it unbelievably beautiful. However, the
repulsiveness of the man sitting next to me in the restaurant car soon
reminded me that it was something else as well.'[14] On 26 June Maria
finally moved their belongings out of the Rue du Bac, from what she
called now 'this ever detested place'.[15] The house at Sanary remained a
building site well into the summer. 'We live in considerable squalor

and discomfort among the ruins – a life of refugees,'[16] Huxley reported to Prentice in early July. With workmen hammering around them, they were reading Fielding's *Tom Jones* aloud: 'such sense, such a tapping of all the nails on the head – knock, knock, knock'.[17]

In September, Huxley rather abruptly left for London, having realised that Matthew was going back to school a week earlier than he had realised. He also wanted to go to the North Midlands, in connection with the Lawrence letters, to see the writer's home at Eastwood, but also to write a piece for *Nash's Pall Mall Magazine* on social conditions in the depressed working class areas. Juts before he left he corrected an article on him sent by a Mrs Theis who had evidently missed a crucial dimension in his work. He told her: 'I wonder if you're right about the absence of ethical bias? I feel myself very much of a moralist.'[18] It was the moralist – in a very well-established tradition of the educated liberal intelligence venturing into 'darkest England' – who wrote the piece for *Nash's*, which was not published until May 1931. In April 1931, another Old Etonian, George Orwell, published his first piece of similar reportage, 'The Spike', in *The Adelphi*. That piece would be reworked into a chapter of *Down and Out in Paris and London*. Huxley's piece, 'Abroad in England', cleverly alluded in its title to the fact that the working class areas of the Midlands and North were a foreign country to most of middle class Britain. 'The notes which follow are the casual jottings of a tourist – a tourist whose home is that remote province of the Great Bourgeois Empire inhabited by Literary Men, Professional Thinkers and the Amateurs of General Ideas,'[19] he wrote. This article, and a companion piece on 'Sight-Seeing In Alien Englands' published the following month, effectively demolish the myth of Huxley the unfeeling toff, indifferent to the fate of what some refer to haughtily as 'the masses'. He showed himself acutely aware of the class-ridden nature of English society. With Orwellian directness he registered the 'Chinese wall' that existed between the Deanery of Durham Cathedral where he was received and the mining village where he had lectured on 10 October on 'Science and Poetry'. The two working men with whom he had arrived from the mining village of Willington he liked very much but he realised how much his class background made it easier for him to relate socially to the Dean because both had been formed in 'those curious hotbeds of bourgeois imperialism, the Public Schools'. Huxley's conclusions from what he saw in Middlesbrough and else-where were that, to avoid a sort of permanent post-imperial, post-industrial mass unemployment, some form of national plan-ning was needed. The vested interests of the few would oppose it 'but if national planning is, by the highest human standards, desirable, then the actual desires of this minority will have to be overridden and the desirable thing imposed by force.' He even spoke warmly of the Soviet Five Year Plan. Since the only plans currently being discussed were Oswald Mosley's 'A National Plan for Great Britain' or the ideas of the Political and Economic Planning group, Huxley's critics have seized on passages such as this in order to expose him as a faintly sinister anti-democratic thinker. In fact, the article makes him look like some form of intellectual Fabian compelled by the spectre of social inequality and suffering to the conviction that Something Must Be Done, probably through some form of nationalisation.[20] Today the solution, from a Labour or Conservative government, would no doubt be privatisation.

On the same trip to England, Huxley broke off to accompany Sullivan to Berlin and Paris on his tour of the 'Great Men' he was pro-filing. He described this as 'a most entertaining piece of sightseeing'.[21] In Paris he himself was interviewed by Frederic Lefèvre who interro-gated him for four hours and who was 'the most crassly vulgar, self-satisfied businessman of letters I ever met'.[22] Lefèvre nonetheless wrote 'the most monstrous flatteries' about him and the two per-formed a dialogue in French for the national radio. Although Huxley talked to Robert Nichols about 'projecting a kind of picaresque novel of the intellect and the emotions – a mixture between *Gil Blas*, *Bouvard et Pécuchet* and *Le Rouge et le Noir*'[23] (an interesting idea that never materialised) and to Prentice about a new volume of verse incorporating *Arabia Infelix* (which had been published in May 1929) and other poems, he was concentrating now on his new play. He told Schiff at the end of December that he had had no success with pro-ducers so far 'owing to its last act'[24] but he hoped he would be luckier in the new year. As 1930 came to a close, the Huxleys felt settled in at

Sanary. In spite of the protracted – and worryingly expensive – works, they had bathed and basked in the sun and were really enjoying it. They were also meeting some of their famous neighbours such as Edith Wharton – 'rather a formidable lady who lives in a mist of foot-men, *bibelots*, bad good-taste and rich food in a castle overlooking Hyères'.[25] He had even been invited to become a Corresponding Member of the local Académie du Var 'which I think is rather distin-guished'.

Huxley's new year reflections for 1931 were informed by the previ-ous autumn's immersion in the life of the depressed mining villages of England, whose fate had touched him deeply. 'What a world we live in,' he exclaimed to Flora Strousse. 'The human race fills me with a steadily growing dismay ... The sad and humiliating conclusion is forced on one that the only thing to do is to flee and hide. Nothing one can do is any good and the doing is liable to infect one with the disease one is trying to treat.'[26] He was, however, still pre-occupied with the relationship of ends and means and his professed desire to escape (written indeed from a rocky point on the Côte d'Azur) was merely rhetorical. He would continue to write his documentary pieces 'abroad in England' for *Nash's* throughout 1931 with their air of bemused and well-meaning puzzlement at the chaos of the contem-porary world, but the growth of a wider political and social awareness that would issue in a more definite public commitment in the middle of the decade was now unstoppable. Meanwhile he was recommend-ing *The Castle* by Kafka as 'one of the most important books of this time'[27] and his own book, about a utopia that wasn't, was beginning to take shape at Sanary. But first he had to go to London to see about production of his first play.

Notes

1   HRC, Letter from Maria Huxley to Mary Hutchinson, 10 March 1930
2   BL, Letter to Sydney Schiff, 28 March 1930
3   *SB*1.230-39. See also: *Mem. Vol.*, pp138–43
4   HRC, Letter from Maria Huxley to Mary Hutchinson, undated, post-marked 1930

5   Quoted in Jeremy Lewis, *Cyril Connolly: A Life* (1997), p236

6   *Ibid.*, p238; p239

7   HRC, Letter to Mary Hutchinson, 17 July 1930

8   HRC, Letter from Maria Huxley to Mary Hutchinson, 28 October 1930

9   *The Letters of Virginia Woolf,* Vol 4. Letter to Dorothy Brett, 10 May 1930

10 *L.*333

11 'Babies – State Property', *Evening Standard,* 21 May 1930. *Hidden Huxley,*
    pp47-50

12 BL, Letter to Sydney Schiff, 19 June 1930

13 *L.*335

14 HRC, Letter to Mary Hutchinson, 28 May 1930

15 HRC, Letter from Maria Huxley to Mary Hutchinson, 26 June 1930

16 Reading, Letter to Charles Prentice, 5 July 1930

17 HRC, Letter to Mary Hutchinson, 17 July 1930

18 HRC, Letter to Mrs Theis, 9 September 1930

19 'Abroad in England,' *Nash's Pall Mall Magazine,* May 1931. *Hidden
    Huxley* pp51–64

20 For a less sympathetic view of Huxley's democratic credentials at this
    point see David Bradshaw, 'Huxley's Slump', in *The Art of Literary
    Biography* (1995) ed John Batchelor. Bradshaw argues, with his cus-
    tomary meticulous scholarship, that Huxley's expressed support for
    national planning was a contradiction of his usual libertarian stance

21 *L.*343

22 HRC, Letter to Mary Hutchinson, 23 October 1930

23 *L.*343

24 BL, Letter to Sydney Schiff, 24 December 1930

25 HRC, Letter to Ottoline Morrell, 18 December 1930

26 *L.*345

27 *Ibid*

XX

Utopia

In January 1931 Huxley plunged back into London society, basing himself initially at the Regent Palace Hotel, Piccadilly Circus (a hotel that left him 'fascinated with horror'[1]) and dining with Virginia and Leonard Woolf, Raymond Mortimer, Robert Nichols, and other old friends. Virginia Woolf spotted him at a concert at the end of January: 'More of a windmill and a scarecrow, more highbrow, purblind and pallid and spavined than ever; but all the same, sympathetic to me.'[2] In spite of the attention his play needed, and notwithstanding his renewed attempt to write some verse for the book he had proposed to Prentice ('what a labour! It absolutely knocks me out.'[3]), Huxley was continuing, not to escape, but to confront the face of the Depression.

On 11 February he went into the Stranger's Gallery of the House of Commons to listen to a debate on the national economy at which Ramsay MacDonald's Chancellor of the Exchequer, Philip Snowden, spoke. Huxley was appalled at the occasion, its tedious speeches and waffle – 'There is a kind of weariness of the spirit, to which I privately give the name of Septic Boredom,'[4] he told the readers of *Nash's Magazine*. 'What in heaven's name,' he pleaded, 'in an age of cheap and rapid printing, are we doing with this mediaeval council chamber?' He was contemptuous of Parliament and its 'twaddling' politicians. 'In the appropriately Gothic hall of the Mother of Parliaments, the old anachronistic bawling continues to reverberate.' What annoyed Huxley was the irrelevance of these old buffers' speeches: 'What is the use of knowing how things were done in the good old days when the bad new days have come along and made complete nonsense of your knowledge?' This impatient iconoclasm came out also in an interview (which had originally appeared under the heading 'The Despair of Aldous Huxley' in *Harper's* Magazine the previous June) published in a new book in May by Sewell Stokes, *Hear The Lions Roar*. Stokes describes Huxley as 'a sad, brave lion' who invites his interviewer to join him in his club, the Athenaeum, where the English male intellectual and clerical establishment had moved about peaceably for a century or more. Huxley made some mocking remarks about the 'bottoms of the august great' which had left their impressions on the antique club chairs, and gave a performance of the stereotypical Huxley of the 1920s, just at the point when he was beginning to bid farewell to this pose of languid contempt and aesthetic revulsion at the world's follies. Huxley confessed his bewilderment at contemporary London: 'The England that I thought I knew has so completely changed, that, for me, it has become a strange country. I can make nothing of it; the harsh music, the blatant vulgarity, the Talkies . . .'[5]

In a large dance hall in the West End, Huxley had watched the listless and graceless dancers and contrasted them with the happy, natural gaiety of a comparable Paris dance hall crowd. The culprit, he told Stokes, was the English class system which made the working class 'copy a model of gentlemanly behaviour which isn't natural' instead of enjoying themselves spontaneously in their own way. Asked by his interviewer if he had read Evelyn Waugh's *Vile Bodies*, which had just appeared, Huxley said he had, 'and it made me feel quite old. It was about a world I do not know, another generation; so different from my own. It made me aware of the terrible *foreignness* of time.' Waugh was to give his opinion of Huxley, much later, in 1955 when he praised the early novels of the 1920s and regretted Huxley's abandonment of the zestful animation of those works in favour of the pursuit of ideas: 'It was because he was then so near the essentials of

the human condition that he could write a book [*Antic Hay*] that is
frivolous and sentimental and perennially delightful.'6 Huxley also
mentioned in the interview Virginia Woolf, praising her language,
but regretting that all her characters were 'observed at a distance,
through a mist; she never seems able to touch them with her fingers.'
He seemed to be putting distance between himself and the world
both of bright social satire and of Bloomsbury aestheticism. With all
the limitations of background and intellectual temper – not to mention the basic fact, so easily overlooked, that he could not *see* very
much – Huxley was beginning to concern himself increasingly with
society and politics and the problems of the contemporary world.
He followed his visit to the Parliamentary mausoleum by a trip to the
East End where he saw a Jewish slaughter house for poultry off the
Commercial Road, and noticed 'a group of male prostitutes, pow-
dered and with scarlet lips, standing round the door of a cheap
lodging house' as he walked back to the Underground. 'I was proposing to spend the rest of the evening in Bloomsbury – not merely
geographically, but also culturally in Bloomsbury,' he reported.
Bloomsbury, when he arrived, was impressed. 'Lord, how little I've
seen, done, lived, felt, thought compared with the Huxleys,'7 Virginia
Woolf confided to her diary a few days later. 'Aldous takes life in hand.
Whether that damages his writing I don't know. He is "modern". He is
endlessly athletic & adventurous. He will be able to say he did not
waste his youth. Some bitterness is the goad which drives him on.
Death comes; nothing matters; at least let me see all that there is to be
seen, read all there is to be read. I fancy no one thing gives him the
immense satisfaction things give me. That's all the comfort I find.' The
next thing she knew, the Huxleys were off to explore the London
docks, the Black Country, down a mine, to Moscow (a trip that didn't
in the end come off). 'Aldous astounds me – his energy, his modernity.
Is it that he can't see anything that has to see so much?'8 Huxley at this
stage had been given what his friend, Robert Nichols, called a 'queer
pair'9 of glasses which Huxley called 'my white poppies'. They had 'a
sort of pebbly lens in the centre surrounded by a sort of silver shield'.

On 19 February Huxley made his first trip down a coal mine, at
Willington in the Durham coalfield, where Charles Wilson, the man

who had first invited him to lecture to his working men on 'Science and Poetry' on 10 October 1930, had been a miner. The mine visit is referred to in another magazine article, 'Sight-Seeing in Alien Englands' in which Huxley explores further his ideas about the dehumanising nature of modern factory work and its robbing of ordinary people of creativity. These would feed into the writing of *Brave New World*. Although the scientist and the modernist in him was fascinated by the extraordinary phenomenon of a factory like ICI's chemical plant at Billingham ('Looked at aesthetically, a well-organised factory is a work of art – a poem of which the technicians and administrators are the joint authors'[10]) he was also at war with Henry Ford whom he blamed for 'creation-saving devices' and mechanistic work. 'For the work performed by the overwhelming majority of my fellows seems to me so dreary, so utterly boring, that I feel ashamed, in their presence, for my freedom from it.' He attacked Ford for propounding the idea that mechanisation left the mind free to think of other things. 'One is left wondering whether, after all, the work which keeps the mind occupied is not better, humanly speaking, than the work which leaves it free.' In the following issue of the magazine, he returned to the theme of the apparent perfection of modern manufacturing process but its underlying human deficit. A price had been paid, he felt, for Fordist production. His piece was called 'The Victory of Art Over Humanity' and it argued that 'Our leisures are now as highly mechanised as our labours; the notion that men can recover, as consumers, what they have lost as producers, is quite illusory.'[11] But he went further than merely identifying the problem. He wanted a solution and the solution was, once again, a plan. 'The art of co-ordinating the separate arts has got to be first invented, then imposed by some strong and intelligent central authority.' Such sentiments have incurred disapproval from Huxley's critics. His call for action by 'a rejuvenated government, equipped with the necessary institutional weapons, and capable of acting swiftly and with a well-informed and intelligent ruthlessness' sounds rather like the rhetoric that was flying around this time from the lips of Oswald Mosley. Huxley had met Mosley in Paris in February, and, according to Robert Nichols: 'Aldous seemed to dislike him and distrust him but said he was very much alive.'[12] Huxley's article goes on to describe a visit to the London docks where he found an example of the intelligent planning he was advocating in the shape of the Port of London Authority. A less sinister form of coercion than the tread of jackboots, one might feel. The upshot of all these social explorations was that when Huxley returned to Sanary to write his utopian novel the sights and sounds and smells of modern industrial society in a depression were fully in his consciousness.

On 30 March, Huxley's play, *The World of Light* opened at the Royalty Theatre, produced by Leon Lion. Once again there were problems with the censor – this time with Enid's line: 'Oh, I admit you still quite like going to bed with me.' Reading the neatly typed playscript today in the British Library and noting the sparing blue pencil marks of the Lord Chamberlain – occurring against phrases such as 'Oh God!' and 'Christ!' or against a line when a character, wishing to illustrate a point about social hierarchy, says: 'I mean you wouldn't mind going to the W.C. with a dog in the room' – one can only smile at the contrast between 1931 and 2002. In this case Huxley stood firm and the Lord Chamberlain backed off. The author was, however, 'nearly mad with the infection of Lion's fantastic nervosity'.[13] Huxley was forced to work with the prevailing conventions of the West End stage, which desired a well-made play with a middle-class setting, and this is what he delivered on the surface. It makes use of spiritualism, whose popularity in the working class areas of the Midlands and North Huxley had noted on his recent travels. The dialogue is witty and sharply intelligent and the drama unfolds neatly enough but the public did not take to it and it closed after a very short run. Huxley's dream of a smash hit would have to be deferred. The critics had been enthusiastic – which led Virginia Woolf to think he had finally made it. 'He bids fair to be the great man in succession to Arnold Bennett,'[14] she told Quentin Bell, but Huxley himself was more realistic: 'the public remains conspicuous by its absence'.[15] He had not been well in February and had gone back to Sanary for three weeks before the opening of the play. The Huxleys were staying at Dalmeny Court, Duke Street, St James. He returned there on 19 March, via Paris, where Maria remained briefly. As soon as they were able, they returned to

Sanary where they were soon up to their eyes in distemper from the painters who were now at work.

On 7 May Huxley wrote to Sydney Schiff, giving the first hint of his new project: 'I write away at a novel of the future – Wells' Utopia realized, and the absolute horror of it, a revolt against it. Amusing but difficult, as I want to make a comprehensible picture of a psychology based on quite different first principles from ours.'[16] A few days later he told another correspondent that the task was proving, 'Very difficult. I have hardly enough imagination to deal with such a subject. But it is nonetheless interesting work.'[17] Interesting work was coming thick and fast. He accepted an offer to deliver the Thomas Huxley Lecture and was approached by the American publisher, George Doran, to produce a series of weekly articles for syndication by the Hearst newspapers in the USA 'which would provide . . . a very comfortable income'[18] at $100 a piece. Huxley told his syndication agent, Pinker, that 'It seems good money for not much work, and of a kind that might be rather interesting.' The Hearst Essays, which were only recently published in a collection, appeared from around September 1931 to April 1935 and would have been seen in papers such as *The Chicago Herald and Examiner*, *The New York American* and *The San Francisco Examiner*. These were the sorts of pieces that Huxley could throw off in his sleep and they added comfortably to his income. He had just had a royalty statement from Chatto which indicated that his last year's income just from English sales had been over £2000. The two previous years it had hovered around £1200 to 1300.

The new book of poems, *Cicadas,* appeared in May, and was to be Huxley's last. He always regretted this, but posterity has never thought of him as a poet, in spite of the beauty of much of the writing in this volume (which incorporated much of *Arabia Felix* from 1929). The closing passage of 'Lines' for example are particularly beautiful: 'Sometimes in winter/Sea-birds follow the plough,/And the bare field is all alive with wings,/With their white wings and unafraid alightings,/Sometimes in winter. And will they come again?' It seemed, alas, that the unafraid alightings of poetic inspiration would not come again. The push from *Brave New World* was driving him on. At the end of May he told Julian he had been overwhelmed by 'a literary catastrophe – the discovery that all I've been writing during the last month won't do and that I must re-write in quite another way. This throws me right back in my work.'[19] He was meant to be delivering by the autumn and was anxious, but needlessly so, because from late June when he told Mary 'It advances slowly – and the future becomes more appalling with every chapter'[20] he arrived at the 24 August with the announcement to his father that he had 'got rid of' it. He described it as 'a comic, or at least satirical, novel about the Future, showing the appallingness (at any rate by our standards) of Utopia and admumbrating the effects on thought and feeling of such quite possible biological inventions as the production of children in bottles (with consequent abolition of the family and all the Freudian "complexes" for which family relationships are responsible) the prolongation of youth, the devising of some harmless but effective substitute for alcohol, cocaine, opium etc. and also the effects of such sociological reforms as Pavlovian conditioning of all children from birth and before birth, universal peace, security and stability.'[21] Reporting progress to Chatto in the middle of August, he told Prentice: 'I've not yet decided what to call it. But that will come.'[22] No sooner had he finished than he was planning some travel essays built on the model of 'Abroad in England' in which the 'sociological element' would play a role, and proposing an anthology with commentaries that would become *Texts and Pretexts* (1932). Chatto were pleased with the novel and Huxley told Prentice: 'I think it goes with a sufficient swing; at the same time has enough pseudo-scientific detail to make it convincing.'[23] Huxley had been told by Bertrand Russell that he was writing a non-fiction book which would make very similar predictions to his. Huxley suggested to Chatto that the appearance of both books together might be reinforcing.

For relaxation, Huxley had been taking up his oil paints again at Sanary. He had also been reading Maine de Biran's *Journal Intime*, abut which he would write an essay. He had been disgusted by John Middleton Murry's 'vindictive hagiography'[24] of Lawrence but his own comments on his former friend, based on editing the letters and thinking about him again, were increasingly mixed. He found his passionate style claustrophobic after a time and his manner 'oppressively visceral . . . One longs for the open air of intellectual abstraction and pure spirituality'.[25] The outside world continued to intrude and the fall of sterling with its consequences for cheap living on the Côte d'Azur continued to worry the Huxleys, who abandoned a planned trip to the United States. In October they returned to London where they would spend the rest of the year. The slump made Huxley feel that he should be in London to see the crisis through. He felt that H.G. Wells was perhaps right 'in supposing that, given a little intelligence now, the world cd really be made quite decent'.[26] The twists and turns in Huxley's intellectual respect for Wells are indeed hard to keep up with.

His autumn publication was the collection of essays, *Music at Night,* a collection which contained *Vulgarity in Literature* published as a pamphlet the previous November. It was another rich collection and its themes reflect Huxley's intellectual and spiritual journey towards engagement. In an essay on 'Art and the Obvious' he regretted the tendency of modernist art to recoil from popular culture, disgusted by its sentimentality and cheapness. But the badness of commercial mass culture was due to its being 'made *for* the people, but not – and this is the modern tragedy – *by* the people'. This meant that the high art was impoverished as a result of cutting itself off from 'the great obvious truths' of ordinary existence: 'By pretending that certain things are not there, which in fact *are* there, much of the most accomplished modern art is condemning itself to incompleteness, to sterility, to premature decrepitude and death.' This was Huxley's farewell to the *avant-garde.* Though perhaps he should have looked again at *Ulysses.* In the title essay he argued that 'The substance of a work of art is inseparable from its form,' and that 'The limits of criticism are very quickly reached.' He did not foresee a time when criticism would so far transcend any sense of those limits as to appear on occasions to rival literature itself and to deprecate its particular claims. In the essay 'To the Puritan All Things Are Impure', Huxley introduced for the first time 'what I may call Fordism, or the philosophy of industrialism'. He had referred to mass production and the writings of Henry Ford several times before but this was the first time he had used it as the name of a philosophy. In his forthcoming novel it would be the new world religion. 'Rigorously practised for a few generations, this dreadful religion of the machine will end by destroying the human race,' he predicted. The collection also includes the essay 'Foreheads Villainous Low' in which he discusses what today is often called 'dumbing-down', the phenomenon of 'intelligent and cultured people doing their best to feign stupidity', a process which has only gathered pace since the essay was written. Again anticipating *Brave New World*, he notes: 'In the modern industrial state highbrows, being poor consumers, are bad citizens.' In the final essay, 'Vulgarity in Literature', Huxley announces his mature aesthetic credo: 'Other things being equal, the work of art which in its own way "says" more about the universe will be better than the work of art which says less.'

Huxley spent the last months of 1931 in London and stayed over into the New Year in order to give two talks on the BBC, one of which was a dialogue with Gerald Heard, whom he first met in 1929. Heard is now a largely forgotten figure – living perhaps only in the autobiographical novels of Christopher Isherwood (who is said to have captured him most successfully in the character of Augustus Par in *Down There on a Visit*). But in the 1930s Heard enjoyed a high reputation as a prodigiously energetic polymath, writer, broadcaster and man of ideas, a natural companion for Huxley – though the latter's reputation has wholly eclipsed the former. In his life of E.M. Forster, P.N. Furbank noted: 'Strangers thought of him, nervously, as a sort of Wellsian supermind or a "man of the future".'[27] Christopher Isherwood describes Heard at this time in *Christopher and His Kind* (1977): 'Gerald Heard was then a prominent figure in the British intellectual world. He knew most of the leading scientists and philosophers personally and he gave BBC radio talks explaining the latest findings of science in popular language. He was interested, agnostically, in the investigations of the Society for Psychical Research but wasn't prepared to say that he had found definite evidence of survival after death. He had written several books on evolution and pre-history and one which was called: *Narcissus: an Anatomy of Clothes*.' Heard's own dress was 'slyly exotic' and he was 'a slim cleanshaven man in his early forties, with a melodious faintly Irish accent . . . He was witty, playful, flattering, talkative as a magpie, well-informed as an encyclopaedia, and, at the same time, life-weary, meditative, deeply concerned, and in earnest.'[28] In an interview in 1985, Isherwood said of Heard: 'If you couldn't get hold of Bernard Shaw, perhaps he was the next best thing . . . the most fascinating person I've ever met . . . He was a very beautiful man to look at . . . the beauty of his voice.'[29] Heard had an enormous amount in common with Huxley, with the exception of his homosexuality. As Isherwood's partner Don Bachardy remarked of Huxley: 'I certainly don't think he had a queer bone in his body.'[30] Huxley had many homosexual friends but always spoke negatively about male, though not female, homosexuality. He shared the Bloomsbury habit of referring cheerfully (and without intended insult) to homosexual friends as 'the buggers'.[31] Huxley himself said of Heard: 'Gerald Heard is that rare being – a learned man who makes his mental home in the vacant spaces between the pigeon-holes . . . At a time when it is becoming more and more difficult to see anything but the trees, he helps us to become aware of the all-embracing wood.'[32]

Huxley and Heard were very close in the 1930s and after they both went to America. Unfortunately any correspondence between them has been lost or destroyed. A key relationship in Huxley's life and intellectual development is thus doomed to be gravely underestimated by biographers. On 9 January 1932 Huxley and Heard took part in a BBC radio programme titled 'Is Cruelty Out of Date?' in which Heard took the role more or less of interlocutor. They were discussing the persistence of violence in the modern world and the broadcast is notable for a remark by Huxley about the future for the use of force: 'It will be out of date the moment our rulers are educated enough to apply the results of modern psychology to their business of governing. The trouble with politicians is that they are always fifty years behind the times.'[33] In a solo BBC talk the following week, Huxley expanded on this theme in a talk on 'Science and Civilisation'. Acknowledging that the world was living through a period of crisis, Huxley blamed the misuse of science but rejected a Tolstoyan or Ghandian back to nature movement: 'The only cure for science is more science not less.'[34] But science, he insisted, must be applied by humanists if it was to be applied wisely. He made reference to the abuses of propaganda by governments and noted the 'systematic mass suggestion by wireless and poster' that had just been used by the Empire Marketing Board in its 'Buy British' campaign in its attempt to sell the idea of 'Englishness' abroad for marketing purposes. He noted the difference between the humanist ideal of the 'perfect all-round human being' and that of the 'economist-ruler' whose ideal was 'the perfect mass-producer and mass-consumer'.

This talk referred to eugenics as 'an instrument for giving to an ever-widening circle of men and women those heritable qualities of mind and body which are, by his highest standards, the most desirable'. Huxley the previous week had lunched with P. J. Blacker of the Eugenics Society and was to flirt briefly with a scientific notion that his brother Julian would adopt as a lifelong belief. *Brave New World* – in which all these ideas would feature – was about to be published. The Huxleys left the Cavendish Hotel in Jermyn Street the next day for Sanary. Matthew wrote a thank you letter to Ottoline Morrell in which he announced: 'Coccola is packing HARD.'[35]

Notes

1   *L*.346
2   *The Letters of Virginia Woolf*, Vol 4, p283. Letter to Clive Bell, 28 January 1931
3   *L*.346
4   'Greater and Lesser London', *Nash's Pall Mall Magazine*, October 1931. *Hidden Huxley*, pp87–95
5   Sewell Stokes, *Hear The Lions Roar* (1931) pp203–14
6   Evelyn Waugh, 'Youth at the Helm and Pleasure at the Prow: *Antic Hay*' in *The London Magazine* 2 (8), 1955: 'A Critical Symposium on Aldous Huxley'
7   *The Diaries of Virginia Woolf*, Vol 4, pp11–12. 17 February 1931
8   *The Letters of Virginia Woolf*, Vol 4, p293. 21 February 1931
9   *SB*1.249 citing a letter from Robert Nicholls to SB
10 'Sight Seeing in Alien Englands', *Nash's Pall Mall Magazine*, June 1931. *Hidden Huxley*, pp65–76
11 'The Victory of Art Over Humanity', *Nash's Pall Mall Magazine*, July 1931. *Hidden Huxley*, pp77–86

12 Quoted by David Bradshaw in 'Huxley's Slump', *The Art of Literary Biography*, p154. Letter from Robert Nichols to Henry Head, 8 February 1931

13 HRC, Letter to Mary Hutchinson, 20 March 1931

14 *The Letters of Virginia Woolf*, Vol 4, p309. Letter to Quentin Bell 11 April 1931

15 BL, Letter to Sydney Schiff, 7 May 1931

16 *Ibid*

17 L.348

18 HRC, Letter from George Doran, 1 June 1931. See *Aldous Huxley's Hearst Essays* (1994) edited by James Sexton

19 L.349

20 HRC, Letter to Mary Hutchinson, 21 June 1931

21 L.351

22 Reading, Letter to Charles Prentice, 4 August 1931

23 Reading, Letter to Charles Prentice, 7 September 1931

24 L.352

25 L.353

26 L.356

27 P. N. Furbank, *E.M. Forster: A Life* (1978), vol 2, p136

28 Christopher Isherwood, *Christopher and His Kind* (1977), pp81–2

29 HL, Oral History Transcripts, Interview with David King Dunaway, 2 June 1985

30 HL, Oral History Transcripts, Interview with David King Dunaway, 18 September 1989

31 SB, in conversation with the author

32 UCLA, Heard Collection, Box 36

33 'Is Cruelty Out of Date?' published in *The Listener* 20 January 1932 and reprinted in *Hidden Huxley* pp96–104

34 'Science and Civilisation', BBC, 13 January 1932, *Listener* 20 January 1932, *Hidden Huxley*, pp105–114

35 HRC, Letter from Matthew Huxley to Ottoline Morrell, 13 January 1932

XXI

Fordism

*B*rave New World is Huxley's most famous book and the one with which his name is always coupled. When college syllabi and newspaper lists of the best or most highly regarded books of the twentieth century are drawn up, it will always find a place. Such fame can be double-edged. A classic has its downside: it deflects attention from other works and makes a writer seem like a one-book name – preposterous in Huxley's case given his fifty or so books, eleven of them novels. The title – Miranda's words in Shakespeare's *Tempest* on first seeing human specimens of the outside world – was inspired and has become the stuff of journalistic cliché. Yet classics are often doomed to be misunderstood. The extraordinary prescience of Huxley's satire – he forecast not only human embryo research but a range of things, great and small (Virtual Reality, the turning of country walks into a branch of 'the leisure industry', the television running perpetually in the corner of the geriatric ward). Yet this was much more than a 'nightmare vision' of babies in bottles. It was the product of all those ideas examined above about science and human freedom, culture and democracy, the manipulation of the citizen by mass media and modern consumer capitalism. We have become accustomed now to the central imaginative concept of its opening pages – the Central London Hatchery and Conditioning Centre of the World State. As I write, geneticists are predicting that parents could soon be able to choose the genetic features of their babies as one might mix up a bespoke shade of paint from a Dulux machine in a decorating shop.

The book, however, is less often acknowledged to be a critique of modern consumerism, of the way that human freedom evaporates in the world of 'Fordism'. In a foreword to a reprint of the novel in 1946, Huxley was at pains to point out that – in contrast to the usual Utopian novel's visions of a violent repressive state the tyranny of the future would come from the existence of 'a population of slaves who do not have to be coerced, because they love their servitude'. The compliant consumers of 2001, loyally obeying brand *diktats*, against a background in which the politics of radical protest are increasingly neutered or abandoned, would strike a contemporary Huxley as a grim vindication. When Orwell wrote *1984* in 1948 he sent a copy to Huxley who replied that he had enjoyed it but believed his book was better prophecy: the making docile of the population by advertising and brainwashing – ensuring that people 'loved their servitude' – rather than the boot smashing down on the face (which was Orwell's image of violent state repression) being more plausible as a picture of the future, at least in late twentieth century Europe.

Huxley's novel was written deliberately to warn against contemporary trends but also against the whole notion of Utopia itself, the idea that one could design a perfect blueprint and then impose it. The book was a bad Utopia, a dystopia, or cacotopia. Needless to say it was not always taken in that spirit. It was said to have been popular with American college students in the 1950s because of its picture of apparently unlimited and guiltless sexual freedom – secured by the 'Malthusian belt', a forerunner of the Pill. Even today, there are readers who take it in this way. The French novelist, Michel Houellebecq, in his 1998 novel, *Les Particules élémentaires*, says that the world of the novel 'is in fact the precise world which we are trying to attain'.[1] One of the book's first readers, Edith Wharton, however, immediately understood what its author was saying: 'It is a masterpiece of tragic indictment of our ghastly age of Fordian culture . . . He wrote to me that I had "put the case" already in *Twilight Sleep* and I own that I was much set up by his recognition of the fact!'[2] Huxley himself, revisiting the book in 1946, his own political outlook having changed, regretted that it was the product of an 'amused, Pyrrhonic aesthete' who struck a pose of not caring whether the Savage – who like the modern intellectual dissenter carries the germ of hope for a better way – could choose only between two alternatives: 'an insane life in Utopia or the life of a primitive in an Indian village'. The later Huxley was not content with such a negative insouciance and was now a believer in finding solutions. His later vision was of a world organised around the principles of classic anarchism – small decentralised communities living in harmony around the beliefs of Kropotkinian mutual aid. Perhaps it is to the benefit of this novel that it was not so 'positive' – as his last 'good Utopian' novel, *Island* (1961), would be. If one is to write a convincingly repellent picture of what to avoid a little bleakness and despair and angry cynicism goes further than warm affirmation. The 1946 Huxley, who believed in 'sanity' predicted that the essential task for modern rulers – making us love our servitude – would be done through 'a greatly improved technique of suggestion' (infant conditioning and drugs); 'a fully developed science of human differences' (ensuring rigid hierarchies that pre-empted the frictions of dissent); 'a substitute for alcohol and other narcotics'; and a 'foolproof system of eugenics, designed to standardize the human product'. That system, in the novel, had been 'pushed to fantastic, though not perhaps impossible extremes'. Huxley's conclusion was that in 1932 he had projected his nightmare six hundred years into the future but: 'Today it seems quite possible that the horror may be upon us within a single century.'

The Utopian or 'science fiction' novel (*Brave New World* has elements of both) does not need to be convincing in the manner of the realistic novel but its internal logic needs to convince. Huxley manages to create and sustain a scientifically credible scenario (reviewing the book in the *Daily Telegraph* Rebecca West wanted him to go further and supply footnotes explaining his scientific sources) as well as injecting his own personal vision. The artificial manufacture of babies, outside the context of family life, enables easier state control of the breeding process, including the 'hypnopaedia' or brainwashing of the young. Like Orwell's 'proles', there are 'Deltas' here who are too insignificant to be worth manipulating and who therefore attain a degree of animal freedom. Consumer capitalism – which makes itself into a religion that reverences 'Our Ford' and 'the sign of the T' – is wittily portrayed, as is the idea that the business world has no patience with private pursuits that bring it no profit: 'we see to it that all country sports shall entail the use of elaborate apparatus'. This is not even any longer a joke: it is present day reality. The propagandist rhymes that the citizens sing are reminiscent of mindless advertising jingles and, freed from the terrible curse of the 'pre-moderns' – feeling strongly – they live an anodyne life underpinned by the dulling drug *soma*. There is a great deal of humour in the book, as in the reference to 'the great British Museum massacre' and the 'college of Emotional Engineering' in Fleet Street, given as examples of the mindlessness of the culture that has been created. It is perhaps significant that the Savage – the most interesting character because he embodies the spirit of defiance, pointing to a way out – chooses a volume of Shakespeare with which to answer this cultural emptiness and its devaluation of solitude and reflection. The comment of the Controller Mond (the name incidentally of a prominent industrialist, Sir Alfred Mond of ICI) that 'you've got to choose between happiness and what people used to call high art', taken with John the Savage's addiction to Shakespeare, has been taken by some critics as evidence of Huxley's cultural arrogance. The assumption appears to be that in allowing that 'ordinary people' might appreciate the benefits of intellectual freedom and the free play of the imagination as opposed to narcotic forgetfulness and mindless obedience, Huxley was being an insufferable 'elitist'. It is a most peculiar argument but one frequently advanced in all seriousness. The book ends with John claiming 'the right to be unhappy' rather than to enjoy a drug induced love of servitude. In his hermitage he practises a kind of orgy of atonement, Christ-like in the wilderness, mortifying his flesh, and then, in the closing pages of the book, he hangs himself in despair.

In so far as Huxley himself is present in this book, his sense, perhaps, of impotence in the face of the suffering and economic deprivation he had witnessed at first hand throughout 1930 and 1931 when writing the book, comes through in the fate of John. Later, he would be a man with answers, solutions. That intriguing feature of the World State – its apparent readiness to allow islands of dissent rather than subjecting *everyone* to thought control – the latter generally considered to be an essential feature of all authoritarian systems – could also be an expression of Huxley's own sense at this time that the life of the intellectual was otiose in a world that seemed to have no use for the thinker or the life of the mind.

When *Brave New World* was published in February 1932, Huxley was in Sanary, painting, reading, and working on a new play, *Now More Than Ever*, (never performed in his lifetime and for many years after his death thought to be lost), the anthology, *Texts and Pretexts*, the introduction to the letters of Lawrence, and, as if this wasn't enough, rereading his grandfather's works in preparation for giving the T.H. Huxley lecture. The coast at this time was filling up with German-Jewish exiles. The Provençal coast at Sanary had long been attractive to writers and artists but the migration from Germany with the rise of Nazism greatly augmented the process. In his book on the subject, *Exile in Paradise* (1996), Manfred Flügge lists some of the literary and artistic visitors to the Huxleys' villa: the art historian Julius Meier-Graefe, the painter Moshe Kisling and his wife Renée, the American writer William Seabrook, whose Villa des Roseaux was almost opposite the Huxleys, Sybille von Schoenebeck, the American writer and artist Eva Herrmann, the psychoanalyst Charlotte Wolff, and the French writers Drieu La Rochelle and Paul Valéry. The Huxleys had preceded the rise of the German colony (though the first Anglo-Saxon arrivals had been Katherine Mansfield and John Middleton Murry as early as 1915, then Lawrence and Frieda in 1928, and Roy Campbell in the same year). From around 1933 the coast became 'Montparnasse-sur-Mer' as Thomas Mann, Lion Feuchtwanger and many other leading German writers arrived.[3] Huxley was in two minds about this emigration. It would provide him with the stimulating company he needed but at the same time he disliked an exclusively literary milieu. The previous spring, when the migration was only just starting and he was trying to write *Brave New World,* he had complained to Ottoline Morrell: 'Swarms of literary Germans infest the countryside like locusts.'[4]

In February Huxley learned of the death of Lytton Strachey and wrote to console Mary Hutchinson: 'How sad, sad, sad it all is; and with such a peculiar pointlessness and meaninglessness, when looked at from without.'[5] Little over a month later he was writing to her again about the ensuing suicide of Carrington, of whom Huxley had been much fonder than of Strachey, and whose death he found very 'distressing'. Old memories of Garsington stirred: 'Her death seems to close such a lot of chapters: she was in some queer way, as one now realizes, a symbolical figure, the paradigm of a whole epoch in the life of a whole generation. I hardly ever saw her during these last ten years – but she was none the less representative for me, and her death is none the less the destruction of something important. It was a touchingly heroic act of devotion.'[6] Huxley was now thirty-seven, that epoch of sleeping out on the Garsington roofs in the summer nights, talking about poetry and art into the small hours, well behind him. He was an acknowledged and successful man of letters, sought out in his French retreat by other successful practitioners. We have a verbal snapshot of him around this time by James Lansdale Hodson: 'Aldous Huxley is so tall – six feet four inches – and slender that he bends when walking; he has a mop of blackish brown hair, a keen, sensitive face and horn-rims with curved lenses. He preserves at thirty-seven something of the Oxford undergraduate's appearance – suede leather shoes, negligent collar, protruding soft cuffs . . . He talks well, leaping from topic to topic, changing his chair and his attitudes also at the same time . . . he types everything, tries to do one thousand words a day, and writes poetry only when he must.'[7] To Flora Strousse – that odd correspondent whom he never met but to whom he was often so disarmingly frank about himself – he wrote: 'I share with you a fear of the responsibilities of relationships – have only one that really counts at all, with my wife – nothing else that commits me in any serious way. It's awful to be committed – but at the same time, if one isn't one gets very little in return: and if one is, and the other party doesn't feel committed . . . The endless possibilities of misery and the few of happiness!'[8] But new social relationships were being formed at Sanary all the time. Charles, the Vicomte de Noailles, a neighbour, and Edith Wharton were frequently seen and Bronislaw

Malinowski (whose *Sexual Life of Savages*, Huxley thought, should be mirrored by a *Sexual Life of Gentlemen and Ladies*[9]) turned up nearby.

Tired out by his literary labours, Huxley took a brief holiday at Cannes (taking in on this trip a visit to an amateur performance in French of his play *The World of Light*). At Cannes he met H.G. Wells, of whose dislike of *Brave New World* he was already aware. His respect for Wells was in a downward cycle again, not least because the latter started to disparage Lawrence. It was back to the Bloomsbury view of Wells as a vulgar little man of the lower orders: 'Wells, if he is a great man, is great in so far as he is a perfect specimen of the *canaille* magnified ten thousand times: so bottomlessly vulgar and insensitive, without the smallest power of discrimination either in the moral or the aesthetic sphere: an *âme mal née* and therefore, in spite of his immense ability, profoundly uninteresting . . . He is as incapable of feeling and appreciating the unique quality of Lawrence as a dog of appreciating music.'[10]

Notwithstanding this devastating – and snobbish – put-down, Huxley was having his own difficulties with Lawrence. All the old misgivings were bubbling up to the surface as he wrestled with the Introduction to the letters. He was having a little more success with his lecture on his grandfather, which was delivered in May.

In spite of his distaste for the English gerontocratic rulers he had observed in Parliament, Huxley was beginning to rediscover an admiration for the eminent Victorians. He told Mary that his grandfather was 'a very remarkable man' who had impressed him more and more on rereading. 'And he had that heroic larger-than-life quality which belonged to the really eminent Victorians and which seems to have disappeared completely in the present age.'[11] The lecture, 'T.H. Huxley As A Man of Letters', defended his grandfather against the view put by G.K. Chesterton that he was more interesting as a writer than as a scientist. Huxley insisted: 'He was a man of science first of all . . . who also had . . . a literary gift.'[12] He argued that Huxley was still a living force and had 'that persistent contemporaneity that is the quality of all good art'. He analysed his prose rhythms and praised his 'astonishingly lucid' way of writing but conceded that one of the major defects of nineteenth century literature was 'its inordinate literariness, its habit of verbal dressing-up and playing stylistic charades'. It was Huxley Senior's 'passion for veracity' that saved him from the excess of this vice. Huxley was finding time to contribute to *Time and Tide* magazine, in a series called 'Notes by the Way' which reflected themes in the fiction. In May he discussed the major theme of *Brave New World* – the way in which modern rulers kept power by thought manipulation: 'The Machiavelli of the mid-twentieth century will be an advertising man; his *Prince*, a textbook of the art and science of fooling all the people all the time.'[13] They showed that – although he professed to read no newspapers at Sanary (except, it seems, the French socialist daily *L'Oeuvre*) – he was fully aware of current developments such as the progress of the Slump and the splitting of the atom in Cambridge. The trip to London to deliver the Huxley Lecture had also enabled a trip to Belgium and one to Germany with Raymond Mortimer. But first he had to sort out his literary affairs. *Brave New World* was doing well in England – selling 13,000 copies in the first year – but not so well in the USA where its jaundiced view of the materialist Utopia would be less welcome. Huxley's Doubleday contract was running out and, after a flurry of contractual letters and bids, he agreed to move to Harper's with a three-year contract involving payment of $7000 a year. He was influenced in his desire to move to Harper's by the presence there of an old friend from the mid-1920s at Doran's, Eugene Saxton. Back in England his next three-year contract with Chatto was renewed more or less automatically, with the annual payment rising from £1000 to £1250. He was now earning a good living (over £2000 in UK royalties alone in the year ending 31 March 1932).

The Huxleys had 'an interesting time'[14] in Germany in May, having enjoyed an unusual occasion in Belgium beforehand. They had been invited by the King and Queen of the Belgians (Maria's uncle, George Baltus, having been the go-between) to lunch at the Royal Palace. Huxley bought himself a pair of white kid gloves and the affair proved pleasant and intimate though King Albert I displayed 'a very thorough, rather ponderous mind, grinding exceeding small and rather slowly'.[15] What is more the Palace was 'mouldy in its splendour: actually moths flew out of the sofas when one sat down!' Huxley was delighted by the absurdity of the court etiquette such as talking in the third person 'which is distinctly cramping to conversation when one isn't used to it'. The royal couple made it easy for the visually-impaired Aldous (who would normally have been required to walk out of the room backwards as etiquette demanded) by themselves taking their leave first. The Huxleys joined Raymond Mortimer in Belgium and went on with him to Germany. They met Sybille Bedford, who felt that Huxley looked on Germany at this tense time 'with a kind of aloof voyeurism'.[16] On a previous visit to Berlin he had visited, out of curiosity, a sleazy night club and had allowed himself, out of politeness, to be steered briefly around the dance floor by a young man.

On his return, Huxley started to write his play, *Now More Than Ever*, which did not receive its first performance until 27 June 1994 during a special Huxley centenary symposium at the University of Munster. The play was published in 2000, edited with an introduction by the leading British Huxley scholar, David Bradshaw, and James Sexton. As the editors demonstrate, this is an important play, that exhibits Huxley's growing political awareness and 'ethical *gravitas*'[17] – although, overburdened as it is by too much exposition, it is not a compelling piece of theatre. Ominously, Huxley told Leon Lion: 'There will be a good deal of talk.'[18] The play was sparked by the suicide in Paris in March 1932 of 'The Match King', the Swedish financier Ivar Kreuger, who turned out to have been a massive fraud in spite of his ostensible record of philanthropy – a sort of 1930s Robert Maxwell. Kreuger would be the model of Graham Greene's Erik Krogh in *England Made Me* (1935) and Huxley saw in the story a way of indicting capitalist greed and chicanery by 'linking the story up with general economic ideas'.[19] No London theatre would do the play but the following June Huxley was revising it for a possible New York production and again in 1934 his hopes were revived in London but all came to nothing and he abandoned it for good. The play was finished by the end of the summer of 1932 when Huxley told Ottoline that Maria was 'indefatigably typing' it up. 'I hope it will attract a few more people than the last one, which made less money than any play since the *Agamemnon* of Aeschylus.'[20] He told Mary it was 'on the theme of Kreuger and Hatry [a British City fraudster imprisoned in January 1930] – a financier who is ambitious to rationalize industry and is led by his excellent intention into gigantic fraud . . . let's hope it may make a bit of money.'[21]

In between his literary projects, Huxley was rereading – *War and Peace*, an eternal favourite of his – and painting: 'It's so nice to practise an art in which all the problems are internal to the art and where one doesn't have to bother about what goes on in the world at large [a view with which the painter of *Guernica*, for example, might want to quibble]. But the more I paint, the more I resent the laziness of modern painters. Why don't they take the trouble to do those large elaborate compositions that the old men did? . . . The moderns seem to me to be inexcusably cheating and shirking difficulties.'[22] He was also arranging for Matthew to enter Dartington School. He told his father that Matthew had the Nys family's 'natural gift for living' but not his own love of abstract thinking: 'He is just the opposite of me; for he knows how to deal with people, but not with abstract ideas: whereas I know how to deal with abstract ideas but not with people.'[23] The autumn saw the publication of two new books where Huxley's role was more that of an editor than a writer. He was glad to get both off his hands: 'We have had a rather crowded summer – always people in the house: which is, *au fond*, a mistake, even if they're nice. At last, however, we're alone.'[24] The two books were *The Letters of D.H. Lawrence* and *Texts and Pretexts*.

Huxley's introduction to this selection of Lawrence's letters represents his final attempt to establish an objective view of his fellow writer. On the positive side he declared: 'Lawrence was always inescapably an artist' who was 'in a real sense possessed by his creative genius'. He added: 'It is impossible to write about Lawrence except as an artist.' When Virginia Woolf read this she protested to her diary: 'And why does Aldous say he was an "artist"? Art is being rid of all preaching: things in themselves . . . whereas L. would only say what proved something.'[25] Huxley identified Lawrence's 'special and characteristic gift' as being 'an extraordinary sensitiveness to what Wordsworth called "unknown modes of being"'. He could never forget 'the dark presence of the otherness that lies beyond the boundaries of man's conscious mind'. Huxley told of how he had failed to convince Lawrence of the importance of science, begging him to look at the evidence. Lawrence would reply: "'Evidence doesn't mean any-thing to me. I don't feel it *here*." And he pressed his two hands on his solar plexus.' Huxley also conceded that Lawrence had 'an extremely acute intelligence' as well as being a man of genius. But, unlike Huxley, 'Lawrence refused to *know* abstractly. He preferred to live.' This made him 'a kind of mystical materialist'. Some of Huxley's comments seem a shade autobiographical: 'His travels were a flight and a search . . . He was at once too English and too intensely an artist to stay at home.' Huxley, having pointed to those areas where Lawrence and he could not agree, concluded: 'To be with Lawrence was a kind of adventure, a voyage of discovery into newness and otherness . . . For an inhabi-tant of the safe metropolis of thought and feeling it was a most exciting experience.' In the end what makes this essay so impressive – and moving in the most dignified way – is both the acute insight into another way of thinking and feeling and the generosity of a tribute being paid by a writer of prodigious talent to a writer of genius.

In October the Huxleys took a brief motoring trip to Italy and met Alberto Moravia at Forte. Rereading Tolstoy on Napoleon made him realise the truth about Mussolini and 'all that stupid unreal rhet-oric of fascism'.[26] On his return to Sanary Huxley began a new novel – the book that would cause him the most anguish and difficulty, *Eyeless in Gaza*. Writing to his new American publisher, Eugene Saxton of Harper's, he seemed to have an intuition of its difficulty even before he had begun to write. He even offered to suspend pay-ments until he was in the right mood: 'for I know by bitter experience that I can't force myself to write anything that isn't ripe'.[27] He carried on reading – Hermann Broch's *The Sleepwalkers*, and Henry Green's *Living* – 'A really very good rendering of that for us bourgeois, most mysterious phenomenon, the mind of the factory worker.'[28] *Texts and Pretexts* appeared in November. It was a sort of anthology *raisonné*, interspersing excerpts with commentaries. His introduc-tion headed off the criticism that to produce such an anthology of mostly poetic texts 'in mid-slump' was mere fiddling while Rome burned by saying, characteristically that: 'Perhaps Rome would not now be burning if the Romans had taken a more intelligent interest in their fiddling . . . They also serve who only bother their heads about art.' The texts are well chosen and the commentaries intelligent and worldly-wise. The Introduction sums up Huxley's belief that this world is the best one that we have and that we had better proceed on the basis of that realisation: 'Personally, I must confess, I am more interested in what the world is now than in what it will be, or what it might be, if improbable conditions were fulfilled.' He groups together in fact a series of aphoristic statements about himself: 'I prefer being sober to even the rosiest and most agreeable intoxication . . . I like things to be said with precision and as concisely as possible . . . Experience is not what happens to a man; it is what a man does with what happens to him . . . Meanwhile, one must be content to go on piping up for reason and realism and a certain decency.' This is, if one will, the seventeenth century side of Huxley, the lover of the maxims of La Rochefoucauld, reason tinged with wisdom, intelligent and unillusioned, hopeful but sanguine, decent but not expecting too much in the way of revelations about changes in human nature or society. In truth, however, he was heading towards a personal crisis through which this gentle optimism would be tested to the limit.

Notes

1 Michel Houellebecq, *Les Particules élémentaires*, (1998), p194. Author's translation

2 *The Letters of Edith Wharton* (1988), ed R. W. B. Lewis and Nancy Lewis. P546. Letter to Margaret Chanler, 25 March 1932

3 See Manfred Flugge, *Exil en Paradis: artistes et écrivains sur la Riviera (1933–1945)* (1996; French edition, Paris, 1999)

4 HRC, letter to Ottoline Morrell, 7 May 1931

5 HRC, Letter to Mary Hutchinson, 3 February 1932

6 HRC, Letter to Mary Hutchinson, 19 March 1932

7 James Lansdale Hodson, *No Phantoms Here* (1932), p258

8 *L.*357

9 *L.*314

10 HRC, Letter to Mary Hutchinson, 19 March 1932

11 *Ibid*

12 *T. H. Huxley As A Man Of Letters* (1932), p1

13 'Notes by the Way', *Time and Tide* 7 May 1932. *Hidden Huxley,* p117

14 *L.*360
15 *L.*360
16 *SB*1.255
17 David Bradshaw and James Sexton (editors) *Now More Than Ever* (2000) University of Texas Press, Austin. The editors, unlike the present author, perceive a 'hard-line elitist ideology' and a 'superior contempt for the masses' in Huxley's earlier work from which the play, in their judgement, appears to mark a retreat
18 *Ibid.* pxvi, citing Letter to Leon Lion, 27 August 1932
19 HRC, Letter to Ralph Pinker, 24 July 1932
20 HRC, Letter to Ottoline Morrell, 13 October 1932
21 HRC, Letter to Mary Hutchinson, 14 October 1932
22 HRC, Letter to Mary Hutchinson, 17 September 1932
23 *L.*361
24 HRC, Letter to Mary Hutchinson, 17 September 1932
25 *The Diaries of Virginia Woolf,* Vol 4, 13 October 1932
26 *L.*363
27 *L.*366
28 BL, Letter to Sydney Schiff, 3 November 1932

XXII

Mexico

At the start of 1933, the Huxleys set off on a five month trip to the West Indies, Guatemala and Mexico. It was their first long trip since 1925–26 and it would issue, of course, in a book, *Beyond The Mexique Bay* (1934). For Huxley the travel book, like the novel, was the continuation of the essay by other means. The relaxed, discursive, inclusive form of modern English travel-writing suited him. They left at the end of January on the *Britannic*, a West Indian cruise liner, but their plan was to leave the ship at Kingston, Jamaica. The sight of middle-aged English people determined to 'have a good time' on the ship filled him with amused horror. There was an entertainment 'commissar' who organised a 'Children's Party for Grown-Ups' for what Huxley termed 'as representative a collection of the elderly *haute bourgeoisie* as you could hope to find'. What these childish elders hoped to find, it seemed, was a sort of 'quaint Peter-Panishness'. From Kingston he wrote to Sydney Schiff: 'The horror is unimaginable. Hundreds of retired colonels, spinsters and widows with incomes, enriched Lancashire business men (including, on our cruise, several bookmakers, who drank nothing but champagne), interspersed incongruously with very *bien* people, who keep themselves from the rest.'[1] The Duchess of Northumberland and her two daughters kept apart 'as though they were Brahmins in a crowd of untouchables' and the infantilism of the elderly people who 'dress up, bloodcurdlingly, as schoolboys and babies' made Huxley exclaim: 'How depressing our compatriots can be!' But the indigenous population – whom Huxley described, uncomfortably to the modern sensibility, as 'the black-amoors' gave him '*en masse* a sense of hopelessness, tho' individually and in moments of excitement they are sometimes more cheering – e.g. when we heard them singing topical songs of their own compo-sition at Trinidad'. In *Beyond the Mexique Bay*, Huxley describes a very striking personal epiphany where this clever facetiousness, which was never far from the surface in his travel writing, is eclipsed by a moment of real transformation. He went into a shop in Speightstown, Barbados and passed through to a back room 'lit by a dim oil lamp' where 'a very old negress' was cleaning flying-fish and beside her 'an incredibly beautiful, pale brown girl was sitting beside her, sewing'. The door behind them was open to the sea. 'There was nothing spe-cially curious or remarkable about the scene; but for some reason it held, and in my memory still holds for me a quality of extraordinary alienness and unfamiliarity, of being immeasurably remote . . . And the girl, so beautiful, with her face shining in the lamplight, as though it were illumined from within, the old negress . . . seemed, of another universe.'[2] Such moments of openness to the rich and strange are all too rare in Huxley's travel writing. Too seldom is he transformed by 'alien' sightings that break in on the composed and ordered land-scape of witty and knowing commentary.

The Huxleys passed on through Trinidad, Caracas, Belize ('a place that is definitely the end of the world'[3]), Quirigua, where they stayed with a Scottish doctor called MacPhail (a surname that would be used later in *Island*) who ran the United Fruit Company Hospital, and from which base they explored the Maya ruins. The Maya culture set Huxley thinking about cultural and racial differences. He con-cluded that theories of racial superiority such as those now prevalent in fascist Europe were nonsense and the idea of racial purity a chimera. 'Considered genetically,' wrote the author of *Brave New World*, 'any given population is a vast roulette table.' Next they trav-elled to Guatemala City, which made him think that Central America was a kind of laboratory in which to study politics. He predicted the

rise of 'nationalistic state-socialism', heralding his growing realisation that militaristic nationalism was the principal political disorder
of the times. This 'philosophy of hate and division' rooted itself in
certain psychological needs, which perhaps a 'World Psychological
Conference' should be constituted to address. He was not particularly
sanguine about the prospects of an intelligent citizenry appearing to
challenge these trends: 'Universal education has created an immense
class of what I may call the New Stupid.' These were the people who
would swallow the thoughts of the 'mob-leaders', Hitler and
Mussolini. The journey went on to Antigua, Lake Aitlan,
Chichicastenango (where the historical accounts of brutality
reminded him of 'the beating, kicking, shooting, starving of Jews and
Communists in Germany'), Oaxaca, and Mexico City. Ottoline
Morrell received a very brief postcard from Mexico: 'Very strange and
sinister country, and dark, savage people. Can't share Lawrence's
enthusiasm.'4

    In Mexico the Huxleys met a coffee planter called Roy Fenton who
entertained them and took them on mules between Pochutla and the
Oaxaca road in southern Mexico. Sybille Bedford reports an incident
told to her by Roy Fenton, but omitted from Huxley's account, of an
occasion at Ejutla where a drunk nearly pulled a revolver on Huxley.
It was the sort of incident that one might expect a writer to treat as
good 'material' but he never explained why he omitted it.5 The coffee
plantations disturbed Huxley: 'Our afternoon tea and our after-
dinner coffee depend on the existence of a huge reserve of sweated
coloured labour. An unpleasant thought.' Mexico City also sparked
thoughts of Lawrence. Huxley rejected his notion that 'the advance
from primitivism to civilization' could be in any degree reversed. He
confessed that he had once thought 'that it was possible to make very
nearly the best of both worlds. But this, I believe, was a delusion.' By
May, the Huxleys were travelling to New York (unaware that Leonard
Huxley had died suddenly on 3 May) where they dined with H.L.
Mencken in the second week of May. New York was expensive and
they couldn't stay long, having now learned of Leonard Huxley's
death. On the SS Statendam sailing back to Europe Huxley wrote to
Eugene Saxton. He admitted to him that he probably had 'an entirely

erroneous view' about fiction. 'For I feel about fiction as Nurse Cavell felt about patriotism: that it is not enough. Whereas the "born story teller" obviously feels that it is enough.'[6] Huxley was always disarmingly frank about his shortcomings as a novelist.

Back in Sanary in July, Maria wrote to their recent host, Roy Fenton, to say that La Gorguette was to be 'our permanent address and en plus – I hope it will be our address for a long time'.[7] The Huxleys' health was not good and the occasionally arduous journey – that mule ride, for instance – had worn them out. Huxley was trying the famous Hay diet, the first of many such ventures into areas that some would find faddish but which he would undertake in his usual spirit of wanting to try something new. His publishers were slow at first to show enthusiasm for his travel book – so much so that he abandoned it briefly to work on the new novel – but they warmed to it during the summer and he delivered the manuscript in November. He told Ottoline Morrell that it was 'a book of travels – which is really a book about everything.'[8] A peculiarly apt description of Huxley's approach to writing. But if he thought that Sanary was a place of escape, he was wrong. The ominous signs of coming cataclysm in Europe were beginning to show themselves. He compared Wordsworth's account of his visit to France during the Revolution with Europe in 1933 – 'the awful sense of invisible vermin of hate, envy, anger crawling about looking for blood to suck'.[9] Central America had persuaded Huxley that psychological factors such as hate were more powerful factors than economic ones. 'In CA there were no economics, only evil passions.' In his sunny retreat, Huxley was harbouring some very dark thoughts. A young Welsh writer, J. Glyn Roberts, asked him to endorse his new book, *I Take This City* (1933) and Huxley agreed to praise its 'uncompromisingness and violence'.[10] He told Roberts: 'About 99.5% of the entire population of the planet are as stupid and philistine (tho' in different ways) as the great masses of the English. The important thing, it seems to me, is not to attack the 99.5% – except for exercise – but to try to see that the 0.5% survive, keeps its quality up to the highest possible level and, if possible, dominates the rest.' Like a contemporary intellectual berating the *Sun* or the *Daily Mail*, Huxley blamed tabloid journalists like Hannen

Swaffer and James Douglas for fostering this 'imbecility'. The word 'dominate' here is plainly a hostage to fortune. Yet those who met Huxley at this time – such as Roy Fenton – found him patient and generous. Gerald Heard told Ottoline Morrell: 'One of the reasons why one is so fond of Aldous is because he is so gentle with cruder people like oneself. No doubt he suffers just as much but his suffering does not make him wild.'[11]

One thing that nearly made Huxley wild was the steady influx of incomers throughout the summer. In August, he complained to Eugene Saxton: 'Sanary swarms with German literary exiles, from Thomas Mann downwards. The place fairly stinks of literature – which is rather distressing.'[12] He told Julian that these exiles were 'Rather a dismal crew, already showing the disastrous effects of exile.'[13] Maria was less tolerant of the German Jewish exiles: 'They are mostly so ugly.'[14] Their closest friends now seemed to be William and Marjorie Seabrook who were very friendly 'when sober'. Huxley, as has been noted above, was both aware of the sufferings of the Jews in Europe, and in the habit of using rather questionable or pejorative terms to describe them. He characterised the German exiles to Julian as 'a rich selection of Jews' at about the same time as he was writing in the Chicago *Herald and Examiner* of 19 August 1933 on 'Apocalypse' and pointing out how persistent was the spirit of intolerance: 'In Hitler's Germany the Jews are being treated as though they belonged to some species of lower animals.' Huxley was generally sceptical of the idea of progress – in the arts and in the remaking of humanity – but in this piece, whilst conceding that progress in realising humanist ideals was slow, he concluded: 'But this does not mean that such hopes are without value. They impel the hopers to do work which, though apparently doomed to failure in the present, may bear good fruit at some future time.' A more pessimistic summer visitor was Gerald Heard 'advising us all to clear out to some safe spot in South America or the Pacific islands before it is too late'.[15] Edward Sackville-West made his first visit to Sanary this summer.

The summer sequestration in Sanary was briefly broken by a trip to Paris. Huxley went to take part in a conference of intellectuals discussing the future of the European spirit and was bored beyond belief by 'the professors'. He told Mary: 'One has no idea, until one attends a congress of "intellectual co-operation", how bottomlessly stupid learned men can be. Like dogs.'[16] He had not intended to speak but sat up one night to prepare a *discours*, which he fired off the next day – 'to the horror and dismay of the professors, who were really pained to hear something that actually meant something'. The only consolation in this event was meeting Julian Benda – 'whom I liked very much'. He complained to Mary that the economic crisis was making the pound fifty per cent less effective in purchasing power with the result that they were having to economise on labour by moving the dining-room next to the kitchen and installing butane gas geysers to heat the water. In November they went off on a tour of Spain where they visited Madrid and Toledo and Barcelona. They looked up the Roy Campbells, who were living in poverty. They had been unable, Roy told Aldous, to buy a book for three years. This was their third Spanish journey and once again they were thrilled by the El Grecos. 'What a pity painters have ceased to believe in God,' he wrote to Mary on a postcard from Toledo showing El Greco's *Assumption of the Virgin:* 'They'll never paint this sort of thing again until they become *croyant* and *pratiquant.*'[17] Huxley was painting furiously again but the results were not always to Maria's taste. 'Sometimes I hide them,'[18] she confessed to Mary, whom she had asked to go and see the revival of *The World of Light* at the Playhouse in London where it had opened on 4 December for a three week run. 'Tell us frankly how that wretch Lion has dealt with it.' Rehearsals had apparently been scant and Huxley used a cold he had caught in Spain as an excuse not to come to the opening night. It was no more successful this time than on the previous occasion.

In January 1934, Huxley resumed his tussle with the novel that would become *Eyeless in Gaza*. But he had not severed his link with journalism. *Nash's Magazine* asked him to write a piece on eugenics 'particularly the sterilization of the unfit'[19] as he explained to C. P. Blacker, General Secretary of the Eugenics Society, when he wrote in December, asking for a briefing on the history of the progress of the bill for the legalisation of sterilisation. Blacker replied that the Bill had in fact been rejected by the Commons in June 1931, mainly because of

Labour opposition. 'The adoption of a drastic eugenic policy by the Nazis had had the effect of still further antagonizing persons of Labour persuasion against eugenics,'[20] Blacker told Huxley. The piece appeared in April, headed, 'What is Happening to Our Population?' The article claimed that mental deficiency was on the increase, owing in part to the fact that infant mortality was in decline and thus: 'An environmental change for the better has resulted, among other things, in a hereditary change for the worse.'[21] Huxley saw that 'half-wits' were on the increase and said the only remedy was in: 'encouraging the normal and super-normal members of the population to have larger families and in preventing the sub-normal from having any families at all'. He advocated – as the Galton Institute does today – use of the family allowance system to encourage some groups and not others to bear children. But he went further in proposing sterilisation of 'certified defectives', pointing out that eugenic sterilisation was already legal in half the states of America. He dismissed the objections of theologians and 'mystical democrats'. The latter he agreed were on strong ground in suggesting that this was 'just another attempt on the part of the rich to bully the poor; that it is an excuse invented by the ruling class for evading its responsibilities towards people it has itself condemned to a life of degradation'. He agreed that such an argument was 'commendable' but he still insisted that it was unscientific because democracy needed intelligent citizens to make its onward march irre-sistible: 'Half-wits fairly ask for dictators.' He also believed that, on humanitarian grounds, 'defectives' made poor parents and were responsible for many acts of cruelty according to the NSPCC. At this point Huxley swerves aside from the eugenic point and moves on to consider the increase in population generally and whether it has reached an optimum level: it may have done so but the need to control it has to be confronted. The piece ends rather flatly on that note. The argument is put with clarity and logic but those who find the notion of eugenics odious are unlikely to be convinced by it. One might add that Huxley's 'scientific' predictions have not been borne out. There is no evidence, seventy years on, that there are more 'half-wits' in the population than in 1933.

What is odd in this piece is the contrast between Huxley's cold

logic and his evident humanitarian sympathies, his fundamentally
progressive orientation, in addressing other social and political issues.
It is true that he was exasperated by the stupidity of the '99.5%' in
tabloid-fed public opinion. But nowhere else in his writing up to this
point is there anything other than an occasional intellectual arrogance or snobbishly superior remark of a kind that one might expect
from one of his background. Very shortly, Huxley was to discover
political commitment of a kind that would banish any worries about
his democratic credentials. The whole episode demonstrates the limitations of the intellectual's fondness for an abstraction that has cut
loose from its moorings in common humanity and common sense.
And as has been copiously demonstrated in recent studies, he was not
alone amongst the 'progressive' thinkers of his time in playing with
this concept. And, finally, he had just published an article for *Time
and Tide* on 'The Prospects of Fascism in England' whose argument is
both acute (recognising the Poujadist roots of petit bourgeois support
for reactionary politics) and exemplary in its rejection of ideas which
were by no means being met with antipathy in many parts of English
upper-class society at the time.

Abstraction was also the starting point of his new novel. 'The
theme, fundamentally is liberty,' he told Julian. 'What happens to
someone who becomes really very free.'[22] His description of the
embryo novel to Mary Hutchinson makes it sound like a treatise by
the Italian sociologist Pareto whose ideas he was buttonholing just
about all of his friends and readers with at this time: 'I dodder along
with my book, rather exasperated because I can't quite get the formal
relations between parts that I'm looking for, but advancing little by
little. I am looking for a device to present two epochs of life simultaneously so as to show their relations with one another – and also
their lack of relationship. For when one considers life one is equally
struck by both facts . . .'[23] Mary, too, was treated to Huxley's passion
for Pareto, though while praising its scientific 'unmetaphysical'
account of human affairs he admitted it was 'the most depressing
book in the world'. He had first read the *Sociologica* in 1924 and was
now going through it again, noting how true to the facts it was: 'Partly
because of the events, which have punctured all the post-war hopes of

lands-fit-for-heroes and reconstruction; and partly, doubtless, because
one is creeping into middle age and is less easily distracted by one's
appetites, which have grown feebler, and by one's passions, which
seem such a bore – all but the consuming desire for knowledge and
understanding. That grows.' If he did not have to earn his living, and
if his eyes could stand it, he would wish to do nothing for the next few
years but read 'and in the intervals travel round, pushing my nose into
things'.

In fact, Huxley was not doing a great deal at all in the lovely, abun-
dant spring of 1934 at Sanary, by his own account: 'Such flowers and
greenery I never saw here. I have been doing little – lying rather fallow,
as I don't seem to be able to get what I want in my projected novel:
reading a fair amount.'[24] He thought little of one new book, T.S. Eliot's
After Strange Gods: A Primer of Modern Heresy (1934). 'I never knew a
writer who spent so much time explaining what he didn't mean to say
and then at last saying so little. The way he makes generalizations
and then slips away without giving examples is incredible . . . And
then the serene way he ignores history.' A lethal exposure of Eliot's
hallowed method that would still be considered controversial today.
In April the Huxleys visited Italy, partly to have a last look at Rome
before Mussolini destroyed it with his triumphalist fascist architecture. He complained to Eliot that 'the strutting of the fascists, the
cringing hypocritical acceptance of fascism by the masses were most
depressing'.[25] In June, Huxley slipped across to London where he
attended a conference of the Society for Sexual Information and
Progress at Welwyn Garden City where sexual reform was being discussed. He visited Virginia Woolf at Rodmell and she found him, at
the age of forty, mellower than ever before. 'A most admirable, cool,
antiseptic, distempered, but humane & gentle man: with age just tem-
pering his brow: experience; but admirably mature, as we are not; has
gone about the world, completely sceptical, all the more humane;
judging everything yet nothing. A little theoretical, about religion &
sex; not for that reason a novelist; infinitely elegant and bony: his
blurred grey eye; his malice & wit . . . He uses every instant to the best
advantage but has somehow solved the problem of remaining just,
gentle, – a very sympathetic mind.'[26]

Two other sketches of Huxley belong to this mid-point of his adult life. The first is by Frank Swinnerton, the man credited with 'discovering' him for Chatto: 'He is the tallest English author I know . . . Naturally this great height has given some of those who encountered him the impression that he lives remote from the world, wrapped in distant hauteur. That is not the case . . . the truth is that Huxley converses easily, and is full of gleeful high spirits. He uses long words because he thinks in long words; and not because he is aware they are long words. The words he uses most often in conversation (or at least in narrative) are "fantastic" and "incredible" . . . He has a happy knack of meeting odd people and seeing odd sights; and while this does not mean that he is himself odd it does mean that he is prepared for every oddity.'[27] Swinnerton decided that after *Brave New World* (he did not yet know what was to come) Huxley had reached a dead end – 'something has gone wrong, it seems to me, with the Huxley alignment'. He risked a prophecy: 'there is a single mind, which is Aldous Huxley, busily transforming multiplicity into unity and so into wisdom. He has a greater capacity for wisdom than any encyclopaedia-stuffed man of this era; and may yet lead his generation, and the younger generation, into a state of grace out of which great things will come.'

The third moral snapshot is from Alexander Henderson's book on Huxley (the first full-length study, approved, and published by, Chatto). Henderson pointed out that Huxley had now been writing for nineteen years and had already produced twenty-five books. Librarians were still ready to ban his books in some places and the stock attitude of reviewers was to label Huxley 'Intellectual – slightly unpleasant'. Henderson felt that Huxley's post war cynicism and attacks on idealism were 'over-compensating' but concluded that: 'The foundation of Huxley's materialism is a natural idealism.'[28] All three views of Huxley agree that here was a brilliant writer who had made his mark but of whom something more was expected. He was being summoned to act as the moral conscience of his generation but before he could do that he would have to resolve his own inner conflicts, to balance his intellectual powers with his moral and imaginative vision of contemporary life. The next twelve months or so, from the middle of 1934 to the end of 1935 when he embraced the pacifist cause, constituted one of the most difficult passages in his life. But he would emerge stronger, more clear-sighted, less self-conscious and more committed than ever before. Just before leaving Sanary to spend the last three months of 1934 in London he gave Mary a hint of what was going on in his thoughts:

> I am more and more struck by the hopelessly primitive
> and uneducated state of our minds – utterly ignorant of
> all rational techniques for encouraging such essential
> states as concentration on the one hand and
> 'decentration' – relaxed quiescence – on the other . . . It's
> a dismal story of wasted talents and unrealised
> potentialities; and I come more and more firmly to
> believe that the most important task before human
> beings is the perfection of a series of psychological
> techniques for the proper exploitation of personality. All
> this famous 'planning' in the social and economic sphere
> will be wasted and useless if we remain barbarously
> unplanned as individuals – at the mercy of the social
> forces we have created . . . we have been content to drivel
> along with our current educational systems, most of
> which neglect all the essential things and leave their
> victims for all intents and purposes quite untrained.[29]

This was Huxley's personal manifesto for the next year or more. He left Sanary for the time being, the memory fresh of meetings with Paul Valéry, who talked of the poets of his youth (Mallarmé, Villiers de l'Isle Adam, Huysmans). He also bade farewell to the summer migrants to the coast who were still capable of exciting his satirical and self-mocking impulses: 'It's sad that all the things one believes in – such as democracy, economic equality etc – shd turn out in practice to be so repulsively unpleasant – hot, smelly crowds; banana skins; building estates like skin eruptions on the landscape; loud speakers and gramophones every ten yards; roads made nightmarish with rushing traffic.' But would winter in 'Pudding Island' for the next six months be an improvement?

Notes

1   BL, Letter to Sydney Schiff, 12 March 1933
2   *Beyond the Mexique Bay* (1934), p13
3   *L.*367
4   HRC, Postcard to Ottoline Morrell, 10 April 1933
5   *SB*1.272–3
6   *L.*371
7   *L.*371
8   HRC, Letter to Ottoline Morrell, 31 August 1933
9   *L.*373
10   National Library of Wales, Letter to J Glyn Roberts, 19 July 1933
11   HRC, Letter from Gerald Heard to Ottoline Morrell, 17 December 1932
12   UCLA, Letter to Eugene Saxton, 4 August 1933
13   *L.*375
14   HRC, Letter from Maria Huxley to Mary Hutchinson, 5 August 1933
15   *L.*375
16   HRC, Letter to Mary Hutchinson, 24 October 1933
17   HRC, Postcard to Mary Hutchinson, 6 November 1933
18   HRC, Letter from Maria Huxley to Mary Hutchinson, undated but probably December 1933
19   Wellcome Trust, Eugenics Society papers, Letter to C.P. Blacker, 1 December 1933
20   Wellcome Trust, Letter from C.P. Blacker to Huxley, 4 December 1933
21   *Nash's Pall Mall Magazine*, April 1934. *Hidden Huxley*, pp147–58
22   *L.*376
23   HRC, Letter to Mary Hutchinson, 25 February 1934
24   HRC, Letter to Mary Hutchinson, 19 May 1934
25   *L.*380
26   *The Diaries of Virginia Woolf,* Vol 4 pp222–23. 18 June 1934
27   Frank Swinnerton, *The Georgian Literary Scene* (1935), p458
28   Alexander Henderson, *Aldous Huxley* (1935)
29   HRC, Letter to Mary Hutchinson, 18 August 1934

XXIII

Albany

On arrival in London in October 1934 the Huxleys took lodgings at 18 St Alban's Place, SW1: 'a studio flat – 2 bedrooms, large studio, kitchen and bath – within 50 yards of Piccadilly Circus, at £5 a week – altogether a miracle. It is very quiet and I manage to do a certain amount of work and even some painting in the afternoons.'[1] 'We propose to be here in London till after Christmas,'[2] he told Mencken (another auditor of praise for Pareto who had just been translated – 'Such a monument of common sense'). Huxley liked above all, Pareto's realism, and disliked, by contrast, the fashionable poses of the young thirties poets. Virginia Woolf noted down his terms of dismissal of Macspaunday: 'A. can't stand Auden. Nothing but a demagogue. Declaims: takes in the young. Something in Day Lewis – hasn't read Spender.'[3] Huxley's fondness for massive works of sociology coexisted with a growing interest in personal development. He had read Geraldine Coster's new book on *Yoga and Western Psychology* and told Julian that yoga might be the way forward because: 'I've always felt that it was vitally necessary for people to have some efficient technique for personal development.'[4] Without achieving full mental and spiritual development people couldn't benefit from improved social and political arrangements. And, preoccupied as he was with *Eyeless*, Huxley was not blind to other people's misfortunes.

His friend J.W.N. Sullivan had just entered the first stages of an incurable paralysis and was having difficulty in meeting his contract with the Viking Press. Huxley immediately offered cash help and wrote to some other writers, including Wells, asking them each to stump up £200. This was a characteristic gesture by Huxley. Whatever his personal circumstances, he always found himself able to help out a range of people – relatives and friends – who were in difficulty.

On 12 November, Huxley surprised himself by announcing to Mary: 'We have taken – for seven years! – a flat in The Albany. Very nice, with central heating, parquet floors, and lots of room. A very decisive step!'[5] Huxley's astonishment was justified. Restless as he was – and what about Sanary, lying empty for the winter? – such a commitment to the future seemed a little inconsistent with his foot-loose record. They would keep the flat for barely two years. The Albany is a very exclusive residential building off Piccadilly with a lit-erary reputation generated by past tenants, real (Byron) and imaginary (Raffles the gentleman thief). Names like Terence Stamp and Bruce Chatwin have continued its twentieth century allure. The Huxleys furnished it cheaply with second-hand furniture and began to receive a stream of guests, including Ottoline Morrell whose visit was marked by an accident in which she scattered a string of pearls on the floor when the string broke. It was an elegant address, though not entirely convenient, with a kitchen in the basement and a servant room in the attic, which they later enabled Sybille Bedford to live in.

It was at this address, E2 Albany, that Huxley first began to suffer from the insomnia that would rack him on and off for the next year – a symptom of his inner stress and unease. They moved in to the flat in mid-December. In January, after Christmas in the country, Huxley went back to France to collect material for some articles he had agreed to write for *Paris-Soir* on the theme of *La France au seuil de 1935*. He managed to get out of this commitment in the end, telling E.M. Forster, 'not having sufficient effrontery to pour out my opinions on a subject of which, the more I look into it, the less I find I know'.[6] He shared with Forster a gloom about the world as it was on the thresh-old of 1935: 'and add to it a considerable gloom about myself: Bertie Russell, whom I've just been lunching with, says one oughtn't to mind

about the superficial things like ideas, manners, politics, even wars –
that the really important things, conditioned by scientific technique,
go steadily on & up (like the eternal feminine, I suppose) in a straight,
un-undulating trajectory. It's nice to think so; but meanwhile there
the superficial undulations are, as one lives superficially, & who knows
if that straight trajectory isn't aiming directly for some fantastic denial
of humanity?' The following month the personal anxiety returned, in
spite of the breathing-exercises which Gerald Heard had recommended for him. 'I've been far from well, suffering from sleeplessness
which is just about to drive me away from London and the country to
another climate,' he told R.A. Scott James. 'This has kept me in a
state of incapacity to do most of the things I ought to have done.'[7] He
had just been to see John Gielgud in *Hamlet* which he thought was
'the work of art with the greatest amount of substance ever put into
words'. In his present impasse, however, this made him ask 'why one
goes on writing when one sees what writing can be – and what one's
own writing is not'.[8]

Huxley was in touch at this time with Strachey's friend, Sebastian
Sprott, now a lecturer at Nottingham University. He told Sprott that
he felt he should really visit the east Midlands again 'to hear a little
about that other England of which we here in London have really no
inkling'.[9] Huxley was aware that Piccadilly was not the place to know
England in the Depression. His insomnia, however, had become so
bad that his doctor recommended a drastic change of climate such as
the mountains near Grenoble and he put off the trip to see Sprott. In
March he put up in the Hotel des Grandes Rousses at Huez in the
French alps – a rather 'god-forsaken little place . . . However I console
myself with the thought that it must be good for me, and take enormous walks on snow-shoes, conscientiously, as one might drink the
waters at Vichy'.[10] From there he went to Sanary where the Huxleys
spent March until October. By early April he was able to report to
Harold Raymond at Chatto that he was gradually sleeping better and
had started working again 'under about half steam & progress slowly
with the book'.[11] At the start of May Maria announced that 'he is
cured, definitely cured . . . work goes well'.[12] He dashed off an article
in May for the *Daily Express* to mark the Silver Jubilee of George V in

which he made some predictions for the next twenty-five years. Huxley was generally a good prophet and his prediction of a 'generation war' as a result of a rapidly ageing population in the later twentieth century was one of the more interesting. He also expressed the hope that 'Europe is spared the war which its Governments seem quite determined to make inevitable'.[13]

The rise of Hitler and the apparent threat of war was increasingly galvanising Huxley's thinking. He addressed an International Writer's Congress in Paris on 21 June to warn about the dangers of propaganda and was disappointed that it appeared to be a Communist front event. Later, during his residence in the United States, the FBI would regularly dredge up his attendance at this event to bolster their thin case against his putatively subversive potential. Earlier in the month he had attended a London rally at Olympia addressed by Sir Oswald Mosley, now the leader of the British Union of Fascists and surrounded by his Blackshirt thugs. Twelve thousand people filled the hall. Sitting with Naomi Mitchison and other friends, Huxley saw the brutal handling of protesters.[14] In a pamphlet published to record the event, Huxley was one of many who described what they saw. Mosley's stewards – many of whom wore knuckle-dusters concealed under bandages or gloves – would pounce on any hecklers and attack them viciously. Mosley would stop speaking and searchlights would theatrically sweep onto the victims. The opposition, however, was equally active. On 16 October 1934, Canon Dick Sheppard had written a letter to the press asking members of the public to pledge their support for peace. Eighty thousand people returned postcards making their pledges in the first year. By the beginning of 1937 numbers in 'Dick Sheppard's Army' had swelled to 130,000. The first sacks of mail in October 1934 contained a postcard from Huxley, then living at 18 St Alban's Place. A rally at the Albert Hall took place in June 1935 and Huxley would eventually write the Peace Pledge Union's first official pamphlet. But at Sanary in the early summer of 1935 he was more preoccupied with his own health and sanity. With a mixture of apprehension and amusement, Maria watched as he implemented a new plan, to take violent exercise for the sake of his health: 'he digs every spare inch of the ground and causes havoc all round him to the despair of the gardener'.[15] He was also taking a mixture of calcium and magnesium as a sedative and mild hypnotic for the continuing 'beastly insomnia'.[16] The novel seemed back on course and he was having discussions with the American writer Ted McKnight Kauffer, who had first met him at Sanary in 1931, about writing some short film scripts on the theme of 'Dreams' for Alexander Korda. He also hoped that Korda might take an interest in *Brave New World*.

Meanwhile Huxley's charitable instincts had been awakened by the predicament of a young woman friend, a partly-Jewish German whose passport was coming up for renewal and who was naturally fearful of being repatriated. He wrote to Sprott to ask if he knew of any 'impecunious Englishman' who would marry her as a purely financial transaction so that she could stay in England. 'The solution, it seems to me, consists in finding someone combining impecuniosity, honesty and homosexuality.'[17] He pointed out that Auden had just married Erika Mann on the same grounds. He wrote to Naomi Mitchison at the same time – with the result that a clutch of potential husbands now presented themselves. 'It is reassuring to know that husbands are in such good supply and at so reasonable a price,'[18] he told Sprott. The wedding took place on 15 November at the Westminster registry office, with Huxley as principal witness. There was a party at the Albany afterwards. 'Party for the German they've married to a postman [actually a doorman at a gentleman's club in Westminster] – for £50,'[19] Virginia Woolf noted in her diary. She had been one of the guests, with Robert Nichols and Naomi Mitchison.

In November, Huxley lunched for the first time with Dick Sheppard. Afterwards he felt that he been rather garrulous and glib in his talk of organising the peace movement. 'When one has been endowed with that curious thing, the gift of the gab, one is sadly tempted to make use of it for elegantly expressing ideas which one knows as ideas and not by experience.'[20] He told Sheppard that it was 'frankly comic' that such an egghead as he should be telling a man like Sheppard how to proceed and that it was only by laughing at himself that he could 'take the edge off my shame. Thinking, reading, talking & writing has been my opium & alcohol, & I am trying to get off them on to listening & doing.' Huxley was making the painful transition from closeted thinker to activist. He was a quick learner and became a very important member of the PPU, and one not without an understanding of the tactics of campaigning. His first public appearance as a peace campaigner was at a lunchtime talk at Friend's House in Euston Road – a stone's throw from the Bloomsbury salons he knew so well. On 3 December he came to the rostrum to 'set forth some of the intellectual justifications for pacifism . . . and . . . discuss what I may call some of the indispensable philosophical conditions of pacifism.' He introduced his familiar argument about ends and means and declared: 'There is nothing inherently absurd about the idea that the world which we ourselves have so largely constructed can also, if we so desire, be reconstructed on other and better lines.' This is a marked change from the intellectual pessimism of the 1920s and early 1930s. What is most significant about this talk, however, is that in it Huxley explicitly brings in a spiritual or religious dimension. He urged that 'the doctrine of the essential spiritual unity of man' be taken seriously. He claimed that humanism 'has as its principal end-product the religion of nationalism', which was part of the problem not the solution. 'There is left the belief in a spiritual reality to which all men have access and in which they are united. Such a belief is the best metaphysical environment for pacifism.'[21]

There was little doubt that for Huxley his adoption of the pacifist cause was not a mere intellectual interest. It was a spiritual discovery. He was undergoing a 'conversion'[22] that would end the mental and physical anguish of the past year. The hard line political activists of the Left were contemptuous. After *Eyeless in Gaza* was published the following summer, Stephen Spender would write to Christopher Isherwood to express anxiety that the religious Auden could be seduced by this approach: 'He has some ideas now but they are all wrong; a sort of half-religious, mystical pacifism. I do hope that Wystan doesn't fall for it.'[23] In a letter to Robert Nichols, telling him about 'the novel that won't get finished', Huxley expressed his anxieties about the coming conflict: 'I wish I could see any remedy for the horrors of human beings except religion or could see any religion that we could all believe in.'[24] Two months later, after returning to Albany from Belgium where Maria's youngest sister, Rose, had been married he was telling Victoria Ocampo that he had been talking to Gerald Heard about ways and means of getting an adequate peace movement on its feet. 'The thing finally resolves itself into a religious problem – an uncomfortable fact which one must be prepared to face and which I have come during the last year to find it easier to face.'[25] For a Huxley, the idea of religious belief was a hard one to swallow, but (while the religion of brass eagle and beeswax would for ever be outside his scope) he was beginning his inexorable journey towards the 'Perennial Philosophy' whose expositor he would become in the next decade.

As well as this re-making of himself as a quasi-religious believer in pacifism (his early writings about peace stress the need for a refor-mation of the individual life as much as they talk about questions of power and military policy), Huxley was also attending to his physical disposition. The torment of the year 1935 (which Maria would refer to later as 'l'année horrible') was the result of several difficulties (and of the conviction that they were all related to each other). There was a sense of indistinct purpose – the need for someone who had been so destructively cynical to find a positive commitment. 'He suddenly felt he must develop. Negative cynicism was not enough.'[26] There were profound aesthetic problems, trying to make the new novel work. He had a writer's block that was starting to raise financial anxieties. What if his writing career was finished? What would he then do? In that gloomy, old-fashioned building, the Albany – where the sound of his typewriter raised anxieties on the part of management that someone might be sullying the dignity of the place by engaging in 'trade' – he sank deeper into depression. And, finally, there were physical prob-lems. Huxley was often in bad health throughout his life but this was something different. He had already, under the influence of Gerald Heard, begun to practice breathing-exercises and various kinds of mental discipline, in order to defeat his insomnia.[27] It was bad enough not being able to see properly but he felt his whole physical deport-ment was wrong. He was in the grip of a feeling of utter physical and artistic dysfunction.

Intellectually and spiritually, however, the peace movement was starting to show him a way out of the impasse. Physically, a saviour appeared in the shape of F.M. Alexander, the therapist and inventor of the Alexander technique. Huxley started to have daily sessions with him from November 1935 in which his whole posture, physical movement, performance of simple daily actions, was subject to a process of 'kinesthetic' re-education. Huxley later wrote an introduction to a selection of Alexander's writings, in which he claimed Alexander had discovered empirically 'that there is a correct or "natural" relationship between the neck and the trunk and that normal functioning of the total organism cannot take place except when the neck and trunk are in the right relationship'.[28] What attracted Huxley to this technique – apart from the fact that it seemed, for him, to work – was the way it highlighted the relationship between body and mind, that old combat which had always preoccupied him. By focussing on 'the data of organic reality' to the exclusion of 'the insane life of phantasy' it made it possible for 'the physical organism to function as it ought to function, thus improving the general state of physical and mental health'. It had certain affinities with the 'straight-spine' position of yoga and so successful did Huxley consider it that Maria also put herself through the process. Alexander in turn put the Huxleys on to Dr J.E.R. McDonagh, whose theory was that intoxication of the intestines was at the root of most disorders. They duly submitted to colonic irrigation, vaccine injections, and special diet. By early 1936 Huxley was able to report victory over insomnia, fatigue (he could now work for eight hours instead of four), normal blood pressure, the vanishing of psychosomatic symptoms and of two patches of eczema that he had had for years, better skin colour, and the disappearance of chronic nasal catarrh.[29]

Huxley returned to The Albany – to a work room that Sybille Bedford described as a 'goldfish bowl' and one that she thought added to his discomfort[30] – and began to write those sections of *Eyeless in Gaza* that dealt with the moral rebirth of Anthony Beavis. Huxley, particularly during his Californian years, would from time to time acquire the reputation of one who was a little too prone to take seriously the claims of quackery but there is little doubt that this therapy worked for him. Around this time the Huxleys started to introduce to their friends the therapist and author of *The Human Hand,* Dr

Charlotte Wolff, whom they had met in Paris, and who had now established herself across the road at Dalmeny Court. At an evening at the Woolfs, Lotte started to read palms. Leonard Woolf was disgusted by this 'humbug' but Clive Bell told him that this was not the proper scientific spirit.[31]

Summing up the past year, Maria wrote in a new year letter to her sister Jeanne (she addressed her sometimes as 'Janin' or 'Jokes', in these letters written in French and now in the Royal Library at Brussels, the latter being a Flemish diminutive) that she hoped sincerely that 1936 would be 'as different from the last as possible. I don't think anyone could grasp how dreadful the last year has been for me'.[32] She reported that the novel was coming to an end and that somehow she had great hopes for it. Aldous's health was 'good but not brilliant' but he was working hard and was 'calm and peaceful'. They were leading a quiet life, seeing only the people they wanted to see. The fever was abated.

Notes

1   L.385
2   NYPL, Letter to H.L. Mencken, 16 October 1934
3   *The Diaries of Virginia Woolf*, Vol 4, 1 November 1934
4   L.382
5   HRC, Letter to Mary Hutchinson, 12 November 1934
6   King's College Cambridge, Letter to E. M. Forster 17 January 1935
7   HRC, Letter to R.A. Scott James, 25 February 1935
8   L.390
9   King's College, Letter to Sebastian Sprott, 5 March 1935
10 HRC, Letter to Mary Hutchinson, 17 March 1935
11 Reading, Letter to Harold Raymond, 9 April 1935
12 L.392
13 *Daily Express*, 8 May 1935. *Hidden Huxley*, pp171–175
14 see *Fascists at Olympia* (1934) by 'Vindicator'
15 L.393
16 L.395
17 King's College, Letter to Sebastian Sprott, 22 August 1935
18 King's College, Letter to Sebastian Sprott, 30 September 1935
19 *The Diaries of Virginia Woolf*, Vol 4, p354 21 November 1935

20 Lambeth Palace Library, Letter to Dick Sheppard 9 November 1935
21 'Pacifism and Philosophy', *The New Pacifism* (1936) edited by Gerald Hibbert
22 SB in conversation with the author
23 Stephen Spender, *Letters to Christopher* (Santa Barbara, 1980) Letter to Isherwood, 27 July 1936
24 *L.*398
25 *L.*398
26 SB in conversation with the author
27 *SB*1.308
28 *The Resurrection of the Body. The Writings of F. Matthias Alexander* (1969) ed Edward Maisel
29 *L.*402
30 *SB*1.294
31 *The Letters of Virginia Woolf*, Vol 5, p452, letter to Julian Bell, 17 December 1935
32 RL, Letter from Maria Huxley to Jeanne Neveux, January 1936. Author's translation

XXIV

Eyeless

The Huxleys were in Sanary for the New Year of 1936: 'Exquisite weather here,' he told Harold Raymond at the beginning of January, 'sun and no wind, and the landscape extraordinarily beautiful.'[1] But Huxley was now actively engaged in contemporary politics and was constrained to add: 'It makes it all the more distressing to reflect that such a short way off, in Spain, they are busily engaged in slitting one anothers' throats.' Young poets were going off to the Spanish Civil War but Huxley returned to London to continue to work with Dick Sheppard and Gerald Heard in the Peace Pledge Union. The novel was nearly finished and Maria wrote to his American publisher, Eugene Saxton, to let him know. She said that Alexander had made 'a new and unrecognisable person of Aldous, not physically only but mentally and therefore morally. Or rather, he has brought out, actively, all we, Aldous's best friends, know never came out either in the novels or with strangers.'[2] That is a very significant remark, for the new Huxley who was now being unveiled – to the dismay of those who preferred him in the guise of the brilliant cynic and destructive satirist – was not so new. Contemporaries, like many present-day critics, missed the constructive undertow, the ethical underpinning, of Huxley's earlier writing. They, but not his close friends, were caught unawares by the emergence of the idealist of peace.

Huxley increasingly found that he had to defend himself. Early in 1936, Leonard Woolf wrote a pamphlet on Mussolini's aggression, *The League and Abyssinia*, accusing pacifists like Huxley of burying their heads in the sand when confronted with Fascist violence, wishing to have 'nothing to do with evil'. On the contrary, Huxley told Leonard Woolf (and Virginia as they circled Kensington Gardens discussing politics and Huxley's refusal to sign a manifesto calling for sanctions against Mussolini because it would simply cause the Italians to rally round the Duce). 'He examines the evil and asks what is the best way of dealing with it. To this question experience gives a clear answer: the worst way of dealing with one evil is to do another evil, or to threaten another evil.'[3] For the rest of the decade this would be Huxley's working philosophy of international affairs. His contributions to *Time and Tide*, which were continuing, show that he was increasingly sensitive to the democratic deficit of some of the ideas he had been exploring earlier in the decade. His passion for strong government, intelligent co-ordination and planning was yielding to an awareness of what could actually happen if power was given to 'men with well-thought out plans for improving the world'.[4] Continuing the anti-Utopian thinking of *Brave New World*, he argued: 'Thinking in terms of first principles has generally entailed acting with swords and rubber truncheons.' The hyper-intelligence had engaged with the real world and discovered the brutal consequences of ill-matched ends and means. His flirtation with eugenics was likewise coming to an end. His final gesture was to second a vote of thanks to Julian's Galton Lecture at the Eugenics Society on 17 February. The next month he was off to the Nottinghamshire coalfields again to go down a pit and visit some unemployed centres.

Huxley's host in Nottinghamshire was Sebastian Sprott, a choice of companion which led Maria to joke to Jeanne that Aldous was going to explore 'the homosexual underworld of Nottingham'.[5] Given Huxley's homophobia this was unlikely. Chatto, no doubt seeing the virtue in encouraging their author's exposure, published in April a threepenny pamphlet in yellow paper covers, *What Are You Going to*

Do About It? The Case for Constructive Peace. All Huxley's gifts of
logic, clarity, lightness of touch and essayistic fluency came into play
in what was his most coherent statement of his pacifist beliefs to date.
'Feeling, willing, thinking – these are the three modes of ordinary
human activity,'[6] he argued. 'To be complete, life must be lived simultaneously on all three planes. In this pamphlet an attempt is made to
provide all those who *feel* that war is an abomination, all who *will* that
it shall cease, with an intellectual justification for their attitude; to
show that their feeling and willing are essentially reasonable, that
what is called the utopian dream of pacifism is in fact a practical
policy – indeed the only practical, the only realistic policy that there
is.' He then proceeds to demolish one by one the familiar arguments
against pacifism that would come from a 'theoretical heckler'.

The theoretical hecklers were not slow to respond. Cecil Day Lewis
spoke for the Communist Party Left in a rejoinder, *We're Not Going to
Do Nothing*, which mocked Huxley's 'big, beautiful idealist bubble' as
singularly useless against 'a four-engine bomber'. Day Lewis then
demanded: 'Where was Mr Huxley when the lights went out in Italy,
in Germany?' [answer, witnessing the rise of fascism at first hand]. He
dismissed Huxley's 'spiritual exercises' and termed him 'the Prophet of
Disgust'.[7] Day Lewis said that Huxley's argument that no change was
useful that did not come from within was 'another form of the doctrine of despair'. The *Left Review* returned to the attack (conscious of
Huxley's intellectual prestige and therefore keen to shoot him down)
in June, with an open letter from Stephen Spender who announced
solemnly that he was 'angry' at Huxley's alleged proposal to sacrifice
'oppressed pacifists and socialists in Italy, Germany, and Austria on
the altar of a dogmatic and correct pacifism'. As for Huxley's doctrine
of ends and means, it had 'muddled you into thinking that one kind
of violence is as bad as any other'. Spender announced in conclusion:
'We had to wait for Aldous Huxley to propose that prayer is an exercise for the soul, like an elastic exerciser or a dose of Eno's Fruit salts.'[8]
By now, in June, *Eyeless in Gaza* had appeared and its 'mystical' parts
would further discountenance the Left. George Woodcock, in a study
of Huxley's writings, recalled how Huxley's pacifist conversion
'seemed to place him within the . . . tradition of radical political

dissent that stemmed in England from Godwin, the Chartists, and the largely pacifist British socialist movement'. But the appearance so soon afterwards of *Eyeless* seemed to signal for this older Left tradition 'a retreat into obscurantism on the part of one of the writers we most admired . . . It seemed another case of the Lost Leader.'[9]

A case, however, can be made that *Eyeless in Gaza* is Huxley's best novel. More than *Point Counter Point* it extends the range of the earlier satirical novels and finds new fields of interest, a more affirmative direction, and a deeper understanding of human beings and their relationship to the contemporary world. But at the same time it suffers perhaps from the circumstances of its composition, the 'mystical' elements not forming part of the original conception. Huxley seldom talked up his books but his comments while writing this novel imply that he had real doubts about its likely success. 'All I'm certain of is that I shd have liked another year to work at it,' he told Victoria Ocampo. 'But I couldn't afford to give the time – and perhaps anyhow it wouldn't have been any good: the book might have gone stale and dead on my hands if I'd gone on.'[10] To another correspondent he confessed it was 'rather a curate's egg – good in parts perhaps'.[11] Its chief formal interest is in the dislocated time scheme it adopts to tell the story of Anthony Beavis – a character very similar to Huxley himself – and the exploration of guilt and remorse centres on certain incidents (a brother's suicide, a father's remarriage) which are mirrored in Huxley's. John Beavis recalls Leonard Huxley, Brian suggests Trevenen, and lesser characters have their echo in originals such as the Reverend Purchas (Dick Sheppard or parts of Gerald Heard) and Dr Miller (F.M. Alexander). Back in 1930, Huxley had told a correspondent that Rampion in *Point Counter Point* (whom everyone had concluded to be based on D.H. Lawrence) was 'just some of Lawrence's notions on legs. The actual character of the man was incomparably queerer and more complex than that.'[12] It was a skilful defence against the charge that he had caricatured and over-simplified to say: look, the real people you detect are infinitely more complex and rich than my poor versions of them. One thing Huxley could not do was to deny the echoes and parallels because they were immediately recognised by others. The portrait of his deceased father,

Leonard Huxley (a dreadful punster, emotionally repressed) was objected to by his step-mother, Rosalind. Huxley tried to persuade her that John Beavis was rooted in an amalgam of sources – a poem by Coventry Patmore ('Tired Memory'), or the philologist first husband of Frieda Lawrence – but he was forced to admit that 'quite unjustifiably, I made use of mannerisms and phrases some of which were recognizably father's'.[13]

As with his protestations of innocence to Ottoline Morrell in 1921 over *Crome Yellow*, Huxley assumed an ingenuous air: 'I had not thought that they would prove recognizable to others and I am most distressed to find that they should have been.' The young man who commits suicide, Brian Foxe, he conceded was 'definitely' based on Trev. But Anthony Beavis in the novel is responsible for Brian Foxe's death. No-one could blame Huxley for the suicide of Trev. Was there here a kind of moral masochism? Was Huxley punishing himself for some unidentified wrongdoing? What did he need to feel guilty and remorseful about? The title of the novel (from Milton's *Samson Agonistes*, 'Eyeless in Gaza, at the Mill with slaves') implies a sense of impotence and inadequacy. The strange, unsettling incident when the naked lovers, Anthony Beavis and Helen Amberley, are shattered by the fall of a dog from a plane above them compounds this sense. The dog dies on impact. They are spattered with its blood. It is a quite horrible scene (Huxley was always good at conveying physical disgust) and the context suggests that human relationships, and sexual ones in particular, are haunted by the possibility of abrupt termination, of disgusted recoil. The Latin tag that Anthony Beavis uses – *Video meliora proboque; deteriora sequor* (I see and approve of the best but follow the worst) also conveys a sense of moral dysfunction. Given that Huxley was self-confessedly inept at devising plots and attending to the normal business of the novelist – inventing, in short – it is neither reductive nor crass to discuss these 'originals'. Defending himself before Rosalind for the creation of Brian Foxe (recognisably Trev but with some disagreeable additions such as a stammer) Huxley argued that 'all deeply good characters in imaginative literature have to be, as it were, diluted with weakness or eccentricity; for only on such conditions are they comprehensible by readers and expressible by writers'. He did not regret the portrait based on Trev 'since it was reproduced entirely in love and in an attempt to understand a character which I profoundly admired'. That love and admiration were beyond doubt. And if Anthony Beavis is Huxley, the portrait is drawn with a ruthless and unsparing crayon: 'That which besets me is indifference. I can't be bothered about people. Or rather, I won't. For I avoid, carefully, all occasions of being bothered . . . One clever man and two idiots – that's what you've made yourself. An admirable manipulator of ideas, linked with a person who, so far as self-knowledge is concerned, is just a moron; and the pair of you associated with a half-witted body.'

All Huxley's sense of himself as a moral and physical mess before Alexander and Dick Sheppard pointed him the way to physical and ethical rebirth is in this portrait. For the rest, it offers much the same picture of the English aesthetes and intellectual upper middle class, the same bold and sometimes shocking frankness about sexual and social mores which his readers had come to expect and to relish. It was his last novel before settling in America where, some readers felt (wrongly I would argue) that his best as a novelist was past. Meanwhile the new life of political commitment had been signalled in the novel and would be followed by Huxley in his personal life. Anthony Beavis, at the end of the novel, discovers the importance of the 'unity of mankind, unity of all life' and the sense that life has meaning. If it does not, 'then he was at liberty to read his books and exercise his talents for sarcastic comment . . . If it weren't nonsense, if there were some significance, then he could no longer live irresponsibly. There were duties towards himself and others and the nature of things.' The last words of the novel are: 'Dispassionately, and with a serene lucidity, he thought of what was in store for him. Whatever it might be, he knew now that all would be well.' Huxley was bidding farewell to his former self. Not all his readers were pleased. They preferred the man who had 'chosen to think it nonsense, and nonsense for more than twenty years the thing had seemed to be'. They had to adjust to the fact that Huxley was now a writer who rejected 'the pointlessness, the practical joke' in favour of a tentative kind of affirmation.

Around this time, Ottoline Morrell, nominally reconciled to Huxley, wrote in her journal a kind of summing up of the writer in 1936: 'what I feel most clearly is that he is now singularly lacking in the imagination of the heart, which alone would enable him really to understand and enter into the lives of the human beings that he writes about. The tentacles of his intellect are incessantly at work collecting detached facts, collecting stories, scenes; he studies queer oddities and tricks of behaviour. He listens to conversations but he listens and looks as if he were looking and listening at the behaviour and jabber of apes. His attitude is always that of an onlooker, a sad disapproving onlooker, a scientific student of human behaviour.'[14] She went on to accuse him of having 'a very limited capacity for admiration' and speculated that his peace campaigning would suffer from 'his want of warmth and passion and humour'. This is a harsh portrait – which goes on to blame Maria for abusing her position as his eyes and ears to attract to them 'the rather degenerate cosmopolitans who collect like bluebottles round any successful literary man'. One senses that there is some unresolved personal matter here, particularly when Maria is brought into the argument. And Ottoline has clearly not appreciated the extent to which Huxley was changing – though she does conclude by saying that has 'a gentle, tender and unself-seeking nature' that might 'give him courage to know himself, to cast aside his superiority and revalue his burden of knowledge, and to conquer contempt by compassion'.

In April the Huxleys had moved back to Sanary, having sublet the Albany flat (Harold Raymond found 'a gentleman from Bermuda' interested in taking the lease but Huxley doubted 'whether the Secretary of the Albany would permit the letting of the flat to a coloured person'[15]). In Paris on the way to Sanary Huxley had met 'an intelligent representative of the Left'[16] who told him that the French were unlikely to adopt total pacifism. 'I suppose this is due to the fact that they have had no Quaker tradition preparing the ground for the idea.' Huxley was not wholly at ease in Sanary and, although the new book was selling well, he was rather short of funds. Not having supplied a novel for four years he was in Chatto's debt. His publishers, however, were pleased with the sales. The subscription sale of 7000 was bigger than for any previous title of his and by the end of June sales had reached 10,000. Foyle's bookshop in London had made it their monthly 'Choice' but, sending Maria a batch of reviews which she knew Aldous would not read, Harold Raymond observed: 'Reviews on the whole are displaying English reviewing at its most pitiable.'[17]

From Sanary, Huxley continued to be involved in the Peace Pledge Movement. He was chairman and Gerald Heard was vice-chairman of the splendidly appropriate Research and Thinking Committee. But Maria noticed Aldous was restless and dissatisfied: 'There's no doubt that he would sell up at the first possible opportunity. Although he is happy and in good spirits I sometimes get the impression that he is bored. He wouldn't say so at any cost nor would he admit it to himself but I am convinced. He isn't even interested in his painting any more.'[18] He was supplementing his Alexander technique and yoga-based methods of meditation now with an examination of Catholic thinking on prayer. He had read a book by a priest, Father Bede Frost, called *The Art of Mental Prayer* and recommended it to T.S. Eliot while agreeing with him that meditation needed to have 'a metaphysical or theological background'.[19] He went to Pontigny to meet a group of thinkers who had formed themselves into a group called the Centre Polytechnique des Études Économiques who were becoming 'unofficially the brain trust of the Blum government'.[20] Huxley was drawn, for the rest of his life, to men and women of this kind – social psychologists, scientists, engineers, sociologists, biologists, economists – experts in all aspects of human society who seemed more attractive to him than the people to be found in literary circles. They were also practically engaged with social problems: his Olympian intellectualism was over and from now on he would recognise that the contribution of the intellectual to society is in collaboration with existing know-how rather than in a speculation that risks becoming self-indulgent. He was proposing, in collaboration with Gerald Heard, to produce 'a kind of synthesis, starting from a metaphysical basis and building up through individual and group psychology to politics and economics . . . a synthesis for human beings, not a synthesis à la mode de Berlin, Rome or Moscow.'[21]

But all this purposeful activity didn't mean that his anxiety about the political situation lessened. The prospects for Europe in 1936 seemed to him 'worse than ever'.[22] France was in 'a very uneasy, disquieted state . . . There might so easily, I think, be a bad financial panic resulting in chaos and a violent reaction from the Right.'[23] Maria, however, was enchanted by the summer bathing and the peacefulness of Sanary. 'We are enjoying it all with added intensity, in comparison to those long, London months.'[24] And so, throughout the summer they enjoyed Sanary – it was to be their last summer there – while Aldous exchanged letters with the leaders of the PPU. These showed a shrewd understanding of tactics – as when he suggested getting round a boycott of a congress on peace in Brussels (brought about by its insistence on collective armed security) by going as a delegate from a movement called 'For Intellectual Liberty' which would enable him to observe what was going on without compromising the PPU. After Brussels, he went to Holland and thence to London where he and Matthew were living in a hotel in Mount Royal, waiting for the Albany tenant to go at the end of September. Maria was left behind at Sanary where she started to sort things out, feeling in her bones that they were about to sell the house. She joined them in London in September, slightly anxious about the cost of the rooms, in part because they had been spending a fortune on doctors.

One of Huxley's tasks at Mount Royal was to write the introduction to a selection of his writings for the Everyman Library. As usual he explained his reasons for writing in very plain terms: 'In the present volume are assembled certain fragments of the books, the all too numerous books, which I have written because I wanted to, because the wolf was at the door and I had to, because the composition of them was a form of self-exploration and self-education, and because I had things to say which I wanted to read. The writing of these books was a pleasant process.'[25] In the event the Huxleys never did get back into the Albany and stayed at Mount Royal until the following March. But at Christmas they returned briefly to Sanary. 'All good wishes for the New Year,' Huxley saluted Lord Ponsonby from La Gorguette, 'tho' the prospects for 1937 look, I must confess, worse than ever.'[26] December also saw the publication of his latest essay collection, *The*

Olive Tree, which gathered up various literary essays – the lecture on his grandfather, the essay on Lawrence – together with more general pieces, several of which display the signs of his new-found commitment. There are frequent excoriations of nationalism and militarism and the dangers of political monomania. He cherishes his status as a freelance intellectual, expressing his horror in 'Literature and Examinations' that he might be studied. The teaching of literature, he believed, often falls into 'grotesque absurdity' and consists of 'the repetition of the *mantras* of fashionable critics'. He lashed out at English snobbery which leads people to 'listen to the privileged class congratulating itself'.

Perhaps the most attractive essay is the title essay, 'The Olive Tree', for it celebrates that love of the Mediterranean which was felt both by Aldous and Maria and which, poignantly, they were about to leave behind, having spent large parts of the last two decades in Tuscany and Provence. He argues that the tree has always been an object of worship and the olive tree in particular is associated with peace and olive oil with joy. Noting that the English are 'essentially mongrels' he judges that: 'Our Saxon and Celtic flesh requires to be constantly rewedded to the Latin spirit . . . the olive tree is, so to speak, the complement of the oak.' English to the core – and never more so than when in the United States – Huxley was ever open to the 'sun-lit clarity' of the south. 'If I could paint and had the necessary time, I should devote myself for a few years to making pictures only of olive trees.' But that was not to be. Already he was making preparations to leave. In October he had been planning a trip to the USA, envisaging a trip of about nine months. He wanted Matthew to enrol as a pre-medical student at Duke University where J.B. Rhine had his Parapsychology Laboratory, which had aroused the interest of both Huxley and Heard. By February 1937 plans were firming up and Huxley was outlining his itinerary to Eugene Saxton at Harper's and 'greatly looking forward' to exploring America. Should he buy a second hand Ford or 'some larger and more majestic vehicle'?[27]

On 19 February, the Huxleys left the house at Sanary for ever. Maria, in particular, was deeply moved by the idea of leaving. She wrote to Ottoline Morrell: 'No country will ever be like this or the

Tuscan hills; with their terraced olives, the vine and cypress at each house . . . Which does not mean that I am not looking forward to our future wanderings.'[28] To Mary, she confessed, on the day that the trunks were shipped off to America from Sanary, that the Mediterranean landscape was 'irreplaceable in my heart'.[29] Huxley himself was preoccupied both with a projected *Enyclopaedia of Pacifism* which he was editing and with preparation of a much larger work that would elucidate his current intellectual obsession – the relationship between *Ends and Means*. He told Dick Sheppard that the latter would be a book 'on the means for realizing desirable changes – such as peace, social justice etc. Reformers ordinarily oversimplify to such an extent; reducing everything to one cause, they think that one reform, or a series of reforms of one type, will remove the cause and lead to desirable change. Whereas it's obvious that there is multiple causation and must therefore be a multiplicity of means for making the desirable changes.'[30] The Huxleys left Sanary and made their way to London via Paris where Aldous started to have teeth problems, which produced an inflammation of the sinus. This involved a visit to hospital to remove the tooth and a miserable Easter in consequence, the only good news being the lifting of the ban on *Brave New World* in Australia which meant a great deal of gratuitous publicity.

On 7 April, after a brief stay in London at the Mount Royal Hotel to tie up loose ends, the Huxleys set sail on the SS *Normandie* for New York in the company of Gerald Heard and his partner Christopher Wood. Just before leaving, Maria wrote a letter to her sister Jeanne which tried to express her mixed feelings about going. If she were alone, she said, she would not go, but she wasn't, and it was 'quite pointless to stay and to risk so much when we are among the few people who have the freedom to be able to escape'.[31] An ambiguous comment that might suggest that the Huxleys sensed a coming catastrophe in Europe and were in part fleeing it – but there is no other evidence that this was in their mind. In spite of having burned their boats at Sanary, the Huxleys were convinced that this was just another bout of wandering, to lecture and to explore, from which they would return probably at the end of the year. There is no sense that they knew that their sojourn in the United States would turn out to be for ever.

Notes

1 Reading, Letter to Harold Raymond, 3 January 1936
2 *L.*400
3 *L.*401
4 'A Horrible Dilemma', *Time and Tide*, 14 March 1936. *Hidden Huxley*, p213
5 RL, Letter from Maria Huxley to Jeanne Neveux. Undated but probably March 1936. Author's translation of 'la basse homosexualité de Nottingham'
6 *What Are You Going to Do About It?* (1936)
7 C. Day Lewis, *We're Not Going to Do Nothing* (1936) *Left Review*
8 Stephen Spender, 'Open Letter to Aldous Huxley', *Left Review*, June 1936
9 George Woodcock, *Dawn and the Darkest Hour: A Study of Aldous Huxley* (1972), p16
10 L.408
11 HRC, Letter to Mrs Kethevan Roberts, 30 July 1936
12 *L.*340
13 *L.*409
14 *Ottoline at Garsington,* p220
15 Reading, Letter to Harold Raymond, 3 January 1936
16 Lambeth Palace, Letter to Dick Sheppard, 6 May 1936
17 Reading, Letter from Harold Raymond to Maria Huxley, 18 June 1936
18 RL, Letter from Maria Huxley to Jeanne Neveux, 19 June 1936. Author's translation
19 *L.*405
20 *L.*407
21 *L.*408
22 *L.*407
23 Lambeth Palace, Letter to Dick Sheppard, 21 June 1936
24 Reading, Letter from Maria Huxley to Harold Raymond, 30 June 1936
25 Eton College, Draft of 'Writers and Readers', enclosed in letter to John Hadfield, 17 November 1936
26 Bodleian, Letter to Lord Ponsonby, 30 December 1936
27 *L.*413
28 HRC, Letter from Maria Huxley to Ottoline Morrell, 25 January 1937
29 HRC, Letter from Maria Huxley to Mary Hutchinson, undated but probably mid-February 1937
30 Lambeth Palace, Letter to Dick Sheppard, 7 February 1937
31 RL, Letter from Maria Huxley to Jeanne Neveux, March 1937. Author's translation

XXV

America

On the SS *Normandie*, as it steamed across the Atlantic, the Huxleys received, on 10 April 1937, a visit in tourist class from one of the literary Germans from Sanary, Thomas Mann. He took tea with them in the salon and later joined them in the ship's cinema, but told his diary later: 'Handicapped by the language.'[1] On arrival, New York struck them with its 'extraordinary beauty'[2] as Maria put it to Jeanne. They stayed briefly at a house in Rhinebeck, NY owned by their old Sanary friend, William Seabrook, the spot to which they would return at the end of the year. 'You can't believe how famous Aldous is here,' Maria reported. He was besieged by radio stations seeking interviews. Maria was still sniffy about the supposed lack of sophistication of the population but bowled over by the beauty of New York State. She admitted to Jeanne that they were pining 'pour notre Europe', but welcoming 'the distance from insoluble political problems'. She urged her sister and her daughter Sophie, as she would do again and again to other family members over the next few years: 'Risque tout et viens ici.' As soon as they could they bought their Ford (the famous Bugatti had been given away to the Kislings at Sanary) and set off – Aldous, Maria, Matthew and Gerald Heard – with Maria at the wheel. They were to spend five weeks on the road, driving through Virginia, Georgia, Florida, Louisiana, Texas to arrive at Frieda

Lawrence's ranch at San Cristobal in the mountains of New Mexico in
May. Exhausted by the driving, Maria had lost weight, discovering on
a Taos drugstore weighing machine that she was down to ninety-
eight pounds. On the way they had visited various universities at
Charlottesville, Black Mountain College, Duke, Dillard, New Orleans
and Knoxville. The last stretch across Texas was a thousand miles of
desert 'with a heat-wave in full blast & wind whirling the dust into the
air in huge grey spirals'[3] to Taos where Huxley was 'rather relieved to
be sitting still. I am starting to work again on the sociological book &
hope to get it done by the end of the summer.'

They had a log cabin on Frieda Lawrence's ranch, nearly nine
thousand feet above seal level among woods with the desert below:
'sage-brush green . . . with the canyon of the Rio Grande running
through the midst and the blue mountains beyond. The sky is full of
enormous dramas of cloud and sunshine – with periodical thun-
derstorms of incredible violence. Boiling hot sunshine alternates
with cold shade and icy nights.'[4] The nearest town to the San
Cristobal ranch was Taos, twenty miles away, so in spite of the unwelcome presence of artists – almost as bad as being surrounded by
writers – they felt well removed from civilisation. Huxley considered he had never been anywhere before so hostile to man: 'Humans
crawl about this savage, empty vastness like irrelevant ticks.' Maria
was making the best of it, as she explained to Edward Sackville-West
who was staying at the house at Sanary: 'no servants whatsoever',[5]
being her main gripe. She made the same complaint to Charles
Noailles in Sanary: 'It started by being so hard that I thought it would
have to be given up . . . I know that I shall be homesick for my
Mediterranean shores with the olives, the terraces and the signs of life
with every cypress.'[6] To Ottoline, although still agitated by the
absence of servants and the need to do housework, Maria was a little
more optimistic: 'we go for long walks, puffing up the hills, then sitting to puff more and pick some strawberries and Aldous may draw
the desert or the clouds'.[7]

Aldous worked in his bedroom which communicated with hers
through an arch, or in a little hut outside, and Matthew slept in the sit-
ting-room from which steps descended to a tiny kitchen. They had to

build on a bathroom themselves, a task made lighter by Matthew's skills. Gerald Heard had a little hut on the other side of a stream. There was hot water from butane gas and a wood-burning range to cook on. Aldous, taken with this primitivism, even made some bread, full of cornflour and treacle and spices, which turned out (more or less) eatable. The ranch's inhabitants included the redoubtable Frieda, her lover Captain Angiolini Ravagli, and Brett (their old friend from Garsington who had not been on speaking terms with Frieda since she tried, with Mabel Luhan, to steal Lawrence's ashes from the cement chapel built by Ravagli. The plan was to scatter them over the ranch in the belief that this was Lawrence's true wish). Brett, Huxley reported, was: 'Deafer and odder than ever, in a Mexican 10-gallon hat, with a turkey's feather stuck in it, sky-blue breeks, top boots and a strong American accent.'[8]

In this setting of striking natural scenery and human eccentricity, Huxley settled down for the summer to write his 'philosophico-psychologico-sociological'[9] book, *Ends and Means*. In July his *Encylopaedia of Pacifism* was published by Chatto in England as a sixpenny pamphlet. It is not clear how much of this was written by Huxley himself as editor. Certainly it summed up his beliefs about nationalism being an 'idolatry' and a 'religion of war'. It repudiated theories of racial superiority, reminding the British that they were formed from 'scores of immigrant waves'. And it declared: 'We are living in critical days. It is not enough to desire peace or to talk peace. We must make a personal decision and live peace.' For Huxley the personal was the political. The entry on 'class war' observes: 'The pacifist's sympathy is naturally with the exploited and the downtrodden. The spirit of the class war and particularly any recourse to violence in the furthering of it are, however, anathema to him.' The *Left Review* was planning to publish a pamphlet, *Authors Take Sides on the Spanish War* (1937), and Huxley was one of the writers whose views were solicited. He told them that he was 'of course' on the side of the Government and against Franco in the Spanish civil war. Like Orwell he preferred the Anarchists ('Much more likely to lead to desirable social change') to the Communists but insisted that violence was no solution. 'The choice now is between militarism and pacifism. To me, the necessity of pacifism seems absolutely clear.'[10] This would be another nail in his coffin as far as Day Lewis, Spender and others were concerned.

Another body that was taking an interest in the pamphlet was the Federal Bureau of Investigation – although they didn't catch up with it until February 1938 when a memo to the director of the FBI headed 'Subversive Activities – General' mentioned Huxley as the author of the *Encyclopaedia*. The spooks were not well-informed enough to know about Huxley's repudiation of Communism but they didn't like the company he was keeping. They ordered a copy. The FBI file on Huxley – declassified in 1984 under Freedom of Information Laws – was kept up throughout his life but in spite of its bulk it is light on evidence. A few months before he died it was reported that Forest Hills High School in Michigan was using *Brave New World* for classroom study and a complainant to the FBI said the book was 'controversial in nature and not a fit subject for high school study'. The Forest Hills Schools Board ordered the book to be banned from the school but when it was discovered that most of them had not read it the decision was reversed. The complainant said that pupils were coming home from school 'with a softened attitude towards Communism'.[11]

It was while he was finishing *Ends and Means* at San Cristobal that Huxley was approached by a Los Angeles bookseller and dealer in manuscripts, Jake Zeitlin, regarding the handling of his work for the movies. Zeitlin came to the ranch in August to discuss the possibility of turning novels like *Antic Hay* ('there is good comic material here'[12] Huxley had told him) and 'The Giaconda Smile' into film scripts. Huxley admitted that *Point Counter Point* and *Eyeless in Gaza* were 'probably a bit long and complicated' to be Hollywood material. The rights to *Brave New World* had been sold off cheap by his incompetent (and, it turned out, crooked) agent, Pinker.

On the face of it this was extraordinary. Throughout the 1920s and 1930s Huxley had fulminated against the new forms of mass entertainment – most memorably in the account of his visit to *The Jazz Singer* in Paris in 1929. He felt that these were 'creation-saving' forms that deprived people of their creativity and made them passive consumers not active participants in art. Yet he was now actively seeking to enter the world of the movies. He told Zeitlin that he might be staying in the USA at the start of the New Year after his lecture tour was completed, and asked him to make some 'tactful enquiries' about the possibility of 'doing work for the films'.[13] As the summer wore on, Huxley was softening both to the idea of the cinema and to America itself – a country which, up until now, he had excoriated as vigorously as he had its mass entertainments. In a letter to Clive Bell consoling him for the death of Julian Bell in Spain he wrote: 'You would find a great deal to astonish, interest, and amuse you in the various parts of the country. I had no idea, till this summer, of the depths of its strangeness.'[14] The new book, meanwhile, was being typed up by Maria, who felt that it was possibly the best thing he had ever done 'spiritually'.[15] She saw it as: 'In essence a practical continuation of *Eyeless*.' She was nonetheless approving of the idea of working in the movies: 'The money would be useful.' *Ends and Means* appeared in November (once again the interval between completing a manuscript and publication astonishes). The new book, he told his friend Koteliansky, was 'rather an important book discussing the sort of things we shall have to do if we want to make the improvements in the world that we all profess to desire. It covers all the ground from politics to philosophy.'[16]

Ends and Means: An Enquiry into the Nature of Ideals and into the Methods Employed for their Realization, became one of Huxley's best-selling books. It was just what he said it was: a comprehensive exploration of how to achieve the desirable ends, 'the ideal goal of human effort ... liberty, peace, justice and brotherly love' that he claimed all ages had identified in the same way. The problem was not the ends but the means, about which there was 'utter confusion'. And far from progress being made in the modern world there was regress – towards 'organized lying' (propaganda) and 'regression in charity'. In particular: 'Technological progress has merely provided us with more efficient means for going backwards.' In 1937, long before the awakening of green movements on the modern scale, Huxley – in spite of his commitment to science – was prepared to question the belief that applied science could address all human problems without negative consequences. This was not then, as it is now, a commonplace. The book begins with a discussion of the nature of explanation which concludes that 'causation in human affairs is multiple – in other words, that any given event has many causes'. This was Huxley's central belief: 'there can be no single sovereign cure for the diseases of the body politic'. The next section of the book was what he called 'a kind of practical cookery book of reform' across a range of issues, and the final section discussed the big questions about: 'What is the sense and point of the whole affair?' He dismissed the idea that the practical reformer could do without such thinking because: 'So far from being irrelevant, our metaphysical beliefs are the finally determining factor in all our actions.' The book had excellent reviews and was an immediate success with 6000 copies sold in the first three weeks in the UK.

No sooner had the book been published than Huxley and Gerald Heard set off on a lecture tour of the States, expounding their gospel of peace. 'Gerald and I are giving a series of duologue lectures this autumn – in a sort of Mutt and Jeff, Harry Tate-cum-Boys manner'.[17] he had told Harold Raymond. In September the Huxleys and Heard had driven in the Ford to Los Angeles – a city which Maria compared to 'a permanent International Exhibition'.[18] They found a flat at 1425½ North Crescent Heights Boulevard in West Hollywood. Matthew was now eighteen and in love with America. It seemed that his parents were beginning to follow his example. Maria had come to terms with 'the barbarousness' of having to live without servants and, having met so many interesting and pleasant people in Los Angeles, they were warming to it. 'We would not mind staying here a while,' she told Roy Fenton. She claimed now that Europe had become 'oppressive' to her just before they left, in spite of her nostalgia for cypress and olive grove. Maria told Jeanne that she could learn to love America but the heat and the endless driving were wearing her out. She was amazed, and rather shocked, when Aldous was offered $750 for a four minute radio interview. Very quickly the Huxleys met some very remarkable people. Edwin Hubble the astronomer and his wife Grace; Gary Cooper ('il a les plus beaux yeux et le plus charmant regard du monde'[19] Maria told Jeanne), Anita Loos, Charlie Chaplin and Paulette Goddard ('Yesterday we had a very *intellectual* dinner with Charlie Chaplin', Maria told Roy) and Upton Sinclair. Chaplin was in the habit of performing for his friends little scenes from his work-in-progress and the Huxleys watched in delight as he did 'a mimic of Mussolini making a speech', a foretaste of *The Great Dictator*. They found Chaplin a rather melancholy man, however, at this first meeting. Huxley later gave Mary Hutchinson a description of this first impact of Hollywood on them:

> Hollywood . . . with its fearful Jewish directors, and the
> actors, and the film writers, who make more money than
> any other kind of author and are generally speaking not
> authors at all. Our chief friends in that world were
> Charlie Chaplin and Anita Loos, both of whom are really
> very charming. We even had a glimpse of the ordinarily
> invisible Garbo, whom we met at Anita Loos's looking
> infinitely ninetyish and perverse, like an Aubrey
> Beardsley drawing dressed up, for added perversity, in a
> very sporty Lesbian tailor-made. Not that she is
> exclusively a Lesb. Rather omnifutuent – her present
> boyfriend being Stokowski the conductor.[20]

Huxley himself received his first offer to become one of those wealthy writers: for an adaptation of the *Forsyte Saga*: 'but tho' I might have earned vast sums in the process, the prospect of living for several months with the ghost of poor John Galsworthy was too formidable. I simply wouldn't face it!' There was, however, the possibility of a film script of his own, which Zeitlin was trying to put around the studios. Huxley's treatment for *Success*, for many years thought to have been lost, is now in the collections of Stanford University. Unusually for Huxley it has a clear and straightforward plot – an advertising executive offers a bet that he can make an obscure sausage manufacturer into a world-famous producer of sausages by the power of advertising propaganda alone. It is a script whose themes are very Huxleyan – the iniquity of advertising and propaganda, the hollowness of material success – and even contains a character who is a young playwright dreaming of success and riches like the author himself. There is also some rather unsophisticated social comedy. He had clearly thought about the filmic treatment and there are 'cinematic' moments, as when human crowds dissolve into a shot of pigs being herded to slaughter, but the script never excited any interest. The overarching irony of the script – that its author was angling for success of his own – lends the whole thing a certain piquancy. Huxley had not yet met the Marx brothers, who would become, especially Harpo, a part of his circle. They might have been able to inject sufficient madness into this to make it work – or perhaps the Woody Allen of *Small Time Crooks* could do something with it.

It is clear from a comment to Mary Hutchinson that Huxley was now changing his view of America. He told her that after the lecturing was finished in early 1938: 'I expect we shall be setting out for Europe; unless by any miracle the movie people wished to make use of a comic scenario I wrote while at Hollywood.'[21] Having intended this as a brief holiday from Europe, the Huxleys were now prepared to consider staying on permanently, especially if *Success* turned into a success. Meanwhile they went on with their exploration of the new world. They visited the only chinchilla farm in the world and saw a Mickey Mouse film being made and oil being drilled and visited a private collection of modern French art 'in the house of a nice mad-man'. They were dazzled but also exhausted by all the endless talk and bustle. It was in the summer of 1937 that Grace Hubble started to record in her journal some of these social occasions at which the Huxleys and the Hollywood stars were present. Within their limitations (there are many gaps) her unpublished journals make her into a sort of minor and occasional Californian Boswell, presenting scenes and sayings of Huxley in the early Californian years. The first relevant entry records Huxley and Heard before setting out to lecture, the latter saying 'Western Europe dying, America must carry the torch. Dubious outlook for the torch.'[22] This was presumably the message they took around America.

'When the time came for Aldous and Gerald to go off together it was cool in the early morning and they went in leather coats, small grey hats and an umbrella. So I laughed and felt just a bit lonely at being left by both at the same time,'[23] Maria told Mary. Huxley hated lecturing – for which he had no natural gift – and especially hated having to say the same things over and over again. What made matters worse was Heard's fall in the snow in Iowa at the end of November (he broke his arm just below the left shoulder and went to a doctor friend in Huntington, Indiana to recuperate) which left Huxley to carry on single-handed, well into the New Year. 'It was more tolerable when we were two and could throw the ball back and forth in a lively discussion,'[24] he told Julian. While Aldous was away lecturing across this winter (Baltimore, Philadelphia, Washington etc), Maria was installed once more in Rhinebeck, NY in a pastoral-sounding address, Dairy Cottage, Foxhollow Farm on the old Dows estate owned by J.J. Astor at Rhinebeck. She had driven on her own all the way from California. She could be near the Seabrooks at this address, which they kept until February 1938. Huxley adored the wooded beauty and the nearby Hudson River and the bright, cold blue days. Maria was slightly less enamoured of the house: 'The place is rather like an ugly old English cottage as compared to the exquisite old little houses which fill this country, but it is warm and comfortable and roomy and only 98 miles from New York.'[25] It was here one December morning that a telegram arrived from Zeitlin: 'MGM INTENSELY INTERESTED IN YOUR STORY NOW ENTITLED SUCCESS WILL HAVE DECISION IN FOUR OR FIVE DAYS.'[26] This turned out to be a false dawn, however, and Huxley ploughed on with his lecturing. Maria wrote to Ottoline that in spite of there being much about American life that was 'alien' to them: 'the whole past months have been a continual *adventure*. There is no other word for the amazement with which we discovered this continent and its people'.[27] As the year drew to a close there seemed little doubt that the Huxleys would be staying for the time being in America. But it would have been unwise for such footloose people to predict at this stage that they would remain – in Maria's case until her death in 1955 and in Aldous's till his in 1963, twenty-five years later.

Notes

1   *The Diaries of Thomas Mann,* p275, 10 April 1937
2   RL, Letter from Maria Huxley to Jeanne Neveux, 30 April 1937. Author's translation

3 Reading, Letter to Harold Raymond, 21 May 1937
4 *L*.421
5 *SB*1.345 quoting letter from Maria Huxley to Edward Sackville-West, 23 June 1937
6 HRC, Copy of letter from Maria Huxley to Charles Noailles, 25 June 1937. Sybille Bedford papers
7 HRC, Letter from Maria Huxley to Ottoline Morrell, 5 July 1937
8 *L*.422
9 *L*.417
10 *L*.423
11 Federal Bureau of Investigation. Freedom of Information/Privacy Acts Section. Subject: Aldous Huxley
12 *L*.423
13 *L*.424
14 King's College, Letter to Clive Bell, 7 August 1937
15 RL, Letter from Maria Huxley to Jeanne Neveux, 20 August 1937. Author's translation
16 BL, Letter to Samuel Koteliansky, 27 July 1937
17 Reading, Letter to Harold Raymond, 26 August 1937
18 *L*.426
19 RL, Letter from Maria Huxley to Jeanne Neveux, 11 October or November, 1937
20 HRC, Letter to Mary Hutchinson, 8 December 1937
21 HRC, Letter to Mary Hutchinson, 8 December 1937
22 HL, Hubble Diary, 3 August 1937
23 HRC, Letter from Maria Huxley to Mary Hutchinson, 15 December 1937
24 *L*.428
25 HRC, Letter from Maria Huxley to Mary Hutchinson, 15 December 1937
26 UCLA, Telegram from Jake Zeitlin to Huxley, 10 December 1937
27 HRC, Letter from Maria Huxley to Ottoline Morrell, 18 December 1937

XXVI

Hollywood

Early in 1938 the Huxleys returned to California, the lecture tour having concluded by the end of January. They had bought a new Ford car which they drove back via Colorado, where Matthew was at school, and New Mexico where they called in to visit Frieda Lawrence at the ranch. They arrived at Los Angeles on Friday 11 February and took a house at 1340 North Laurel Avenue. Huxley had taken ill on the journey, at Tucson, experiencing an attack of bronchial pneumonia that troubled him for most of the rest of the year. He had met several doctors and scientists already in the States (including, at Chicago, Dr William Sheldon whose classification of human beings into types so enthralled him) but now he was less the enquiring mind, more the patient. It wasn't really until April 1938 that Huxley was out of bed and active again. He was at work on a novel 'which threatens, if I am not careful, to turn into the *Comédie Humaine*'[1] but which was destined never to be finished. He was also 'collecting whatever information I can pick up in regard to the technique for giving a viable economic and social basis to philosophic anarchism'.[2] The film scenario was getting nowhere because 'the whole picture industry is in a state of neurasthenia and panic, and it's impossible for anyone to make any decision'. The news from Europe was also depressing for someone who desired peace. Its opposite seemed more and more likely.

At home the Huxleys lived their usual quiet life – in spite of their small but glittering circle of acquaintances in Hollywood. Maria, for the benefit of Jeanne, described their daily routine at North Laurel Avenue. In the morning they both rose early. Maria made the beds and cleaned the apartment which was brand new with new carpets and waxed parquet flooring. Then she went out shopping in her large Mexican hat. A maid called Hazel arrived at 1.30 to cook lunch. Leaving her to clean, they went out for a walk in the hills between lunch and tea. At 7.30 they took their baths and at 8.30 ate: 'Then Aldous goes to bed and we read Herodotus for a long time. As you can see, I live the life of a princess.'[3] Aldous was in such good spirits – after weeks of illness when he couldn't sleep and when she read to him endlessly (skipping what she judged to be the cruder passages in Aretino) – that when she went in with his early morning tea 'he smiles so lazily in waking up that I cannot believe it possible'. But the sense of impending crisis in Europe haunted them. Gerald Heard told them that what was happening in Austria – the persecution of the Jewish population – was entering into their subconscious and Maria told Jeanne that she felt 'so French' that she felt a draw to go over there until the crisis was over: 'which is crazy'. In another letter she told Jeanne of their 'anxiety and horror' about the Austrian persecutions: 'But here we are so far away.'[4] There seems no justification for the view that Huxley had smugly insulated himself from the coming crisis in Europe.

The Hubbles became regular visitors and Grace watched Huxley asking Edwin questions about astronomy: 'He had left off his glasses and his eyes had a tragic, blinded look and his face without the glasses was quite beautiful, and youthful looking, very white, the mouth large and sensitive, the mass of dark, thick hair, he and Edwin talking together, would have given a painter a chance . . . Aldous like a blasted angel, in a place that is somehow wrong . . . They like America better than they did.'[5] But they were still learning to understand it. At one of the first lunches where Huxley met Harpo Marx he was full of ideas for movies and suggested the Marx brothers make a film about Marx with Groucho as Karl Marx, Chico as Bakunin, and Harpo as Engels. Harpo hadn't realised Huxley was being facetious in the Anglo-Saxon manner and told him seriously that such a movie could not be made in this town.[6] Huxley had another idea for a film about astronomy in which the audience would find themselves looking into the 100-inch telescope and seeing Harpo's face.[7] On another evening at Harpo Marx's the dinner developed a mad surrealist Marx Brothers quality. Someone upset a plate of canapés, then Huxley, not being able to see clearly, put his hand deep into a platter of fish and mayonnaise, and all through the meal the sound of dishes being broken and smashed came from the direction of the kitchen.[8]

Another important friend of the Huxleys throughout their American years was Anita Loos, who smoothed Huxley's way into the film studios and offered to be his protector there. They were frequent visitors to her beautiful house on the sea 'which reminded me of mine at Sanary,' Maria told Jeanne, 'but grander and with Chinese servants, one of whom is the best cook I know. It is a pleasure to go to her house as if we were part of the family.'[9] One day they went walking on the beach with Thomas Mann and his wife, Katia. Maria pointed out the litter of white objects on the beach, which turned out to be condoms. The incident would turn up in an essay by Huxley, 'Hyperion to a Satyr' in *Adonis and the Alphabet* (1956). Something of Huxley's conversational subject matter and his trenchant judgement comes out in Grace Hubble's reports of these evenings in Los Angeles during the Huxleys' first year in America. He conceded that James Joyce wrote well – 'even his unintelligible things read musically' – but Gertrude Stein 'had no ear'.[10] Ronald Knox was the most brilliantly precocious boy he had known at Eton and Oxford but T.S. Eliot 'didn't know nearly as much as he pretended, with his literary allusions and his pompously serious essays'. Ezra Pound was another questionable scholar, 'an impostor'.[11] He talked also of Noel Coward in 'a high voice that breaks and is colourful – expressing shades of amusement' and concluded that Coward's plays were 'strangely successful' given that they were whipped up 'like a soufflé in a vacuum'.[12]

At one lunch in June 1938 Huxley and Heard started talking about Krishnamurti and the Theosophical Society. Under Heard's influence Huxley was beginning to take a serious interest in what he had mocked as a young writer, 'the wisdom of the East'. Grace Hubble, the scientist's wife was not impressed: 'Aldous and Gerald seem to me, in this pursuit of religion, like two small boys working over a conjuror's box of parlour tricks. No, that isn't quite it, they are looking for magic and power, for the secret words, the open sesame that rolls back the door. It is not religion, it is magic. Aldous, like D.H. Lawrence, has no great love for his fellow-man and he has a lot of rancour to get out of his system, also like D.H. Lawrence. He is somehow cold-blooded. He has read too much.'[13] At another dinner he talked about the ability of owls to detect infra-red waves in the dark to locate their prey by their heat: 'I think that is so-o-o [rising] lovely.'[14] He was excited too by Edwin Hubble's telescope. One lunchtime he arrived 'full of happy interest, smelling flowers and staring into things with his nose against them'. Gazing at the great device, he announced: 'Look at the pilasters and fluting. It is Roman, it is like the tomb of a great queen.'[15]

The oddities and quirks of scientific knowledge, particularly zoological rare knowledge, were the staple of Huxley's dinner-table conversation. Huxley and Heard – who were now seeing a lot of each other, swapping intellectual ideas, and energising each other – are glimpsed at the Hubbles' table, 'singing uninterruptedly like birds in an aviary' of mystical knowledge and the thinkers of that tradition. Maria, 'in gray slacks, sandals, red socks and short leopard-skin coat' and 'looking like a very thin mouse, but quite sweet'[16] watched the chattering pair. And then a new topic of conversation arose. Huxley had managed to secure a contract from MGM to write a screenplay for a biopic of Madame Curie. It would be directed by George Cukor with Garbo in the title role. He had put the idea to Anita Loos in May and the MGM screenwriter Salka Viertel had already suggested it to Garbo who was enthusiastic. According to those who have studied Huxley's screenplays this was not a bad effort for a beginner. 'Surprisingly, it was rather good,' thinks Virginia Clark, author of *Huxley and Film* (1987). But in spite of being highly remunerative (in the end Huxley pocketed $15,000) his script was thrown away and when the film was eventually made in 1943 (with Greer Garson not Garbo in the lead) Huxley's name was nowhere on the credits. He told Julian that he wasn't sure whether this activity was for him, 'since this telling of the story in purely pictorial terms doesn't allow of any of the experimentation with words in their relation to things, events and ideas, which is *au fond* my business'.[17]

Huxley was required initially to spend eight weeks at the studios on the script which meant he had to repulse an offer from Dr George Bell, Bishop of Chichester, to join a hand-picked group of eminent people (Anthony Eden, Sir Francis Younghusband) for a weekend in Chichester examining 'the connection between the spiritual view of life and the application of that view to concrete conditions of the present day'. The angry young man of the 1920s was now being courted by bishops for his views on the means whereby the Church of England could 'be more closely related to life', which is a measure of how far his spiritual 'conversion' had been recognised. He wrote back to Bishop Bell that he could not take part because he was 'trying to get the life of Mme Curie made into a film with the minimum of distraction and vulgarisation'.[18]

In July the Huxleys moved from North Laurel Avenue to a house in North Linden Drive, Beverly Hills for the summer. In August they drove up the coast to see about putting Matthew into Berkeley. Maria told Grace Hubble that she was not very keen on sewing name-tags into her son's clothing: 'I always prefer gardening or electric repairing or fiddling with a carburettor to sewing.'[19] She made a confession to Jeanne, unjust to herself, that: 'things are difficult for Aldous. Left to himself he could very easily live permanently in a world of intellectual abstractions. Thanks to me he is constantly forced to confront the brutal naked reality of life.'[20] Though when they went out for a night with Chaplin to Chinatown (where the star was mobbed by the crowds) she was shocked by the stripper in a night club who 'left nothing to the imagination'.[21]

In September they moved again to 1320 North Crescent Heights Boulevard in Hollywood, awaiting news of the script. Huxley was learning how to be cynical, like everyone else, about the studios: 'After being extremely enthusiastic for a while, they seem now to have forgotten all about it like chimpanzees that concentrate with terrific intensity on something, then drop it and are totally unaware that it ever existed.'[22] He turned away and began to write the novel that would draw on his new knowledge of Hollywood and the life of

Southern California, *After Many A Summer*. The political situation, and the absence of any positive political signs of improvement, the 'progressive deterioration of the remaining islands and oases of decency'[23] were depressing him (quite apart from the continual ill-health that dogged him throughout 1938). More and more he was being drawn towards the consolations of religious philosophy: 'To find a psychology covering the whole range of human potentiality, not merely the range known to the homme moyen sensuel, one must study the religious philosophers.' Practical steps like joining public protests or writing letters to the press seemed to him inefficacious. Declining one such initiative from Jake Zeitlin, he told him: 'The persecution of the Jews in Germany is horrible in the extreme; but it is not by proclaiming the fact in a loud voice that this particular persecution will be stopped . . .'[24] It could not be stopped until 'the habits of thought feeling, action and belief' which created such evils were changed.

Changing those habits was increasingly to be Huxley's mission. Gerald Heard would be his abetter in this but Maria was occasionally frustrated by Heard's other-worldliness (refusing to own a car but expecting her to drive him around) and his criticising the Huxleys for seeing too many people of the wrong sort. Maria felt certain courtesies were owed but Aldous was not always keen on socialising, and put the burden onto her. On one occasion a distinguished liberal lawyer rang up asking them to supper. Huxley picked up the phone and said: 'Mrs Huxley is away. I do not know our engagements. She will let me know.'[25] Maria was effectively Aldous's secretary, the excuse she gave to Mary Hutchinson for not writing so frequently – 'do you remember the days when we exchanged endless letters and constantly . . .?'[26] She told Mary that the new house on North Crescent Heights Boulevard was 'the ugliest house probably in Hollywood. Ugly and comfortable . . . Furnished about twenty years ago by comfortable Jews . . . But the garden was planted even before that and it is delightful and very private and we love it . . . It has a terrace and Aldous worked outside until yesterday . . . Aldous is so much better . . . he still rests twelve hours a day . . . a night out is an event and as a result we enjoy it.' Maria added: 'We have made no new friends;

but we see the old ones quite regularly.' Anita Loos on Sunday was now 'an institution' and they met her once a week for lunch as well. The Chaplins were seen less frequently but they were very fond of the English actress Constance Collier who lived nearby. Maria said she often reminded her of Ottoline Morrell, whose death had been reported in April. Although they saw Ottoline rarely, 'she was an essential part of England for us; a solidity in England.' They had paid their first visit to a night club (though Maria had come home early at ten) but generally they went to bed early and read. 'We are alone nearly always.' It has often been assumed that the Huxleys enjoyed a glittering Hollywood life-style, seeing and knowing everyone, but the reality was quite different. Early nights with a book were much more the pattern than carousing with famous writers (few of whom in America Huxley met during his twenty five-year residence). It is true that the Huxley circle – Loos, Garbo, Harpo Marx, later Stravinsky, Isherwood – was far from lustreless but it was a small interior company, and the life was modest and fairly austere. Anita Loos wrote a reminiscence of one of the picnics that this small group took 'with *dramatis personae* so fantastic that they might have come out of *Alice in Wonderland*'.[27] Krishnamurti, Garbo (in male disguise), Paulette Goddard, Chaplin, and Isherwood were of the party which sat down in the sandy bottom of the Los Angeles river, ignoring a no trespassing sign. Soon, a sheriff armed with a gun turned up and the party, in spite of its celebrity cast, was unceremoniously moved on.

Huxley's energies in early 1939 were thrown into the new 'short phantasy, in the manner, more or less, of *Brave New World*'.[28] It would be finished by July when he would describe it as 'a kind of fantasy, at once comic and cautionary, farcical, blood-curdling and reflective'.[29] He was greatly encouraged, early in 1939, by the apparent improvement in his sight as a result of seeing Margaret Corbett, a disciple of Dr W.H. Bates, whose controversial method of exercising the eye Huxley would later write a short book about. In April the Huxleys moved yet again, to a furnished house at 701 South Amalfi Drive, Pacific Palisades. Garbo lived on the other side of the street. Maria called it 'a terrestrial Paradise . . . The house is crazy, ugly, full of frightful German and Chinese knick-knacks, with not many bedrooms, but, that rare thing in America and so important for us, it is spacious . . . more peaceful for Aldous.'[30] Anita Loos described its bizarre furnishings – a life-sized facsimile of King Kong, a stuffed crocodile, a hideous bar. Grace Hubble found it 'a rambling house, rambling garden above the canyon . . . We lunched in the garden . . . Bertrand Russell thin, old and ill-looking with flushed face.'[31] A month after moving in, Garbo arrived for dinner. 'She was ravishing.' Another regular guest was Salka Viertel, the Polish-born actress who ran a sort of salon at her home in Santa Monica Canyon, which brought together many of the highly talented European exiles. Maria loved her and told Jeanne that she was very 'us' because 'above all she is a European. She loves perfume and takes lovers.'[32] Her existence proved that 'Europeans can live in Hollywood while retaining their charm and their personality'. The names of the surrounding drives – Napoli, Corsica, Toulon – awakened Maria's nostalgia – 'names that make one melancholy for things we loved and have left' – but she told Grace Hubble that 'really California *is* still calmer and quieter. And it is beautiful and it has been kind and anyway we do like it.'[33]

The most important news, however, was that Aldous, on a visit to the oculist, had demonstrated near-normal vision: 'C'est un miracle, Janin!' Maria exclaimed to her sister. Huxley had told Harold Raymond, two months earlier, that the Bates exercises had raised his vision from fifteen per cent of normal to fifty per cent and further improvement was expected. 'I am already doing all my reading (as much as two hours a day or more) without glasses, which is rather remarkable.'[34] When he delivered the manuscript of *After Many A Summer* in August he claimed that: 'I wrote it and revised the script (always a very trying job) entirely without spectacles – a remarkable tribute to the efficacy of the eye-training I have been taking.'[35] He was, however, using a typewriter with a large typeface to make this assertion. In a long account of the details of the improvement sent to Julian, he claimed to be able to read the seventy-foot line on the oculist's chart at six feet and large nursery print at the near point. He claimed the scar-tissue was clearing up and hoped that the bad eye would get up to the level the good eye used to be at.[36] Meanwhile: 'We live very quietly, see a minimum of people.' Huxley was becoming very enthusiastic about linguistics and told Julian: 'There is no hope of thinking and acting rationally about any of the major issues of life until we learn to understand the instrument we use to think about them.' Huxley was seeking to understand language through the science of linguistics rather than through his own linguistic experiments.

In spite of Huxley's protestation that he lived a quiet life, there was a surprise lunch party at South Amalfi Drive on 30 July to celebrate his forty-fifth birthday. The guests included Helen Hayes, Charlie Chaplin and Paulette Goddard (who staggered in with a birthday cake from an English confectioner's weighing eight pounds, Charlie bearing a dozen bottles of Mumm champagne), Christopher Isherwood ('dark and slight'[37] – this was possibly the first time he met Huxley), Charles MacArthur, Gerald Heard, and Matthew. After lunch everyone sat under the eucalyptus tree. Then Orson Welles arrived. Then Lillian Gish. It was seven in the evening before all the lunch guests departed. Huxley clearly enjoyed all this, though that Sunday, coming away from Charlie Chaplin's where everyone had sat eating lunch in a crescent-shaped arbour by the swimming pool – and where he had confessed he didn't really like playwriting 'because he was too discursive and liked to ramble'[38] – he paused to look back at Chaplin's pile as he was leaving: 'Isn't it the ugliest house you ever saw?' he asked Grace Hubble. One of his last social engagements before the official declaration of war on 3 September was a dinner with the Hubbles. 'Aldous at dinner said, about the poetry of Auden, Spender, Day Lewis *et al* that he didn't like it and he thought the contemporary admiration of it was a curious passing phase, just a while ago Stephen Phillips was thought a great poet and dramatist.'[39] In the course of the past year, at dinner parties Huxley had rubbished all the leading poets of the day: Eliot, Pound, Auden and others. A week after war broke out a letter arrived from the *New Yorker* asking if he had any poems to offer the magazine. 'Alas,' he replied, 'I have not written any verse for a long while, as I find it a more-than-whole-time job which can't be combined with any other activity – and unfortunately I have been much involved in a variety of occupations.'[40] It is hard to think of a better summing up of Huxley's position at the start of the war.

Notes

1   *L*.432
2   *L*.434
3   RL, Letter from Maria Huxley to Jeanne Neveux, March 1938. Author's translation
4   RL, Letter from Maria Huxley to Jeanne Neveux, 15 March 1938. Author's translation
5   HL, Hubble Diary, 13 March 1938
6   HL, Hubble Diary, 11 June 1938
7   HL, Hubble Diary, 1 April 1938
8   HL, Hubble Diary, 5 June 1938
9   RL, Letter from Maria Huxley to Jeanne Neveux, 4 April 1938. Author's translation
10 HL, Hubble Diary, 1 April 1938
11 HL, Hubble Diary, 18 April 1938
12 HL, Hubble Diary, 17 May 1938
13 HL, Hubble Diary, 16 June 1938
14 HL, Hubble Diary, 5 July 1938
15 HL, Hubble Diary, 7 July 1938
16 HL, Hubble Diary, 29 November 1938
17 *L*.437
18 Lambeth Palace, Letter to Bishop Bell, 8 August 1938; Letter from Bishop Bell to Huxley, 26 July 1938
19 HL, Letter from Maria Huxley to Grace Hubble, 4 September 1938
20 RL, Letter from Maria Huxley to Jeanne Neveux, 27 September 1938. Author's translation
21 RL, Letter from Maria Huxley to Jeanne Neveux, 5 October 1938
22 HRC, Letter to J.B. Priestley, 21 October 1938
23 *L*.438
24 *L*.439
25 RL, Letter from Maria Huxley to Jeanne Neveux, 11 December 1938. The quotation is given by Maria in English
26 HRC, Letter from Maria Huxley to Mary Hutchinson, 15 December 1938
27 *Mem. Vol.*, pp91–3
28 *L*.440
29 *L*.441
30 RL, Letter from Maria Huxley to Jeanne Neveux, 3 April 1939. Author's translation
31 HL, Hubble Diary, 2 July 1939
32 RL, Letter from Maria Huxley to Jeanne Neveux, 31 July 1939. Author's translation

33 HL, Letter from Maria Huxley to Grace Hubble, 28 June 1939
34 Reading, Letter to Harold Raymond, 1 June 1939
35 Reading, Letter to Harold Raymond, 1 August 1939
36 L.442
37 HL, Hubble Diary, 30 July 1939
38 HL, Hubble Diary, 4 August 1939
39 HL, Hubble Diary, 23 August 1939
40 NYPL, Letter to C.A. Pearce, 16 September 1939

XXVII

Wartime

As 1939 drew to a close and England prepared for war, Huxley was settling down at MGM to write a script for *Pride and Prejudice*. 'I work away at the adaptation . . . for the moment – an odd crossword puzzle job,'[1] he told Eugene Saxton. 'One tries to do one's best for Jane Austen; but actually the very fact of transforming the book into a picture must necessarily alter its whole quality in a profound way.' Specifically, he felt, stressing the 'story' at the expense of the 'dilute irony in which the characters are bathed' was 'a major falsification of Miss Austen'. But this is how Hollywood works and Huxley was doing it, not for love of the art of the motion picture but for the cash, as he explained to his English publisher this time, Harold Raymond: 'The systems of production are such that it is hardly possible for a picture of this kind to be anything but frightful . . . However, the job pays well & permits one to help a few people involved in the nightmare in Europe.'[2] That help went mostly to Maria's family. Jeanne's daughter Sophie was the first to be helped, arriving from France in November. She lived with the Huxleys until 1944 and during the early part of the war they thought about formally adopting her.

As far as his own writing went, Huxley was offering Raymond either of two ideas for a new novel: 'a kind of experimental dissection of people & situations, pushed to the limits attainable through analysis of language [how Huxleyan!] or, alternatively, a kind of *Brave New World* describing a society better than the present, not worse.' It was to be more than twenty years before this project of a good utopia was finally realised with the publication of *Island* in 1961, two years before he died. But first, November would see the publication of his first novel since arriving in America, *After Many A Summer*. American editions would complete the Tennyson quotation by adding 'dies the swan' to the title. It has sometimes been suggested that Huxley's move to America – which is how his presence there should be regarded from late 1939 on, talk of return to Europe having fallen silent – coincided with his decline as a novelist. One doesn't have to endorse Christopher Isherwood's view – that Huxley actually wrote his best novels in America – in order to say that this is erroneous. It is true that there is a quality of zest and energy and satirical daring in those early English novels that was never quite recaptured. And even if either *Point Counter Point* or *Eyeless in Gaza* remains his most ambitious and successful novel (*Brave New World* existing in a category of its own) *After Many A Summer* turned out to be a witty, sunlit novel that was certainly not the work of a writer in decline. 'In some ways I think it is Aldous's best work: a superb mixture of excellent fooling and serious thought,' Harold Raymond wrote from Chatto in London to Eugene Saxton at Harper's in New York. 'I know no writer with the same power of mixing his ingredients.'[3] Although the English reviews were lukewarm it sold well and *Harper's Magazine* paid $2500 for the serialisation rights. There were worries about the similarities of the novel's plot to the real life affairs of William Randolph Hearst – his lover Marion Davies was thought to be hinted at in the name Dowlas, which was changed to Maunciple, and the shooting was reminiscent of real events, but no law suits were launched.

The novel opens with the arrival of the English writer, Jeremy Pordage, at the mock-mediaeval castle of the magnate, Mr Stoyte. The out-of-place literariness and old-world manners of Pordage inevitably make us think of Huxley. Pordage's new habit of 'deriving a curious wry pleasure from the recognition of his own shortcomings' may reflect Huxley's growing ease with himself in southern

California. He mocks Pordage's 'small, fluty voice, suggestive of even-song in an English cathedral' and there is a good comedy of manners in the Englishman arriving in America, a vein that Huxley would not be the last English novelist to exploit. Stoyte/Hearst is represented as emotionally infantile and paranoid and his mistress, Virginia Maunciple, as silly and vain as a character from *Gentlemen Prefer Blondes*. But the comedy soon starts to make way for the 'ideas', which are about the clash of the old world and the new, about the culture of modern mass entertainment, and programmes of social reform. The 'progressive' thinker, Mr Propter, who has more than a dash of Gerald Heard about him, sounds off about the need to escape from the bondage of personality, and about the shortcomings of conventional socialism for solving social problems. Propter dismisses conventional schemes of social improvement because they ignore the fact that 'Good is a matter of moral craftsmanship. It can't be produced except by individuals.' However perfect the social machinery nothing can be achieved without reforming the individual: 'No human society can become conspicuously better than it is now, unless it contains a fair proportion of individuals who know that their humanity isn't the last word and who consciously attempt to transcend it.' These are the ideas which Huxley and Heard were starting to explore around this time through various alternative communities in southern California. Pordage's work on the archives, the Hauberk Papers, which he has come to catalogue in the castle, takes him back to the world of the English eighteenth century and the Fifth Earl's researches into human longevity. The parody of Augustan prose recalls passages in *Crome Yellow*. Huxley's view of the pursuit of eternal life is Swiftian: the dream of living for ever is in fact a nightmare and the final discovery of the 201 year old Earl in the cellar of his English house – a 'foetal ape' – is both well told and unambiguous in its moral point of view. The visit to England in the final chapter makes its old-world deca-dence appear every bit as absurd as the Hollywood-mogul personal and architectural excesses of Stoyte.

Just before the novel was published, Maria told Jeanne: 'Aldous has no wish ever to go to England. He has almost a horror of it. In these circumstances Sanary no longer has any appeal for us. The climate here is good; the countryside is admirable. The people are welcoming. I think that we will stay in America and make it our permanent country.'[4] But not necessarily Los Angeles itself. They were toying with the idea of purchasing a twenty acre estate at Chatsworth in the San Gabriel Valley, the setting for Mr Stoyte's castle in the novel. 'It's the most beautiful spot we know.' But work at the studio and on other projects would keep them in the city for another two years or more. The tension that always existed in Huxley between retreat and social engagement was behind this desire to leave the city. The war was making things worse, making him turn in on himself to some degree. From his desk at MGM's Culver City studio he wrote a note to Zeitlin declining some unspecified commitment: 'I am at the studio all day and too much pre-occupied with the war and its implications to want to do anything at night but meditate in solitude.'[5] At Christmas, Gervas and Elspeth Huxley paid a brief visit to them at South Amalfi Drive and he approved of their plan to live in Kenya 'in a world you will be a little freer to remake according to the heart's desire than obsessed, hallucinated Europe can ever be'.[6]

Huxley's initial contract with MGM was for eight weeks but the slowness of the process on what the studios called 'Pee and Pee' meant he had to stay on at the studio on half-pay from February 1940 ready for revisions, though he spent as little time actually at the studios as possible, not liking the physical conditions of his office. In the same month he discovered from Harper's that he actually owed them money and found himself in a temporary financial crisis. The studios indicated that there would always be work for him there (he seemed to be proving competent at this 'jigsaw puzzle' craft of adaptation) but he wanted to get back to his other writing. 'The worst thing would be if he wrote just to make money,'[7] Maria told Jeanne. *Pride and Prejudice* was released by MGM in August 1940 with Greer Garson as Elizabeth Bennett and Laurence Olivier as Mr Darcy. The director was Robert Z. Leonard. Huxley's name was on the credits alongside Jane Murfin and the film was sumptuously produced and successful. MGM was happy with Huxley's contribution because, Maria told Jeanne, 'Aldous has learnt to do their kind of thing extremely well, as he does anything he really wants to do.'[8]

Anita Loos, who had found Huxley the job in the first place, and who continued to be a favourite neighbour at Santa Monica, later recalled that he had at first wanted to refuse the job because it was paying $2500 a week: 'I simply can't accept all that money to work in a pleasant studio while my family and friends are starving and being bombed in England.'[9] Anita told him this was nonsense because he could use the money to help those very people. Maria, who had been listening in to the conversation on the telephone extension, thanked Anita for her realism. Loos replied: 'The trouble with Aldous is that he is a genius who just once in a while isn't very smart.' The financial problem of early 1940 must have been very quickly resolved because Maria was telling Grace Hubble at the end of February: 'Aldous is very rich now.'[10] The Huxleys sent food parcels to Europe and continued to be anguished by the plight of those suffering. 'The accounts I get of London now have a strange similarity to those which Homer gives of Hades – a place of diminished life, of vagueness and uncertainty and sub-acute despair.'[11] He thought that after the war all the tyrannous forces he had been identifying in large scale organisation, in social and industrial planning, would be released, making impossible his ideal of a decentralised society.

Early in 1940 Huxley had lunch with Christopher Isherwood, whom he had first met the previous summer. Isherwood was also working at MGM and wrote in his diary: 'How kind, how shy he is – searching painfully through the darkness of this world's ignorance with his blind, mild, deep-sea eye. He has a pained, bewildered smile of despair at all human activity . . . He is still very much the prize-winning undergraduate, the nervous, fastidious, superintellectual boy. Stupidity afflicts him like a nasty smell – and how eagerly he sucks at the dry teats of books! I see how utterly he must depend on Maria, how blessed must be the relaxation in her thin Belgian arms – and I like them both, much better than before.'[12] The two writers saw a lot of each other during the writing of Pride and Prejudice. Huxley admitted to Isherwood his inability to make up plots and they discussed the possibilities of a mathematical formula for doing so. Huxley, needless to say, had heard of a Russian composer who had invented a machine for writing fugues. Isherwood felt an intellectual barbarian in Huxley's presence and thought: 'We get along best when gossiping.'[13] Isherwood also heard about the two rival plans for the next book project: a positive utopia and an ambitious 'philosophical Summa, couched in fictional form'[14] as he called it to Julian. Huxley gave a little more detail to Harold Raymond: 'The fable will be that of a man who offers himself as a *corpus vile* for a prolonged experiment in the hibernation treatment which they are now using for cancer & heart disease – & who is kept on ice for a couple of centuries when he is woken up, and finds himself in a different and better kind of world. The book will take the form of a record of his experiences in both worlds, the present and the future, and of his reflections on them.'[15] In fact neither of these two ideas came to anything.

Huxley was in very poor health throughout the spring, as was Maria. They were anxious about the fate of Maria's mother and sister, Rose, who had got out of Brussels but whose whereabouts, in early June, were unknown. Sybille Bedford arrived in Southern California in July 1940 and was shocked to see her old friends: 'I found Aldous and Maria very changed.'[16] Although Aldous was not wearing spectacles any longer 'this was not as impressive as it might have been because of his looking so drawn and strained, with a great burden of unhappiness severely locked away . . . And poor Maria was so thin, so worn, so nervous – and so resolutely cheerful.' This was not apparently a personal or domestic unhappiness. Like Shakespeare's Miranda, who had once supplied the title of his most famous work, Huxley could say: 'I have suffered with those I saw suffer.' It was as if the Huxleys, apparently in fortunate exile in the sun, had taken on themselves the anguish of their family and friends in Europe. When he started work again in July, however, he resolved on a completely different project – the idea given to him by Gerald Heard – of writing a biography of Père Joseph, the original *eminence grise* of seventeenth century France.

The presence of English writers in sunny Southern California in wartime was obviously a provocation to adverse comment at home. The British popular newspapers got up something of a campaign against the exiles in Hollywood, 'Gone With the Wind Up', accusing them of shirking their patriotic duty. Huxley – and even the much younger Isherwood – was over draft-age and there was little a forty-five year-old, half-blind, gangling intellectual could be expected to offer any conceivable fighting force. But he did what he could with food parcels, gifts for charity auctions, and small individual acts of help, which were all he believed he could do. Charlie Chaplin said at the Hubbles that he had been a pacifist in the last war but was now a war-monger: 'I am a little man and I have always got along by being acquiescent, conciliatory, anxious to please, that has been my way of avoiding trouble – but before I'd submit to these bullies I'd be shot and so help me – I'd take as many of them with me as I could.'[17] Anita Loos was active in William Allen White's 'Help the Allies' fund-raising activities and there was no question of Huxley burying his head in the sand though events seemed to have depressed him considerably.

One sunny evening in July 1940, Huxley and Maria dined at a new restaurant on Sunset Boulevard called the Player's Club, with Anita and the Hubbles. Grace wrote afterwards: 'Aldous silent when war discussed.'[18] One must take this not as callous and selfish indifference but as an expression of Huxley's inability to come to terms with the dashing of all his high ideals for peace and international co-operation expounded from the mid-1930s onwards. As Isherwood had pointed out, he was hypersensitive to such things and – writing in the middle of his illness in May – he warned Suzanne Nicolas, Maria's sister, not to dwell too much on the bad news in the media. He told her – in his impeccable and fluent French – that to allow oneself to be overcome by anxiety from too much exposure to news bulletins was to allow the war to make yet more inroads, weakening you and your family without actually mitigating any evil. He advised her to limit her exposure to 'one or two doses a day'.[19]

When Huxley began work again in August – telling Frieda Lawrence that he couldn't consider doing an adaptation of *Lady Chatterley's Lover* for the stage because he had lost nine months through prolonged work at the studio and his illness – the film had just been released and he was very pleased with its success. He told the Hubbles that he would have preferred Cukor as director: 'I barely stopped my director from having Mrs Bennett fight a duel with Wickham!' He thought the principals '*so* bad'.[20] But the atmosphere, the climate of ideas, of seventeenth century France was much more to his taste and he pressed on with research for *Grey Eminence*. Huxley moved quickly and three months after starting his research in July was writing in October, finishing the book in May 1941. He told Lewis Gielgud that the book was 'a strangely apposite study of Père Joseph, collaborator of Richelieu, the most astounding case of a power politician who was also a mystic'.[21] Blithely informing Harold Raymond that he had abandoned his previous projects, he commended the new one as having 'an obliquely topical interest; for Joseph was as much responsible as anyone for prolonging the Thirty Years War, which is on the direct line of ancestry to the present disasters. And he brings to focus in the most dramatic way the whole problem of the relations between politics and religious insight.'[22] Getting hold of the needful books when wartime France and its libraries were out of the question was a headache. Chatto was asked to get books for him from the British Museum.

Meanwhile, the eye-exercises were continuing, providing some morsel of optimism. But this in turn was threatened by a new financial crisis caused by the alarming news that Ralph Pinker's literary agency was going into liquidation, owing money to many people, including Huxley (£548, a substantial sum in 1940s terms). Pinker had embezzled money and would eventually be jailed in Wormwood Scrubs (like his brother Eric who had earlier used client account money for gambling and ruined the New York operation).[23] Since Huxley was not writing any articles or short stories at this time, and could deal with Chatto direct, he made no immediate steps to acquire a new agent. He carried on writing and by February 1941 he was able to tell Raymond that the book was threequarters done: 'How tame and unfantastic mere fiction is, compared with history! Actual facts and people are inexpressibly strange.'[24] But those facts were also 'very depressing' because there seemed 'very little evidence to justify a belief that there can be any merely political and economic solution to the chronic and the periodically recurrent problems of human beings'.

Huxley was increasingly drawn towards a mystical or religious solution for rebuilding the world after the war. Around this time both

Huxley and Heard were becoming involved with the Swami Prabhavananda who ran the Vedanta Society of Southern California at 1946 Ivar Avenue, Hollywood, an 'intentional community'. In his account of the Swami, *My Guru and His Disciple* (1980), Christopher Isherwood claims that Huxley was initiated into the Society at the Swami's temple in 1940 but says that he and Heard drew apart from the Swami because of a dislike of his devotional bias. They preferred the meditational approach of Krishnamurti who had broken away from Hinduism and who objected to the guru–disciple relationship. He was based at Ojai, about a couple of hours' drive from Los Angeles. Isherwood confesses in the book to some tension between him and Huxley as a result of the latter's pronounced homophobia (which doesn't seem to have been a problem, however, in the case of Gerald Heard). He was very fond of Maria, however, and her 'charmingly outspoken'[25] inquiries into his personal life.

Père Joseph – a practising mystic who was drawn fatally into the compromises of power politics, could not have been a more suitable field of inquiry for Huxley. He now believed that anyone with 'a gift for the knowledge of ultimate reality' could do far more good 'by sticking to his curious activities on the margin of society than by going to the centre and trying to improve matters there'.[26] The Huxleys, however, were continuing their love affair with California. They had lunch in April with the novelist May Sarton who reported back to Koteliansky: ' I liked Aldous extremely, his quiet and simplicity, his interest in what people are doing – it was a very pleasant and easy lunch . . . They have a small butterfly dog and she [Maria] was blowing up balloons for him to play with . . . They both love California . . . they live in a very queer house, a Victorian idea of Hollywood with lots of oriental knick-knacks and hideous sofas but big windows opening onto the steep green valleys and a lovely garden. It is on the very crest of a hill. But they are forever and ever wanderers and strangers examining America as if it were an insect, having no *part*.'[27] Like Sybille Bedford, she noticed Maria's exhausted look – she used the French word, *usée*. Possibly to refresh their existence, the wanderers continued to eye their estate in the Valley. The owner had rejected their offer but they still had hopes of his entertaining another bid. Because Aldous had now accepted some more film work, the MS of *Grey Eminence* having been finished, they wouldn't have been able to live in the desert yet and leaving it empty in the summer would not have been advisable because of the danger of fires (they had seen three on a recent weekend visit) but the beauty of the desert drew them, especially Maria: 'An intense sky and blue yet not a deep blue; but the same tone as the expanse of sage-brush which being young was very silvery so there was silver in the sky and silver at our feet and the whole effect exhilarating and peaceful at the same time.'[28]

The film work was at a new studio – Twentieth Century Fox – only ten minutes drive from their Santa Monica home and with occasional freedom to work from home. Maria was amused by Aldous setting off with his packed lunch concealed in a dispatch case 'like an English clerk'. At Fox he was working on a treatment of a story by Charles Morgan ('Morgan, so phoney baloney'[29]). Fox had paid $27,000 for the story and Huxley's job was to rewrite it. Around this time the Huxleys were seeing more of Krishnamurti and Rosalind Rajagopal at their community at Ojai and Gerald Heard at Laguna. Huxley was saying relatively little in his letters about his growing interest in Hindu philosophy and the idea of an 'intentional community' of a kind Gerald was soon to found at Trabuco. He would not himself ever consider living communally but the ideas interested him. At Ojai Krishnamurti lectured under the trees in the manner of an Indian sage. Another, more western kind of sage, was the medium Eileen Garrett, who met the Huxleys for the first time in the summer of 1941 shortly after her arrival in Hollywood. A neighbour, Mercedes de Acosta, introduced them (Garrett would later taken an interest in Huxley's mescaline experiments). De Acosta would often accompany the Huxleys on their evening walks at sunset and she used to ask him 'endless questions'.[30] In turn, the Huxleys introduced de Acosta to Eva Hermann, 'a lovely and sensitive person', who lived in Santa Monica Canyon.

The Huxleys' circle of friends was expanding. De Acosta, though married, was a high profile Hollywood lesbian and a friend of Garbo and a member of what were known as the 'Sewing Circles', a sort of underground lesbian network. In his study, *Huxley in Hollywood*

(1989), David King Dunaway asserts that Maria was part of this network. But there is no concrete evidence to support this.[31] Sybille Bedford is highly sceptical about the notion of Maria as a frequenter of the lesbian bars of Sunset Boulevard and Santa Monica Canyon. It hardly fits with the Huxleys' modest and early-to-bed lifestyle and their close companionship.[32] More convincing is the tone of a letter to Suzanne at this time, pining for escape to the desert: 'Our cabin in the desert is still just a dream.'[33] Maria's bisexuality is a fact, but the evidence for her involvement in any sort of lesbian scene is circumstantial and seems to rest simply on her friendship with Garbo, De Acosta and others. For Huxley's forty-sixth birthday, Anita Loos invited many of these to her house on the ocean and there was a magnificent birthday cake and candles.

By the autumn, *Grey Eminence* had appeared and Huxley was immediately at work on a new novel, *Time Must Have A Stop*. At the end of October, Maria told Suzanne that she and Aldous would be taking possession of their 'cabanon au désert',[34] on New Year's Day. In fact they were in residence by 19th December: 'My desert, look at the address on the top of this,'[35] Maria wrote to Jeanne. The address was Llano del Rio.

Notes

1   *L.*447
2   Reading, Letter to Harold Raymond, 8 November 1939
3   UCLA, Letter from Harold Raymond to Eugene Saxton, 5 October 1939
4   RL, Letter from Maria Huxley to Jeanne Neveux, 15 October 1939. Author's translation
5   UCLA, Letter to Jake Zeitlin, 9 November 1939
6   *L.*448
7   RL, Letter from Maria Huxley to Jeanne Neveux, 12 February 1940. Author's translation
8   *SB*2.8. Quoting letter from Maria to Jeanne Neveux, 1940. Date not given
9   *Mem Vol.*, p95
10 HL, Hubble Diary, 26 February 1940
11 *L.*451

12 Christopher Isherwood, *Diaries* Vol 1, 1939–1960, pp77–8, 9 January 1940

13 Isherwood Diaries, 29 January 1940

14 *L.*452

15 Reading, Letter to Harold Raymond, 14 February 1940

16 *SB*2.11

17 HL, Hubble Diary, 22 December 1940

18 HL, Hubble Diary, 2 July 1940

19 RL, Letter to Suzanne Nicolas, 22 May 1940. Author's translation

20 HL, Hubble Diary 23 August 1940

21 *L.*460

22 *L.*461

23 For a fuller account of the misdeeds of the Pinkers see the memoirs of Huxley's American publisher, Cass Canfield, *Up Down and Around: a publisher recollects the time of his life* (1971) p90ff

24 Reading, letter to Harold Raymond, 21 February 1941

25 Christopher Isherwood, *My Guru and His Disciple* (1980), p51

26 *L.*464

27 *May Sarton Selected Letters* (1997) edited by Susan Sherman. Letter to Samuel Koteliansky, 13 April 1941

28 HL, Isherwood Papers, Letter from Maria Huxley to Christopher Isherwood, 16 July 1941

29 HL, Hubble Diary, 26 July 1941

30 Mercedes de Acosta, *Here Lies the Heart* (1960), p304

31 David King Dunaway, *Huxley in Hollywood* (1989) pp70–1. David King Dunaway's thoroughly researched account both of the lesbian scene in Hollywood and of Huxley's time in Southern California, and his valuable interviews with many who knew Huxley (some, unfortunately, currently under embargo at the Huntington Library at the request of Huxley family members) makes one reluctant to seem to dismiss his linkages too casually but I feel some more concrete evidence, other than circumstantial evidence, would be required to connect Maria to the world he describes

32 SB in conversation with the author

33 RL, Letter from Maria Huxley to Suzanne Nicolas, 13 July 1941. Author's translation

34 RL, Letter from Maria Huxley to Suzanne Nicolas, 30 October 1941

35 RL, Letter from Maria Huxley to Jeanne Neveux, 19 December 1941

XXVIII

Llano

Less than a fortnight after the Japanese bombing of Pearl Harbor on 7 December 1941 – an event which ensured that the United States would enter the war – the Huxleys took possession of their new retreat in the desert. Indeed, they had been picnicking there on the day of the raid itself. This might have looked like a withdrawal, but the ostensible reason was Maria's health. For the sake of her lungs doctors had recommended the hot dry air of the desert rather than the fume-laden atmosphere of Los Angeles. Aldous, too, was determined to make progress with his eyes and the unsparing light of the Mojave desert, fifty miles north of Los Angeles, where they had bought the forty acre ranch at Llano del Rio, was perfect. And the Huxleys had never really been happy in cities. To read Maria's many letters from Llano is to register her delight at the beauty of the desert scenery – however much the domestic chores and the complex demands of the simple life weighed on her. They brought with them the continuing worries about Maria's family – her mother and Rose still wrestling with paperwork in France – and Aldous's continuing studio commitments made them think of taking also a flat in Beverly Hills. The address at 701 South Amalfi Drive was not in fact abandoned until the middle of February. Llano, therefore, may have been a change of scene. It was not a running away.

The publication at the end of 1941 of *Grey Eminence* was a further step on Huxley's path towards the exploration of religion in general and the mystical tradition in particular. On New Years's Day Harold Raymond wrote from Chatto to Eugene Saxton in New York to point out that 'scarcely a year goes by without my being rung up by some idiot in Fleet Street who wants to know if it is true that Aldous has joined the Romish church'.[1] There was scant likelihood of Huxley joining any of the established Christian churches – the intellectual agnostic in the twentieth century invariably turns eastwards – but his new field of intellectual exploration worried some of his admirers. A Catholic priest and a trained mystic who assisted Cardinal Richelieu was not the sort of subject they would have expected him to choose. His reasons for doing so have already been mentioned above and the subtitle, 'A Study in Religion and Politics', indicates the book's scope. Huxley wanted to explore the relationship between the new religious ideas he was beginning to investigate and the world of affairs with which, as a peace activist, he had been engaged. The opening chapter of *Grey Eminence* which finds the barefoot friar Père Joseph walking towards Rome, meditating on such thoughts as the self being 'An active nothing that had to be annihilated into passive nothingness if God's will was to be done,' must have raised some puzzled eyebrows. One cannot, either, escape a sense of self-identification as the forty-six year-old Huxley describes 'the face of a man in middle life, weathered, gaunt with self-inflicted hardship, lined and worn with the incessant labour of the mind' and 'his myopic eyes'. As a boy, the friar 'loved . . . to be left alone, so that he could think his own thoughts'.

Huxley set out to challenge the 'fashionable' or Marxist view that economic factors determined political events. For obvious reasons, he wanted to explore the notion that ideas – and in particular mystical ideas, ideas that challenged the world of realpolitik – were as powerful as economics. He describes the religious background, and gives a sample of those ideas which he would explore more systematically in *The Perennial Philosophy* five years later. These included the notion that mystical theories were based on 'the empirical facts of mystical experience' and that 'selfhood is a heavy, hardly translucent medium, which cuts off most of the light of reality and distorts what little it permits to pass'. This is Huxley's central notion, that we should 'stand out of our own light' in order to see the eternal truths. In a revealing moment, Huxley says that the appeal of the mystical tradition was that it provided the non-Christian with 'a religion free from unacceptable dogmas, which themselves are contingent upon ill-established and arbitrarily-interpreted facts'. In other words the natural objections of a Huxley to Christian theology could be side-stepped neatly. Some theologians, like Karl Barth, see this mystical tradition as 'esoteric atheism'. We might also call it religion without tears. Huxley's English admirers might also add that it was more than a little Southern Californian. But Huxley believed firmly that a world without the light from mysticism would be 'totally blind and insane'.

The purely historical sections of the book are told in a fairly conventional textbook fashion and it is the theorising – about religion and politics – that gives it most interest. The conclusion – from Père Joseph's failure to prevent power politics conquering his religious instincts – was that we must cultivate 'the art of what may be called "goodness politics", as opposed to power politics'. Political reforms were useless without the inner reform exemplified by the contemplatives: 'Society can never be greatly improved, until such time as most of its members chose to become theocentric saints.' In the contemporary world, however, the work of the theocentrics – like the work of the peace-campaigner in the circumstances of 1941 – 'is always marginal'. Reviewing the book in *The Spectator*, the historian C.V. Wedgwood saw it as 'the authentic voice of Mr Huxley' and concluded that it was 'incontrovertibly the work of a thinker, whose undeviating integrity is one of the few spiritual torches left burning in the black-out'.[2]

Just before leaving Santa Monica for Llano, Huxley wrote a letter to two correspondents (known only as 'Miss Hepworth and Mr Green') in which he gave a fascinating account of himself in 1942:

I am an intellectual with a certain gift for literary art, physically delicate, without very strong emotions, not much interested in practical activity and impatient of

routine. I am not very sociable and am always glad to
return to solitude and the freedom that goes with
solitude. This desire for freedom and solitude has led not
only to a consistent effort to avoid situations in which I
would be under the control of other people, but also to
an indifference to the satisfactions of power and position,
things which impose a servitude of business and
responsibility . . . As a young man, I cared supremely for
knowledge for its own sake, for the play of ideas, for the
arts of literature, painting and music. But for some years
now I have felt a certain dissatisfaction with these things,
have felt that even the greatest masterpieces were
somehow inadequate. Recently I have begun to know
something about the reality in relation to which such
things as art and general knowledge can be appraised.
Inadequate in and for themselves, these activities of the
mind can be seen in their true perspective when looked
at from the vantage point of mysticism . . . The secret
here, as in the fields of morals lies the indirect approach.[3]

Not for the first time the biographer ruefully reflects that this
supremely intelligent and self-aware man was invariably his own best
critic.

One bad piece of news from France in early 1942 was that Drieu La
Rochelle, the young Frenchman whom Huxley had so much admired,
had become, as editor of the *Nouvelle Revue Française,* 'an ardent
advocate of collaboration'.[4] Huxley did not try to apologise for him.
'He is an outstanding example of the strange things that happen when
a naturally weak man, whose talents are entirely literary, conceives a
romantic desire for action and a romantic ambition for political
power and position.' Huxley's thoughts were running in the opposite
direction from political ambition and he was now busy trying to
make the ranch at Llano viable. He slightly strained his heart at the
beginning of February doing some unaccustomed heavy work which
caused a chronic fatigue, exacerbated, as he told Isherwood, by 'having
reached an impasse in my writing, where I don't know whether I can

achieve what I want to achieve, or how exactly to do it. I would like to do something else altogether for a little; but my physical condition makes it difficult for me to do anything but the usual sedentary work.'[5] He must have looked on with amazement at the practical success of Gerald Heard in establishing a 'monastery, at Trabuco College near Laguna on a 360 acre estate, which he had just visited, where contemplatives could be nurtured. Huxley sometimes thought he was in a kind of limbo between worldliness and pure contemplative spirituality – his irrevocable commitment to 'analysis' seeming to him to be inimical to both.'[6]

Meanwhile the work on the house at Llano continued. The word means a level field or even ground in Spanish and it was situated in the Antelope valley close up to the San Gabriel Mountains. It was more like an oasis than a ranch, with a small orchard, a pool they could swim in, and a vineyard from whose grapes the couple once tried to make wine, treading the grapes with their bare feet. Huxley may have been unaware at first (though he would later write on the topic) of the socialist community founded at Llano in 1915 by a radical lawyer, Job Harriman. They secured water rights and cleared the area of its characteristic creosote bush, burro bush and Joshua tree but, as Huxley's later essay showed, the community fell apart as a result of internal quarrels.[7] Today this area of desert is, as a recent writer, Mike Davis, put it, 'prepared like a virgin bride for its eventual union with the Metropolis'.[8] Subtopia is on the march and when I visited it in early 2000 there was a sense – in the windswept homesteads heavily fortified by wire against which packs of dogs hurled themselves at unwelcome visitors – that this territory now partook more of paranoid America than of utopian experiment. I finally retreated at a sign which read NEVER MIND THE DOG WATCH OUT FOR THE OWNER over the picture of the end of a gun barrel.

The Huxleys lived near to an oasis and they improved the house – which Anita Loos said was 'just like the shack where Huckleberry Finn's father died'[9] – by adding another storey and constructing a hexagonal unit where Huxley slept and worked. They had to install a new pump after the caretaker managed to destroy the existing one and they buried an electricity generator out in the yard, keeping the trapdoor in position with a terracotta bust of Gerald Heard. This was referred to as 'Gerald's Tomb'. Christopher Ishwerwood was once a guest and, forgetting an injunction not to use the lights in the night, he flicked a switch and the engine 'started up with a clatter like a motor-bike and woke everybody else up'.[10] Maria spent the first weeks and months at Llano often alone because Aldous was working on a new film project – *Jane Eyre* – for Twentieth Century Fox. Directed by Robert Stevenson, it would eventually appear in 1944, with Huxley gaining his second screen credit jointly with Stevenson and John Houseman. Orson Welles would play Rochester and Joan Fontaine Jane Eyre. Maria worried about the financial burden they had taken on in buying the property: 'I hope we won't come to regret this house . . . We are almost prisoners here . . . I am full of worries and anxieties.'[11] Huxley cabled Chatto for information about his royalties and was told that 1941 had yielded £843 in English royalties alone. The rebuilding and the endless round of domestic chores such as cleaning windows (not really Maria's *forte*) was a bit much for her but she consoled herself that she was at least 'in my desert now'.[12] And as spring came, after the blizzards and hurricanes, the blossom and the signs of green on the trees became 'so beautiful that it catches one's breath to look at it'.[13]

The studio gave Huxley a week off in the second week of March because he was exhausted and at the end of the week Maria found it 'melancholy' to see him going to get the bus at Palmdale in the first sun. Matthew was spending a lot of time with her and was looking well. He helped with the work on the house and she gloried in the quiet time: 'How awful that life in L.A. was. Spending my time rushing and catering for a crowd; and being in the crowd and talking to the crowd.' Her dog Loulou and the five kittens played freely in the spring sunshine and both she and Matthew were reading the writings of Vivekananda, the chief disciple of Ramakrishna, founder of the Hindu sect which had established the Vedanta Society of Southern California where Isherwood spent so much time with the Swami Prabhavananda. The work had advanced sufficiently by the spring for Maria to have a 'bright and cheerful'[14] kitchen which doubled up as a dining-room, a small office almost entirely taken up with a desk they had bought cheaply, her own bedroom which, after the bed and dressing-table left no room to move. She slid along the edge of the room to a bow window which gave a view of the snow-covered San Gabriel mountains and her almond trees in blossom and the irrigation ditch. In Huxley's bedroom his bed was covered with the same blue and red fabric that had been at Sanary. There was a tiny bathroom. The caretaker who lived in the former post-office helped with all the big jobs. There was a worry about water because intensive wartime cultivation was using up all the available supplies.

But in spite of all these little difficulties the Huxleys were happy at Llano at this period. 'The desert beyond is always immense and calming,' Maria told Grace Hubble. 'So you see I do feel very happy even if my hands ache with so much unused muscle stretching and squeezing.'[15] They were almost self-sufficient and bottled and preserved their own fruit and engaged in permanent warfare with the rabbits and desert hares, squirrels, rats and coyotes who came to feast on their produce. By April, Aldous was there more or less permanently and the film work must have been quite light for he was at work again on a novel, or trying to be at work on one: 'Writing has been at something of a standstill for some time. Or, to be more accurate, I have been going round and round, and poking my nose into a succession of alleys that turned out, after exploration, to be blind.'[16] As a way out of the block he proposed to write a short book of 'pure utility' about the Bates method of visual education. His aim was to produce something of practical benefit to millions of people and also to strike a blow for the Bates method in the face of determined opposition from the optometric establishment. The book was written quickly and finished in July, after which Huxley went to spend three weeks with Gerald Heard at the monastery in Trabuco. He now turned his mind towards another 'biographico-historical subject'.[17] He told Chatto: 'I have in mind one of the most fantastically strange stories in all French history – the story of the demoniac possession of the nuns of Loudun . . .' But it was to be another five years before *The Devils of Loudun* was published (in part because Llano in wartime was hardly the place to find research materials for such a book). *The Art of Seeing*, meanwhile, came out in October.

The book's account of Huxley's own predicament has already been discussed but this was not meant to be an uplifting confessional self-help manual. It was intended as a scientific – but also practical – attempt to 'correlate the methods of visual education with the findings of modern psychology and critical philosophy'. He complained that ophthalmologists were 'obsessively' preoccupied with 'only one aspect of the total, complex process of seeing – the physiological'. They had paid exclusive attention to the eyes 'not at all to the mind which makes use of the eyes to see with'. He said he had been treated by men with the highest eminence in their profession 'but never once did they so much as faintly hint that there might be a mental side to vision, or that there might be wrong ways of using the eyes and mind as well as right ways, unnatural and abnormal modes of visual functioning as well as natural and normal ones'. The book set out to show how a different approach might be adopted. It is written with all Huxley's exemplary clarity and, to the lay person, is very persuasive. Chatto was inundated after publication with requests from readers for names of Bates practitioners and the book sold very well. Sixty years on, however, Huxley would seem to have failed in his aim of altering the professional approach of ophthalmology. Bates remains a fringe character for most specialists. What is interesting perhaps, is that Huxley at this time was thoroughly immersing himself in Eastern philosophy and Hindu scripture, involving himself in the Vedanta Society which studied those scriptures, and exploring the transcendental 'mind over matter' dimension of this tradition of thought yet, in spite of the central premise of *The Art of Seeing* that 'the human mind-body is a single unit', the book is written in a wholly scientific register. There is no explicit disclosure of Huxley's private agenda.

In the autumn of 1942 an article appeared in *The American Scholar* with the title, 'The Trouble with Aldous Huxley'. The author, W.Y. Tindall, lamented 'the decline of the novelist or, better, his ascent from novelist to mystic'. And the article laid the blame on Gerald Heard. Although this article is written in a would-be urbane tone of dry mockery, it is not without insight. It claims that Huxley's infatuation with Lawrence was a dry-run for his infatuation with Heard. 'For all his intelligence, Huxley cannot resist a dominant personality.'[18]

Moreover, 'beneath the desperate frivolities of Huxley had lurked the moralist and the disappointed idealist whose complaint against the world was that it had failed to conform to his standards of truth and beauty'. As a professional literary critic Tyndall was appalled at the introduction of moral issues into aesthetics, claiming: 'the beautiful has been sacrificed to the good and the true'. He went on: 'master and disciple retired to California where, when they are not walking with Greta Garbo or writing for the cinema, they eat nuts and lettuce perhaps and inoffensively meditate, Huxley in Hollywood and Heard on a convenient mountainside'. This article is interesting as an early example of that marriage of academic conservatism and popular prejudice that has been the making of so many successful second careers in the media for dons right up to the present day.

Huxley almost certainly didn't read Tyndall's piece and was anyway preoccupied with his health. From Llano he informed Julian that his nervous system had thrown up a catalogue of ailments: 'heart irregularity, intestinal spasm, hives, bronchitis and the continuous falling off of one of my finger nails, which was evidently innervated and so inadequately supplied with blood'. Fortunately, 'an excellent and rather crazy Viennese doctor'[19] had put him on a 'stringent meatless, [the Huxleys had been vegetarian for some time now] milkless, sugarless and saltless' diet. The autumn weather was another balm. 'Here it is the most beautiful season,' Maria wrote to Suzanne, 'warm and crisp and golden.'[20] Aldous told Mary Hutchinson, 'Meanwhile one writes and one does what infinitesimally little one can to help in alleviating the misery of the world. Of books I don't read much outside the field of mystical religion, which is what now interests me beyond anything else and in which, I believe, lies the sole hope of the world.' Building up arms would not stop conflict only 'some sort of common belief, the holding of which makes people reluctant to embark on these enormous suicides'. Because the world of global politics affected everyone this common belief could not be Christian or any other dogma 'but must be based on something that all people can experience and that has a place in all the existing religious traditions. Mysticism is the only thing that meets the requirements.' He refined this argument in a letter to Julian, saying that: 'Mysticism also has the enormous merit of being concerned with the eternal present, and not, as humanism is, with the future.'[21] By contrast political religions like Nazism and Communism or any kind of Utopianism were ruthless and ready to liquidate 'the people it happens to find inconvenient now for the sake of the people who are going, hypothetically, to be so much better and happier and more intelligent in the year 2000'.

Huxley spent most of 1943 based at Llano, working at a new novel, reading further in the mystical tradition. The war meant that royalty funds in England could not be released – which gave some financial anxiety because the Huxleys now had Maria's youngest sister Rose staying with them with her four year old daughter Olivia and her new baby, Sigfrid. There were also sporadic food shortages and gasoline rationing. Continued good sales of *Grey Eminence* and *The Art of Seeing* meant, however, that English royalties for 1943 would be £3,679, considerably more than in recent years, and by April Huxley was actually offering to invest some money in shares in Chatto.

At Llano the Huxleys were discovering, if not self-sufficiency, then a modicum of husbandry skills. The previous year Maria had bought ten pounds of sunflower seeds, not realising what a vast crop this would yield, and now they were planting radishes. Maria looked out through the kitchen windows (the only ones she bothered to clean because 'their eyes open on all I love'[22]) on 'a queer fellow of an author wearing blue jeans and thinking he can grow radishes. But Aldous waters them from such a height and with such gusto that the head gets buried and the tails stand in the air as if they were doing yogi exercises and so all we get are dry roots and laughs'. Huxley was looking well and enjoying his Tolstoyan labours. Matthew, now back in the US Army medical corps after an appendicitis operation, wrote letters which delighted his parents. 'He loves us both, that is so obvious in the letters, and the year we spent together here has meant much to him.' In spite of their bouts of ill-health and the hard work of living in the desert, and the horror of the war, there is a sense that this was a nearly idyllic time for the Huxleys. They ate their own potatoes, red peppers, onions, carrots, aubergines, tomatoes. But then, some time in the early summer, Aldous, 'who was supremely well and happy'[23] in Maria's words, plucked at some poison ragweed in the orchard and caught a rash which seemed to react badly with the dry air of the desert and so he left for town. Then in July he went to stay yet again with Gerald Heard at Trabuco throughout July and August. Maria stayed behind at Llano, swimming in the oasis pool 'with the bull-bats drinking in swoops in spite of my presence and the doves timorously looking from the edge and never risking a drink till I am gone . . . The desert is still beautiful and I still love it more than anything.'[24] The only real cloud was Matthew's health. He had been invalided out of the army with German measles and other complications and came back to Llano to rest. By September his father was writing to him suggesting that it was now time to be a little more directed and giving him a rather long and uncharacteristic talking-to that had about it some of the earnest censoriousness of a Victorian *paterfamilias*. He was encouraging Matthew to go to Ojai and to make his reading more purposeful and systematic. 'Promiscuous reading can become a really pernicious addiction, like oversmoking or drinking.'[25]

Huxley was directing his own efforts more or less successfully and, by the end of the year, the manuscript of *Time Must Have A Stop* was almost completed. He told his new American publisher at Harper's, Cass Canfield (Eugene Saxton had died in the summer) that the new novel 'may be described as a piece of the *Comédie Humaine* that modulates into a version of the *Divina Commedia*'.[26] He added that he had deliberately 'kept light' the story and that overall it was 'an odd sort of book'. To Harold Raymond in London he also promised that the end was in sight for a book 'which has been riding my back, like the Old Man of the Sea, for the past eighteen months'.[27] The truth, however, was that Huxley wasn't wholly satisfied with it and he agreed with Maria when she read the manuscript at the end of January that they should seek a second opinion. Accordingly, Maria wrote to Christopher Isherwood telling him that Aldous had never before sought an opinion in this way. But he had now told Maria: 'I will ask Christopher to read it. I would like him to. He has very good judgement.'[28] And so Isherwood came out to Llano at the beginning of February 1944: 'It's the kind of spring day on which you feel that perhaps you will live for ever. Everything seems eternally alive . . . There is no sign of the war, except the olive-drab army trucks, moving almost invisibly through the landscape, along the road below the house.'[29] Before supper Maria was in the kitchen 'cooking wildly, with everything boiling over'. She was glad to be back at Llano away from 'that horrid town' though the rash problem had made them reluctantly move back to Los Angeles, to a 'large comfortable and gay'[30] flat at 145½ South Doheny Drive, Beverly Hills. 'How blissfully happy we are again in a curiously and hitherto unsuspected, dove-grey or wrath grey or even English-grey desert,' she told Isherwood.

The Huxleys would keep Llano on until February 1947. It was clear, however, that it was not just the allergy that had sent them away. Maria suddenly realised during the summer that the size and remoteness and sheer difficulty of managing the ranch 'would always make me remain a hustled slavy. Aldous made it quite clear on one of our talks that never could he take an interest in material things; that if he did it intruded on his work and disturbed him.' The decision was inevitable but still hard for Maria: 'It is a pang! Nobody loved the place as much as I do. No-one knows it as I got to know it through so many silent and peaceful days.' And so their dream ended, a dream of escape and tranquillity. Aldous was about to celebrate his fiftieth birthday.

Notes

1   UCLA, Letter from Harold Raymond to Eugene Saxton, 1 January 1942
2   C.V. Wedgwood, *The Spectator*, 5 December 1941, p538. Watt, pp335–36
3   *L.*473–4
4   *L.*472
5   *L.*474
6   *L.*476
7   See Robert Hine, *California's Utopian Colonies* (1983) and Mike Davis, *City of Quartz* (1990)
8   Mike Davis, City *of Quartz* (1990) p3
9   HL, Hubble Diary, 4 January 1942
10   *Mem. Vol.*, p157
11   RL, Letter from Maria Huxley to Suzanne Nicolas, 29 January 1942. Author's translation

348 Aldous Huxley

12   HL, Letter to Grace Hubble, 24 February 1942
13   HL, Isherwood papers, Letter from Maria Huxley to Christopher Isherwood, 17 March 1942
14   RL, Letter from Maria Huxley to Madame Nys, 17 March 1942. Author's translation
15   HL, Letter from Maria Huxley to Grace Hubble, 20 April 1942
16   Reading, Letter to Harold Raymond, 14 March 1942
17   L.480
18   W.Y. Tindall, *The American Scholar*, Autumn 1942, 11 (4), pp452–64
19   HRC, Letter to Mary Hutchinson, 2 November 1942
20   RL, Letter from Maria Huxley to Suzanne Nicolas, 9 November 1942. Author's translation
21   L.483
22   HL, Letter from Maria Huxley to Grace Hubble, 10 April 1943
23   HL, Letter from Maria Huxley to Grace Hubble, 9 August 1943
24   *Ibid*
25   L.497
26   L.498
27   Reading, Letter to Harold Raymond, 17 January 1944
28   HL, Isherwood papers, Letter from Maria Huxley to Christopher Isherwood, 30 January 1944
29   Isherwood Diaries, p334, 7 February 1944
30   HL, Letter from Maria Huxley to Grace Hubble, 9 January 1944

XXIX

Atman

Back in Los Angeles at the start of 1944, Huxley expressed the hope that the year would see 'the end of the horror in Europe'.[1] He feared that the consequences of masses of dispossessed people in Europe might be a growth of 'totalitarian centralization' – for the Jeffersonian democracy of self-sufficient individuals he advocated 'cannot exist where there is not a wide distribution of private property in land, utilizable goods and means of production'. For himself, his skin condition was still raw but the fact that the weeds at Llano would now have died down for the winter encouraged the Huxleys to think that they could return 'experimentally'.[2] A summer season there, however, was out of the question: 'It is all a great nuisance and shows how dangerous it is for men of letters to do a little honest work for a change.' His work in Beverly Hills was now an anthology with comments, along the lines of *Texts and Pretexts*, 'devoted to what has been called the Perennial Philosophy – the Highest Common Factor underlying all the great religious and metaphysical systems of the world'.[3] Since Huxley's view of a peaceful world order was predicated on a shared outlook by all world citizens 'it would seem useful and timely to produce such a book'.

Work on this project began in April or May but first he was seeing what he could do with an original story for the movies in collaboration with Christopher Isherwood. 'I hope we shall be able to sell it, as it will solve a lot of economic problems and will make it unnecessary to go into temporary slavery at one of the studios,'[4] he told Frieda Lawrence. The story was *Jacob's Hands* and it concerned a faith healer in the Mojave Desert. It was published for the first time in 1998.[5] Although Isherwood as a young man had been a delighted consumer of film in contrast to his friend who began by deploring the movies, he was not really any more successful in the long run as a film-writer – which can be said of most of the famous-name writers employed by the studios in the 1930s and 1940s. Isherwood went out to Llano in early March to talk about the script, which was based on a real character, an old man in the desert who healed animals. Although both writers had high hopes for this script, it cut no ice at the studios who no doubt felt at that time that such a 'cranky' subject was unsuitable. Isherwood later recalled: 'Nobody liked the story – least of all James Geller, who'd been practically prepared to buy it sight unseen: he was the story editor at Warner's, and one of Aldous's warmest admirers. Either they thought it was goody-goody, or that it was superstitious, or both. Nevertheless, I still think it really had something.'[6] Huxley wrote to Leon Lion that the writing of film scripts could be: 'Rather interesting for a short time, but after that maddeningly irritating. It is always a great relief to be able to get back to the solitude and *laissez-faire* of writing for print and paper rather than celluloid.'[7]

Huxley was spending quite a lot of time in the desert 'hoping to outwit the weeds'[8] and indulging increasingly gloomy (and some-what over-stated) reflections on the current state and future prospects of England as the war drew to a close. He was dependent for infor-mation on a Quaker investigation of conditions in England whose author he had just met in Los Angeles and who seems to have rather over-egged his account. He was now deep in a reading of the mystical tradition and regretted that the educational system seemed to ignore the classics of this tradition such as William Law. He told Isherwood that the anthology would be 'like the outline of a system . . . a kind of miniature *summa*',[9] adding that the methods of science 'are still those of Descartes, which positively guarantee the scientist against dealing with more than a small part of reality and force him to deal even

with that in a very unnatural and unenlightening way'. Huxley's conviction that the truths of mysticism were profounder than those of
science had never before been stated so unambiguously.

The good news as the spring advanced was that the allergic itch was
seemingly under control and Huxley could spend more and more
time at Llano. Plenty of rain in the desert at the start of the year had
produced a fine show of spring flowers and the grazing was good for
the cattle. Their caretaker, the 'blue-eyed Texan handyman, in his big
hat and western belt slung low around his hips'[10] who had caught
Isherwood's attention, was running his own herd so the ranch was
'agreeably lively with calves, cows, steers, horses, not to mention the
inevitable dogs and cats that inevitably pullulate in the country'.[11]
Matthew was now fully recovered and working as a reader for Warner
Brothers (he would be radicalised during this time and was acting as
a press officer for the union) and Maria was well. The only disappointment was what looked like a final rejection from the William
Morris Agency of *Jacob's Hands*. 'It appears that the reason for the
hitherto universal rejection of it is fear of the doctors,'[12] Huxley told
Isherwood.

At the end of July Maria wrote to Jeanne that 'Aldous is more
adorable than ever and today his new novel appeared,'[13] repeating this
a month later: 'He is the most adorable of all the Aldouses I have ever
known and I want you to know it.'[14] Better health, a chance to return
to the desert, the prospect of the war ending, or dividends from the
wisdom of the East, or a combination of all of these, appeared to be
creating a more serene fifty-year-old Huxley. *Time Must Have A Stop*,
much like its predecessor, *After Many A Summer*, was in some measure
a reversion to the sprightly wit of the novels of the 1920s. Huxley said
it was his favourite amongst his novels and Maria agreed. The satire
on 'sentimental old dodoes' or unfeeling professed humanitarians,
and the occasional spasm of sexual disgust in the earlier chapters are
reminiscent of the old concerns. Indeed, the Californian sun, which
had brightened the previous novel, is absent entirely from this English
and Italian setting. Chapter Four, in particular, is a searing indictment
of stuffy bourgeois family life in England. But John Barnack says at
one point: 'Cynical realism – it's the intelligent man's best excuse for

doing nothing in an intolerable situation.' When the scene moves to Italy, Eustace Barnack encounters a radical bookseller who holds forth on the reasons why the French Revolution modulated into tyranny: 'this sort of thing was bound to happen wherever people tried to do good without being good'. This is the new Huxley not the old, no longer content with destructive satire but seeking for the positive way forward. But at the same time the 'ideas' in this novel are more well-integrated into the story compared with preachier antecedents. It is also bolder in including hallucinatory sequences and streams of consciousness. At its heart is the character Bruno Rontini, who tells the young poet Sebastian Barnack that writing can be 'an obstacle in the way of further knowledge. And that, maybe, is one of the reasons why most men of genius take such infinite pains not to become saints – out of self-preservation.' Huxley was not quite at the point of renunciation, of abandoning writing in order to become a pure contemplative, but he was putting into the mouth of Rontini the notion that if a writer 'spends all his energies on writing and doesn't attempt to modify his inherited and acquired being in the light of what he knows, then he can never get to increase his knowledge'. Brontini and Sebastian later visit the frescoes of San Marco and the Medicean tombs whose exalted art teaches him 'the unutterable wearisomeness, the silly and degrading horror, of being merely yourself, of being only human'. Once again a book has ended with a perception that mystical knowledge is the only indispensable knowledge and that political amelioration, the doctrine of progress, are ineffective until they have achieved this realisation.

The novel sold well but Maria was complaining towards the end of the year that the cost of living had soared since the outbreak of the war. Nonetheless her health and that of Aldous was good. She was no longer thin, nor was she suffering from migraines. In a letter to Jeanne she said that they had no plans to return to Europe once the war was over and that for now she wanted only to spend more time at Llano: 'autumn being the most beautiful season there'.[15] During the stays in Beverly Hills she pined for the snows of the San Gabriels 'which are as close as the Apuan mountains were at Forte'. At Christmas, hoping this would be the last time they did so in wartime, they despatched to

Mary Hutchinson in rationed England a packet of figs, tinned tongue, cherry jam, gelatine dessert, orange juice, cocoa and onion flakes.[16] Another Christmas gift was a story for Olivia called *The Crows of Pearblossom*, which was published posthumously in 1967. It is a pleasant children's story full of local colour from Llano and Pearblossom where Olivia lived with her mother, Rose. There are cottonwood trees, alfalfa grass and rattlesnakes and the tale – about a rattlesnake who steals crow's eggs – could be seen perhaps as a pacifist parable for the snake is defeated by intelligent strategy rather than by being killed. There is possibly a touch of self-mockery in the character of Mr Crow: 'This is serious,' he said. 'This is the sort of thing that somebody will have to do something about.' Mr Crow consults the owl for advice: 'Owl's a thinker. His ideas are always good.' Mr Huxley at the end of 1944 was at work on his anthology of good ideas, *The Perennial Philosophy*, knowing that after the war there would be plenty of people wishing to 'do something' and in need of the right intellectual basis on which to found their actions.

In January, Maria's wish was granted and they were back in the desert. She told Sybille Bedford that Aldous was about to embark on a painting bout, not having painted since arrival in the USA. He had also been, in spite of his eyes, learning to drive the car in the desert: 'He will not take a licence or drive on the main highways and in town but he adores it and still likes speed . . . Even the cattle stare in wonderment when he drives through them . . . And he smiles and his cap is always on one side or the other for the setting sun and you know how comic and rakish and adorable he looks then.'[17] She said how much they had been enjoying Christopher Isherwood's new novel, *Prater Violet*, which Maria had been reading aloud. '. . . he is a sort of *habitué sans habitudes*. Part of the family. But no successor to Eddy [Sackville-West] . . . or Raymond [Mortimer]. Somehow those days are all over and things change . . . We have long walks in the evenings and after dinner we read. But we dine very late and until then we live in our houses. The nights under the same roof but the days well apart. It suits us.'

Eating their own eggs and bread and cream from neighbours they delighted in their routine of 'monotony' for in truth: 'Everything is wonderful about my life.' Soon she was telling Jeanne about Aldous painting in a long white smock: 'You would not recognise Aldous. So serene and above all sweet . . . He *helps* in the housework now, drying up while *Don Juan* plays on the gramophone – a cracked record we can't afford to replace . . . All his wonderful qualities that you know so well are developed to the point where even I am surprised.'[18] Unaware of this praise, Huxley was busy deprecating himself as usual, telling E.S.P. Haynes, who had liked his last novel, that he was 'sadly aware that I am not a born novelist, but some other kind of man of letters, possessing enough ingenuity to be able to simulate a novelist's behaviour not too unconvincingly'.[19] Still in the grip of Sheldon's theory of types about which he had just written for *Harper's*, Huxley said he was 'the wrong shape for a storyteller and sympathetic delineator of character within a broad social canvas. The fertile inventors and narrators and genre painters have all been rather burly genial fellows . . . So what chance has an emaciated fellow on stilts?' Sheldon's analysis of the relationship between shape and mind was, he claimed, 'the first serious advance in the science of man since the days of Aristotle'. He was also corresponding at this time with the German novelist Hermann Broch, whose trilogy he had greatly admired and whose book *The Death of Virgil* he was reviewing for the *New York Herald Tribune*. He told Broch that his book was valuable 'socially' because it pointed to the profound dangers of the 'aesthetic temptation'[20] which led intellectuals away from the most valuable kinds of knowledge. He told Henry Miller that his new book would present the doctrine 'taught by every master of the spiritual life for the last three thousand years – a doctrine of which the modern world has chosen to be ignorant, preferring radios and four-motored bombers and salvation-through-organization, with the catastrophic consequences that we see all about us.'[21] His publisher, too, was bombarded with these solutions from the desert: 'Personally I come more and more to believe in decentralization and small-scale ownership of land and means of production.'[22] But Huxley feared that the need to reconstruct would result in at best an outbreak of *dirigisme* at worst state tyranny.

During the summer the Huxleys decided to buy a chalet in the mountains at Wrightwood, not too far from Llano, but without the risk of allergenic flora. The move was rather an abrupt one, as Maria confessed to Rosalind Rajagopal, the Huxley's Californian friend: 'We have actually bought, rather suddenly and vaguely the most hideous little house at Wrightwood.'[23] The Huxleys' genius for acquiring unsuitable houses on the spur of the moment had not deserted them. Wrightwood is nearly six thousand feet above sea level and a very attractive spot in the mountains today – a resort for walkers, and, a little higher up, those using ski and snowboard. As with Llano, the Huxleys did not move in immediately – the cabin needed work to make it properly habitable. They did not take up full-time residence until early 1947. In July they paid a visit and climbed to eight thousand feet, entranced with the view, until they heard the sound of a rattlesnake in the undergrowth. Maria was greatly disappointed because she knew that this meant Aldous could not be allowed to go on his customary walks in case he did not see one of the coiled snakes (a reminder that for all the praise of Dr Bates, Huxley *never* had perfect vision). On their descent they came across two bears ambling across the road, another hazard (although the ever-informative Huxley pointed out that bears were vegetarian)[24] From Maria's point of view Wrightwood was not as attractive as her desert paradise: 'The windows do not open on to any horizon. At night I can see neither the moon nor the stars; in the morning there is no huge and golden awakening.'

The following month Maria suddenly announced to Jeanne that they had crazily bought a second house at Wrightwood. 'To the degree that the other one is gloomy, ugly, stuffy, sombre, cramped, and horrible, the new one is glorious, in the open air and full of light with windows, sky, and views (relative, as all views will be for the rest of my life, in comparison with Llano).'[25] Huxley wrote to Krishnamurti at Ojai offering him the chance to use the first cabin as a mountain retreat: 'Wrightwood itself is at six thousand feet and the temperature is always agreeable, never going above ninety, when there was a heatwave in the neighbouring desert of over a hundred. Mornings and evenings are cool and the air is stimulating.'[26] There was a nearby store and electricity in the cabin. The new house, a former forest ranger's station on Highway Two, had an adjoining stable for the ranger's horse, which the Huxleys altered into a studio for Aldous. Wrightwood's local historian, Pat Krig, who was a child when the Huxleys arrived, told me that she remembered them as being rather 'sombre' and 'remote' residents who kept themselves to themselves. She felt that their alterations had detracted from the 'mountainy' feel of the cabin but its present owner – like the Huxleys a refugee from city life, on the East Coast – was delighted with the house and its setting of pine trees: 'It's good to see the seasons again!' he told me. The house was situated in ten acres of land and, just a little way down the hill there was a silver-fox farm, which they were assured would not smell. It was certainly small, but conversion of the stable block could solve that problem. Maria struggled to be philosophical about the loss of Llano: 'It could have been a beautiful dream but in reality it was a nightmare and I couldn't live that way. I believe the physical work helped to get me through the war, ill-health, Matthew going away . . . it was there that for the first time in my life I found steady and reliable health.'[27] By October 1945 the ranch at Llano was up for sale (though it wasn't sold until early 1947) and Huxley was at work again at the studios on a new film.

The Perennial Philosophy, which appeared in September 1945, should not have surprised his readers – a respect for the mystical tradition having been present in his work for a decade – but it clearly did so. A typical reviewer was C.E.M. Joad in the *New Statesman* who lamented that the Huxley of 1929 who could write in an essay in *Do What You Will* that he was 'a worshipper of life who accepts all the conflicting facts of existence' had now become a devotee of the Highest Common Factor. 'If a choice must be made,' Joad declared, 'the unregenerate Huxley of sixteen years ago seems to be infinitely preferable to the sour-faced moralist of today. The trouble with Huxley is and always has been intellectual whole-hoggery. Ideas will go to his head. He should read Aristotle on moderation.'[28] To call Huxley a 'sour-faced moralist' seems a little excessive but the charge of 'intellectual whole-hoggery' has a grain of truth in it. In practice, Huxley's politics – after the bumpy confusions of the late 1920s – had emerged very clearly. He was a decentralist, a believer in self-governing small communities, and a hater of state socialism and state fascism. Utopian politics of right and left he saw as inescapably totalitarian – because they wished to steamroller opposition to *their* imposed blueprint – and he was a libertarian and a pluralist in politics.

But his attachment to what Leibniz had called the *philosophia perennis* did indeed rest on the conviction that there was One Answer – however rich and eclectic the material he assembled turned out to be. In Huxley's exaggerated predictions of what would happen after the war, and in his Cassandra-like ejaculations about the state of the world throughout the 1940s and 1950s, there is the sense of a man who has conceived of the contemporary problem and its solutions in intellectual terms perfectly satisfactory to him and who is disappointed at the world's inability to follow his lucid directions for saving itself. The intellectual, Joad seems to be saying, runs the risk of simplifying the world into a set of watertight theorems, ignoring its complexity which is founded often in contradiction and the resistance of the human material to logical straightening out. Too readily, sometimes, Huxley would happen on the work of a thinker with a Big Idea – such as William Sheldon and his theory of human types – and immediately see in it a comprehensive and sufficient explanation. Such a disposition is the pure intellectual's occupational hazard. But the new philosophy that Huxley was presenting in the book – in fact a very old philosophy as he was at pains to point out – was a great deal more complex than anything he had embraced to date. What exactly was it?

'The Perennial Philosophy is primarily concerned with the one, divine Reality substantial to the manifold world of things and lives and minds. But the nature of this one Reality is such that it cannot be directly and immediately apprehended except by those who have chosen to fulfil certain conditions, making themselves loving, pure in heart, and poor in spirit.' In direct contrast to the knowledge that is in books or encyclopaedias, the perennial philosophy needs a prepared human instrument on which to play its melodies. 'Knowledge is a function of being. When there is a change in the being of the knower, there is a corresponding change in the nature and amount of knowing . . . What we know depends also on what, as moral

beings, we choose to make ourselves.' Two paradoxes play throughout this argument: Huxley's stress on the limitations of words, of the
need to tune in to the ineffable, comes from a dazzlingly proficient
wordsmith; and his pre-occupation with 'seeing' and the invisible-
ness of God, comes from a man who wrestled all his life with the
difficulty of seeing in the plain physical sense. Later, he would seek
to explore consciousness in a drug-induced manner, to 'see' with
chemical assistance. His whole life was, as I suggested in the opening
pages of this book, a search for light, for means of knowing and
seeing that did not depend on the shortcomings of the human
machinery. More than most, he would value the words of Dionysus
the Areopagite: 'For this darkness, though of deepest obscurity, is
yet radiantly clear.' But he insisted in *The Perennial Philosophy* that
all this was not escapism. A key theme of the book is that the
insights of mysticism are *data*. They are real elements in life and not
abstractions.

The book is written, it hardly needs saying, with absolute clarity
and avoids the sort of luminous waffle that such subjects can invite.
It is true that concessions are made to the portentous initial capital
(Reality etc) but the book – essentially a series of extracts from the
great mystical works of the world 'chosen mainly for their significance . . . but also for their beauty and memorableness' – introduces
and explains each extract, linking it to others. Anyone new to this tradition would find it hard not to be seduced by the way the material
is presented and it remains a valuable primer for this body of
thought. The extracts combine the wisdom of East and West, from
Christian mystics like William Law, St John of the Cross, Thomas
Traherne, Meister Eckhart, to Chinese Tao and Indian scripture,
Buddhism, Hinduism, Islam, and Dionysus the Areopagite. Huxley's
education, since arriving in America in 1937, at the hands of Gerald
Heard, the Swami Prabhavananda, and Krishnamurti, bore fruit in
the essentially Eastern bias of his presentation. Central to his exposition is the Sanskrit phrase *tat tvam asi* ('That art thou'), the
perception that the Atman, or immanent eternal Self discoverable in
each of us, is one with Brahman, 'the Absolute Principle of all existence'. The purpose of life, for the mystic, is to connect with the

divine 'ground' of all existence. 'It is from the more or less obscure intuition of the oneness that is the ground and principle of all multiplicity that philosophy takes its source. And not alone philosophy, but natural science as well. All science, in Meyerson's phrase, is the reduction of multiplicities to identities.' Huxley was not about to turn his back on science, however much he knew its current limitations.

Although this is a book which explores the ineffable and the unseen, it is far from insulated from the real world. Again and again, Huxley tilts at his old targets, such as the need to love the earth and respect nature instead of following the example of those 'who chopped down vast forests to provide the newsprint demanded by that universal literacy which was to make the world safe for intelligence and democracy, and got wholesale erosion, pulp magazines, and the organs of Fascist, Communist, capitalist and nationalist propaganda'. He attacked 'technological imperialism' and the mechanisation which was 'increasing the power of a minority to exercise a co-ercive control over the lives of their fellows' and 'the popular philosophy of life . . . now moulded by advertising copy whose one idea is to persuade everybody to be as extraverted and uninhibitedly greedy as possible, since of course it is only the possessive, the restless, the distracted, who spend money on the things that advertisers want to sell' – the argument of *Brave New World* recapitulated. He talked of non-attachment, 'standing out of one's own light', and turning one's back on the 'universal craving' that consumer capitalism has fostered (in an exponential way since 1945, we might add, and with much less opposition, at the turn of the twentieth century, from the intellectual class). But this was not to articulate a programme of flight from the world. As noted earlier, the book was written specifically as a contribution to the work of post-war reconstruction: 'The politics of those whose goal is beyond time are always pacific; it is the idolaters of past and future, of reactionary memory and Utopian dream, who do the persecuting and make the wars.'

But for many of Huxley's admirers the spectacle of their former iconoclastic hero talking about God – in however vague and non-institutional a way – was profoundly unwelcome.

Notes

1 *L.*500
2 Reading, Letter to Harold Raymond, 17 January 1944
3 *L.*502
4 *L.*502
5 Aldous Huxley and Christopher Isherwood, *Jacob's Hands* (1998) edited with introductions by David Bradshaw and Laura Huxley
6 Isherwood Diaries, Vol 1, p336, 11 March 1944
7 Reading, Letter to Leon Lion, 28 March 1944
8 Reading, Letter to Harold Raymond, 4 April 1944
9 HL, Isherwood papers. Letter to Christopher Isherwood, 13 June 1944
10 Isherwood Diaries, Vol 1, p334, 7 February 1944
11 *L.*505
12 *L.*510
13 RL, Letter from Maria Huxley to Jeanne Neveux, 23 July 1944. Author's translation
14 RL, Letter from Maria Huxley to Jeanne Neveux, 22 August 1944. Author's translation
15 RL, Letter from Maria Huxley to Jeanne Neveux, 19 November 1944. Author's translation
16 HRC, Copy of customs declaration. 25 November 1944
17 RL, Letter from Maria Huxley to Sybille Bedford, 15 January 1945. In English
18 RL, Letter from Maria Huxley to Jeanne Neveux. Undated but probably Easter, 1945. Author's translation
19 *L.*516
20 *L.*525
21 *L.*529
22 *L.*531
23 *SB*2.59 Citing letter from Maria Huxley to Rosalind Rajagopal. Undated
24 RL, Letter from Maria Huxley to Jeanne Neveux, 4 July 1945. Author's translation
25 RL, Letter from Maria Huxley to Jeanne Neveux, 17 July 1945. Author's translation
26 HL, Letter to Krishnamurti, 19 July 1945
27 RL, Letter from Maria Huxley to Jeanne Neveux, 12 October 1945. Author's translation
28 C.E.M. Joad, *New Statesman and Nation*, 5 October 1946. Watt pp363–65

XXX

Gioconda

Shortly before returning to the film studios in the autumn of 1945, Huxley had become, briefly, a political canvasser for President Roosevelt. The Welsh writer George Ewart Evans was told by his son, Paul, who was a friend of Matthew – the latter currently on strike at Warner Brothers' studio and a Roosevelt campaigner – that Matthew had been struck down by 'flu and had prevailed upon his father to do some doorstep leafleting. As Paul Evans put it: 'I daresay that many of the people of Beverly Hills would be surprised to learn that the cadaverous, courtly, half-blind gentleman who knocked at their door and left a political tract was Aldous Huxley.'[1]

The new film project was far from a political tract as Huxley explained to Anita Loos: 'I am about to sign up with Disney' – a delicious leap from Meister Eckhart to the creator of Mickey Mouse – 'for the script of *Alice in Wonderland*, which is to be a cartoon version of Tenniel's drawings and Carroll's story, embedded in a flesh-and-blood episode of the life of the Rev. Charles Dodgson. I think something rather nice might be made out of this – the unutterably odd, repressed and ridiculous Oxford lecturer on logic and mathematics, seeking refuge in the company of little girls and in his own phantasy. There is plenty of comic material in Dodgson's life, and I think it will be legitimate to invent some such absurd climax as a visit of Queen Victoria to Oxford and her insistence on having the author of *Alice* presented to her, in preference to all the big wigs . . .'[2] Dorris Halsey, the current agent for the Huxley estate, whose husband Reece Halsey dealt with Huxley over this contract, told an interviewer that her husband described a story conference with Disney 'who had no idea who and what Aldous Huxley was'. The meeting was 'on two different planes: the two personalities were so dissimilar, and while Aldous was forever courteous – the tone was one of *noblesse oblige* – here was this man who had made a success out of a mouse . . . It was sort of weird.'[3]

While waiting for a non-existent film version of *Brave New World* to materialise, using the talents of Loos, Burgess Meredith and Paulette Goddard (and worrying whether the Hays Office which censored films would tolerate babies in bottles on screen), Huxley threw himself with enthusiasm into the Lewis Carroll project, according to Maria, who noted that he was being paid $5000.[4] His own mother, Julia Arnold, had been one of the little girls photographed by Charles Dodgson and he probably had more of an instinct for the milieu of Victorian Oxford than anyone else in Hollywood at that time. It took him some time to realise that this was probably the last thing wanted by Walt Disney. Rather more quickly he found that 'as usual, it turns out to be impossible to make any of the documentary points which it would be so amusing (at any rate for me) to elaborate . . . it would be nice to reconstruct the university of the period . . . But alas, there is no time in an hour of film – and even if there were time, how few of the millions who see the film would take the smallest interest in the reconstruction of this odd fragment of the forgotten past!'[5] By now, too, the film of *Brave New World* had bitten the dust, in spite of Huxley's being convinced that it had 'a fearful topicality'.[6] RKO, who had been sold the film rights by the crooked agent, Pinker, were now demanding so much that it was unviable. It was later made as an NBC mini-series and the musical rights were later sold – though the musical remains unmade. It is a pity that no one at the BBC thought of approaching Huxley to do *Alice*. The film was eventually made by Disney in 1951 with Huxley's earlier involvement nowhere acknowledged.

Huxley was able to do much of the work at Llano with occasional visits to Wrightwood, which was being steadily improved. The stable block was converted into a writing studio for Aldous, and Maria seemed happy. She told Harold Raymond at Chatto about the house and about Llano, with which she was obviously still in love. She confirmed that Aldous was seeing much better and could read large print with the eye that was once blind: 'If you notice on the photographs, the eyes are never re-touched now.'[7] She aired with him their thoughts about going to Europe, which they had not seen since before the war. 'Sometimes I long to. To go to Florence again. To see the roofs on the French houses. The mists over the dark trunks of the London parks.' But she wondered whether it was 'fair to go and eat your food' (rather injudiciously following this remark with the information that she was feeding her eleven cats with Californian sardines).

Meanwhile, Aldous was looking on the wider world with his usual dismay, telling Middleton Murry that he was forced to wonder whether 'there may not, after all, be some truth in the notion of diabolic possession'[8] to explain the world's madness. It is conventional to describe Huxley as 'pessimistic' in these later years yet it was not the pessimism of hopeless resignation. He kept on hoping that reason and good sense would prevail and did what he could to prepare for that eventuality, notwithstanding his Cassandra-like exclamations of woe at the world scene. In March 1946 he published a little book called *Science, Liberty and Peace*. This short treatise is highly significant for in it Huxley, the inheritor of a great proselytising scientific tradition, makes his most powerful statement of a belief that science has negative as well as positive consequences (though with the stress on the positive). He said the book's aim was to show 'how and by what means applied science has contributed hitherto toward the centralization of power in the hands of a small ruling minority, and also how and by what means such tendencies may be resisted and ultimately, perhaps, reversed'. He was exploring the paradox that science had enabled man in one sense to 'conquer nature' but 'as Tolstoy foresaw, man and his liberties have sustained a succession of defeats'. Faced with the post-war arms race, pre-war pacifists must express their opposition through civil disobedience. He believed that the mass media and 'the spread of free compulsory

education' have created not Mill's enlightened democracy but propaganda for the powerful.

Even if one accepts Huxley's contention that 'never have so many
been so much at the mercy of so few', and even if one endorses his
indictment of the abuses of literacy, there is something disquieting
about his repeated attacks on universal free education (a theme played
repeatedly since the 1920s). A privately-educated upper-middle class
Eton and Balliol man from a distinguished intellectual family cuts a
poor figure denouncing the very means by which those less intellectually privileged – but equally intellectually gifted – than himself
might achieve their fulfilment. Even his great uncle, Matthew Arnold,
in his writings on culture, understood (though popularly thought to
have argued the exact opposite) that the goal of social equality
demanded access to education by all. One wonders at Huxley's progressive friends, particularly in America, not having pointed these
things out to him. In the book he argues once again for decentralisation and small-scale applications of science for self-sufficiency and
supplying local markets, revealing himself yet again as a proto-Green.
One rather relishes his reference to 'the note of bumptious self-con-
gratulation' that began to be sounded with the rise of modern science
in the seventeenth century and notes his first public reference – albeit
fleeting – to the Holocaust. He argues that the rise of nationalism and
centralisation means inevitably that science will serve the ends of
militarism. 'The collective mentality of nations . . . is that of a delin-
quent boy of fourteen, at once cunning and childish, malevolent and
silly, maniacally egotistical, touchy and acquisitive, and at the same
time ludicrously boastful and vain.' He wants scientists to oppose the
arms race and concentrate their skills on tackling instead problems of
food production and of fostering regional self-sufficiency in food
production. He concludes by advocating a Hippocratic oath for scientists.

During the summer of 1946, Huxley began work on yet another
film project: to turn his short story from *Mortal Coils* in 1922, 'The
Gioconda Smile' into a movie. The story had been bought a year previously, 'badly handled by an inexperienced writer, and then brought
to me for a revision which has turned into complete re-writing'.[9] He

had just turned down an approach from another producer to acquire the rights to *Point Counter Point* – 'a costume piece, I suppose, about the idyllic nineteen-twenties'[10] – but was chary of making the same mistake as with *Brave New World* and letting the rights go for a song. He had also managed to commit himself 'to compile an anthology of essays and criticism for the *Encyclopaedia Britannica* people. I wish I hadn't, but there it is.' The director of the new film, which would eventually be called *A Woman's Vengeance*, was Zoltan Korda and the salary was a comfortable $1500 dollars a week. Probably one of the strongest plots in film-maker's terms from the self-professed uncongenital novelist, 'The Gioconda Smile' was also worked on towards the end of the year by Huxley as a stage script, its third generic version – though he would admit cheerfully to Jeanne that summer: 'I know nothing about the contemporary theatre, not having been to a play for years'.[11] Huxley spent the summer at Wrightwood in his stable-studio working on it for Korda, 'a very nice fellow who has good ideas and who doesn't interfere'.[12] As soon as it was finished he talked of reworking it into a stage version and then announced his plans to write an historical novel about St Catherine of Siena (abandoning a slightly more ambitious plan to mix it with contemporary material). This idea in the end came to nothing.

As Huxley pressed on with all these projects in seclusion in the mountains at Wrightwood, Maria wrote to Suzanne: 'I think Aldous is a little down without his mixed harem.'[13] As autumn drew on to winter the first snow came at Wrightwood and Aldous was out shovelling in order to get to his studio. He and Maria spent their last Christmas at Llano – where life was a little more spacious – before moving permanently to Wrightwood on 26 February 1947. From here Huxley sent the play to John Van Druten, who collaborated (secretly, he didn't want his role acknowledged) in rewriting it. According to Beth Wendel, who later collaborated with Huxley on another of his plays, Huxley had no visual imagination whatsoever and the collaborator had to be the one who visualised it on stage and who supplied details of sets, action, entrances and exits. Huxley confessed to Van Druten that he wasn't 'artist enough' to put what he called 'the whole truth' into a play. But maybe that couldn't be done at all: 'That is why,

I think, I have never cared profoundly for the theatre.'[14] A disarming admission from someone trying to run two scripts at once and from one who would continue to dream until his death of the possibility of theatrical success. In January 1947 he wrote to Ted McKnight Kauffer that work on both scripts of *Gioconda* was progressing in the usual jig-saw puzzle way: 'It is rather maddening work ... But having embarked on it, I feel I had better finish the damned thing as well as I can – even though it probably won't be much good, as I am far from a born playwright.'[15] Huxley's modest view of his abilities both as novelist and playwright – he thought he lacked the necessary innate talents for supreme distinction in both – does not seem to have led him to believe he should lay down his pen. He would be working at Wrightwood (though keeping on the South Doheny Drive flat for the rest of the year) and bidding farewell finally to Llano in February, 'very sadly, but feeling that it is the sensible thing to do, in view of the difficulties and troubles it involves'.

On the first night at Wrightwood, Maria wrote to Jeanne that Aldous was delighted with the new house now that his library was installed and the central heating working. It was a more practical house than the one at Llano, with its electricity and hot water: 'But it is ugly.'[16] A few days later Maria wrote again to give Jeanne some names of people in London she could contact. Jeanne had gone to London to train as a teacher of the Bates method of visual education. Maria's list is a roll-call of the old friends from the 1920s and 1930s, beginning with Mary Hutchinson, who was living in Charlotte Street and whom Maria claimed not to have been in contact with since the outbreak of war. (She started a letter to Mary but abandoned it, saying broken threads are 'very difficult to re-knot'.[17]) She told Jeanne that she had no desire to renew the acquaintance and described her former friend cuttingly as a 'nymphomaniac'.[18] Raymond Mortimer was another contact who also occupied an interesting milieu but it was one 'like all of Bloomsbury very difficult to penetrate, and I always had a horror of it'. Eddy Sackville-West, she said, like Raymond, 'always had a weakness for me'. Yvonne Franchetti from Forte was now married to Hamish Hamilton, the publisher: 'All that is so far in the past that it's like the memory of something read in a novel.' Naomi Royde-Smith could introduce Jeanne to the world of the theatre. And finally, there was Constance Collier who had been a Hollywood neighbour and close friend: 'Aldous and I love Constance. She sees life in the same way as we do and loves us also.'

In her cold chalet in the mountains, Maria was looking back on this world without apparent regret. But there was always a sense of fragility in Maria's moods. She told Christopher Isherwood that they had been to see Peggy and Bill Kiskadden: 'One of those wonderful Californian evenings when the sun is just warm enough and the air cool enough and there is the promise of so much happiness if we did not mar it.'[19] The Huxleys had read Isherwood's letter from England, sitting in the sun in one of their favourite spots in Los Angeles, the Farmer's Market, where they so often lunched and where Huxley first met Stravinsky: 'and suddenly all was covered by the English greyness which made me suffer so much always because I was not born in it'. A key perhaps to the Huxleys' life of wandering? Isherwood was also told of another evening with Evelyn Waugh, arranged by Sir Charles Mendl: 'Waugh was wearing a little black hat on top of his little face and a striped suit over his little body; terrible.' Maria thought she had put her foot in it by asking Waugh's wife what was making her so melancholy – 'they walked off, all three, and we were left – uncomfortable. When I think of our lives I realize that we know only very nice people.'

These days she passed the ranch at Llano on the way to Wrightwood 'without a pang . . . almost . . . But when I come down from that gloomy shut-in valley (where at night I see only three stars and an electric pole in the narrow sky) into the large desert which is a mass of sun and colour as well as luminous large clouds in spring and where the eye goes further and further and the heart with it endlessly, then I mind more than I should.' But Aldous, in spite of a brief health scare (when his heart beat suddenly increased) was happy, as was Matthew, in spite of the fact that his mother was slightly scandalised at his living with his partner at the other house in Wrightwood. Maria was tired: 'Having two houses, and Aldous being the most absent-minded of men, he never realises quite what is going on with me. That has had its advantages (in the past when I was young) as well as disadvantages. A. is so good and so loving that my whole life is filled with it. But the tiredness caused by human beings is unbearable and insurmountable. A mere walk is enough for me. That is one of the reasons why I fear so much a trip to Europe.'[20] Aldous himself was happy and full of brightness, 'and we walk alongside the dark lakes under a menacing sky. He started the new novel the day before yesterday and talks to me about it with passion; I tell myself, however, that it must be very disappointing for him to talk to someone who understands so little about the subject . . . But Aldous never complains about lack of friends. We have none. None with whom he can exchange "intellectual fireworks" as an American woman put it to us . . . Aldous has become a very remarkable and significant person.'

Maria realised that life would be easier in Los Angeles, with easily available domestic help: 'But it is our double life and our love of LIBERTY which ensures that I am a slave. I am not seriously complaining. For we have chosen this and it is very sweet and very peaceful to be alone during the whole day and just the two of us together in the evening.' And so she put up with the house, 'ugly, uncomfortable and far too small', as it was. Perhaps if Aldous had a secretary . . . But he did not. Her tiredness was 'because Aldous, who is worth the whole world to me, is still a physical burden in the sense that he is totally impractical and doesn't even want to do anything. He has absolutely no wish to concern himself with practical matters. He doesn't want to talk about them or even think about them.' Maria felt that this exhaustion and lack of inward calm that was being imposed on her was in direct contradiction to the ideas being argued out in his books. But in spite of all this 'he is the sweetest and most adorable and most intelligent man in the world'. That serene Huxley was the one seen by Cyril Connolly, who arrived to write about him for *Horizon*. He saw Huxley's case of 'intellectual adaptation' to Hollywood as exceptional: 'The Californian climate and food creates giants but not genius, but Huxley has filled out into a kind of Apollonian majesty; he radiates both intelligence and serene goodness, and is the best possible testimony to the simple life he leads and the faith he believes in, the only

English writer, I think, entirely to have benefited by his transplantation and whom one feels exquisitely refreshed by meeting.'[21]

Towards the end of March, Huxley began to signal that a projected historical novel about Catherine di Siena was foundering (he had also abandoned an attempt to do a new version, with Anita Loos, of Goldsmith's *She Stoops to Conquer*). Loos was told that he was now thinking of a novel about 'a post-atomic-war society'[22] and Harold Raymond was promised something 'half grotesque and half serious' along these lines: 'A strictly contemporary novel seems very difficult to write, as the present world is so obviously provisional and makeshift, so that individual actions have an air of pointlessness, while anything in the nature of satire falls far short of everyday reality.'[23] Against this background he struggled on with the script, replacing his usual jigsaw puzzle metaphor for screenwriting with a new one which compared it to carpentry. The censors were giving problems because of the mention of pre-marital sex and divorce, 'the principle of the Johnson Office's morality being that nothing may be said in a decent way but all may be suggested indecently'.[24] In the Rank studio where he was working on *A Woman's Vengeance*, (that title having been bestowed by 'the all-powerful Jewish gentlemen in charge of distribution'[25]) Huxley overheard a remark that would end up in his next novel. The Studio casting manager told his director, Zoltan Korda: 'In this studio not even Jesus Christ could get a raise in salary.' The Korda brothers tried to revive the idea of filming *Point Counter Point* but without any outcome. Jeanne's husband, the French playwright Georges Neveux, was also working on a version in French of *The Gioconda Smile*.

As soon as Huxley could get free from the studio, which was at the end of September, he set off with Maria by car for New York. This was the first time since 1938 that they had left California and, for Maria at least, it was a welcome break. She told Rosalind Rajagopal that she now had 'an absolute horror of California. I would not mind if I never went back.'[26] *The New Yorker* ran Huxley down during his stay, interviewing him in his Central Park South apartment. 'His sight is still poor, but he continues to eschew glasses and goes in for the optical exercises he thinks have helped him,'[27] the magazine's diarist noted. Describing the simple life of Wrightwood, it noted how he

370 of Aldous Huxley

wrote in the mornings, again in the afternoon for a couple of hours, and then after dinner 'he and his wife play phonograph records or she reads to him – generally novels like *War and Peace* or *The Brothers Karamazov*, which he likes to re-read or re-listen to, every few years.' Huxley spoke warmly of Korda's work on *A Woman's Vengeance*. 'We didn't suffer from the extraordinary Hollywood assumption that twelve incompetent writers equal one competent one.' He recalled working on *Pride and Prejudice:* 'finding forty or fifty scripts on the story piled up in my office. It gave one the most peculiar feeling – all this wasted energy, this huge pile of pulp that no one looked at.' He then described the new post-atomic novel and declared: 'It's extraordinarily difficult to write a novel today. There's such a sense of general precariousness . . . Now the whole social order is running down in the most hopeless way, with no prospect of amelioration in the immediate future . . . It's Malthus's nightmare come true . . . The touching assumption that man has conquered nature is absolute bosh.' This was vintage Huxley, telling the world, in exquisitely modulated accents, how awful things were. Like the Buddha, in his favourite quotation from that source, he would tell the media: 'I will show you sorrow, and the ending of sorrow.'

With Maria at the wheel of the Ford, they drove back to Los Angeles – finding themselves marooned briefly in the Blue Bird Motel at Little Rock, Arkansas during torrential rains – and to Wrightwood where Maria announced to Matthew: 'I cannot tell you how wonderful it is to have decided we do give up Wrightwood . . . Now Aldous and I long again for the desert.' She added: 'I could leave California in an hour, forever, without one regret! Including all the people it contains, which is very unkind of me.'[28] The house was cold, it needed to be kept warm to avoid freezing-up, and it tied up all their capital in a house that they could not spend all their time in – as Aldous saw no prospect of being relieved of movie-work for the time being. Maria had punished herself for Aldous's sake and wanted to do so no longer. In fact the house would be kept on for more than a year but they would spend most of their time at the flat in Beverly Hills and in travelling: for the next year, 1948, would see their first visit to Europe since the mid-1930s.

Notes

1 National Library of Wales, Letter from Paul E. Evans to George Ewart Evans, 25 September 1945
2 *L*.535
3 HL, Oral History Transcripts, Interview between David King Dunaway and Dorris Halsey, 12 August 1985
4 RL. Letter from Maria Huxley to Jeanne Neveux, 20 October 1945
5 *L*.537
6 *L*.539
7 Reading, Letter from Maria Huxley to Harold Raymond, 21 May 1946
8 *L*.545
9 UCLA, Letter to Reginald Pole, 14 September 1946
10 Reading, Letter to Harold Raymond, 26 May 1946
11 RL, Letter to Jeanne Neveux, 29 July 1946
12 Reading, letter to Harold Raymond, 23 July 1946
13 RL, Letter from Maria Huxley to Suzanne Nicolas, 23 October 1946. Author's translation
14 *L*.560
15 *L*.565
16 RL, Letter from Maria Huxley to Jeanne Neveux, 26 February 1947. Author's translation
17 RL, Cancelled draft of letter from Maria Huxley to Mary Hutchinson on part of sheet used to write to Jeanne Neveux, 20 March 1947
18 RL, Letter from Maria Huxley to Jeanne Neveux, 3 March 1947. Author's translation
19 HL, Isherwood papers. Letter from Maria Huxley to Christopher Isherwood, 6 March 1947
20 RL, Letter from Maria Huxley to Jeanne Neveux, 20 March 1947. Author's translation
21 Cyril Connolly, *Horizon*, October 1947, p11
22 *L*.569
23 Reading, Letter to Harold Raymond, 1 April 1947
24 *L*.572
25 *L*.576
26 *SB*2.84 quoting letter from Maria Huxley to Rosalind Rajagopal, October 1947
27 *The New Yorker*, 25 October 1947, p27
28 RL, Letter from Maria Huxley to Matthew Huxley, 21 December 1947

XXXI

Europe

Huxley hoped, at the start of 1948, that the Korda brothers, pleased with the success of *A Woman's Vengeance,* would want to film, on location, another of his short stories with an Italian setting, 'The Rest Cure'. During the war he had not stirred out of California and his comments on Europe, while full of compassion for those suffering in the war and its aftermath, had not evinced any desire to go there. Some in England felt resentful of those who, as they saw it, had sat out the war in the sun and as late as February the following year when *Ape and Essence* was offered to the Times Book Club its manager, Andrew Shirley, told Chatto that not merely was the book's futuristic setting unpopular: 'I am also bound to observe that Huxley's only solution is the one he adopted himself in World War II, namely escape',[1] When Chatto responded promptly that Huxley had gone to the USA long before the war 'solely because he would have been stone-blind within a year if he had stayed here',[2] Shirley apologised.

This was a common criticism of Huxley, that his meditations in the desert were merely escapist. He saw them, by contrast, as direct engagements with the real issues. He told Krishnamurti: 'How strange that we should be so much more conscious (once we have reached civilisation) of the artificial problems we ourselves have fabricated than of the cosmic problems presented by the nature of things – more conscious of political and social relations than of the relations between man and Nature, material and spiritual. And yet if the relations between man and his spiritual and material environment can be put on a satisfactory basis, all the other, the man-made problems will tend to solve themselves.'[3] He objected to schoolchildren being taught 'civics' but not the 'much more fundamental ideas' he had expounded in *The Perennial Philosophy*. 'These last are *data* over which we have no control, but to which we must adapt ourselves. "Civics" are home-made.'

On 24 February, Huxley announced that his novel was finished – the title from *Measure for Measure* alluding to the 'angry ape' who 'plays such fantastic tricks before high heaven'. For the first time ever, Aldous agreed to Maria reading it to him. She did this in one sitting, ending, she told Matthew, at one thirty in the morning – a four and a quarter hour marathon. She was awed by it and looked at her husband: 'Though he so often looks old now he looked young and a bit shy and pleased: you know his air of a little boy. Honest, innocent, humble and so clever and knowing so much.'[4]

In mid-June the Huxleys sailed from New York to Europe, travelling from Cherbourg to Paris on 29 June to see Jeanne and Georges Neveux. On 4 July Aldous was interviewed by Georges for the radio and on 13 July they set off for Italy. Just before leaving France, Maria wrote to Mary Hutchinson at last: 'I am so radiantly happy . . . we are so completely part of Europe and at home.'[5] They encountered a political disturbance in Siena when Communists fired on the funeral procession of two policemen. Maria was forced to take shelter in a nearby house. The clashes between fascist-sympathising landlords and peasants were seen by Huxley as further confirmation of his current belief that there was a crisis of population and resources worldwide. He told a local writer, Alberto Bonnoli, that world leaders were fiddling while Rome burned: 'They play power politics and prepare for new wars . . . while the population of the world increases at the rate of 55,000 a day and while erosion destroys every day an equal or perhaps a greater number of acres of fertile land.'[6] He also referred to the findings of Sir Cyril Burt that the average IQ of children was falling which revived the sleeping spectre of Huxley's

eugenicist sympathies: 'The question arises: can one have a democratic way of life in a population which is, biologically speaking,
degenerating?'

In August the Huxleys stayed at the Hotel de la Ville in Rome and,
towards the end of the month they travelled to Sanary, staying for a
couple of weeks at the Villa Rustique. Then it was back to Paris –
where they stayed with Mimi Gielgud – and London, Huxley's first
visit to England since 1937. He was interviewed in his suite at Claridges
by Cyril Connolly for *Picture Post*. Connolly remarked that someone
of his background might have been expected to have become a traditional pillar of the establishment: 'Instead, we find a religious
reformer, a secular mystic, beautifully-dressed, installed at Claridges
with a play running in the West End and a lucrative job writing film
scripts in Hollywood, to which he is on the way back.'[7] Connolly's
comments on the serenity and wisdom of Huxley at this interview
have already been cited. He went on to trace the history of his relationship with Huxley, and his meeting him in Hollywood where he
was 'at once struck by the strange new quality of sublimated sensuality, intellectual pity, spiritual grace. There was nothing of America
about him . . . He dressed like an Argentine dandy who moves
between Oxford and Rome.' Huxley told his interviewer: 'I am not a
Christian but if I were, the sect which would appeal to me most would
be the Quakers.' The English audience must have been as perplexed as
Connolly by this new manifestation of Huxley the elegant sage, pouring tea from a silver Claridges pot and talking about Zen and Tao.

The writer Robert Payne, in a description written around the same
time, also noted Huxley's aura of well-bred sanctity: 'He has the air
of a young archbishop, and nothing is so surprising as to see him sitting decoratively in a film studio, a film script on his knee, his blue
suit flowing like full canonicals, and the man himself, with his rare
elegance and that nonchalance which is the fruit of a practised art,
and even of a kind of vision, somehow gives the impression of continually blessing the place . . .'[8] Payne discovered there in the
Universal studios 'an Englishman who gave all the appearance of
being a saint, a real saint . . . and with this extraordinary air of calm
and sanctity there went a voice so grave, so gentle, so delicately and

impenitently modulated that it came like a shock on exposed nerves.' This observation was all the more striking given Payne's admission that he had loathed Huxley's writing, finding it at first superficial and callow. Huxley told Payne that Zoltan Korda was the only thing that kept him in Hollywood: 'that, and the knowledge of all the good that could come out of here if only men would set their minds to it.' Payne noted that Huxley, for all the profundity of his reflections – his belief that only 'mercy' could now save us – was utterly without sententiousness and the old wit repeatedly broke through. He went back to Huxley's flat and took tea then left him 'groping a little at the edges of the pavement, the grey hair like a wave and the half-blinded eyes gazing through the darkness'. And it occurred to Payne that he was seeing Oedipus at Colonus.

The Huxleys sailed back from England in October to New York, where Huxley remained alone until the end of November. Maria went on to Wrightwood, leaving him to take treatment in New York from a German doctor, Gustav Erlanger, who introduced certain drugs by means of 'a very mild galvanic current' which had some slight effect in clearing up the opacities.[9]

Ape and Essence was as far from the historical novel of fourteenth century Italy centring on the life of St Catherine of Siena as one could conceive. It is a nightmare projection of a post-atomic Los Angeles, a strange, disturbing novel with none of the occasional humour of *Brave New World*. Unusually for Huxley it begins with a first person narrative and in the milieu of the Hollywood studio, in 1947, where the screenwriter-narrator is told by the studio boss, Lou Lublin, that 'in this Studio at this time, not even Jesus Christ himself could get a raise'. He then speculates about how such a scenario, 'Christ before Lublin', would get made if the commission were given to a great artist like Rembrandt or Piero. Then he notices a two-ton truck loaded with scripts for incineration and in particular a treatment titled 'Ape and Essence' by a William Tallis who lives in the Mojave desert. The narrator and a colleague go out to the desert – described in such a way that Llano comes immediately to mind – but the man is dead. The second part of this very short novel prints the script. One wonders whether, if the Studio bosses had given Huxley his head and

Hollywood was not Hollywood, this is the script Huxley would have wanted to write.

The audience for this movie of the future consists of baboons and what appears in it is a vision of a society after the Third World War, a nightmare projection of the ideas expressed in *Science, Liberty and Peace*, about irresponsible science serving militarism and nationalism ('A choking scream announces the death, by suicide, of twentieth century science'). The atomic explosion is referred to as 'The Thing' and the new society practises brutal human sacrifice on 'Belial Day' where deformed babies are murdered (Huxley's last word on eugenics?). The society is misogynistic – women are unclean vessels who produce these deformed babies – and both sex and procreation, as in *Brave New World*, are divorced from parenthood and family life. Culture is equally valueless: fuel for the communal ovens is supplied by books from the Los Angeles Public Library. The ritual of Belial Day, presided over by His Eminence the Arch Vicar of Belial, Lord of the Earth, Primate of California, Servant of the Proletariat, Bishop of Hollywood, is a parody of institutional religion. It takes place in the Los Angeles Coliseum and exhibits 'the groundless faith, the subhuman excitement, the collective imbecility which are the products of ceremonial religion'. The script inveighs against war and the plundering of the planet's resources (Huxley believed that if nuclear war did not destroy the human race it could accomplish the task itself by allowing population to overtake a dwindling stock of natural resources) and the notion of Progress – 'the theory that you can get something for nothing'. The Arch Vicar, who in a twisted and cynical form gives voice to some leading Huxleyan notions, argues that after the First World War traditional values disappeared 'and the resulting vacuum was filled by the lunatic dreams of Progress and Nationalism' and scientists 'ceased to become human beings and became specialists'. Normality in this hideous society is provided by the visiting New Zealander, Dr Poole, who falls in love with an indigenous woman, Loola, and the two eventually escape to the Mojave desert as 'Hots', the tiny minority which does not obey the rules of seasonal mating and which is free (which, of course, is always what happens in the movies).

In a letter to Sir Richard Rees in March 1949 George Orwell, who found the book 'awful', asked: 'And do you notice that the more holy he gets, the more his books stink with sex. He cannot get off the subject of flagellating women. Possibly, if he had the courage to come out & say so, that is the solution to the problem of war. If we took it out in a little private sadism, which after all doesn't do much harm, perhaps we wouldn't want to drop bombs etc.'[10] There are traces of sado-masochism to be found in other parts of the Huxley oeuvre but no evidence to suggest that this was a personal disposition rather than that rather cruelly bleak way he had of reporting on human oddity. Other reviewers wondered whether Huxley's bleak vision was anything more than that and whether, simply by piling on the horrors, he was actually displaying a lack of human compassion. The disgust was powerful but were the prescriptions being adumbrated potent enough to escape the charge of practising a sort of pornography of repulsion?

Juliette Huxley wrote to Brett that she had found the book: 'Too crude and juvenile. The still undigested libidos torment him yet.'[11] Reviews generally were lukewarm and Huxley expressed his sorrow at this to Chatto: 'Perhaps the book is bad? Who knows? I know it cd be better & see now how I could have made it so; but I still think it's a reasonably decent piece of work & that it says some important things. But perhaps one is mistaken.'[12] No one could accuse Huxley of being an arrogant author or a *prima donna*. In a letter to the writer Philip Wylie he admitted the difficulty inherent in the novel of ideas for those who had neither the elevated genius of Dostoevsky nor the contentment with the small-scale of a Peacock: 'We fall between two stools and find it horribly difficult to make a satisfactory marriage between ideas and a middle-sized, non geniusish novel.'[13] In an interview in *The Listener* at the end of 1948 he had told John Davenport: 'I don't feel I am really a novelist; it seems to be all a slight fraud, the whole thing, that I am saying something in fictional terms. I think, frankly, a good novelist has to be in some sense rather larger than life . . . the big novelist has to have this gargantuan capacity for experience and enjoyment; and unfortunately I don't feel I have that.'[14]

In November 1948 Huxley had a severe attack of bronchitis and on doctor's orders spent the winter months in the Palm Desert at an

address called the 'Sage and Sun Apartments'. He was working on a
stage version of *Ape and Essence* and preparing a volume of essays.
'After that, I hope, will come the historical novel.'[15] He described the
Palm Desert location to Victoria Ocampo: 'We are . . . surrounded by
sand and date palms, very glad to be out of the rains, snows, frosts and
tempests which have prevailed in the rest of California . . . It is quiet
and one works well.'[16] He found it 'most surprising and gratifying' that
The Gioconda Smile had done very well in London and was still playing after nine months. It was also to do tolerably well in Paris in a
version by Georges Neveux in early 1949. One of the pieces in the
planned volume of essays was to be on the French writer Maine de
Biran whose *Journal Intime* he had discovered again at Sanary in the
summer, covered in his own annotations of fifteen years previously.
Memories of Sanary, however, did not awaken any desire to return to
France. Maria discussed it with Jeanne and concluded: 'I don't think
we will ever come to live in France or Europe . . . Aldous and I envis-
age ourselves here in our later years.'[17] She added: 'Suddenly, yesterday,
Aldous and I were both tempted by a house in a street with a garden
and designed to our taste. Everything about it persuades us and it is in
our price range.' The Huxleys were always impulsive about choosing
houses (even if they repented at leisure) and 740 North King's Road,
Los Angeles thus became their latest address, although as usual they
did not move into it permanently at first, spending May to September,
their last summer, at Wrightwood. The house in the mountains had to
go but it was still beautiful – in spite of diesel lorries carrying 'man-
gled redwoods' and filling the air with carbon monoxide 'so that the
road for miles at a stretch, is worse than Wilshire Boulevard. But one
can still get off the highway and walk – and then it is paradise.'[18] It is
one of the inconveniences of paradises, however, that they invariably
prove unsustainable. The move back to Los Angeles had become
inevitable. The new house would be 'large, commodious' the garden
'with big trees and plenty of privacy' and the location 'in that curious
country lane between Santa Monica and Melrose, full of huge estates
and enormous trees'.[19] It was considered not too expensive – $10,000
down with $13,000 to pay in ten years at $135 a month.

　　The Huxleys moved in to the new house in the summer. In July they had dinner with the Stravinskys, an event minutely recorded by the music critic and conductor, Robert Craft. Craft noticed Huxley's 'silver-point features' and his eyes: 'The right cornea is covered by a milky film, like a clouded glass, and it is the unflawed but rapidly nictitating left eye which he turns to us, though its powers of sight are hardly greater. His skin has a desiccated appearance – from the desert sun during his anchorite period, one would suppose, except that it is deathly white. Everything else about the man except the big weedy brows suggests not the out-of-doors, however, but the tightly-sealed edifices of intellectual respectability.'[20] Craft noted how poor was Huxley's sight ('he *feels* for his knife, fork and plate, with the palpitations of the blind'). Maria helped him to find his food and quietly directed him throughout ('Un tout petit peu à gauche, chérie'). The Huxleys spoke French to each other at home but also on this occasion, because Stravinsky was not really used to the 'lambent, culture-saturated purr' of Huxley's version of the English mandarin dialect. Stravinsky still saw Huxley as a man of science and a rationalist rather than as a mystic and was worried that he would be unable to keep up with a scientific discourse. Huxley's after dinner conversation was extraordinarily learned and multifarious. His hands gesticulated hugely. 'But he is the gentlest human being I have ever seen, and the most delightfully giggly.' The Stravinskys returned to the Huxleys for tea on 19 August, rather intimidated by the austerity and gloom of the surroundings at North King's Road ('the sepulchral lighting and raftered baronial hall') where they were offered 'parsley tea with crystal sugar, and a tray of molasses cookies, wheat germ, raw carrots, small wedges of non-fattening fruit cake'. Craft felt that Huxley was better to listen to than to read because one was absolved of the Tolstoyan sermons and treated to wonderful digressions of a kind that a writer would feel the need to rein in or edit out. Craft thought that Huxley saw in Stravinsky what he also saw in Lawrence – evidence of a great creative genius that he did not himself possess.

Almost the last letter Huxley wrote before quitting Wrightwood was to George Orwell – whose essays and letters are full of rather condescending references to Huxley (as if the world had room for

only one Old Etonian dystopian novelist and contemporary commentator). Huxley was thanking Orwell for the gift of *1984*. He agreed
how 'fine and how profoundly important the book is'[21] but doubted
that future authoritarian rulers would adopt the brutal repression of
those in Orwell's book. 'My own belief is that the ruling oligarchy will
find less arduous and wasteful ways of governing and of satisfying its
lust for power, and that these ways will resemble those which I
described in *Brave New World*.' Huxley's belief that liberty would be
surrendered through conditioning, through populations coming to
'love their servitude', rather than 'clubs and prisons', would indeed
seem much more in line with what has actually happened in the West
in the second half of the twentieth century.

Finally established in North King's Road, Huxley reviewed his current projects. The essays were virtually complete, the one on de Biran
having run to 40,000 words. 'If the thing comes off as I hope, it will be
an example of what I think is a new literary form,' he told Harold
Raymond, 'in which philosophical discussion is enlivened and given
reality by the fact of its being particularised within a biography.'[22]
This was to be Huxley's aspiration for the future – to find forms
which provided adequate vehicles for the things he wanted to say. He
had long ago abandoned any purely aesthetic speculations or experiments. The de Biran essay appeared as part of *Themes and Variations*
in May 1950. It was the longest essay in the book, almost book-length
(and might profitably have been reissued as such). It was based on
Maine de Biran's *Journal Intime* and was written very much in the
style of *Grey Eminence*, with the attempt at historical portraiture soon
giving way to intellectual exposition. De Biran (1766–1824) was obviously a very sympathetic spirit to Huxley, a cerebrotonic and a realist
or 'empiricist of the spirit'. Like the visually-impaired Huxley, de
Biran's constant illness made him what he was: 'Health impels us
towards the outside world, sickness brings us home to ourselves.' He
was also a thinker who saw the coming of the modern threats to liberty in the culture of the machine and in the ideologies of nationalism
and progress. Every reasonable person, Huxley concluded, should try
to 'escape from history'. De Biran was 'concerned to establish the irre-
ducible and primordial faculty of the inner world' and set it against

the outer world of history. Huxley predicted what he called a 'third revolution' following on from the political and economic revolutions: 'The third revolution is that which will subvert the individual in the depths of his organic and hyper-organic being, is that which will bring his body, his mind, his whole private life under the control of the ruling oligarchy.' This was the prediction of *Brave New World,* written sixteen years previously, and assuming it would not happen for 'five or six centuries'. Writing in 1949: 'Today that estimate seems to me excessive.' Apart from the de Biran essay, 'Variations on a Philosopher', the book has essays on art and religion, on the inability of Western art in the main to handle adequately the theme of death, on El Greco (in truth a much more successful combination of aesthetic analysis and philosophising in a biographical context than the de Biran essay), on Piranesi's 'Prisons' ('Today every efficient office, every up-to-date factory is a panoptical prison in which the worker suffers . . . from the consciousness of being inside a machine'), on Goya, and on 'The Double Crisis' ('The human race is passing through a time of crisis, and that crisis exists, so to speak, on two levels – an upper level of political and economic crisis and a lower level of demographic and ecological crisis').

In spite of these high intellectual preoccupations, Huxley was thinking of the studios again. He was working with Christopher Isherwood and a screenwriter called Lesser Samuel on an idea for a script. Long thought to have been lost, this treatment recently turned up in the Isherwood papers acquired in late 2000 by the Huntington Library in California. *Below the Equator* was described succinctly by Isherwood (whose hand is the main one in this script) in a letter that May to Gerald Heard: 'Am still working on the S. American movie story I devised with Aldous. It is about a meeting between Peggy Kiskadden, Mr Norris, Julian Huxley and Eileen Garrett, in a tin-mine at 17,000 feet. No-one gets seriously injured, but a bridge is blown up.'[23] Huxley's contribution seems to have been to propose the title 'Armed with Pity' for the script. The script got nowhere. Meanwhile, Huxley pressed on with the never-to-be-written historical novel on St Catherine of Siena. It persuaded him to return to Italy to gather more material and in May 1950, after the marriage of

Matthew to Ellen Howde in New York, the Huxleys set off on the *Queen Mary* to France. One person Huxley hoped to meet in France was Hubert Benoit, a French thinker with whom he had been corresponding extensively. Aldous and Maria attended the wedding in New York, he in a suit tailor made in Rome (in London he would order another of his immaculate suits from Studd and Millington in Piccadilly) and Maria in a quilted black dress. They entertained the Hubbles in the Raleigh Room of the Warwick Hotel in New York where a waiter tripped and spilt a tray of green salad and boats of French dressing down Aldous's back. He was cleaned up in time for the party to move on to the Ziegfeld Theatre to see the musical of *Gentlemen Prefer Blondes.*

From Cherbourg the Huxleys went straight to Paris to stay with Jeanne and Georges Neveux at 82 Rue Bonaparte. 'And here we are again in Europe as if we had never left it,'[24] Maria wrote to Mary Hutchinson. Aldous wrote to Harold Raymond that he was thinking of another historical study 'this time on the famous devils of Loudun . . . It is a most extraordinary story, illustrating the whole gamut of the religious life from its most infernal depths to its sublimest heights.'[25] This would require further researches in France during the trip. They made another visit to Siena in June 'exploring the incredibly beautiful countryside in a dwarf car'[26] then Aldous left Maria in Sanary at the Villa Rustique where Matthew and Ellen were honeymooning and crossed to England to stay with Julian and Juliette at Pond Street in Hampstead. This provided an opportunity to catch up with old English friends and acquaintances such as Stephen Spender, Edith Sitwell, T.S. Eliot, Cyril Connolly and Osbert Sitwell who was in the first stages of Parkinson's disease. Spender was 'white-haired and distinguished-looking' and Sybil Colefax 'bent double with her broken back, but indomitably receiving guests and going out'.[27] Julian gave a party at which twenty-seven Huxley relatives were present, 'a pleasant and touching experience'. But the sight of all these old society figures from the 1920s and 1930s, ageing, balding, full at the midriff, struck the Californian exile as inescapably 'Proustian'. Although he found England 'much more cheerful than it was 2 years ago'[28] he was still gloomy about the world outlook. His friends were now used to exclamations such as 'What a world!' being used to sign off letters and the endlessly repeated conceit of diabolic possession being the only explanation of the Western world's rush to destruction. From Pond Street Huxley wrote to thank Isherwood for all the work he had done on *Beyond the Equator,* which sounded very much as though Huxley's input was slight. 'You must have put an enormous amount of work into it – which makes me feel rather guilty.'

From London, Huxley returned to Sanary where Maria was preparing to sell the house. They both loved the south of France and were struck by its perennial quality: 'How amazingly tough the French way of life has proved itself!'[29] But they did not seem tempted to remain. They next joined the Neveux family at Juillac, then returned to Paris to see Mimi Gielgud before sailing back to the USA on 22 September. At New York they watched the final rehearsals for *The Gioconda Smile.* 'I found everything in the most frightful mess – the actors at daggers drawn with the producer-director, the rendering of the play unsatisfactory in the extreme'.[30] The play opened on Broadway at the Lyceum Theatre but survived only five weeks. Back in Los Angeles, Huxley told Harold Raymond this was a pity 'for I think, if it had been well cast, it might have gone. And also it is a bore; for it wd have been nice to make some easy money.'[31] Maria had driven them by car from New York stopping to see Frieda Lawrence at Taos and finding her remarkably well and lively – she was now in her seventies. As the year ended the Huxleys were discovering a new fad: dianetics and its language of 'engrams' and being 'clear' etc. Huxley found that there was 'a complete shutting off of certain areas of childhood memory, due, no doubt, to what the dianeticians call a "demon circuit".'[32] This is extremely interesting, for Huxley's later drug-induced explorations of consciousness centred for him on attempts to recover some occluded – and unspecified – childhood memory. 'Hubbard, the author of the book, is a very queer fellow – very clever, rather immature, far from being a "clear" himself ... and in some ways rather pathetic; for he is curiously repellent physically and is probably always conscious of the fact, even in the midst of his successes.'

After the failure of the play and the lack of news about the script with Isherwood, Huxley looked to the new year to settle down to work on *The Devils*, an historical example of the diabolic possession he seemed to detect in the geo-political world of the 1950s.

Notes

1   Reading, Letter from Andrew Shirley to Ian Parsons, 11 February 1949
2   Reading, Letter from Ian Parsons to Andrew Shirley, 14 February 1949
3   HL, Letter to Krishnamurti, 13 January 1948
4   *SB*2.91 Quoting letter from Maria Huxley to Matthew Huxley 22 February 1948
5   HRC, Letter from Maria Huxley to Mary Hutchinson, 6 July 1948
6   *L*.587
7   Cyril Connolly, *Picture Post*, 6 November 1948, 41 (6). pp21–3
8   Robert Payne 'Aldous Huxley' in *Now More Than Ever: proceedings of the Aldous Huxley Centenary Symposium, Munster 1994.* (1995, Frankfurt), pp1–6
9   HRC, Letter to Mary Hutchinson, 23 November 1948
10   George Orwell, Letter to Sir Richard Rees, 3 March 1949, *The Collected Essays, Journalism and Letters of George Orwell, Volume 4, In Front of Your Nose 1945–50* (1970), p539
11   HRC, Letter from Juliette Huxley to Dorothy Brett, 10 December 1949
12   Reading, Letter to Harold Raymond, 20 March 1949
13   *L*.600
14   *The Listener*, 4 November 1948, pp686–87
15   Reading, Letter to Harold Raymond, 16 December 1948
16   *L*.589
17   RL, Letter from Maria Huxley to Jeanne Neveux, 1 May 1949. Author's translation
18   HL, Letter to Grace Hubble, 30 July 1949
19   *L*.597
20   Robert Craft, 'With Aldous Huxley', *Encounter*, November 1965, p10
21   *L*.604
22   Reading, Letter to Harold Raymond, 12 September 1949
23   UCLA, Heard Papers, Letter from Christopher Isherwood to Gerald Heard, 6 May 1950
24   HRC, Letter from Maria Huxley to Mary Hutchinson, 19 (?) May 1950
25   Reading, Letter to Harold Raymond 21 May 1950
26   HL, Isherwood papers, Postcard to Christopher Isherwood, undated but probably mid-June 1950

27 *L.*629
28 *L.*627
29 *L.*630
30 *L.*630
31 Reading, Letter to Harold Raymond, 16 November 1950
32 RL, Letter to Jeanne Neveux, 30 December 1950

XXXII

Devils

Huxley spent the whole of 1951 researching and writing *The Devils of Loudun*, his second full-length historical/biographical study in which he sought to explore ideas in the concrete context of a specific life. Conscious of a lack of complete success with the 'novel of ideas', this seemed to him a solution to the problem of how to present ideas in a form that would prove more attractive than the abstract thesis: the story was graphic and extraordinary but it also gave an opportunity for 'trying to formulate a coherent picture of the mind'.[1] Meanwhile his own intellectual explorations were continuing. Dianetics, taken up at the end of 1950, was followed by a renewed interest in parapsychology. He suggested to Professor J.B. Rhine, whose Parapsychology Laboratory at Duke University had been one of the first places he had visited when arriving in the USA in 1937, that he should publish an anthology of basic parapsychology texts – experimental material and philosophical background material.

All this was done against a background of continued struggling with eye problems. In March 1951 both Aldous and Maria caught a bad 'flu virus that was prevalent in Los Angeles and it attacked Huxley's right eye, the poor one, with the result that he lost all sight in that eye for a period. He was given a treatment that was intended to break down some old scars covering the pupil but it produced some disturbing side-effects and great pain. Huxley was very shaken by the state he was in. 'He was so rattled. It really was horrible,'[2] Maria told Matthew. Although he recovered by May there were further problems throughout the year and generally he was, as Maria put it, 'in an off mood', disappointed in part by the failure of the play which would have given him some freedom.

In June Huxley went to Ojai, where Krishnamurti and Rosalind Rajagopal ran the Happy Valley School, to give the Commencement Address on the theme of the school's motto – which he had probably given them because it was a favourite of his own – *aun aprendo*, I am still learning. His sister-in-law Rose's son, Sigfried Wessberg, attended the school and remembered that although it was run generally on what would be called 'progressive' lines (if you didn't want to go to lessons you didn't have to) there was no rock and roll or junk food and the day began with readings from the Prophet. Huxley gave lectures there, sage-like in the oak grove. Sigfried, as a thoroughly American teenager, was sometimes baffled by his famous relative. He recalled for an interviewer how Huxley watched a young man across the street lovingly waxing and polishing a red Alfa Romeo every Sunday morning. 'How red can it get?' Huxley asked, perplexed at the passion for consumer goods, cars, material possessions that gripped 1950s America. 'That kind of culture, he couldn't grasp it.'[3] It was for similar reasons that he employed Anita Loos as an interpreter of America and its mores. Until she enlightened him he thought an ice-cream sundae was a drink. Sigfried also remembered the house at North King's Road: 'They'd have all these séances and all these mushrooms and big pots of seeds and God knows what.' The house smelt of cloves and other herbs and spices and there was 'a big dish in the main living room full of all kinds of dried seeds and dried bushes and jars of things'.

The house became the focus of Tuesday evening sessions, exploring various forms of parapsychological phenomena and hypnotism. The participants started off by dining at the World's Largest Drugstore (now demolished but familiar to readers of *The Doors of Perception*, a book whose groundwork was being prepared in these sessions) after which they gathered in the long living room of the house to explore such things as 'magnetic passes' and the work of mediums. L. Ron Hubbard himself was a visitor. Around this time Gerald Heard published an article on flying saucers which caused Huxley to say: 'I have no settled opinion so far, but keep my trap shut and wait.'⁴ That captures the essence of Huxley's outlook at the time: his mind was open and he wanted to find out about these unusual phenomena which others would dismiss out of hand or mock. These Los Angeles years, after the desert and the mountains, which were to be Huxley's last decade, were filled with more ordinary kinds of social life. They had open air lunches twice a week at Yolanda's in the Town and Country Market (still flourishing and a favourite haunt of elderly Los Angeles residents) with Vera and Igor Stravinsky, Robert Craft, Christopher Isherwood, Gerald Heard, Peggy Kiskadden (whose husband Bill, a doctor, took an interest in Huxley's health) and Betty Wendel (screenwriter and collaborator with Huxley on *The Genius and the Goddess*).

It has already been noted that Huxley is popularly assumed to have been in Hollywood at the centre of a dazzling web of social contacts. But, notwithstanding the distinction of some of these names, it was a small circle. Huxley's modest lifestyle and distaste for swanky restaurants and raucous living and endless socialising meant that his range of acquaintance was not large. Moreover, in the twenty-five years that he spent in America, from 1937 to his death in 1963, he seems to have met very few of the writers who dominated the epoch in literary terms. If one were to draw up a list of the key works of mid-century American writing during these years none of the names would figure in Huxley's published essays or in his published and unpublished private correspondence – though we cannot be certain that he did not read them. He did, by contrast mention frequently works like *The Organisation Man* or *The Hidden Persuaders* and enthusiastically recommended them to friends. He seems to have preferred the company of scientists and social thinkers – and, some would say, quacks. A book like *Human Personality and its Survival of Bodily Death* excited him more than *A Streetcar Named Desire*. Pressed on this by interviewers in 1959 he admitted that he had little interest in contemporary fiction. He had read Kingsley Amis but thought he was 'repeating himself'.[5] John Braine's *Room at the Top* was 'quite good, don't you think?' It seems he had tried Kerouac's *On the Road* but, 'I got a little bored after a time. I mean, the road seemed to be awfully long.'

In April, Huxley asked Robert Craft one day if he would read to him because his good eye was overtaxed. The picture Craft paints is not the one of a triumphant disciple of Dr Bates: 'I find him typing the witchcraft book . . . in the den at the end of the darkened corridor, and on a table stacked ominously with publications in Braille. He is wearing his 'Chinese glasses', black cellulose goggles with perforations in place of lenses: they force the pupils to perform a kind of stroboscopic movement, and consequently prevent staring; Aldous has taped a bandage over the pin-holes on the right side, which means that he no longer has any sight at all from his opaline right eye.'[6] Talking to Huxley about his new book, Craft was puzzled, as many have been, by the contrast between the searching, lucid, rational intelligence which was Huxley's most obvious characteristic and the most striking evidence of his Victorian inheritance, and the credulity with which he greeted (though he did not necessarily swallow whole) each new Southern Californian fad of mind and consciousness. As the year went on he went deeper and deeper into the horrible events and cruelties of the Loudun story – forced to pass over an invitation to go to India with Robert Godel and his wife to visit the holy places of the Himalayas – and pausing only to offer his extreme reflections on a world that seemed, as usual, to be going to the dogs. The Cold War was now raging and on 23 May the House Committee on Un-American Activities heard testimony that Huxley was one of a number of writers involved in an organisation called 'Friends of Intellectual Freedom'. The purpose of this organisation, according to an FBI briefing note in Huxley's file, was 'to raise funds to help former Communist writers rehabilitate themselves'.[7] It was not until 15 May 1953, however, that the FBI finally grasped what should have been obvious from the outset. A confidential memorandum from the Los Angeles Field Office (which had been monitoring his activities) to the Washington Bureau noted: 'Aldous Huxley is well known, highly respected, and far removed from any pro-Russian or Communist Party sympathies.'

In spite of the hard work on the new book, which was only half-complete by the end of May, Huxley managed to break off in July to revise the dialogue of what he called 'a very ingenious and effective stage adaptation' of *After Many A Summer* by a writer called Ralph Rose, whose radio version had already been broadcast. And then he succumbed to more trouble, an attack of iritis, which incapacitated him for five weeks, keeping him in the house and in darkness because he could not stand any light. The doctors thought that this could have been connected to a long-standing chronic bronchitis, which may have been a focus of infection for the eye trouble. The summer was hell. Back on course in October, he was gladdened by the news that he had become a grandfather (to Mark Trevenen Huxley). There was also talk of a new film project on the life of Gandhi 'which perhaps I may tackle when the book is done. Interesting – but dreadfully difficult. Still, a challenge.'[8] This was another project, planned by the director Gabriel Pascal, that would come to nothing. On 23 January 1952 Huxley announced at last to Chatto: 'My book is finished.'[9]

All should have been well but now it was Maria's turn to be ill. She had been taken to hospital for treatment of a cyst, which, though Huxley does not seem to have acknowledged or to have been told this, turned out to be a malignant tumour. In fact he told Jeanne: 'The doctors are confident there will be no recurrence as the trouble was taken in good time and got rid of very thoroughly. No radiation will be necessary.'[10] Maria was said to be well and to have become 'a reformed character in regard to eating and consumes large quantities of meat – the proteins of which have speeded up the healing of the wound in a remarkable way.' Aldous and Maria went out at the start of the year for a brief holiday in the Arizona desert, glorying in the sight of snow on the higher mountains and the carpets of spring flowers and the remarkable desert lilies: 'It is an unforgettable spectacle – the good will of life, the tenacity of it in the face of the most adverse circumstances, the patience of it (the lilies will lie dormant for as much as ten or fifteen years, if there is a drought, and then come bursting through the sand at the first moisture), the profusion, the beauty. And the yearly miracle takes place in an enormous, luminous silence.'[11] For the first time Huxley wrote explicitly of the desert as a place associated with mystical vision: 'as a means to purifying insight into the divine otherness, there is nothing to compare with that silence'. On his return he struck Robert Craft as 'refreshed and in high spirits'[12] when he dragged him off for his favourite walk over the summit of Doheny Hill, pouring out abstruse dendrological information and ending with a drive to an ice-cream parlour in Beverly Hills where he ordered a banana split. 'Cerebrotonics should eat bananas very day,' he informed Craft.

As well as banana splits, Huxley was treating himself to a newly invented pressure-breathing treatment which he was taking at home with an oxygen tank and a special attachment. This seemed to have eliminated the chronic bronchitis that had been 'a source, over many years, of general under-parness and various troubles of an acuter nature'.[13] He continued to haggle with Pascal over a contract for the Gandhi film. And in London, Chatto were looking over the manuscript of *The Devils of Loudun*. They were not completely happy and felt that it was not going to be as successful as *Grey Eminence*. 'In places the tangential discussions produce a somewhat excessive interruption to the story' and the story itself 'might occasionally prove more than a queasy stomach could assimilate'.[14] Harold Raymond asked Huxley to delete some of the more gruesome details in the torture of Urban Grandier such as 'there was a sound of splintering bone . . . ooze of marrow'. Huxley agreed happily, as he agreed at the same time to a proposal for a book by Robert Hamilton about his work. He said that he would not be among its readers because he never read criticism which was 'always unhelpful, since the critic cannot, in the nature of things, know what the writer is working with and against, what his resources are, what his handicaps and special obstacles . . . That I am not Dostoevsky or Goethe is admittedly deplorable but it is not by deploring that one can add a cubit to one's stature.'[15]

The Huxleys' psychic explorations continued. Maria had a few years earlier been helped by hypnosis after an intestinal infection and Aldous claimed to have become 'a rather good hypnotic operator'[16] who was able to help Maria again after the tumour was removed in January. He thought he was not, as regards himself, 'a particularly

good hypnotic subject' but when he was suffering from iritis the previous year he had received hypnotic treatment from the UCLA
Psychology Department and from Leslie LeCron, a psychotherapist.
The ego, under hypnotherapy, was able to 'let go, to get out of the
way, to stop interfering with the beneficent action of the "entelechy",
which is at once the physiological sub-conscious that sees to the
proper functioning of the body, and the higher, non-personal sub-
conscious . . .' Huxley had discovered 'E' therapy and immediately
began to proselytise amongst his friends, sending them copies of a
pamphlet by A.L. Kitselman describing the technique. He was also
using various kinds of auto-hypnosis on himself to cure insomnia.
Maria was every bit as enthusiastic and she wrote to tell Jeanne that
all this therapy was transforming him: 'You know how all these years
we have loved Aldous, and known his kindness, sweetness and honesty . . . but you also know how, in spite of all that, he was exhausting
to live with, and sad to live with. Well, now he is transformed, trans-
figured . . . Aldous no longer looks the same, or has the same moral
and intellectual attitude towards animals, people, the clouds, or even
the sound of the telephone (which is remarkable).'[17] He was helping
out in the house, proposing ways of acting practically to help others,
in short coming out of his protective shell, all of which she put down
to his exposure to these various therapies. Maria wrote to Matthew at
this time a letter which tried to explain all these changes and to reas-
sure him that they had not become 'Faddists'.[18] In a spirit of great
frankness – did she know the real truth of her illness by now? – she
talked about her first meeting with Aldous at Garsington in terms
that have already been described in an earlier chapter. From now on
both Maria, in the brief time left to her, and Aldous would strike
others as having gained a greater serenity.

The Devils was about to be published in October and Huxley was
planning a book of reflective essays on the American West as well as
negotiating for a trio of short stories for cinema and television to be
played by Laurence Olivier and Vivien Leigh. He was toying as well
with the script of 'a popular science movie on the sun'.[19] When The
Devils appeared it was considered 'horrible'[20] by Basil Blackwell. The
Odhams Press Book Club also turned it down as the subject 'would

cause much raising of eyebrows among the members'. But Huxley
was convinced that it had worked and that his notion of embodying
general ideas in a particular case was the reason it had done so:
'Because they ignore the particular case, the facts of individual life in
a body, science, philosophy and philosophical history are always inadequate to reality as we know it by direct experience,'[21] he told Mary
Hutchinson. The book, set in seventeenth century France, tells the
story of Urban Grandier, the priest who is accused of witchcraft, and
the possession by devils of the nuns of Loudun. As with Arthur
Miller's *The Crucible* of the same year, the persecution of Grandier has
an obvious contemporary resonance. Huxley was named in
November 1952 by an hysterical anti-Communist newsletter
Counterattack as one of a number of authors who had signed an
Authors' World Peace Appeal and by doing so had 'fallen for one of
Moscow's biggest lies'.[22]

The violence of the torture scenes is excessive and the overall picture
of human affairs is profoundly pessimistic, notwithstanding the mel-
lowing of Huxley the man at this time. Successfully transferred to stage
and to film (by Ken Russell after Huxley's death) the story is gripping in
outline but it is the scaffolding onto which Huxley loads reflections on
the seventeenth century mind, excursions around his mystical preoccupations, and dissertations on his view of the world. He was at pains
to stress, in the philosophical passages, that mystical experience is above
all *real*. 'The heavenly kingdom can be made to come *on earth*; it cannot
be made to come in our imagination or in our discursive reasonings.
And it cannot come even on earth, so long as we persist in living, not on
the earth as it is actually given, but as it appears to an ego obsessed by
the idea of separateness, by cravings and abhorrences, by compensatory
phantasies and by ready-made propositions about the nature of things.
Our kingdom must go before God's can come.' In these and many other
passages we hear the voice of Huxley the essayist and the moralist, as it
were grafted on to the story, transparently using the story as a device to
enable him to do so, where one might wish the artistic creation itself
might accomplish the task implicitly. Only those who can accept that
strategy will find it a wholly successful book.

After publication of *The Devils*, Huxley spent the first half of 1953 engaged on miscellaneous film and journalistic projects – such as his one hour documentary on the Sun which taught him that 'one must read 100% in order to be able to leave out 99%, as has to be done in this medium'.[23] Increasingly, his contacts were with scientists, doctors, social scientists, academic specialists in a range of disciplines. His reading, likewise, was in the works of such men and women. Having spent much of his career as a freelance writer tilting at 'the professors', he was now increasingly in their company, trying in some cases to persuade them – ironically, in the case of a proposal to Alan Watts of Stanford for a 'post-graduate school for the study of synthesis and all its methods of practical application to the education process on all its levels',[24] intending to bankroll the plan with funds from 'Our Ford'. These would all be designed to launch programmes of study designed to further Huxleyan grand notions. Huxley was becoming aware of the power of institutions and the big foundations to co-ordinate work on a large scale. One of the last things he would do in the weeks before he died was to try to draft a programme for the World Academy in Stockholm on 'Human Possibilities'. The imbalance of elements, the artistic failure, of his last great attempt at a fictional synthesis of his ideas for a better world, the novel *Island,* has its roots in this omnivorous intellectualism, this pursuit of good ends that ran too eagerly ahead of the necessary artistic delight in means.

Early in January 1953, Huxley's old friends Sir Osbert and Edith Sitwell arrived for tea. Edith was in Hollywood, working with the screenwriter Walter Reisch and George Cukor on a screenplay for her *Fanfare for Elizabeth.* 'It's so nice seeing dear Aldous and Maria Huxley – two of my oldest friends,' she told Geoffrey Gorer. 'Aldous hasn't changed at all since he was 23 (when I knew him first). He drove me to tea with Dr Hubble, the astronomer, the other day, and on the way kept up a long grumble – the drive took 40 minutes – on the subject of Coleridge and Wordsworth. "Really, Edith, that any man *reputed* to be sane should have written, *quite* deliberately, 'I need not say, Louisa dear,/How glad we are to have you here,/A lovely convalescent."'[25] Grace Hubble was present at two of these tea parties, the first of which disclosed Edith Sitwell in her full splendour: 'Today she wore a black turban with a border that reached her shoulders, so that only her face, framed in its borders was to be seen. Fresh, fair, transparent complexion, slanting blue eyes with pale gold lashed, aquiline nose, with thin-lipped curling mouth. Her dress was of masses of black drapery to the floor, concealing her figure completely. She wore one ring, of two aquamarine stones set one above the other, as big as walnuts.'[26] This astonishing phenomenon rose again ten days later to demolish what Aldous described as 'the monstrous Victorians, who became increasingly alien and unnatural. More and more they seem like characters in *Alice in Wonderland* and *Through the Looking Glass*.'[27] Eavesdropping on this tea-party today, as Huxley and the Sitwells – relics of upper-middle class intellectual England in the Californian sun – proceeded to demolish, not only Carlyle and Elizabeth Barrett Browning among the Victorians but Christopher Fry, Arthur Miller's *Death of a Salesman*, and Ford Madox Ford ('and his dreary wife'), a certain narrowness in this patrician taste is revealed. Poor old Sir George Colefax, husband of Sybil, was dismissed as 'a bore'[28] at the next tea party, having tried to elucidate the Swiss banking system to Aldous. 'He told *me* the entire story of Joyce's *Ulysses*!' complained the apparition in black drapery.

Huxley was approaching the age of sixty and told Julian: 'Age, I find, has its compensations – but also a great deal which has to be compensated for.'[29] He quoted 'Uncle Matt' – Matthew Arnold's – poem 'Growing Old' and noted that Maria was well 'so long as she doesn't overdo it. Her margin of reserve strength is small, since last year's operation.' In February he learned of the death of a very old friend, Lewis Gielgud, which was 'a great shock'.[30] He told Juliette: 'We had been friends for half a century, and he was part of the order of things.' They had first met as prep-school boys in 1903. His own powers were being tested for a series of lectures on art at the National Gallery of Art in Washington which he had been invited to give the following spring. The necessary reading was putting a strain on his eyes. He had resumed his siege of the Ford Foundation, hoping to persuade it to fund research into the role of language in international relations, 'intemperate and improperly used'[31] language being the cause of many problems on the world stage. It was for this reason that he withdrew from the Author's World Peace Appeal, membership of which had been noted by the FBI. He felt that the duty of writers was to the language and he was not a joiner and had not realised the Appeal was an ongoing organisation rather than a one-off gesture.

The same month Huxley received a letter from an English doctor in Canada called Dr Humphry Osmond. He wrote back, telling Osmond that: 'Under the current dispensation the vast majority of individuals lose, in the course of education, all the openness to inspiration, all the capacity to be aware of other things than those enumerated in the Sears-Roebuck catalogue which constitutes the "real" world.'[32] It may be, Huxley reflected, that the drug mescalin might have a role to play in opening minds. Osmond was due to visit Los Angeles for a conference. Huxley offered to put him up.

Notes

1   L.633
2   SB2.120–21. Citing letter from Maria Huxley to Matthew Huxley, March 1951
3   HL, Oral History Transcripts, Interview between David King Dunaway and Sigfried Wessberg, 3 February 1988
4   SB2.122. quoting letter to Matthew Huxley. Undated
5   UCLA, West Wind, Fall 1959 Interview
6   Robert Craft, 'With Aldous Huxley', Encounter, November 1965, p12
7   FBI file on Huxley
8   Reading, letter to Harold Raymond, 10 December 1951
9   Reading, Letter to Harold Raymond, 21 January 1952
10 RL, Letter to Jeanne Neveux, 26 January 1952
11 L.642
12 Robert Craft, 'With Aldous Huxley', Encounter, November 1965, p14
13 L.644
14 Reading, letter from Harold Raymond to Aldous Huxley, 6 March 1952
15 Reading, letter to Harold Raymond, 24 March 1952
16 L.646
17 RL, Letter from Maria Huxley to Jeanne Neveux, 16 April 1952
18 SB2.135–37. Quoting letter from Maria Huxley to Matthew Huxley, 1952
19 Reading, letter to Harold Raymond, 26 December 1952
20 Reading, Letter from Basil Blackwell to Harold Raymond, 19 September 1952

21 HRC, Letter to Mary Hutchinson, 2 November 1952
22 *Counterattack*, 7 November 1952, Vol 6, No 4
23 *L*.663
24 *L*.657
25 *Selected Letters of Edith Sitwell* (1998) edited by Richard Greene, Letter to Geoffrey Gorer, 21 February 1953, p353
26 HL, Hubble Diary, 20 January 1953
27 HL, Hubble Diary, 30 January 1953
28 HL, Hubble Diary, 5 March 1953
29 *L*.663
30 *L*.665
31 *L*.667
32 *L*.669

XXXIII

Doors

Humphry Osmond was working in 1953 in a mental hospital on the Canadian prairies, the Saskatchewan Hospital at Weyburn, specialising in schizophrenia. With his colleague, Dr John Smythies, he had contributed an article to the *Hibbert Journal* on the present state of psychological medicine. Huxley had read it and it was this that caused him to write to Osmond. The idea of taking up Huxley's offer to stay seemed rather remote until Osmond suddenly found himself invited to attend a meeting of the American Psychiatric Association at Los Angeles. Maria later told Osmond that her first response to Aldous's proposal to invite this 'Canadian psychiatrist who works with mescalin'[1] was to announce: 'But he may have a beard and we may not like him.' Aldous thought for a moment then replied: 'If we don't like him we can always be out.' As it turned out a deep and lasting friendship was quickly cemented. Osmond had known Huxley's work – taking *Texts and Pretexts* with him on Atlantic convoys during the war and reading it in the London Blitz – but was slightly apprehensive on arrival at North King's Road. Maria put him at his ease by saying: 'I knew that you and Aldous, being Englishmen, would get along well.' Osmond later commented: 'To Maria, Englishmen were largely incomprehensible except to each other.' Out of the inner darkness of the house Huxley materialised to offer a handshake 'sketchy and uncertain, as if he did not enjoy the custom', the cerebrotonic not relishing physical contact. Osmond was astounded by 'the range, boldness, flexibility and sheer playfulness of his splendid mind. When he was at ease he would toss ideas about with the grace, elegance and sense of fun that a trained dolphin has playing with a ball.'

When Huxley had written offering to collect Osmond from the airline bus-stop at the Hollywood Roosevelt Hotel he had anxiously inquired whether he would be bringing any mescalin with him 'for I am eager to make the experiment and would feel particularly happy to do so under the supervision of an experienced investigator like your-self'.[2] Mescalin – the mind-altering drug derived from the Mexican root, peyote – had been available since 1918 and had been used in psychiatric medicine to try to understand patients' mental processes. Huxley seemed positively eager to be a guinea pig and his doctor declared that he saw no objection. He had already spoken on the tele-phone to Gerald Heard asking him to join the experiment. Heard was unavailable but joined him in November for a second session.[3] Heard, who later referred to Huxley's 'successive passionate convic-tions that some particular therapy, some specific exercise, could prove a panacea' seemed nonetheless to be taking the latest enthusiasm seri-ously. Huxley always stressed the seriousness of the experiment and was keen to dissociate himself from those who came in his wake in the 1960s determined to 'turn on and tune in'. Before broaching the topic with Osmond, Huxley went with him to a session of the APA confer-ence and sat there crossing himself mockingly every time Freud was mentioned.

And so it was that at eleven o'clock one morning, 4 May 1953, the most famous English literary drug taking since De Quincey took place in Huxley's Hollywood home. A Dictaphone was switched on. Osmond swirled the silvery white mescalin crystals in a glass. 'It was a delicious May morning in Hollywood, no hint of smog to make the eyes smart, not too hot,' Osmond recalled. The bitter chemical was slow to take effect but within two and a half hours Osmond saw that it was working, and after three hours he saw that all was well. The ses-sion lasted for eight hours. In the short book, *The Doors of Perception*, published in February 1954, Huxley takes up the story: 'I was on the spot and willing, indeed eager, to be a guinea pig. Thus it came about that, one bright May morning, I swallowed four-tenths of a gramme of mescalin dissolved in half a glass of water and sat down to await the results.' The book, for the first time ever, had a dedication to 'M'. Why did he choose, at this point, to dedicate a book to Maria? It is not certain how much he knew of her prognosis or how much he was simply refusing to face – or to discuss – facts. 'We live together, we act on, and react to, one another; but always and in all circumstances we are by ourselves . . . The mind is its own place,' he wrote before describing what he hoped to see.

Huxley was convinced in advance that the drug would admit him 'into the kind of inner world described by Blake and AE', but this did not happen. He did not see 'visions of many-coloured geometries, of animated architectures, rich with gems and fabulously lovely, of landscapes with heroic figures, of symbolic dramas trembling perpetually on the verge of the ultimate revelation'. He had not reckoned with the simple fact that: 'I have always been a poor visualizer.' But then, half an hour after swallowing the drug, he became aware of 'a slow dance of golden lights' then similar colours and patterns but no visions. 'The great change was in the realm of objective fact. What had happened to my subjective universe was relatively unimportant.' By 12.30 he was looking at a small glass vase containing three flowers. He had noticed them earlier in the day but now he saw with different eyes. 'I was not looking now at an unusual flower arrangement. I was seeing what Adam had seen on the morning of his creation – the miracle, moment by moment, of naked existence.' This was the 'Isness', the *Istigkeit* of Meister Eckhart's mystical philosophy. His mind was perceiving the world 'in terms of other than spatial categories', it was concerned 'not with measures and locations, but with being and meaning'. And all this was happening because the massively functional Huxley brain was being outwitted and bypassed. The 'cerebral reducing-valve' (mescalin reduces the supply of blood sugar to the brain) was being prevented from denying access to 'Mind at large'.

He later ate a meal, went for a drive, crossed Sunset Boulevard, visited the World's Largest Drugstore where he pulled down a book on Van Gogh and looked at his picture *The Chair* but the photographic representation was as nothing to the sense of 'manifested Suchness'. It was only an emblem – as art might be for the mystic, something to be gone beyond, a symbol rather than the deeper reality that the symbol signifies. He looked down at his grey flannel trousers seeing 'a labyrinth of endlessly significant complexity' in the folds of material. (In her biography, Sybille Bedford reported a friend's assertion that Huxley had been wearing, in fact, blue jeans, but that Maria thought grey flannel sounded more appropriate. Osmond, however, subsequently said he had a photograph of the day of the session which vindicated Huxley.[4]) *The Doors of Perception*, with its companion volume, *Heaven and Hell*, is probably Huxley's best known book after *Brave New World*. It was popular in the 1960s with the drug generation that he deplored. It even gave the name to a rock-band, The Doors, and Huxley is in the crowded picture that is the sleeve illustration for *Sergeant Pepper's Lonely Heart's Club Band*. But in spite of its celebrity, it can be seen, from one point of view, as a rather sad book for it is the story of an attempt to reach by artificial means what Huxley could not find by the route of artistic perception alone. Blake could see what Huxley sought by the light of his own extraordinarily fertile and visionary imagination. The heightened awareness reported in this mescalin trip is no more impressive to the reader, to the non-participant, than a canvas of Bosch seen in ordinary daylight in the Musée des Beaux Arts. Huxley was aware of this: 'I am not so foolish as to equate what happens under the influence of mescalin or of any other drug, prepared or in the future preparable, with the realization of the end and ultimate purpose of human life: Enlightenment, the Beatific Vision.'

When Huxley sent the manuscript to Chatto, Harold Raymond replied: 'You are the most articulate guinea pig that any scientist could hope to engage.'[5] The book was a success and went through many impressions but critics were of two kinds. The first, like the Swami Prabhavananda, thought it illegitimate to take a short-cut to enlightenment by popping a pill. 'To Swami, this was a deadly heresy, and he regarded Aldous and Gerald as its originators,'[6] wrote Isherwood. Spiritual discipline was the only proper way. From the other standpoint of non-mystical rationalism, Thomas Mann's view is representative. He told Ida Herz who had sent him a copy of the book that he could not share her enthusiasm: 'It represents the last, and I am tempted to say, the rashest development of Huxley's *escapism*, which I never liked in him . . . Now, given the eloquent endorsement of this famous writer, many young Englishmen and especially Americans will try the experiment. For the book is selling like mad. But it is an altogether – I do not want to say immoral, but must say irresponsible book, which can only contribute to the befuddlement of the world and to its incapacity to meet the deadly serious problems of the times with intelligence.'[7]

After the experiment Maria and Aldous took a motoring trip for three weeks to the American North West in which they covered five thousand miles ending with 'a couple of radiant days at Tahoe'[8] in June. There is a description in *Adonis and the Alphabet* (1956) of a visit to Salt Lake City on this trip. Once home, Huxley polished off *The Doors* in a month and started to work on some essays. He celebrated his fifty-ninth birthday in June at a party with the Stravinskys, Hubbles, Gerald Heard and Christopher Wood, and Eva Herrman. At the end of the summer Edwin Hubble died suddenly. He had been a great friend and someone Huxley admired as an all-round scientific humanist.

On 3 November 1953 the Huxleys presented themselves for examination as part of an application for American citizenship. They had lived in California for fourteen years and, partly because Matthew and his family were doing the same, wanted to become citizens. It seemed to symbolise the impossibility now of any return to Europe. Their two character witnesses, Betty Wendel and Rosalind Rajagopal, drove them to a court in the Rowan Building in Downtown Los Angeles where they answered all the necessary questions on American history and the Constitution. The judge asked Huxley if he would be prepared to bear arms in the US Army and he replied that he would not. By all accounts the judge tried to be accommodating. He offered Huxley the opportunity to say that his objection was religious but he refused to use the get-out – in spite of whispered promptings from Maria. This left the judge no option but to adjourn the proceedings. According to Betty Wendel, who wrote an account for Sybille Bedford:

'When they left the building Aldous's face was white. He said with an entirely uncharacteristic show of feeling, "They don't want us here!"'[9] He asked to go home to bed. They subsequently decided not to pursue the application, although worried that continued 'resident alien' status might affect their plans to go to Europe in 1954. Huxley actually thought of leaving the United States if he were to be rejected but he did not, in the end, take the matter far enough for his application actually to be refused. More worrying at this time, perhaps, was Maria's health. He told Eileen Garrett, President of the Parapsychology Foundation and an old friend of both of them, that Maria had been having a series of X-ray treatments, 'which she finds tiring and nervously trying. Vitamins and hypnosis help; but it is a bit of an ordeal.'[10] Huxley was no longer making light of Maria's illness.

Early in 1954 Huxley told Chatto that he was at work on a long story and some essays: 'And in the distance lies the project of a novel, to cover three generations from the mid nineteenth century, to the present. This is still obscure but I seem to see it coming.'[11] Probably the most interesting fictional prospectus for a long time, this was another idea that would never reach fruition. The fragment of an unfinished novel published in his second wife, Laura's, memoir *This Timeless Moment*, could be a remnant of this ambition.[12] For now, *The Doors of Perception* was published in February and, after noting some hostile reaction, Huxley told Harold Raymond: 'How odd it is that writers like Belloc and Chesterton may sing the praises of alcohol (which is responsible for about two thirds of car accidents and three quarters of crimes of violence) and be regarded as good Christians and noble fellows, whereas anyone who ventures to suggest that there may be other and less harmful short cuts to self-transcendence is treated as a dangerous drug fiend and wicked perverter of weak-minded humanity.'[13] In a letter to his old friend Professor Rhine (their mutual interest in parapsychology alive, for Huxley had just written a piece for *Life* on ESP and psychokinesis) Huxley said that the topic raised by *Doors* of 'the fauna and flora of the deeper subconscious' continued to fascinate him. He believed that the deep levels reached by mescalin-takers constituted a world 'which has little or nothing to do with our personal or collective human interests – the world from which poets and prophets have derived their descriptions of hell and heaven and the other, remoter areas of the Other World.'[14]

From the Other World, he turned to the Old World. The Huxleys had decided to revisit Europe in April – it would be Maria's last experience of her beloved continent – and they set sail from New York for Cherbourg on 7 April. They planned to attend Eileen Garrett's conference on parapsychology and philosophy in the south of France at St Paul de Vence and then to fly to Egypt to visit their old friends Dr and Mme Paul Godel (he was head of the Suez Canal Company's hospital at Ismalia). Before he left, Huxley had started work on a new novel, *The Genius and the Goddess*, which would be his penultimate essay in fiction. The Huxleys left with the citizenship question in the air. They were not even sure, in the months preceding departure, whether they would have their papers and passports ready by April. 'It is all very tiresome, all the more so as we have got into this imbroglio quite gratuitously and of our own volition,'[15] he told Matthew. After a brief stay at their usual hotel in New York, the Hotel Warwick, and having seen Matthew and Ellen and the grandchildren who delighted them, and having conferred with Humphry Osmond, the Huxleys set sail on the *Queen Elizabeth*. They went straight to St Paul de Vence where Huxley read a paper on 'The Far Continents of the Mind'. He reported to Osmond after the conference: 'There were no conclusions, of any kind, of course; but a lot of interesting things were said.'[16] He also met 'some very remarkable people', mostly French, doctors, philosophers, and psychologists. Then they went to the Godels at Ismailia: 'a very extraordinary place in company with a very extraordinary man'.[17] Each day he went to the hospital with Godel 'disguised as a visiting doctor in a white gown' and marvelled at the doctor's approach, teasing out the psychosomatic symptoms by 'Socratic questioning' of the patients. The Huxleys loved the climate and the people of Egypt and were overwhelmed by Cairo. They tried to persuade Matthew – who was now starting a career in public health administration – to come out and study the work of Godel.

From Cairo the Huxleys went on to Beirut, again delighted by what they saw and playing with the idea of coming to live there. Their visit to an Armenian Church in the northern suburbs of Beirut where a miraculous patch of light was said to appear is described in an essay in *Adonis and the Alphabet* (1956).[18] Huxley saw nothing, he said, because of his poor eyesight and the experience prompted reflections on the difference between spirituality and superstition, and the ways in which the State could use parapsychological knowledge to brain-wash citizens. In spite of his researches into parapsychology, Huxley remained 'appalled by the superstitious passion for marvels displayed even by intelligent and well educated men . . . What may be called the Baconian-pyramidological-cryptographic-spiritualist-theosophical syndrome afflicts a large part of the human race.'[19] He never ceased to think of himself as a scientific investigator of these phenomena, not a credulous faddist. After Lebanon, the Huxleys went to Jerusalem, Cyprus, Greece and, just before going on to Rome, Huxley summed up: 'It has been a very wonderful journey through space and time – wonderful but depressing; for I have never had such a sense of the tragic nature of the human situation, the horror of a history in which the great works of art, the philosophies and the religions, are no more than islands in an endless stream of war, poverty, frustration, squalor and disease.'[20] It was a further illustration of the Buddha's tenet: 'I show you sorrow and the ending of sorrow.'

In Rome (Huxley had nothing to say about his stay in Athens – the great English phil-Hellenic passion never stirred him) the roar of scooters and traffic upset him. 'Walking in Rome used to be one of the great pleasures of life; it is now one of the pains.'[21] They spent a week-end in Florence where Maria saw Costanza for the last time, in a very ill state, dying of lung cancer. They visited the Etruscan tombs at Tarquinia and the set of *Helen of Troy* at the Ciné Città film studios in Rome. Also in Rome they had lunch with a young Italian former vio-linist, Laura Archera, whom they had first met in 1948 at Wrightwood when she came to see them about making a film on the Palio at Siena (not realising that Huxley had written an essay on the subject, a fact which he was tactful enough not to refer to). She met Huxley again in 1952 at a dinner party given by the movie producer Gabriel Pascal, and discussed psychotherapy with him. That was to be her subsequent career. Maria, a few days later, came to see Laura at her studio for a therapeutic session. This was after her operation and she told Laura she was completely at peace with the idea of dying: 'To me, dying is no more than going from one room to another.'[22] Laura later returned for sessions with Aldous who was desperate to retrieve a childhood memory of a two-year period around the age of eleven. The session actually ended up with his demonstrating on her the hypnotic technique of 'magnetic passes'. Now in Rome, the acquaintance was renewed. Maria was exhausted by the travelling, 'pale and thin'.[23] They met Sybille Bedford who was also living in Rome at this time in the Via della Fontanella.

It has been suggested – and the evidence is fragmentary and anecdotal – that Maria, in June 1954 in Rome, knowing that she was soon to die, made arrangements for Aldous to be cared for by, as it were, designating a successor. Various women in Hollywood – Peggy Kiskadden, Beth Wendel, Maria's sister, Rose, for example – who knew and cared for Aldous have been considered as possible candidates. All three women were interviewed in the 1980s by David King Dunaway and Betty Wendel told him that Maria, shortly before she died, had rung her up to say: 'Don't let X get him.'[24] Peggy Kiskadden, for her part, said that the idea that she was X was 'implausible'.[25] Sybille Bedford says that, on one of those balmy nights in Rome, Maria took Laura to one side and spoke to her out of earshot.[26] She assumed that Laura was being told that Maria was dying. 'Maria very much wanted him not to be alone . . . It was a kind of consecration.'[27] Maria had devoted her life to Aldous, caring for a man who was not easy, exhausting herself in the process. She did not want the business to halt with her death. Sybille Bedford is convinced that the marriage to Laura was 'more or less engineered by Maria'.[28] It has also been suggested that Aldous was unwilling to deal with what was happening: 'He couldn't face certain things. He couldn't, for example, face Maria's death. He was a very strange man,'[29] says Sybille Bedford. Perhaps this was yet another example of his excessive intellectualism – an incapacity in ordinary things and emotions that could start to look like but was not callousness.

From Rome, the Huxleys went to Paris and then to the Drôme where the Neveux family had taken a house for the summer at Dieulefit. Here Aldous managed to do a little more work on *The*

Genius and the Goddess. Three weeks later they went to Vaisons-la-Romaine for a theatre festival which was presenting one of Georges' plays. Then they returned to Dieulefit to celebrate Aldous's sixtieth birthday on 26 July. But, happy as Aldous was at work in the garden, Maria was visibly tense and suffering. Eventually she went to see a doctor in Paris who advised immediate return. They could not book a return passage straightaway so Aldous left her in Paris with Sophie and crossed to England to see Julian and Juliette and to meet his publisher and old friends. He dined with John Lehmann and V.S. Pritchett and met a new psychotherapist called Eeman in Baker Street. At Julian's house in Pond Street he made light of Maria's condition saying, Juliette remembers, that she had had 'a "small" relapse but was now recovered'.[30]

On 21 August they sailed for New York on the *Mauretania*. On the ship, Huxley wrote to Juliette about how happy he had been with them: 'Thank you for all your sweetness and goodness.'[31] They spent a fortnight in New York and in October Huxley lectured at the Institute for Modern Art in Washington and again at Duke University on the theme of visionary experience and art, the germ of *Heaven and Hell*. Then he returned to Los Angeles to finish *The Genius and the Goddess* as well as some new essays. Maria told Matthew that the new novel was 'his best ever . . . there is Trev in it . . . I can't help feeling that this love for Trev extends and makes the story so good.'[32] Almost immediately, during lunch with Betty Wendel at the Town and Country Market, he asked her to collaborate with him in a stage version of the story. Humphry Osmond went back to Canada, and they missed him greatly. Because of Maria's medical treatment and Aldous's shingles they had not been able to repeat the mescalin experience before he left. Maria was having a long series of X-ray treatments combined with a recurrent and very painful lumbago.

On 9 January 1955, Huxley had his second mescalin experience. 'This experience was no less remarkable than the first – but entirely different; for since I was in a group, with three other people [including Gerald Heard, a man called Captain Hubbard who supplied the drug on this occasion, and possibly Laura because she mentions taking it with him in 1955[33]] the experience had a human content, which the earlier, solitary experience, with its Other Worldly quality and its intensification of aesthetic experience, did not possess.'[34] The trip lasted five hours and may have been Huxley's last experiment with mescalin: 'I was given a series of luminous illustrations of the Christian saying, "Judge not that ye be not judged", and the Buddhist saying, "To set up what you like against what you do not like, this is the disease of the mind".'

In the real world, the collaboration with Betty Wendel in the American stage production of *The Genius and the Goddess* – an unconscionably tedious story – was beginning to unfold from the start of 1955. And Maria's lumbago – which, for Huxley, was what he judged her illness to be – continued to give trouble and need constant hospital treatment. He told Osmond on 22 January that he hoped 'all will be well within a short time'.[35] Was he deceiving himself? Or was he being kept in the dark? By the beginning of February he was forced to admit that something else was going on, and asked the doctor if there was some malignancy in the liver. He was apparently told that they were not sure. Maria had told the Kiskaddens several times: 'Aldous doesn't know; he doesn't want to know,'[36] even though the truth must have been apparent since the summer of 1952. He kept on talking of trips to be taken when Maria was better until, on 5 February 1955, the emotional dam broke and the truth burst in on him.

Notes

1   Humphry Osmond, *Mem. Vol.* pp114–22
2   *L.*670
3   Gerald Heard, 'The Poignant Prophet', *Kenyon Review*, 1965, p65
4   Humphry Osmond, 'Preface' to *Moksha: Aldous Huxley's Classic Writings on Psychedelics and the Visionary Experience.* (1977) edited by Michael Horovitz and Cynthia Palmer, pviii
5   Reading, Letter from Harold Raymond to Aldous Huxley, 31 August 1953
6   Christopher Isherwood, *My Guru and His Disciples*, p219
7   *Letters of Thomas Mann*, Letter to Ida Herz, 21 March 1954, p464
8   *L.*675
9   *SB*2.152
10 *L.*692

11 Reading, Letter to Harold Raymond, 21 January 1954
12 Laura Archera Huxley, *This Timeless Moment* (1968), pp205ff
13 *L*.701
14 *L*.693
15 *L*.696
16 *L*.705
17 *L*.705
18 *Adonis and the Alphabet* (1956), 'Miracle in Lebanon', pp195–203
19 *L*.719
20 *L*.709
21 *L*.709
22 *This Timeless Moment*, p9
23 *Ibid.*, p17
24 HL, Oral History Transcripts. Interview between David King Dunaway and Betty Wendel, 2 June 1985
25 HL, Interview between David King Dunaway and Peggy Kiskadden, 3 June 1985
26 *SB*2.172–3
27 SB, in conversation with the author
28 SB, in conversation with the author
29 SB, in conversation with the author
30 *Leaves of the Tulip Tree*, p230
31 *L*.711
32 *SB*2.179, quoting letter from Maria Huxley to Matthew Huxley (undated)
33 *This Timeless Moment*, p117
34 *L*.720
35 *L*.725
36 *L*.731n. No further source given

XXXIV

Sorrow

On 5 February 1955 Huxley wrote an extraordinary letter to Jeanne Neveux. Extraordinary because this fluent and copious letter writer rarely gave vent to exposed, personal feeling. The letter begins:

> Dear Jeanne, I write to you from the depths of an
> immense sadness. Maria is very, very ill – ill, if the
> doctors are to be believed, without hope. What appeared
> to be a lumbago is in fact the symptom of a cancer of the
> spine; and, for two weeks the liver has been attacked, also
> the lungs, and probably the spleen and the intestine.[1]

At last, Huxley had admitted the truth that must have been apparent to everyone else for a long time (Humphry Osmond had broken down in tears when he discovered the truth from Maria during his 1953 visit). He wrote to Matthew on the same day that 'I try not to cry when I see her, but it is difficult after thirty-six years.'[2]

Maria returned home in an ambulance on Monday 7 February to the care of a nurse, Helen Halsberg, who had looked after her in 1952, after her mastectomy operation. Huxley himself treated her by hypnosis, conquering the nausea that had prevented her from eating. She was weak from having received intravenal injections of glucose and vitamins. 'Think of her with all your love, and of me also,' Huxley ended his letter to Jeanne. Matthew flew out to be with his mother on the Tuesday but when Suzanne arrived on Wednesday she was only just conscious.[3] Suzanne told Jeanne how Aldous had been constantly on the verge of tears but had tried to distract them by offering tea and playing 'beautiful' gramophone records.[4] Maria could hardly speak or recognise anyone. Aldous sat with her, 'sometimes saying nothing, sometimes speaking' and practising hypnotic suggestion and 'passes' to ease her pain. He recalled her mystical experiences in the Mojave desert: 'This was the reason for her passionate love of the desert. For her, it was not merely a geographical region; it was also a state of mind, a metaphysical reality, an unequivocal manifestation of God.' All her mystical experiences were associated with light. 'Light had been the element in which her spirit had lived, and it was therefore to light that all my words referred.' He would ask her to 'look at these lights of her beloved desert' which he had conjured up by describing for her the desert scenery.

A little before three on the Saturday morning the nurse said her pulse was failing. Aldous went and sat with her, leaned across and spoke into her ear 'that I was with her and would always be with her in that light which was the central reality of our beings'. And then 'there was peace . . . How passionately, from the depth of a fatigue which illness and a frail constitution had often intensified to the point of being hardly bearable, she had longed for peace!' For the last hour he sat or stood with his left hand on her head and the right on the solar plexus to create 'a kind of vital circuit'. The breathing became quieter 'and I had the impression that there was some kind of release'. In her ear he continued to whisper, '"Let go, let go . . . Only light . . ."' When the breathing ceased, at about six, it was without any struggle.' Matthew and Peggy Kiskadden were also present as these words from the *Tibetan Book of the Dead* were uttered. Matthew later told his wife that these were 'the most anguishing and moving hours of my life . . . It was over so quietly and gently with Aldous with tears streaming down his face, with his quiet voice not breaking.'[5] Gerald Heard observed: 'She has been wonderfully and gently brave through it all.'[6] Everyone said that the end had been swift and painless but Maria's anxiety not to be a burden to anyone may have led her to minimise her suffering. The Huxleys' Breton cook, Marie Le Put, one of those devoted family servants who enjoyed such a good relationship with the Huxleys, was interviewed in 1986. She said that, at a lunch party at North King's Road, Maria had said to her when they were on their own: '"Marie, I can't take it any more. Only you understand what I am going through . . ." She was in such pain.'[7] But at the same time, according to Jeanne, 'she was not afraid of death'.[8]

Maria was buried on 14 February in Rose Dale Memorial Park in Los Angeles. There were only a few mourners in addition to the family: Christopher Isherwood, the Stravinskys, Gerald Heard, Eva Herrmann. For some reason the service was in an Episcopalian church not, as might possibly have been expected, a Catholic one. 'Aldous ashen and worn-looking and there was uncontrolled crying here and there,'[9] reported Eva Herrmann. After the funeral, Aldous stayed on at the house for more than two months. It seemed that he wanted to be alone. Eva Herrmann paid a visit on the night of the funeral: 'The house was dark when A. opened the door. No one else was at home. He had a strong light in his study and was just correcting proofs. You might have thought Maria was in the next room, everything seemed so peaceful.' A month later Christopher Isherwood organised a dinner for Aldous, Gerald Heard and friends. Huxley was tired after a visit to Grace Hubble at Pasadena. 'He yawned and kept closing his eyes, and his face was thin and grey . . . Aldous refers without hesitation to Maria and the times they were together, but he is utterly lacking in any other kind of intimacy.'[10] Another month later, just before he went to New York, he was looking no better: 'He looked so thin and worn. Almost a death mask.'[11] On this occasion, Huxley talked about a new kind of radiation that had produced an entirely new kind of cancer in mice. 'Aldous no longer has the right to mention cancer at all,' wrote Isherwood angrily. Another, less obtrusive, visitor during these two months was the Huxleys' friend, Laura Archera. 'In the months that followed Maria Huxley's death in 1955, I dined quite often at Aldous's home,' she wrote in *This Timeless Moment*.[12] She said he was going through the most difficult period of his life but he got through it by trying to follow the exhortation he had given Maria: 'Let go.' He made a point of accepting all social invitations to keep his mind from brooding and Marie Le Put carried on cooking for him, leaving meals in the fridge. Not knowing about Laura's visits, she was puzzled at how much he was eating.

In April, having worked all this time at finishing the play with Betty Wendel, he decided to go to New York to discuss a production and to stay with Matthew and his family. It was decided that he would be driven by Rose – in Maria's Oldsmobile – to New York, a twelve-day trip that Rose was nervous of taking because, without Maria's constant facilitating, how would people now learn to approach Aldous directly? He had been lent the playwright George Kaufman's apartment on Park Avenue in New York where he stayed for eight weeks, working on the play and living 'in a style to which I am not accustomed – penthouse with terraces overlooking the City, French butler and wife (admirable cook) Siamese cat and an enormous library of plays'.[13] In the months before this trip, Matthew had written to Jeanne that he had to respect Aldous's wish for solitude 'so left him alone in the house'.[14] He had been left, as Huxley put it to Edith Sitwell, with 'this daily and hourly presence of an absence'.[15] To Mary Hutchinson, he wrote: 'And now her absence is a kind of insistent presence – I am conscious of it constantly. However, I work a great deal, and the mechanics of life have been well-settled.'[16] To Jeanne he talked of his loss as an 'amputation',[17] a metaphor repeated to several correspondents, insisting to Lady Sandwich that life, nonetheless, must go on 'a life that seems, after the thirty-five years of being two in one, strangely amputated'.[18]

In July, leaving his New York apartment, Huxley went to stay with Matthew and his family in Guilford, Connecticut in 'a pleasant 18th century house on a tidal river 2 miles from the sea in the midst of woods & green fields'.[19] It was there that he finished off the appendices of *Heaven and Hell*. To Rina Montini, their favourite old member of staff, he wrote in Italian that: 'I do not know what I will do next,'[20] and to Reginald Pole he said bereavement was 'a kind of physical shock, as after an amputation, and a continuing sense of the absence of something which *ought* to be there but is not'.[21] In response to a poem on Maria written by Maria's niece, Claire, Huxley told her: 'She was more capable of love and understanding than almost anyone I have ever known, and in so far as I have learned to be human – and I had a great capacity for not being human – it is thanks to her.'[22] The precise extent of the contribution that Maria made – from those first tentative days at Garsington to her death in 1955 – to the growth and humanisation of Aldous Huxley is immeasurable.

It was during the early summer that Huxley learned from Eileen Garrett that Maria had, as Huxley solemnly reported, 'appeared to her several times since her death'.[23] Perhaps this sort of thing was what he had in mind when he told Julian on the latter's birthday that: 'We both, I think, belong to that fortunate minority of human beings, who retain the mental openness and elasticity of youth, while being able to enjoy the fruits of an already long experience.'[24] He had a further sitting in New York with a medium called Arthur Ford, who also reported on Maria's progress into 'lightness, youth, gaiety, freedom'.[25]

In July, Huxley began to write a series of regular articles for *Esquire*, a magazine which allowed him to combine the sort of fluent lucubrations on the great issues which he did so well, and so effortlessly, with the traditional concerns of a gentleman's magazine. His efforts to find a producer for the play – there were hopes that Ingrid Bergman would star – continued and *The Genius and the Goddess* appeared in July after being serialised in *Harper's Magazine*. The novel – hardly more than a long short story – is Huxley's briefest and in its subject matter connects with his earlier novels: the family, lost childhood experiences, the hint of troubled sexuality. It is told in flashbacks (he was once going to call it *The Wrong End of the Telescope*) and makes much of the unreliability of fiction. 'The trouble with fiction,' says John Rivers, 'is that it makes too much sense. Reality never makes sense.' Early in the novel, Rivers picks up *The Life of Henry Maartens* the scientist, the 'genius' of the title. It is the official biography, or what he calls 'The official fiction . . . an unforgettable picture of the Soap Opera scientist – you know the type – the moronic baby with the giant intellect; the sick genius battling indomitably against enormous odds . . . the absent-minded Professor with his head in the clouds but his heart in the right place . . .' Maartens is described as: 'An idiot where human relations were concerned, a prize ass in all the practical affairs of life.' Maarten's wife, Katy, the 'goddess' (who may have had something in her of Frieda Lawrence) comes to Rivers while her husband is dying. The sexual relationship which ensues restores her. 'I was indirectly responsible for a miracle,' observes Rivers. Maartens is restored 'to a state of animal grace through satisfied desire', a rather Lawrentian conclusion. The book seems to have been a success, selling 20,000 copies in England very quickly with a second printing ordered by August.

Huxley returned to Los Angeles in September, fleeing from the heat of the East Coast in August to an equally hot California with temperatures of over 110 degrees. He had told Grace Hubble that he wanted some time to 'chew the cud',[26] but the play – and the endless need to rewrite it to please the producers (especially Joseph Anthony whom he liked) – denied him that creative pause. 'All this jigsaw work entailed in shaping a play for stage production is extremely boring,'[27] he complained to Humphry Osmond. After reading about the oddity of the composer Gesualdo, he told Osmond: 'I always have the feeling, when I read history, or see or listen to or read the greatest works of art, that, if we knew the right way to set about it, we could do things far more strange and lovely than even the strangest and the loveliest of past history.' This is a characteristic expression of Huxley's sense of being *unsatisfied* aesthetically. He was constantly seeking some new sensation that the mere practice of his art would not yield him. He wanted visions, perceptions, mystical experiences that he could not gain unaided by the force of the creative imagination alone. He needed other keys to unlock the doors of perception.

On his return to Los Angeles he was keen to extend his experiments. At lunch with Isherwood on 5 October he was 'thin and pale but lively and full of talk. He urged me to get him some mescalin in New York, spoke of his play, and discussed money – practically asking me outright how much I have. I told him at once, of course. He has $80,000.'[28] A fortnight later he wrote to Humphry Osmond to tell him about another 'extraordinary experience with mescalin the other day'.[29] After reading about a Canadian engineer who had thrown off some childhood traumas through taking LSD, Huxley decided 'it might be interesting to find out why so much of my childhood is hidden from me, so that I cannot remember large areas of my early life'. What exactly were these childhood experiences Huxley was denied? He seems to have been preoccupied with the notion – which is of course a commonplace of therapy – that something in childhood was blocked off. In this instance, he took half the contents of a 400mg capsule (the rest forty minutes later) in the company of Laura 'the first one, as far as I know, alone with an individual, and one which was not a planned scientific experiment,'[30] she wrote.

He reported to Osmond: 'There was little vision with the eyes closed, as was the case during my experiment under your auspices, but much transfiguration of the outer world.' The desired recovered memory did not come but instead 'the direct, total awareness, from the inside, so to say, of Love as the primary and fundamental cosmic fact'. He admitted that this sounded like 'twaddle' but 'the fact remains'. Unlike previous experiences this meant that he did not feel cut off from the human world. The experience convinced him that 'mescalin does genuinely open the door'. According to Laura Huxley, he had his first LSD experience with her in the same month, October 1955 (though she did not join him in taking it). Huxley, however, told Osmond that the first LSD experiment was in mid-December 1955, with Gerald Heard and two others. At this he took 75mg of LSD and found it more potent than mescalin. The results were very similar to mescalin, with no visions, only 'external transfiguration'.[31] In the experiment described by Laura Huxley they listened to Bach's First Brandenburg Concerto together and she quotes directly from descriptions in *Island* his last novel, that mirror this experience. When the music stopped, Laura got up to deal with the record player and suddenly felt a sense of Maria in the room and then inside herself. It seemed for a moment that she actually *was* Maria. Then Huxley spoke, extremely firmly yet gently: 'Don't ever be anyone but yourself.' There were numerous further experiments of this kind which can be found in *This Timeless Moment*, especially in the chapter, 'Love and Work'.

At the end of the year the play was still 'in a state of suspended animation',[32] and Huxley reported that he saw few friends and that Maria's death had 'deprived me of a pair of vicarious eyes'.[33] His relationship with the play's director, Joseph Anthony, deteriorated in the new year with the director accusing Huxley of being unwilling to co-operate with him. In January Huxley had yet another mescalin trip in which he thought of Maria 'and was overwhelmed by intense grief . . . It was something very painful but very necessary.'[34] In February, *Heaven and Hell* – in a sense a sequel or companion piece to *The Doors of Perception* with which it was subsequently reissued – was published. Its foreword honestly states Huxley's need to make use of the artificial road to paradise: 'For a person in whom "the candle of vision" never burns spontaneously, the mescalin experience is doubly illuminating. It throws light on the hitherto unknown regions of his own mind; and at the same time it throws light, indirectly, on other minds, more richly gifted in respect to vision than his own.' He anatomised the kinds of visionary experience reached in these experiments, which were 'strange with a certain regularity, strange according to a pattern'. The visions were not 'our personal property' but an Other World into which we were admitted, making contact with 'the animal otherness underlying personal and social identity' at 'the mind's antipodes'. The book is less personal than *The Doors of Perception* but more informative about the iconography of visions and their artistic correspondences.

Huxley had sent off to Chatto his latest essay collection, *Adonis and the Alphabet,* and was continuing to pump out his monthly contributions to *Esquire* – 'the only magazine that will print an essay about anything or nothing'[35] – at $1000 a time. And then, with astonishment, his friends caught sight of a headline in the *Los Angeles Times* : 'NOVELIST HUXLEY WEDS VIOLINIST'. The report was datelined Yuma, Arizona, 20 March and it was the first anyone, including his son Matthew, knew about his proposal to remarry barely a year after Maria had died. Realising his oversight, Huxley sat down on 19 March to explain to a range of correspondents. To Matthew and Ellen he described Laura as 'a young woman who used to be a concert violinist, then turned movie-cutter and worked for Pascal. I have come to be attached to her in recent months and since it seemed to be reciprocal, we decided to cross the Arizona border and call at the Drive-in Wedding Chapel (actual name). She is twenty years younger than I am [he was sixty-one, she was forty], but doesn't seem to mind. Coccola was fond of her and we saw her a lot in Rome, that last summer abroad. I had a sense for a time that I was being unfaithful to that memory. But tenderness, I discover, is the best memorial to tenderness.'[36] Matthew was very hurt by the suddenness of this announcement and the fact that he had to learn of it when people quoted a newspaper report to him. It shows a side of Huxley that was either very insensitive or simply unaware, in his cerebrotonic universe, of what was going on down below in the world of normal human relations. The day before the wedding he had lunch with his old friend Gerald Heard and there was no mention of it. He claimed that his desire for privacy had been ambushed by the press and told Anita Loos: 'I think some day we shd write a farce called '"The Drive-in Wedding Chapel"' . . . with Jimmy Durante starring as the Minister and various lesser lights driving up, and honking, for a quick nuptial.'[37]

In her book, Laura wrote that Huxley, early in 1956, had asked her: 'Have you ever been tempted by marriage?'[38] and she was frank about not wanting to surrender her liberty as a young woman who had already had several careers. The choice of venue seems to have been a combination of frivolity and cocking a snook at convention. A ladies room attendant was pressed into service as one of the witnesses but by the time they emerged some quick-witted local newspaper reporters recognising a good story were on the case. Because Laura was not Maria and could never be, and because she had a career of her own (Maria's being the full time one of supporting, protecting, managing Aldous) she was always going to risk a certain amount of coolness from friends of Aldous and Maria. The Nys family in particular have tended to make disparaging comments in interviews and letters. But significantly, close friends of Maria and Aldous such as Christopher Isherwood and Anita Loos did not share this view. 'It is such a pleasure to have a happy event in one's life like Aldous's marriage,' Anita Loos told Betty Wendel. 'I have seen Laura twice and find her absolutely enchanting. I don't suppose anyone will ever know the origin of the romance, but how lucky for all of us that she is so divine. When I think of the women who were after him it makes me shudder.'[39] Far from being repentant, Huxley enjoyed recounting the tale of

the 'broken-down cowboy' who accompanied the ladies room attendant as a witness – for the benefit of Isherwood who found him
'deeply happy and in a most benign state of mind'.[40]

The couple soon thought about moving and found a house at 3276
Deronda Drive in the Hollywood Hills, not far from the house of
Virginia Pfeiffer, with whom Laura had been living, 'with virtually no
smog and an incredible view over the city to the south and over completely savage hills in every other direction, hills which remind me of
Greece by their barrenness, their steep-sided valleys and the unsullied
sky overhead'.[41] There were raccoons, coyotes and snakes in the vicinity and there were good walks in the firebreaks, a sign that this
countryside was at risk of fire. Huxley was telling everyone that Laura
was getting on with his friends and that as he put it to Mary
Hutchinson: 'The pain and sadness of those last months have lost
their intensity and my memories of Maria are now predominantly
happy memories.'[42] He was still convinced, however, that Maria's spirit
was in touch. He told Victoria Ocampo that he was sure 'she survives
and develops'[43] and that several people who, unlike himself, were not
opaque to voices from beyond, on the basis of 'contacts' with her,
concluded that 'she has achieved an extraordinary degree of liberation – that she gives an overwhelming impression of youthfulness
and happiness'. The Huxley of the chapel at Beirut who frowned on
superstition was not the Huxley of this letter.

He was now at work on his new 'phantasy', the revived project of a
'good Utopian' novel which would be his last, *Island*. Revisions to the
play still kept breaking in on this task and there was even talk of
reviving a musical comedy version of *Brave New World*. And there
were the endless letters to and from Humphry Osmond – the two
men having now invented the word 'psychedelic' to describe the
visionary consequences of the drugs they were exploring. Julian and
Juliette came over to visit, and in October he flew to New York to give
a speech on 'The History of Tension' to the New York Academy of
Sciences. The Academy's publicist was so effective that he had lined up
no less than seven television and radio appearances for him. Huxley
was beginning to emerge as an adornment of the sort of serious television interview that went out in the 1950s on the networks – less

frequently today – and his brand of elegant and lucid commentary was perfectly adjusted to the format. At the same time he was disinclined to preach, telling a member of the Vedanta Society who asked him to do so, 'I am not a religious man – in the sense that I am not a believer in metaphysical propositions, not a worshipper or performer of rituals, and not a joiner of churches –and therefore I don't feel qualified or inclined to tell people in general what to think or do.'⁴⁴

In October, Huxley's new essay collection, *Adonis and the Alphabet* (in the US it would be titled *Tomorrow and Tomorrow and Tomorrow*) appeared. It was a summing-up of Huxley's intellectual concerns since the last essay collection in 1950, *Themes and Variations*. The opening essay advocating 'non-verbal education' wanted educators to recognise the 'world of the unconscious intelligences immanent in the mind-body' as well as the 'world of self-conscious verbalized intelligence'. It was called 'The Education of an Amphibian' and based on the assumption that, 'every human being is an amphibian . . . we inhabit many different and even incommensurable universes'. Of no-one was this more true than Huxley. The scientific investigator was also a believer in the spirit world, the non-Christian talked about God, the logical analyst wrote fiction, the unremitting highbrow wrote scripts for Walt Disney, the indicter of 'the fantastic over-valuation of words', was a consummate literary artist. And in spite of his obsession with encyclopaedias and factual knowledge, his second essay argued for the vital distinction between 'Knowledge and Understanding'. Denouncing 'the learned foolery of scholars' he praised the dictum of St John of the Cross: know yourself, empty the memory. But there was one word which he was anxious to retrieve for proper use: 'Bawled from a million pulpits, lasciviously crooned through hundreds of millions of loudspeakers, it has become an outrage to good taste and decent feeling, an obscenity which one hesitates to pronounce. And yet it has to be pronounced; for, after all, Love is the last word.'

Huxley the pessimist is again present in these essays. While casting, however, a gloomy eye over the arms race, the ecological ruin of the planet, the rapid growth of world population in relation to food resources, he also exhibited faith in the ability of human beings to transfigure themselves. 'I am still optimist enough to credit life with invincibility, I am still ready to bet that the non-human otherness at the root of man's being will ultimately triumph over the all too human selves who frame the ideologies and engineer the collective suicides.' Yet, in the essay on the early twentieth century socialist experiment at Llano of Job Harriman and his followers, 'Ozymandias', which foundered as human selfishness arose to destroy the co-operative idea, one perhaps has a right to expect more from Huxley. His wryly amused account ('Except in a purely negative way, the history of Llano is sadly uninstructive') is all very well but he was an advocate of Utopia who perhaps should have had some answers to the all too common phenomenon of failed idealism. Huxley the futurologist is present in these essays, too. In the essay on 'Censorship and Spoken Literature' he seems to anticipate both Internet publishing and the talking book. In the best of these essays, Huxley combines attention to the contemporary world with a sense of wider possibilities. Looking, in the World's Largest Drugstore, at the appalling Mother's Day card verses he asks: 'How is it that we have permitted ourselves to become so unrealistic, so flippantly superficial in all our everyday thinking and feeling about man and the world he lives in?'

At the end of December another newspaper headline was set up in type, this time in the British tabloid, *The People*. It read: 'HE HOAXED THE WORLD WITH AN EYESIGHT CURE.' The story beneath was based on a book called *The Truth about Eye Exercises* by Dr Philip Pollack, a leading American eye specialist who set out to demolish the claims of Dr Bates and in particular to describe 'the great Aldous Huxley tragedy'. Pollack described a lecture given by Huxley in the middle of which he faltered and began to bring his eyes closer and closer to the manuscript. 'At last he took a magnifying glass out of his pocket to decipher the words. Huxley was not cured. But he had tried to convince himself that he was. He had memorised the script, but had forgotten one passage.' The moral drawn by *The People* was that one should not throw away one's glasses if one did not wish to fall victim to 'a great American hoax'. Chatto told Huxley that the article and the book might well be actionable but he told them that it was best to do nothing about it, either because he felt the issue too trivial or because he feared that there might well have been a grain of truth in what was described. Although this was clearly part of an anti-Bates backlash, he admitted that he had 'never claimed to be able to read except under very good conditions'.[45] This was not necessarily what was claimed on Huxley's behalf. This incident was probably the address given by Huxley in April 1952 to the Screen Writers' Guild of America, without glasses. The diarist of *The Saturday Review* who described it, said it was: 'An agonizing moment, not improved by scattered titters from embarrassed onlookers.'[46] Such accounts raise the puzzling question of why Huxley put himself in this position and what he hoped to achieve – if the reports are true – by attempting to create a false impression. It remains doubtful whether he had anything other than the briefest of intermissions in his struggle to see adequately.

Notes

1   RL, Letter to Jeanne Neveux, 5 February 1955. Author's translation
2   *L*.731n
3   Huxley's own account of the death is given in *This Timeless Moment*, pp20–25
4   RL, Letter from Suzanne Nicolas to Jeanne Neveux, 3 March 1955
5   *SB*2.187. Letter from Matthew Huxley to Ellen Huxley. Undated
6   UCLA, Letter from Gerald Heard to Lucille Kahn, 10 November 1955
7   HL, Oral History Transcripts, Interview between David King Dunaway and Marie Leput, 10 July 1986
8   Reading, Letter from Jeanne Neveux to Harold Raymond, 5 September 1955
9   UCLA, Letter from Sybille Bedford to Allanah Harper, 25 February 1955 quoting Eva Herrmann's words
10 *Isherwood Diaries*, p482, 18 March 1955
11 *Ibid.* p490, 18 April 1955
12 *This Timeless Moment*, p27
13 *L*.742
14 RL, Letter from Matthew Huxley to Jeanne Neveux, 26 February 1955
15 HRC, Letter to Edith Sitwell, 6 March 1955
16 HRC, Letter to Mary Hutchinson, 7 March 1955
17 RL, Letter to Jeanne Neveux, 27 March 1955

18 HRC, Letter to Amiya Corbin, Lady Sandwich, 17 April 1955
19 Reading, Letter to Ian Parsons, 18 April 1955
20 RL, Letter to Rina Montini, 27 May 1955. Author's translation from Italian
21 NYPL, Letter to Reginald Pole, 17 June 1955
22 *L.740*
23 *L.746*
24 *L.749*
25 *L.756*
26 HL, Letter to Grace Hubble, 26 July 1955
27 *L.766*
28 Isherwood Diaries, p535, 5 October 1955
29 *L.769*
30 *This Timeless Moment*, p138
31 *L.779*
32 *L.778*
33 *L.781*
34 *L.788*
35 Reading, Letter to Ian Parsons, 3 January 1956
36 *L.794*
37 *L.795*
38 *This Timeless Moment*, p35
39 HRC, Letter from Anita Loos to Betty Wendel 23 April 1956
40 Isherwood Diaries, p598, 25 March 1956
41 *L.800*
42 HRC, Letter to Mary Hutchinson, 10 July 1956
43 *L.801*
44 *L.811*
45 *L.815*
46 *The Saturday Review*, 12 April 1952

XXXV

Celebrity

Huxley's unquenchable belief in the possibility of theatrical success ensured that he would persist throughout 1957 in the struggle to get *The Genius and the Goddess* staged on Broadway. This would finally happen on 10 December but the play survived for only five nights. 'Why does anyone write for the theatre? It's just asking for trouble,'[1] he declared in January. Two years of his writing life had been wasted – it seems the appropriate word – on this project (not to mention work on rewriting Ralph Rose's stage version of *After Many A Summer* and attempts to buy back the rights of *Brave New World* from RKO, which also involved approaching Stravinsky about writing a few numbers for the musical, then Leonard Bernstein). Two years that might have been put to more interesting creative use. It was also exhausting. At a dinner party in April, Christopher Isherwood found him 'tired and sleepy'[2] though one of his other guests, the young English poet Thom Gunn, was thrilled to meet the legendary older writer. Early in 1957 changes at *Esquire* meant his services were no longer required but the loss of $1000 a month ('this convenient and well-paid pulpit'[3]) would not have troubled him for royalties continued to be high – English earnings alone being in excess of £4000 a year. In the spring he got together with a group of friends – Julian, Harrison Brown, Kingsley Davis, Fred Zinneman, Bill Kiskadden – in order to make a documentary film on population, concentrating on the illustrative example of Egypt.

Huxley was also beginning to accept offers to lecture. In his youth this had been a painful duty and he had hated it but in his last years in California he took to it and offers increased steadily. In April he spent three days at Stanford talking to students 'of Creative Writing, whatever that is'[4] and was then at the University of New Hampshire and in New York. Stanford went well and he became involved with the comparative religion and post-graduate English classes. He told Osmond that 'the young people were nice and some of their elders were very interesting'.[5] He was now the senior man of letters, the itinerant intellectual and visiting campus guru, always a commodity in demand.

On 18 July Huxley left for New York to supervise the play (earlier Peter Brook had read the script but declined it) and spent the rest of the summer there, also making 'slow progress'[6] on a book of essays, *Brave New World Revisited*. Laura, who was in her native Turin seeing her father, wrote to Jeanne that there was 'a shadow of tiredness'[7] in Huxley's letters from New York where he was staying at the Shoreham Hotel. He managed to see the Picasso exhibition at the Museum of Modern Art – 'what a lot of slapdash shoddy stuff surrounding the twenty or thirty masterpieces!'[8] In November, however, things started to go badly wrong with the play. The producer Courtney Burr made changes that were unacceptable and Huxley and Betty Wendel threatened to withdraw. What one commentator described as 'a weak, conventional domestic comedy' created by Burr and his collaborator Alec Coppel out of their play opened in New Haven on 13 November and the following week at Philadelphia – where it turned out Burr had inserted lines secretly rehearsed. Betty Wendel and Laura Huxley attended a performance on 23 November and Huxley threatened to terminate rights. On the eve of the short, disastrous New York run Huxley declared at last: 'I have wasted more than four months, which might have been profitably employed in doing my own work. The experience has been unpleasant and . . . boring. It has also been highly educational. We live and learn.' But Huxley was unwilling to learn from the new practitioners. He could not comprehend the 'consistent

mindlessness'9 of the characters in Tennessee Williams' plays and was
stuck in a more conventional playwriting mould. He flew back to Los
Angeles with Laura, suitably chastened.

A few days later, a group of students from the Los Angeles School
of Journalism arrived at Deronda Drive to interview the celebrity
author. He told them about his blindness and how he had conquered
it and how it cut off the medical career he had aspired to: 'I happen to
like writing very much . . . I feel quite sure that if I had been a doctor
I should have been a pretty bad doctor and got out of it pretty
quickly.'10 They asked him whether the old, satirical Huxley had been
lost to the new thinker: 'I don't think I've sacrificed the old one. I hope
I still write fairly funny things from time to time. I hope I've added
another dimension; this is what I've been trying to do. I've maybe
failed. I think in a certain sense the satirical side is the necessary complement to the other.' Before the students left he warned them of the
pitfalls of journalism: 'It's an awfully good field to get into, if you
make very sure that you get out of it.'

In the spring of 1958 Huxley finished *Brave New World Revisited*,
many of whose chapters had already appeared in the press during
1956 and 1957, and planned a trip to South America at the invitation
of the Brazilian government. He was complaining to Julian about
being too busy: 'Why does one have to be? It seems absurd and unnecessary; but there it is.'11 A little later he told Matthew's wife, Ellen, 'I am
sick and tired of this kind of writing; but at the same time find it frustratingly difficult to find the right story line for my projected Utopian
novel.'12 This was to be Huxley's last major fictional work, *Island*, the
novel he had promised for so long, the story that would show the
mirror image of *Brave New World*, the picture of the good and right
society – or, as he put it to Jeanne: '*Le Meilleur des Mondes* à rebours,
créatif, positif.'13 Just before the Huxleys left for Brazil in July Huxley
was interviewed on television – the first of several television interviews over the ensuing months – by Mike Wallace. It was essentially an
opportunity to publicise some of the ideas about 'over-organisation'
in modern societies that he would develop in *Brave New World
Revisited*. 'Huxley Fears New Persuasion Methods Could Subvert
Democratic Procedures' was the headline in *The New York Times* on

19 May. The FBI tuned in and took notes, an internal memo dredging up yet again Huxley's attendance in 1935 at the International Authors Congress for the Defence of Culture in Paris, which according to a French publication turned up by the spooks had been exposed as 'a Communist plot to take over France' – a singularly ineffective one it would seem. Since the ideas expounded in the Mike Wallace interview were about the defence of freedom of the individual against the state one can't help feeling that the FBI was wasting its time monitoring the broadcast.

The trip to Brazil taught Huxley how much of a celebrity he now was. 'I was simultaneously touched and appalled to discover that I am now, as the result of having been around for so many years, a kind of historical monument, which sightseers will come quite a long way to inspect, and which radio and press reporters find newsworthy,'[14] he told Osmond on his return. 'In Brazil it was as though the Leaning Tower of Pisa had just come to town, wherever I blew in; and even in Italy I found myself in large theatres. It was really very odd and embarrassing.' Laura Huxley, in her book, describes stopping off in the middle of the Brazilian jungle on the way to Brazilia and meeting members of a primitive tribe. A 'frail-looking' white man arrived and, realising it was Huxley: 'With tears streaming down his cheeks, he approached him saying, "Uxley, Uxley . . . *Contrapunto* . . ." The two men embraced. Aldous too was moved.'[15] After Brazil they went to Italy and to Turin. Laura left Aldous at a café table in Corso Vittorio Emanuele while she went shopping. When she returned, he handed her a letter he had written: 'A letter to tell you that you really must be a *strega* [sorceress] – otherwise why should I keep falling more and more in love with you? . . . I love you very much and only wish I could love you more and better – could love you so that you would be well always, and strong and happy; so that there would never be that discrepancy between a tragic suffering face and the serenity of the nymph's lovely body with its little breasts and the flat belly, the long legs . . . that I love so tenderly, so violently.'[16] Whatever the truth of Huxley's second marriage – whether it was indeed as 'open' as his first on both sides – the genuineness of his love for Laura is beyond doubt from this letter.

After Italy, Huxley (at first on his own) went on to see Julian and Juliette in London. This visit was 'very agreeable, and I saw vast numbers of people from Bertie Russell to Rose Macaulay . . . and . . . Tom Eliot (who is now curiously dull – as a result, perhaps, of being, at last, happy in his second marriage)'.[17] Jeanne's daughter, Noële, met Huxley in London: 'A strange feeling about Aldous, he hasn't changed, he has only aged. The English climate doesn't suit him. No cutting of the Nys link. Coccola isn't forgotten. He speaks of her frequently and tenderly . . . He is dressed in a grey suit with a red tie.'[18] While in London, Huxley was interviewed by John Lehmann on 12 October for the BBC television programme, *Monitor*. He told Lehmann, disarmingly, that he would be 'flattered' to be considered a novelist but perhaps the claim was 'fraudulent' and he was no more than an essayist. But he had not lost faith in the novel: 'You can do whatever you like with it. There are no rules except to do it well.' On 26 October he made another appearance, with Julian, the philosopher Freddie Ayer, and the neurologist, Grey Walter on another BBC programme, *The Brains Trust*. The four gentlemen, with their well-bred voices and public school forms of address ('What do you think, Ayer?') discoursed on a number of questions that seemed to have been tailored to Huxley's concerns. He was more precise than Julian and relaxed and fluent in his answers, eminently reasonable in tone. He brought out some of his hobby-horses about over-population and the exhaustion of natural resources, and made several references to eminent American scientists and researchers at the highest levels with whom he was evidently in close contact. He defended his interests in the paranormal ('The evidence in favour of telepathy seems fairly solid . . . And clairvoyance') and in mysticism. The author of *Language, Truth and Logic* listened politely, only pointing out that mystical knowledge was all right so long as it wasn't regarded as 'cognitive'.

After London Laura joined him in Paris and they went on to Venice. Huxley lectured in Turin, Milan, Rome, and Naples – in spite of an attack of 'flu. He wrote from Turin to Julian and Juliette to say how much he had enjoyed the 'delightful' joint television appearances. 'When shall we three meet again? In these days of jets and international congresses, almost anything may happen . . . I shall always remember these weeks in London as a specially happy and significant time.'[19] He would make three more visits to London in the years that now remained to him and it is clear that California had not erased his love for the pleasures it could still offer him. But when he returned to Deronda Drive in December he admitted he was 'glad to be back in a quiet place after 5 months of globe-trotting, interview-giving, TV appearances, lectures and meeting people'.[20] He was coming back to a great deal of work – on the novel and on the lectures he was to give at Santa Barbara. He told Chatto he was working 'like a termite' at the lectures. 'I am not attempting to write them out, but am feverishly collecting & organising materials, so that I may be able to deliver them *extempore*, but with some measure of sense.'[21] These lectures at the University of California at Santa Barbara would be published posthumously in 1978 as *The Human Situation* and they reveal the full breadth of his concerns about 'this push towards catastrophe'[22] of the contemporary world. But at the start of 1959 he told Julian: 'The trouble with all these talks about culture is that they distract one from doing the things that make a culture worth having and eat up the time and energy that should go into one's work.'[23]

In October 1958, while in London, *Brave New World Revisited* was published. This short book displayed once more Huxley's gift for concise and clear argument and is powerful evidence for his own case that he was more effective as an essayist than as a novelist, at least by this stage in his writing career. Where his last novel would creak under the weight of its exposition and disappoint in its lack of fictional invention and imagining, his last two prose works, *Brave New World Revisited* and *Literature and Science*, were models of pellucid reasoning. The subject of the book was announced as 'freedom and its enemies'. He pointed out that when *Brave New World* was being written in 1931, 'I was convinced that there was still plenty of time. The completely organized society, the scientific caste system, the abolition of free will by methodical conditioning, the servitude made acceptable by regular doses of chemically-induced happiness, the orthodoxies drummed in by nightly courses of sleep-teaching – these things were coming all right, but not in my time, not even in the time of my

grandchildren . . . Twenty-seven years later . . . I feel a good deal less
optimistic than I did when writing *Brave New World* . . . The blessed
interval between too little order and the nightmare of too much has
not begun and shows no sign of beginning.' He predicted a 'nightmare
of total organization' and in so doing revealed himself as essentially a
liberal humanist thinker, defending the freedom of the sentient individual, resistant to bullying by the State, propaganda, conditioning by
advertising and marketing, and brainwashing. This was a tradition
that had its roots among the Victorian intellectuals from whom the
Huxleys sprang, and, in spite of the best efforts of late twentieth century academic theorists, it remains a strong and pertinent and
remarkably resilient tradition.

In his chapters on 'education for freedom' Huxley sketched a mode
of resistance, 'an education first of all in facts and values – the facts of
individual diversity and genetic uniqueness and the values of freedom, tolerance and mutual charity which are the ethical corollaries of
these facts'. He called for decentralisation and small self-organising
communities (even within the great metropolises where people were
increasingly forced to live) to resist 'the current drift towards totalitarian control of everything' and turn back the powers of 'Big
Business and Big Government'. He knew that many people were not
interested in such a resistance ('Give me television and hamburgers,
but don't bother me with the responsibilities of liberty') but he
knew – as we know nearly fifty years later – that without such a
resistance movement the enemies of freedom would triumph.

Huxley spent the whole of 1959 lecturing at Santa Barbara and
working on his last novel, *Island*. In January he invited Christopher
Isherwood and Don Bachardy to lunch. 'He looked tired and older,'[24]
thought Isherwood, who was slightly resentful of Huxley and Heard
for implying, it seemed to him, that their visionary insights under
mescalin and LSD were somehow spiritually superior to his. Huxley
may also have been upset by the news that Matthew and Ellen were
splitting up. In a letter to Matthew, counselling him to show understanding to his ex-wife, he wrote: 'Huxleys especially have a tendency
not to suffer fools gladly – and also to regard as fools people who are
merely different from themselves in temperament and habits. It is

difficult for Huxleys to remember that other people have as much right to their habits and temperament as Huxleys have to theirs . . . So do remember this family vice of too much judging.'[25]

In May Huxley flew to New York to collect the award of merit for the novel presented by the American Academy of Arts and Letters – further evidence of his status as a 'historical monument'. His eyesight continued to create problems. He was fond of walking and, one night in August, while doing so alone near the house, he stumbled and fell and considered that he had had 'a providential escape'.[26] He hurt his back and was in pain for two or three weeks. But it did not stop him working away at 'my Utopian novel, wrestling with the problem of getting an enormous amount of diversified material into the book without becoming merely expository or didactic. It may be that the job is one which cannot be accomplished with complete success . . . I am trying to lighten up the exposition by putting it into dialogue form, which I make as lively as possible. But meanwhile I am always haunted by the feeling that, if only I had enough talent, I could some-how poetise and dramatise all the intellectual material and create a work which would be simultaneously funny, tragic, lyrical and pro-found. Alas, I don't possess the necessary talent . . .'[27] Once again Huxley's searingly honest powers of self-criticism had accomplished what the critics would later merely echo. Chatto must have had some apprehensions when he told them that the book was developing 'a horrid way of going backwards as new ideas occur to me and have to be incorporated into earlier chapters, so that what lies ahead still remains unexplained'.[28] Throughout the summer and autumn he worked away stoically: 'my subliminal self always tends to work rather sluggishly – creating not in first fine careless raptures, but in a series of second and third thoughts, which compel me to go back and change or add to or cut out from the material provided by my first thoughts.'[29] And offers to lecture poured in – from India and from the Menninger Foundation at Topeka. The latter, he told Osmond, was 'the holy of holies of American psychiatry'.[30]

Huxley broke off one morning in the autumn to admit some stu-dents from UCLA who interviewed him for *West Wind*. They found him 'astonishingly tall and gaunt – like one of Daumier's spectral studies of Don Quixote. His face is bloodless, lined. The aristocratic, aquiline nose of all the photographs is there. A nervous, long-fingered hand passes and repasses through his receding hair . . . His manner is at all times patient, polite – and absolutely detached.'[31] Huxley confessed: 'Unfortunately I don't read nearly as much fiction as I would like. I have to ration my reading due to the fact that I have this visual handicap, and so I don't read as many contemporary novels as I ought to.' That 'ought' is significant. They asked him about television and he replied in the same tone of mandarin courtesy: 'I'm not in a position to talk about TV because I don't own a set . . . I like seeing Mr Khruschev and things like that on TV . . . It's a sort of Moloch which demands incessant human sacrifice . . . the people who write for it just go quietly mad.' Huxley may have been reflecting the view of many screenwriters who had not successfully managed the transition to the small screen and who saw cinema under threat from television in the 1950s.

The interview encapsulated Huxley's public image at this time: the grave and courtly intellectual speaking in the accents of another time and place, almost preternaturally cerebral. Around this time he received a letter from Rosamund Lehmann who had developed an interest in spiritualism and who seems to have sent him some sort of report of Maria. He felt that the account was uncharacteristic of her. He conceded that she might have said that 'my excessive intellectuality was a bar to mystical experience'[32] but in a different tone. He told her that Maria would sometimes compare him to the eponymous hero of the Chinese story *Monkey* who was 'too unmitigatedly cerebral'. He added: 'Her great desire was that I should be less isolated, more closely in contact with more kinds of people.' And for good measure he rejected the 'legend' that he was in the habit of travelling with all twenty-eight volumes of the *Encylopaedia Britannica* and using it for information in lieu of a guidebook.

Throughout the next year it would be 'Monkey', the walking cerebellum, that would take centre stage as Huxley lectured far and wide. Progress on the novel would be slow as he moved from one campus to another elaborating his warnings about the planet and the careless custody of it exercised by its human stewards.

Notes

1 UCLA, Letter to Mrs Leon Lazare Roos, 21 January 1957
2 Isherwood Diaries, p744. 2 April 1957
3 *L.820*
4 *L.820*
5 *L.823*
6 Reading, letter to Ian Parsons 16 July 1957
7 RL, Letter from Laura Huxley to Jeanne Neveux, 26 September 1957
8 *L.826*
9 *L.873*
10 UCLA, Interview with Aldous Huxley by students of LA School of Journalism, December 1957, 'Library of Living Journalism'
11 *L.845*
12 *L.848*
13 RL, Letter to Jeanne Neveux, 29 March 1958
14 *L.858*
15 *This Timeless Moment*, p126
16 *Ibid.*, p128
17 *L.858*
18 RL, Note by Noèle Neveux in Nys family papers. Author's translation
19 Eton, Letter to Julian and Juliette Huxley, 21 November 1958
20 HRC, Letter to Ralph Rose, 6 December 1958
21 Reading, Letter to Ian Parsons, 4 January 1959
22 *The Human Situation* (1978) edited by Piero Ferrucci, p83
23 *L.859*
24 Isherwood Diaries, p797, 10 January 1959
25 *L.870*
26 *L.874*
27 *L.875–76*
28 Reading, letter to Ian Parsons, 20 October 1959
29 *L.879*
30 *L.881*
31 UCLA, *West Wind*, Fall, 1959
32 King's College Cambridge, Letter to Rosamund Lehmann, 16 November or December, 1959

XXXVI

Fire

In January 1960, in an unusually cold Southern California – snow down to 2500 feet and frost on the oranges – Huxley resumed work on 'my Utopian fantasy',[1] telling Julian that it 'presents extraordinary difficulties'. A few days later he was informing Matthew that it 'already runs to more than 200 pages and shows no sign of coming to an end – indeed, I don't yet know how the damned thing is going to end'.[2] This sounded rather inauspicious. He admitted to Ian Parsons at Chatto that he had been 'disturbed by the low ratio of story to exposition',[3] and, after discussions with Christopher Isherwood, he had tried to remedy the defect 'by the introduction of a brand new personage'. Jeanne was told that the book was 'horriblement difficile à écrire'.[4] The now certain dissolution of Matthew's marriage was another lowering event, and Huxley found himself having to do what he did not do best, advise on the conduct of ordinary life, which he did by quoting Dante at the couple and telling them that they must find a way out of the 'dark wood'. This same gap between 'the conceptual and constitutional' was one he highlighted in John Midddleton Murry, whom he had not seen since the late 1930s, and whose biography had just appeared. He said that Murry was 'divided against himself (as so many intellectuals are)',[5] a fact that had so provoked Lawrence.

Huxley spent March and April 1960 as a Visiting Professor at the Menninger Foundation at Topeka, Kansas, which he described as 'this curious world centre of psychiatric training. There are more lunatics here per square mile and more analysts than anywhere else, I imagine, in the solar system. My stay will, I hope, be educational, at least for me.'[6] Never an admirer of Freud, Huxley felt that Freudian ideas held too much sway at Topeka 'as tho' a multiple amphibian cd be cured of his troubles by psychology alone, and psychology of only one, not too realistic brand'.[7] The Middle West was under eighteen inches of snow, now melting, so he had to wade about in rubber boots 'like a salmon fisher'. No sooner had his spell in Kansas finished than Huxley was off to lecture to a capacity audience at Berkeley and to the Idaho State College at Pocatello. Huxley was receiving good financial news from his publishers and was clearly in funds so it is not clear why he accepted so many of these speaking engagements when he had a book to write – unless it was a means of escape from a novel that refused to respond to his touch.

In May, Huxley flew with Laura to San Francisco to the Moffitt Hospital to be examined. Although he asked everyone, including Bill Kiskadden who knew all the details, to keep it a secret, including from Matthew, he was suffering from cancer of the tongue. Surgery would have involved removing half the tongue, a possibility which Huxley rejected, preferring to explore the potential of radium needle treatment, which would leave his speech unaffected. Dr Max Cutler, who had been a consultant to Maria during her cancer, was brought in. Cutler later said he found Huxley a 'remarkable' man. 'His interest in his own case was minimal, but he had a tremendous interest in the creative aspects of science and medicine. He considered his own illness as a curious phenomenon which extended his own capacity for experience.'[8] The tongue responded to treatment and healed completely, but within a year and a half Cutler found himself having to remove a cancerous gland from Huxley's neck for diagnosis. Other glands appeared soon afterwards. Unfortunately news got out that he was in hospital and he had to write to Matthew saying he had been suffering from 'a laryngitis that has made eating and talking very hard'.[9] By September, however, he was well enough to attend a

'Convocation on the Great Issues of Conscience in Modern Medicine' at Dartmouth College, followed by a flight to Boston and then a visit to New Hampshire where he received an honorary degree. He also lectured at the University of Pittsburgh. He was not one of those enthused by the election of John F. Kennedy as President, in part because of the 'distasteful' presence of old Joe Kennedy and his millions 'lurking in the background of the young crusader'.[10] He was still taking LSD, though disappointed as always by his inability to visualise.

And in September a new reason for not writing *Island* came along – a Carnegie Visiting Professorship at the Massachusetts Institute of Technology. The residency would be for nine weeks and it paid $9000. It was 'an interesting job in an interesting place'.[11] He told Chatto that the book might be finished by the end of the year, depending on the amount of leisure left to him by MIT. He was very much looking forward to Cambridge, Mass., because 'MIT has a galaxy of topflight scientists on its payroll'.[12] Humphry Osmond paid him a visit at Cambridge and was shocked by the first signs of the cancer and his appearance, 'worn, tired, and pale'.[13] From Cambridge he corresponded with the English dramatist John Whiting who was adapting *The Devils* for the stage at the Royal Shakespeare Company at Stratford-on-Avon. Huxley gave plentiful and detailed comments on Whiting's script. The lectures which Huxley gave at MIT – on the topic, no less, of 'the problem of human nature'[14] – were hugely popular. He spoke from a sheaf of notes and loudspeakers had to relay his voice outside when the hall was full. On some of these Wednesday nights the traffic across the Charles River was jammed, with extra police being called out. He generously invited students back to his campus apartment at 100 Memorial Drive but found time also in the mornings to press on with the novel.

Back in Los Angeles for Christmas he worked 'like a madman'[15] on the novel which he hoped to finish by the spring. In January 1961, he and Laura went to Hawaii for a week 'the excuse being some lectures, the motive a wish to look at the islands which I haven't seen for many years'.[16] This was followed by a conference on Control of the Mind at San Francisco. If he was tired and unwell, he was not slackening his pace. Hawaii would also give him some time with Laura whom he would not have seen a great deal of during these last months. He admired her work in psychotherapy, telling Jeanne about her 'remarkable results – for she is full of resource and has a real intuitive gift'.[17] He would later write an introduction to her book of 'recipes for living', *You Are Not The Target* (1963).

In January 1961, Huxley was approached by Claire Eschelbach, who was working on a bibliography of his writing. He agreed to write a foreword but confessed, 'I stand appalled at the thought of all I have written over the years'.[18] What he had not written was *Island*, but he told Ian Parsons: 'I hope to have the damned thing done by May'.[19] After that he planned to go to London and he asked Parsons to fix him up with a service apartment with kitchen so that he could make his own meals, 'for one gets very bored with unmitigated Club or restaurant food, & likes to do a little picknicky cooking for a change'. He told Ian Parsons that he was 'weary'[20] of the novel but had had a sudden inspiration to call it *Island* – 'Brief & to the point as the phantasy is placed in a hypothetical island between Ceylon & Sumatra, & the society described is an island of relative sanity in a world of madness.' He had to go back to MIT in early April to deliver a centennial address but he did finish the book by June. Even before he finished it he was planning a travel book on the West Coast of America, paid for by a Ford Research Professorship at Berkeley to be taken in 1962. This was another volume that would never materialise. More immediately, he planned to be in Copenhagen for a psychology conference in mid-August, then Italy, then India for a few weeks in late October. But in May all these plans were to receive rather a severe jolt.

May began well, with Max Cutler giving Huxley a clean bill of health and pronouncing him one of his most successful cases. Radical surgery had been avoided. But on 12 May, in the early evening, Laura was returning from a psychotherapy session she had been giving when she stopped at the nearby house of her friend Virginia Pfeiffer to feed the cat (Virginia was away). Then she suddenly noticed the red car of a fire chief and saw smoke and flames coming from the canyon below. The wind was up and she heard a siren. What followed next depends on Laura's account; Huxley gave no details himself. She herself described it as 'unexplainable'. Normally she acted decisively, but in this instance, in spite of the fact that two houses were threatened – her own and Virginia's (the latter the house of her closest friend where she had spent 'some of the most momentous years of my life'[21]), she 'stood immobile, fascinated by the wild grace of the flames, by the ever changing voice of the wind'. She went into Virginia's house and took out some papers then drove home to tell Aldous who was upstairs at work. They then drove down the hill to attend to the fire before realising that it might spread to their own home. The roads were blocked by fire vehicles but a stranger came forward to offer to drive them back to Deronda Drive. Huxley had the presence of mind, when he saw the flames approaching, to seize the manuscript of *Island* while Laura walked through the house, seemingly mesmerised by the flames, incapable of seizing anything. Aldous appeared with some suits on a hanger which jolted her into doing the same and then she remembered her Guarneri violin, which she rescued, along with a Chinese porcelain statue. And they were driven away – 'I was unaware of anything except how beautiful everything was'.

This whole episode is very strange. Why, when the flames had not yet reached the house, did they not rescue more items? Why was there this paralysis of will? The fire destroyed so much that was precious to Huxley (including, effectively, the archive of his entire first marriage). It was material which would have made the work of biography so much easier: Maria's pre-war journal, her letters to Suzanne which had been sent to Aldous because he was thinking of writing an autobiography, the love letters between Aldous and Maria which, in a tin box, had followed them in all their journeys through Europe and Southern California. And there was Huxley's library with its copious annotations on every book. There was the manuscript of Lawrence's 'St Mawr', fragments of two unfinished novels, letters from Lawrence, Paul Valéry, Max Beerbohm, Wells, Virginia Woolf, H.L. Mencken. There was Thomas Huxley's first edition of *Candide*, Huxley's Proust, in the original 1915 Mercure de France edition, and of *Lady Chatterley*, as well as his own first editions and editions signed by T.S. Eliot, Gide and others.[22]

The television cameras and reporters were immediately on the scene and some colourful fictions were woven, including one that

Huxley had 'wept like a child' (in fact, in another odd episode, he had gone off in his car with a local teenager with the plan, at such a moment, to fill up the car with gas). Huxley wrote to *Time* magazine to challenge this account. 'As an old hand at fiction, may I congratulate the write-up artist who penned the account of my actions.' In the aftermath of the fire the couple checked in to a hotel in Franklin Avenue for two weeks, then Huxley went to stay with Gerald Heard at Santa Monica until he left for London on 15 June. He carried on writing and the book was finally finished before he went to England. On 17 May he had written to Matthew: 'I am now a man without possessions and without a past. This last I regret as much for you as for myself; for what has gone is a piece of your life and heart and mind as well as of mine. But there is nothing to do except try to start from scratch.'[23] To a friend, Robert Hutchins, he wrote: 'I am evidently intended to learn, a little in advance of the final denudation, that you can't take it with you.'[24] To another friend, Alan Napier, he said that what he missed most were his telephone and appointment books: 'One is lost! I think I'm supposed to go to India in September to talk about something – but I've no idea where, when, or what about.'[25] When asked by Sybille Bedford how he had coped he said simply: 'One goes out and buys a toothbrush.'[26] To Anita Loos, he described the denuded feeling as a sensation of being 'clean' and to Humphry Osmond he declared: 'I took it as a sign that the grim reaper was having a good look at me.'[27] His response was truly oriental. Among the first titles with which he wished to restock his library were, significantly, Mallarmé, Gide, Baudelaire, Rimbaud, Verlaine and Apollinaire.[28]

More worryingly, however, than the losses in the fire, he had discovered that the cancer in the mouth had returned, though at first he kept it from Laura, thinking that she had enough anxiety to cope with. From London, where everyone noticed his tiredness and greyness, he wrote to Laura from his flat at 4 Ennismore Gardens, 'a fantastically quiet apartment overlooking a large garden full of trees'.[29] He was met by Julian and Juliette at the airport and went out to Surrey with Julian one day to see Prior's Field again. 'There are trees in the school garden which I remember being planted and which are now 60 feet high with trunks 6 feet round. They look as if they had been there for 300 years . . . After California everything is extraordinarily green and luxuriant.' Revisiting his childhood home, Laleham, he reflected 'How posthumous one feels!' Although Huxley came to England on his own he poured out a series of long, loving letters to Laura throughout June and July, telling her of his activities, which included visits to Gervas and Elspeth Huxley in Wiltshire, and attempts to plan a trip to Russia, which foundered over visa delays.

It was in London that Huxley gave a long television interview to John Chandos. Astonishingly neither the BBC nor the National Sound Archive has managed to preserve a copy of this interview but long extracts from it are printed in Sybille Bedford's biography.[30] He told Chandos that 'One can be agnostic and a mystic at the same time' and regretted that the modern world lacked potent symbols, 'cosmic symbols', only nationalist flags and swastikas. He accepted that it was not possible to have 'the flower of mysticism without the drug of superstition' and argued that religion is *infinitely* ambivalent . . . there are good and bad sides to it'. He said he had remained in California because he had found someone who could help him with his vision and because Maria needed a hot, dry climate. He revealed he had taken mescalin twice and LSD five times: 'I'd like to take it once a year. I wouldn't want to wallow in it.' All his drug experiences had been 'very positive' and the 'gratuitous grace' it gave (a term from Catholic theology of which he was very fond) yielded an experience which he characterised as: 'The Universe is All Right. Capital A, Capital R.'

The Devils was now playing in London and he was pleased with it. And the manuscript of *Island*, which had crossed the Atlantic at about the same time as his BOAC jet, was now being examined by Chatto in London and Harper's in New York. Correspondence between the two publishers had indicated they felt it 'too rambling', especially the 'Notes on What's What' section. They also felt the characters were 'wooden' and were simply vehicles: 'I guess we have to accept that, for this book is really a long essay in fictional form and I doubt that he would take the time to put more flesh on the characters.'[31] Chatto had rightly surmised that Huxley wanted no more to do with the novel. He did, however, accede to the cuts and promised to send a revised version. Huxley never disagreed with his publishers on such matters and was always very co-operative.

On 15 July, the book now off his hands, he left for a parapsychology conference organised by Eileen Garrett at Le Piol, St Paul de Vence in the South of France and went from there to stay with Jeanne and Georges Neveux at Vaison-la-Romaine. From there he went to Gstaad in Switzerland, where he was at last joined by Laura at the Palace Hotel. They met Krishnamurti at Gstaad, who had not seen Huxley for five years. According to Laura, he immediately noticed the improvement in Huxley's vision, references to his 'blindness' at this time and later, striking her as highly inaccurate.[32] He also met Yehudi Menuhin and his wife at Gstaad. From there the Huxleys went on to Italy to see Laura's family, then Copenhagen for the conference on applied psychology where Huxley gave a paper on the visionary experience. Then they went to Zurich to meet Albert Hofmann, the discoverer of LSD, then Bergeggi and Turin. They arrived in London on 12 September. Huxley remained there for another three weeks while Laura returned to Los Angeles. The Huxleys would stay thereafter at Virginia Pfeiffer's house in Mulholland Highway. The couple had exchanged letters in the summer, drawing facetious plans for the house they would build on the site of the one destroyed, but they never did so and remained at Mulholland Highway until Huxley's death. Laura Huxley lives there still. In November they were off again to India for the Tagore Centenary celebration at New Delhi. At Madras they stayed with Krishnamurti then returned via Colombo, Hong Kong, and Tokyo. India he found 'almost infinitely depressing' because of its social and political problems. He predicted a military dictatorship when Nehru went.

Huxley spent January and February 1962 at Berkeley as 'a visiting Ford Professor with no functions',[33] hoping that it would allow him to do his West Coast travel book in the manner of *Beyond the Mexique Bay*. This idea might be interesting and educational, he thought, 'for how little one knows, really, about anything! And how grossly incurious one remains about so many things, what an enormous number of intrinsically astonishing achievements one merely takes for granted!'[34]

Huxley knew a great deal more than most people but was true to his motto, *aun aprendo*. I am still learning. With some foreboding, he corrected the proofs of his last novel, 'wondering if the book is any good'. He was not alone in that apprehension.

Notes

1   *L*.884
2   *L*.885
3   *L*.886
4   RL, Letter to Jeanne Neveux, 11 January 1960
5   *L*.888
6   Reading, Letter to Ian Parsons, 26 March 1960
7   *L*.888
8   *Mem. Vol.*, p125
9   *L*.892
10 *L*.893
11 *L*.898
12 Reading, letter to Ian Parsons, 30 August 1960
13 *Mem. Vol.* p120
14 *SB*2.265–72 gives a full account of the professorship
15 RL, Letter to Jeanne Neveux, 27 December 1960. Author's translation
16 *L*.901
17 RL, Letter to Jeanne Neveux, 11 January 1960. Author's translation
18 *L*.903
19 Reading, Letter to Ian Parsons, 12 March 1961
20 Reading, Letter to Ian Parsons, 8 January 1961
21 *This Timeless Moment*, pp69–82
22 UCLA, inventory compiled by Jake Zeitlin, 6 June 1961
23 Cited in *This Timeless Moment*, p82. Letter to Matthew Huxley, 17 May 1961
24 *L*.912
25 Quoted in Christopher Rand, *Los Angeles: The Ultimate City* (1967), p46n
26 SB, in conversation with the author
27 *Mem. Vol.*, p121
28 RL, Letter to Jeanne Neveux, 4 June 1961
29 *This Timeless Moment*, p84. Letter to Laura Huxley, 17 June 1961
30 The National Sound Archive has an unofficial tape of part of the interview from which quotations here are drawn

31 Reading, Letter from Ian Parsons to Cass Canfield at Harper's, 19 June
    1961
32 *This Timeless Moment*, p63
33 L.926
34 L.927

XXXVII

Island

Island was the book that Huxley had to write. Famous for a dystopian projection of human society written before his 'conversion' to a more positive world view, he had meditated for many years on how to produce a 'good Utopia' to balance the picture of *Brave New World*. It was a book into which he was determined to put everything.[1] It would be a *Summa* of all his beliefs about the world, about human potential, about the meaning and purpose of life. But it was a novel, his eleventh and last, not a philosophical treatise, and even he was asking himself, as he pored over the English and American page proofs in Mulholland Highway at the start of 1962, 'if it is any good'. On 2 January he confessed to Chatto: 'I am feeling quite disgusted with the book. I hope it isn't as boring as all this proof-reading makes me think it is?'[2] Ian Parsons replied gently: 'But it's an infernally difficult kind of book to write, as who should know better than you, and I can't believe that serious readers won't gladly forgo some narrative impetus for the sake of the interest of what you have to say. Anyway, we shall see.'[3] That hardly sounded reassuring. He told his German translator, Herbert Herlitschka, that it was 'an odd sort of book, neither novel nor essay-collection – a set of expository episodes and conversations'.[4] John Rosenberg of MGM's office in London had already returned the proof with the comment that it 'offers no possibility for filming . . . one does, as well, miss the old bitterness and incisiveness'.[5] Twentieth Century Fox was a little more positive but made no offer to film it.

Huxley left Berkeley to attend a conference on 'Technology in the Modern World' at Santa Barbara at the beginning of March as the reviews began to appear. Cyril Connolly in *The Sunday Times* was the most positive. He claimed that Huxley had 'succeeded in infusing life into what might otherwise prove a succession of short essays and sermons'.[6] Less sympathetic critics of the novel would argue that this was precisely what he had *not* succeeded in doing. P.N. Furbank in *The Spectator* found the Utopian islanders of Pala 'priggish and arch, sententious, censorious and smug. They are some of the most disagreeable Utopians I have met.'[7] It was left to Frank Kermode in *Partisan Review*, however, to administer the *coup de grace:* 'Reviewers ought to watch their superlatives, but *Island*, it is reasonable to say, must be one of the worst novels ever written.'[8] Kermode simply said what Huxley himself had been saying for all these months: that the ideas overwhelmed the fiction, but he did concede that, in spite of the poorly drawn characters, 'the verbosity, the over-intellectuality', *Island* 'is a stimulating visit'. Kermode, disappointed in the book as fiction, approved of its attempt to advocate 'more imaginative, more utopian ideals'. This seems the right judgement on the book. It is full of worthy thoughts and ideas. It is indeed a statement of the mature Huxley's philosophy. It is sincerely meant. But it lacks the imaginative *brio*, the vigour – even the occasional rough crudity of humour and bizarre invention – of *Brave New World*. Readers will differ in the extent to which they can take their Utopianising raw, without the compensations of fictional inventiveness. The last section of the book, which has been praised as a remarkable account of a mescalin trip, some of us may find merely tedious but the book is undoubtedly stimulating. It cost Huxley much pain to write. He was full of doubts about it, rightly so, but it was a book that he could not have ducked out of writing, and it would have been wrong for it to have been consumed in the flames from which he snatched it a year earlier.

Pala, the island run on vaguely Mahayana Buddhist lines, has certain interesting parallels with *Brave New World*. Here sex is not an

opium of the people, a way of safely channelling potentially chal-
lenging or destructive feelings towards the rulers of the World State,
it is an instrument of enlightenment (though once again the conventional family and the Awful Mother are indicted, and sex and
child-rearing happen outside the family in Mutual Adoption Clubs).
Likewise, the drug *moksha* is a means to that same end rather than a
mind-numbing pacifier. Will Farnaby, the shipwrecked Westerner, is
a representative of the fallen species, the damaged man from the West
with its overpopulation, environmental prodigality, war mentality,
and materialistic consumerism. Slowly he is taught, by these endlessly wise and philosophically correct islanders, the goal of 'Good
Being'. The Ambassador remarks at one point: 'So long as it remains
out of touch with the rest of the world, an ideal society can be a viable
society.' Pala, of course, is not ignored by the rest of the world, which
wants its oil. And on the inside there are those who would prefer a
dose of consumer capitalism to beatific isolation, like young Murugan
who devours the Sears, Roebuck and Co. *Spring and Summer Catalog*
and wants to parley with the oil companies. Huxley attempts to inject
a degree of wit here and there to lighten the endless dialogues in
which the theories of Enlightenment on the way to the Clear Light of
the Void are expounded (sometimes, as in the case of Dr Robert, with
insufferable smugness).

His own experiences as well as his own ideas are deposited in the
book. The death of Lakshmi is very close to the descriptions of the
death of Maria: 'Let go now, let go. Leave it here, your old worn-out
body, and go on. Go on, my darling, go on into the Light, into the
peace, into the living peace of the Clear Light . . .'

In the final chapter, where Will – who as a young man, like Huxley,
'refused to take yes for an answer' – achieves enlightenment through
moksha, the moment of illumination is seen in a way which under-
lines the reasons for Huxley's own search: 'Like a blind man newly
healed and confronted for the first time by the mystery of light and
colour, he stared in uncomprehending astonishment.' It is impossible
to disentangle the real and the metaphorical uses of the word vision
in Huxley's lifelong quest. Like Will he found that: 'The answer was
just plain God – the God one couldn't possibly believe in, but who was

self-evidently confronting him.' He weeps tears of knowledge and, on the last page of Huxley's last novel: 'Disregarded in the darkness, the fact of enlightenment remained.' And the mynah birds of Pala, who repeat endlessly the Buddha's call to awareness (in contrast to the mind-numbing advertising jingles of *Brave New World*) have the very last word indeed: 'Attention.' This was Huxley's 'message' to the modern world: be aware.

From February to April 1962 at Berkeley Huxley enjoyed the same capacity audiences though generally the experience was quieter than the months at MIT. 'I was always amazed at the ease with which he made public appearances,'[9] Laura Huxley recalled. In spite of continuing LSD sessions – a long description of one such on 22 January is described by Laura Huxley[10] – 1962 had been 'a troubled and confusing year'. For: 'Aldous had lost his books, notes, diaries in the fire, lost the home where we had lived for the best period of our life together; he had had a debilitating flu and the future state of his health was uncertain; *Island* had been little publicized and grossly misunderstood; when we would have the home I was designing was problematical.' In spite of these setbacks he threw himself into an extraordinary programme of lecturing and conference attending, at Alabama, Philadelphia, Syracuse (a conference on hypnosis), Alamos (where he looked at the Apollo moon-shot capsule and the latest plane-to-ground missiles and shook his head over the millions spent 'in the service of vast collective paranoias'[11] while hunger persisted), Anaheim, New York (a talk at the American Academy of Arts and Letters). He was publicly honoured as a Companion of Literature by the Royal Society of Literature. He had also been corresponding with Timothy Leary, who would famously become an advocate of the sort of unrestrained LSD use which Huxley deprecated. Later in the year he told Peggy Lamson: 'If only Tim cd get into a Summit Meeting and give some mushroom to the two Mr Ks – the result might be world peace through total lucidity and breaking out by both parties, from the prison of their respective cultures and ideologies! Alas, such a consummation wd be too good to be true, and what in fact we shall go on having is a state of things too dismally true to be good.'[12] In February, Huxley wrote enthusiastically to

Leary about 'the sacramentalizing of common life . . . the ultimate yoga – being aware, conscious even of the unconscious – on every level from the physiological to the spiritual'.[13]

But in June the cancer returned and in July Huxley had a minor operation followed by cobalt treatment from which he was slow to recover. A gland had been removed and Max Cutler said it was not too serious. He reported to Laura, who was in Italy: 'perhaps just because death seems to have taken a step nearer – everything seems more and more beautiful, the leaves on the trees, the flowers, the sky, the green unwrinkled sea as we flew over it this afternoon, and my memories of you and all the people I have loved or felt concerned about'.[14] One cheering thing appeared to be the revival of the play *The Genius and the Goddess* put on by Frank Hauser, which toured at Oxford, Manchester, Leeds ending up in the Comedy Theatre in London, in spite of lukewarm appreciation by the critics and using an altered script from the Oxford one. In August, he accepted an invitation from 'a new World Academy of Arts and Sciences, started by a lot of Nobel Prizemen who would like to see that their science is used in a relatively sane manner'.[15] Huxley's was becoming a mandatory presence at such gatherings. He flew to Brussels at the end of August, caught another dose of 'flu which obliged him to stay in Amsterdam with Suzanne and Joep Nicolas, and then flew to London where he stayed with Julian and Juliette at Pond Street as usual.

On his return to Los Angeles, Huxley started work on what would be his last book, a short study of *Literature and Science* – a topic on which he was probably uniquely qualified to write. He felt that his grandfather Thomas Huxley and his great uncle Matthew Arnold in the 1880s remained the best thinkers on this topic and that the recent contributions by C.P. Snow and F.R. Leavis, which had stirred the intellectual waters in England, were 'too abstract and generalized'.[16] This was fitted in with a paper for a conference at the Centre for the Study of Democratic Institutions and lectures across the Middle West and the East Coast, ending up in New York. He looked out at the new year, 1963, which would be his last, asking: 'Will the few scores of people who decide the world's immediate fate permit it to be a tolerably good year?'[17] Having completed the essay on literature and science, he told Rosamund Lehmann that he was 'ruminating a kind of novel'[18] and reflecting on the death of Phil Nichols, brother of his old friend Robert: 'One ages into progressive solitude and a curious state of segregation – as though one belonged to an alien minority group merely tolerated by the younger majority.' He asked Juliette: 'Do you find, as I do, that the older one gets, the more unutterably mysterious, unlikely and totally implausible one's own life and the universe at large steadily become?'[19] In March, the imperious conference agenda resumed and he was off to Rome for a UN Food and Agricultural Organisation conference as part of its Campaign Against Hunger in the course of which he had an audience with the ailing Pope John XXIII. On the way back he stopped at New York for the wedding of Matthew and Judith Wallet Bordage, then it was more lecturing at Oregon, Berkeley and Stanford.

In April 1963 Huxley had another relapse and in May went into hospital. He spent most of June and July recovering from the radium treatments but was well enough to fly in August to yet another conference – the World Academy of Arts and Science at Stockholm. From there he went to London where his old friends found him much changed in outward appearance (while still in California Gerald Heard had found him on the telephone 'very tired & indeed to have difficulty in talking'[20]). When Julian and Juliette came to meet him at Heathrow: 'We knew at once that there was something terribly wrong with him: he was ashy-complexioned, very thin, and his voice had but half his usual volume.'[21] Huxley insisted that he had been up half the night drafting a memorandum at Stockholm and had caught a cold. He would recover. When he did not recover, Juliette prevailed upon him to see a consultant at Bart's Hospital, which he did. He did not tell them the truth about the cancer and they put his weariness down – wrongly, for he had faced up to and conquered it – to the loss of his house and possessions in the fire.

They took him to see his old friends, the Elmhirsts at Dartington ('Dartington is one of the few places in this bedevilled world where one can feel almost unequivocally optimistic,'[22] he later told Dorothy Elmhirst), Phyllis Nicols, Philip's widow, and Kenneth and Jane Clark at Saltwood Castle. 'I shall always remember Aldous, tall and so pale,

wandering round the rooms and grounds, and stooping to smell the
scented roses,' wrote Julian in his memoirs. One night he described his
next book 'a revaluation of history which he would hold together by
recounting the tale, told by the Florentine of the fifteenth century,
Vanzetti, about the priest who was castrated by order of a Sienese
potentate (whom he had disobeyed) and who got back his severed
balls so he could continue to officiate as priest, wearing them in small
bag about his person.' Juliette, quoting her diary record of this event
for 18 August, continues: 'Aldous loves this story, and I remember his
telling it to me last year, in a grave penetrating voice, as we were riding
home together in the number 24 bus. The rest of the passengers listened spellbound as the velvet voice pursued the episodes all up Fleet
Road.'[23]

After this visit they took him back to Heathrow ('You are getting
terribly remote,' Juliette had told him. 'I feel remote,' he had
answered.) 'We left him in the crowded, noisy waiting-room, already
gone really, stooping over his brief-case to extract *The Times* after
saying goodbye – so grey, so ghost-like, so truly remote from us all.' He
had dined with Sybille Bedford on this visit, the last time she too
would see him, at Rules in The Strand. Afterwards, he had insisted on
one of his long evening walks, stopping at a shop window to ask:
'Why do all the manikins look like Jackie Kennedy?'[24] From London
he flew to Turin to rejoin Laura – where they went up into the mountains – and they arrived back in Los Angeles at the end of August and
the start of what she called a 'slow but unrelenting diminuendo'.[25]
There was a flare-up of what Cutler thought was a secondary inflammation in the radiation-weakened tissues which made him feel very
low. In addition, his voice was affected, the nerve leading to the right
vocal chord having been knocked out. Huxley cancelled his lecture
tour in the East and suspended work on a volume of essays on human
resources. Then he wrote to Julian and Juliette, who were deeply
shocked at the revelation, that he had been suffering since 1960 with
cancer of the tongue. At last he gave them the full story.

During his last weeks he continued to work in so far as he could.
'He worked in his pyjamas and wrote sitting at a typewriter as long as
possible. Then, when he felt too weak to sit up, he would lie in bed

and write in large block letters on a yellow folio pad. If he felt too weak for writing he would dictate into a tape-recorder that stood by his bed.'[26] This is Max Cutler's account and he recalls how Huxley was confident that he was going to get well. He did not, and eventually went into hospital under an assumed name to avoid publicity. He returned to Mulholland Highway and told Laura: 'We can't impose on Ginny any longer. We must leave here.' The next day he started to deteriorate rapidly.

Literature and Science was published in September. It was an honourable termination of a life spent writing, ceaselessly, productively, with unbounded reserves of energy, clarity and determination to seek out what was wise and true. It addressed itself to the 'two cultures' debate, pouring scorn equally on C.P. Snow's *The Two Cultures* with its 'bland scientism' and F.R. Leavis's 'violent and ill-mannered' Richmond lecture, which had replied to Snow. This short book displays all the virtues of Huxley's non-fictional style. It is formidably learned, wide-ranging, utterly without the shrill or peevish tone that can creep into academic writing on these subjects, and elegantly and simply written. It discusses the different ways in which scientists and poets use language and proposes a *rapprochement* between the two: 'Man cannot live by contemplative receptivity and artistic creation alone . . . he needs science and technology.' Steeped in the English poetic tradition, Huxley had spent the last decade at least in the company of scientists rather than literary men, and it shows. He concentrates principally on the failure of writers to reflect the extraordinary scientific developments of the modern world rather than rebuking scientists for neglecting the insights of art. He looked forward to the arrival of 'some great artist' who would achieve the task of incorporating 'the hypotheses of science into harmonious, moving and persuasive works of art'. He called upon both scientists and artists (recognising that neither's language could ever be 'adequate to the givenness of the world') – the words are the final ones of his final book – to advance together, 'men of letters and men of science, further and further into the ever expanding regions of the unknown'.

And, as 1963 drew to a close, Huxley was moving inexorably towards another 'region of the unknown', the last human frontier he had to cross. As with Maria's mortal cancer so with his own, he min-imised its threat, not wishing to make himself a burden to others, having hoped for so long that mind would triumph over body. But by the end of October it was obvious to everyone around him that the end was coming. On 5 November Christopher Isherwood went to see Huxley at the Cedars of Lebanon hospital where he was under obser-vation. Isherwood was told by the surgeon that the cancer was spreading rapidly and that there was no hope: 'Aldous looked like a withered old man, grey-faced, with dull blank eyes. He spoke in a low, hoarse voice which was hard to understand. I had to sit directly facing him because it hurt him to turn his head.'[27] Huxley seemed the only person who did not know that he was dying, seeming to accept it only on the day itself. But he spoke obliquely to Isherwood about old age, 'and I couldn't help suspecting that this was a kind of metaphor, a way of referring to his own death'. Huxley told him he would never write another novel: 'I feel more and more out of touch with people.'

Shortly afterwards, Huxley was taken home to the house at Mulholland Highway. Like the true writer he was, he had a commis-sion to the very end and had half completed an essay on 'Shakespeare and Religion' for *Show* magazine in New York. He went on with it using pencil and paper only, no longer being able to type. He was sur-rounded by friends – Virginia and Laura, and Peggy Kiskadden who brought roses daily from her garden and Rosalind Rajagopal who brought oranges from the ranch at Ojai. Huxley had spent a lifetime inquiring into every aspect of human life and his own illness and imminent death was not to pass by in any other spirit. His last days and hours have been written about extensively – in Sybille Bedford's biography, in Laura Huxley's book, and in her letters to the Huxleys. 'If I get out of this,' he told Laura, 'those few years will be very impor-tant, because this experience that I am going through now will be of the greatest significance.'[28]

There were two nurses providing round-the-clock care and friends read to him constantly. Max Cutler, an exceptional doctor, it seemed to Laura, did not just ask the usual questions but asked what the patient was thinking and feeling about his situation. There was a tape-recorder by the bed and in *This Timeless Moment* a very detailed account is given of the last days and the conversations that passed between Aldous and Laura, and his accounts to her of his dreams. She also gives an account of the composition of what was now the final third of the essay on 'Shakespeare and Religion'. It is a short but beautifully written and illuminating essay. In it he reviews Shakespeare's attitude to religion and to death. Like Huxley the prophet in California, battling in his last decade with a range of obstacles from the studios, to the FBI, to the insentient reviewers, 'the Shakespearian hero has to fight his ethical battles in a world that is intrinsically hostile.'[29] Shakespeare – unlike Huxley – had 'no ambition to be a systematic theologian or philosopher' and preferred to 'hold a mirror up to nature'. His religion, if it is to be equated with the accepting vision of Prospero in *The Tempest*, is 'the doctrine of Maya' that 'our business is to wake up'. On his deathbed, Huxley framed his last expression of a world view which had been evolved over a lifetime:

> The world is an illusion, but it is an illusion which we
> must take seriously, because it is real as far as it goes, and
> in those aspects of reality which we are capable of
> apprehending. Our business is to wake up. We have to
> find ways in which to detect the whole of reality in the
> one illusory part which our self-centred consciousness
> permits us to see. We must not live thoughtlessly, taking
> our illusion for the complete reality, but at the same time
> we must not live too thoughtfully in the sense of trying
> to escape from the dream state. We must continually be
> on our watch for ways in which we may enlarge our
> consciousness. We must not attempt to live outside the
> world, which is given us, but we must somehow learn
> how to transform it and transfigure it. Too much
> 'wisdom' is as bad as too little wisdom, and there must be
> no magic tricks. We must learn to come to reality
> without the enchanter's wand and his book of the words.
> One must find a way of being in this world while not

being of it. A way of living in time without being
completely swallowed up in time.

On the next day, Sunday 17 November, they returned to the task,
which was of the most extraordinary difficulty. He was hardly able to
breathe, he was interrupted by coughing, his voice was faint, and he
had never composed in this way, by dictating. He would sometimes
bring out his magnifying glass to look at the written section of the
essay. Eventually he got the hang of operating the machine and managed to dictate a letter – his last to be published – to Max Kester of
Fosters' Agency in London about a possible television version of 'The
Tillotson Banquet' and a stage version of *After A Many Summer*. He
took to his death the hope of theatrical success.

Laura Huxley described the last week – from 15 to 22 November –
as 'a period of intense mental activity for Aldous'.[30] Until the last day
he 'had not consciously considered the fact that he might die very
soon'. She went on: 'He was mentally very active and it seemed to me
that some new levels of his mind were stirring.' Around noon, on the
last day, Friday 22 November, he asked Laura for a writing tablet and
wrote on it: 'Try LSD 100mm intramuscular'.[31] She left the bedside
and walked into the room across the hall to fetch the LSD from the
medicine cabinet. She was rather surprised to see the doctor and
nurses watching TV – hardly an appropriate moment to be doing so.
Only later would she discover that they had been watching, shocked,
the first footage of the assassination in Dallas of President John F.
Kennedy. Laura, dismissing the doctor's professional caution, admin-
istered the injection herself. It was 11.45 a.m. Some time later she gave
him another 100mm shot because the first injection seemed not to
have had any appreciable effect. She spoke to him – in the words he
used to Maria, in the words used at the death of Lakshmi in *Island* –
about letting go, about moving towards the light. 'You are going
towards Maria's love with my love,' Laura said. At around 3.15 p.m. he
acknowledged her with a squeeze of the hand. At 5.20 p.m., peacefully,
he died.

Nearly three weeks earlier, Isherwood had come away from the
hospital 'with the picture of a great noble vessel sinking quietly into

the deep; many of its delicate, marvellous mechanisms still in perfect order, all its lights still shining'.[32] A few days after the death he wrote to the Swami Vidyatmananda that Laura 'was and is shattered but behaved marvellously. I think she has been much misjudged.'[33] He was one of the small group of people who met at Mulholland Highway – the body had been quickly cremated on the day after the death with no-one present and without any kind of service – on Sunday afternoon. This group included Laura and Virginia, Matthew and Judy, Maria's mother, Rose and her son Siggy, Betty and Sanford Wendel, Peggy Kiskadden and Isherwood. As Sybille Bedford puts it: 'They went for the walk Aldous had gone for every day as long as he was able to stand up, the track along the canyon with the view over the Hollywood hills and the tree-lined reservoir he had called the Lake.'[34] On 17 December, at Friends House in London, there was a Memorial Gathering at which many of those who knew him spoke and at which Yehudi Menuhin played the Bach *Chaconne*. On 27 October 1971 Huxley's ashes were buried in his parents' grave at Compton in Surrey, close to the Watts Memorial Chapel. On 10 October 1972, Maria's ashes joined him there.

The anonymity of that interment – today the grave is untidy and neglected and the fact that Huxley's remains are buried in it is not disclosed – seems an ungrateful coda to the life of one of twentieth century England's most distinguished writers, a constantly inquiring spirit, an intellectual presence with no parallel in the current literary scene, a 'multiple amphibian' living in all the elements of art and science and perception that his omnivorous mind could gather into itself.

Notes

1 Laura Archera Huxley in conversation with the author
2 Reading, Letter to Ian Parsons 2 January 1962
3 Reading, Letter from Ian Parsons to Aldous Huxley, 12 January 1962
4 Reading, Letter to Herbert Herlitschka, 22 March 1962
5 Reading, Letter from John Rosenberg to Ian Parsons, 21 November 1961
6 Cyril Connolly, *The Sunday Times*, 1 April 1962, p30. Watt, pp446–49

7   P.N. Furbank, *The Spectator,* 30 March 1962. Watt, pp449–50

8   Frank Kermode, *Partisan Review,* Summer 1962, xxix, pp472–73. watt pp453–54

9   *This Timeless Moment,* p197

10   *Ibid.,* pp163-86

11   *L.*936

12   HRC, Letter to Peggy Lamson, 29 December 1962

13   *L.*929

14   *This Timeless Moment,* p261 quoting letter to Laura Archera Huxley, 31 May 1962

15   *L.*936

16   *L.*942

17   *L.*946

18   King's College Cambridge, Letter to Rosamund Lehmann, 20 February 1963

19   *L.*949

20   HL, Letter from Gerald Heard to Christopher Isherwood, 10 August 1963

21   Julian Huxley, *Memories II* (1973), p220

22   Reading, Letter to Dorothy Elmhirst, 24 August 1963, typed copy of letter written from Turin

23   Juliette Huxley, *Leaves from the Tulip Tree,* pp232–33

24   SB in conversation with the author

25   *This Timeless Moment,* p241

26   *Mem. Vol.* p127

27   *Mem. Vol.* p161

28   *SB*2.354. Quoting from Letter from Laura Archera Huxley to 'the family', 17 November 1963

29   'Shakespeare and Religion' in *Mem. Vol.,* pp165–75

30   *This Timeless Moment,* p298

31   *Ibid.,* p303. *SB*2.358 gives a slightly different form of words: 'LSD- Try it intermuscular 100mm'. In an appendix (p372) SB appears to differ with LH about Max Cutler's interpretation of the efficacy of the LSD. MC told SB that he had allowed the injection because it would make no difference at this stage. LH was surprised when told of this conversation and believed MC to have been of the opinion that it had a marked beneficial effect

32   *My Guru and His Disciple,* p259

33   HRC, Letter from Christopher Isherwood to Swami Vidyatmananda, 25 November 1963

34   *SB*2.359

Chronology

1894
26 July: Huxley born Godalming, Surrey.

1901
Huxley family leave 'Laleham', the house at Godalming for Prior's
Field nearby where Huxley's mother, Julia, opens a school the
following year.

1903
Huxley goes to Hillside Preparatory School (to June 1908).

1908
Huxley goes to Eton in September as King's Scholar; his mother
dies, 29 November.

1909
Huxley's father, Leonard, moves to Westbourne Square, London.

1911
Huxley forced to leave Eton in March because of an eye infection;
tutored at home; stays with various relatives; nearly blind for at least
a year; learns Braille.

1912

Leonard Huxley remarries to Rosalind Bruce; Huxley possibly writes first (lost) novel; travels to Marburg, Germany.

1913

Stays with brother, Trevenen, at Oxford; visits Grenoble with Lewis Gielgud; enters Balliol College, Oxford in October.

1914

Suicide of Trevenen, 23 August; October lodges with Haldanes in Oxford for second year.

1915

First visit to Garsington, 29 November; first meeting in same month with D.H. Lawrence in Hampstead; meets future wife, Maria Nys, at Garsington in December or early the following year.

1916

Rejected on health grounds by Army; helps to found *Palatine Review*; gains First in English; July and August temporary master at Repton School; September first book published, *The Burning Wheel* (poems); September goes to stay at Garsington for next seven months working on Philip Morrell's farm; proposes to Maria on lawn at Garsington during late summer or autumn.

1917

April to July clerical job at Air Board; living with father and stepmother at 16 Bracknell Gardens, Hampstead; 18 September takes up post as master at Eton (until Feburary 1919); December, *Jonah*.

1918

The Defeat of Youth (third book of poems), August; at work on first piece of fiction, 'The Farcical History of Richard Greenow'.

1919

Leaves Eton in April and visits Maria Nys (after a separation of more than two years) at her parents' home in Belgium; officially engaged; April starts work on *The Athenaeum* magazine (until October 1920); May moves into 18 Hampstead Hill Gardens, London; 10 July marries Maria at Bellem in Belgium.

1920

February first volume of short stories, *Limbo*; April, Matthew born; dramatic critic of *Westminster Gazette*; May, *Leda* published; part-time job with Chelsea Book Club; October moves from *Athenaeum* to *House and Garden*; December leaves Hampstead flat; Maria and Matthew go to Belgium for winter.

1921

January to March lodges Regent Square, Bloomsbury; begins to see Mary Hutchinson; April rejoins Maria at Villa Minucci, Florence; May to August writes first novel on Tuscan coast at Forte dei Marmi, *Crome Yellow* (published November); October returns to London to flat at 155 Westbourne Terrace (to December 1922) working again for Condé Nast.

1922

May, *Mortal Coils*; August to September holiday at Forte in Villa Tacchella.

1923

January, move to flat at 44 Prince's Gardens, London; signs first three-year publishing deal with Chatto; May, *On The Margin*; June to July, summer in Forte dei Marmi, writes *Antic Hay* (published November); August moves to Florence, Castel a Montici (to June 1925).

1924

May, *Little Mexican* and *The Discovery*; travels in France and Italy; writing *Those Barren Leaves*.

1925

January, *Those Barren Leaves*; March to April travels in Tunisia; July, London; August Belgium; September, *Along The Road*; 15 September Huxleys sail from Genoa (leaving Matthew for eleven months) on a round-the-world-trip beginning in India, then south-east Asia, United States until June 1926.

1926

May, *Two or Three Graces*; July, London; August, St Trond, Belgium;

August to December, Cortina d'Ampezzo, Italy;
renews acquaintance there with D.H. Lawrence; December,
Essays New and Old.

1927

January and February, Cortina; starts *Point Counter Point*; March to
May, London and Belgium; May to December, Forte at Villa
Majetta; November, *Proper Studies*; December, spends Christmas
with D.H. and Frieda Lawrence in Florence.

1928

January to February, Les Diablerets, Switzerland; March to May,
Onslow Mews, London; June takes house (until April 1930) at 3 Rue
du Bac, Suresnes, Paris (but not in full residence until October,
spending summer in Forte); November, *Point Counter Point*.

1929

January, Bandol with Lawrence; February, Florence; April, Spain;
May, *Arabia Infelix*; in London; June to September, final summer at
Forte; August, Apuan mountains; September, Suresnes; October, *Do
What You Will*; October to November, motor tour of Spain.

1930

London production of *This Way to Paradise* at Daly's Theatre;
March, with Lawrence on his deathbed at Vence; April move in to
Villa at La Gorguette, Sanary-sur-Mer until February 1937; May,
Brief Candles; September to October, London, Paris, Berlin,
Nottingham; November, *Vulgarity in Literature*.

1931

January to March, London, Dalmeny Court, Duke Street; March
The World of Light at Royalty Theatre; May, *The Cicadas*; May to
August at Sanary, writing *Brave New World*; September, *Music at
Night*; October to December, London.

1932

February, *Brave New World*; May to June, Belgium, Germany; June
to December at Sanary writes play *Now More Than Ever* (finished in
October); September, *The Letters of D.H. Lawrence* edited by Huxley;

November, *Texts and Pretexts*; starts *Eyeless in Gaza*;
December, London.

1933

January to May, travels in West Indies, Guatemala, Mexico; 3 May
Leonard Huxley dies; June to December at Sanary; November,
travels in Spain.

1934

April, *Beyond the Mexique Bay*; at work on *Eyeless in Gaza*; October
to December in London at 18 St Alban's Place, Regent Street;
December, takes out seven year lease on flat at E2, Albany, Piccadilly
whilst retaining Sanary; Huxley in poor physical and mental health;
beginning of crucial turn in his life.

1935

January to March, Albany (with visits to Paris); March to October at
Sanary working on *Eyeless in Gaza*; October to December at Albany,
taking lessons with F.M. Alexander; November joins Dick
Sheppard's Peace Pledge Union; 3 December gives address on
pacifism at Friend's House, London.

1936

January to March at Albany active in PPU; March finishes *Eyeless in
Gaza*; April to September, Sanary; April, *What Are You Going to Do
About It?*; June, *Eyeless in Gaza*; October to November, London;
December, *The Olive Tree*; at Sanary.

1937

19 February finally leaves Sanary; 7 April Huxleys sail with Gerald
Heard for New York; five week journey across states by car to San
Cristobal, Taos, New Mexico, to stay the summer with Frieda
Lawrence at her ranch; July, *An Encyclopaedia of Pacifism*; October
to November, Colorado and Hollywood (North Crescent Heights
Boulevard); November, *Ends and Means*; November to December,
Huxley and Heard lecture on peace; December, Maria at Rhinebeck
NY where Huxley joins her.

1938

February studio accepts screenplay so cancels plans to return to Europe; takes house at North Laurel Avenue, LA; Huxley in hospital with bronchitis for weeks; April begins never to be completed novel; July house at North Linden Drive, Beverly Hills; August to September works on script about Madame Curie at Metro-Goldwyn-Mayer; November, explores the Bates method of improving eyesight.

1939

February to July working on *After Many A Summer*; April move to 701 Amalfi Drive, Pacific Palisades (to February 1942); summer first meeting with Christopher Isherwood; August works on screenplay of *Pride and Prejudice*; October, *After Many A Summer*.

1940

August, after earlier ill-health, begins work on *Grey Eminence*.

1941

May finishes *Grey Eminence* (published October); works on screenplay of *Jane Eyre*; starts on *Time Must Have A Stop*.

1942

February, Huxleys move to desert house at Llano del Rio; at work on *Jane Eyre*; April starts *The Art of Seeing* (published October).

1943

Resumes work on novel; July stays with Gerald Heard at Trabuco College; October, Huxleys take a flat at South Doheny Drive, Beverly Hills in addition to Llano (to 1945).

1944

February finishes *Time Must Have A Stop* (published August); May starts *The Perennial Philosophy*.

1945

March, finishes *Perennial Philosophy* (published September); June buys mountain chalet in Wrightwood, California; writing *Science, Liberty and Peace*; November to December works with Walt Disney on *Alice and Wonderland*.

1946
Spending most of time at Llano in Mojave Desert; March
Science, Liberty and Peace; July to October at work on script of
The Gioconda Smile for Universal; September, at work on stage
version of same story.

1947
Finally abandons Llano for Wrightwood; March starts historical
novel on Catherine of Siena which is never completed;
September leaves California for first time since 1938 by car for
New York; November to December returned from New York to
write *Ape and Essence*.

1948
February *The Gioconda Smile* published as play in US as *Mortal
Coils*, released as film with title *A Woman's Vengeance*; 3 June, stage
version of *Gioconda Smile* opens in London for nine month run; 24
June, Huxleys sail for Europe (not seen since 1937) from New York;
Paris, Siena, Rome, London; August, *Ape and Essence*; October
return to New York; November to December in Palm Desert on
doctor's orders; at work on stage version of *Ape and Essence*.

1949
February Paris stage version of *Gioconda Smile*; May buy house
at 740 North King's Road, Los Angeles (but May to September
at Wrightwood).

1950
April, *Themes and Variations*; Matthew marries Ellen Howde in New
York; May sails on *Queen Mary* to France; Paris, Rome, Siena,
London, Villa Rustique at Sanary; Paris; September, returns to New
York; October, New York production of *Gioconda Smile*; visits
Frieda Lawrence on way back to LA; November to December, starts
work on *The Devils of Loudun*.

1951
March, virus infection followed in July by severe attack of iritis.

1952
January, Maria seriously ill, has treatment for breast cancer;
October, *The Devils of Loudun*.

1953
May, first mescalin experience with Dr Humphry Osmond; June
tour through northwestern states followed by work on
The Doors of Perception.

1954
February, *The Doors of Perception*; 7 April, sails to Cherbourg;
attends parapyscholocy conference, Vence; then Paris, Ismailia,
Cairo, Jerusalem, Beirut, Cyprus, Athens, Rome, Paris, London; 21
August sails for New York; 7 September, returns to Los Angeles;
October, lecturing, finishes *The Genius and The Goddess*;
November, collaborates with Beth Wendell on stage version of
The Genius and the Goddess.

1955
12 February, Maria dies; April to May drives by car to New York via
Southern states; May to June at 1035 Park Avenue, New York
working on stage production of *The Genius and the Goddess*; novel
appears June; July to August, summer with Matthew at Guilford,
Connecticut; September to December back in Los Angeles

1956
February, *Heaven and Hell*; 19 March, marries Laura Archera at
Yuma, Arizona; July, couple move to 3276 Deronda Drive, Los
Angeles; starts work on *Island* (not published until 1961); October,
Adonis and the Alphabet.

1957
July to November, at Shoreham Hotel, New York working on stage
version of *The Genius and The Goddess*; December, begins
Brave New World Revisited.

1958
July to August, travels in Peru and Brazil; September, Italy; October,
London, Paris, Venice; October, *Brave New World Revisited*;

November, lectures at Turin and other Italian cities;
December, returns to Los Angeles.

1959
February to May, first course of lectures at Santa Barbara on 'The
Human Situation'; July, serious fall; September to December, second
series of lectures at Santa Barbara.

1960
March to April, Visiting Professor at Menninger Foundation,
Kansas; May, cancer diagnosed; June, radium treatment;
September to November, Visiting Professor at Massachusetts
Institute of Technology.

1961
January, visits Hawaii; February, control of the mind conference,
San Francisco; 12 May, Deronda Drive house destroyed by fire; June,
finishes *Island*, visits London; July at Vence; August, Switzerland,
Copenhagen; September, returns to Los Angeles to stay at 6233
Mulholland Highway; November India, Japan.

1962
February to May, Visiting Professor at Berkeley; March, *Island*,
conference at Santa Barbara on technology in the modern world;
April to May, addresses further conferences in the US; June, illness
recurs, *The Genius and the Goddess* performed in England; July
minor operation; August to September, Brussels for meeting of
World Academy of Arts and Sciences; September, London;
November, lectures in Mid West.

1963
March, at Rome conference of UN Food and Agricultural
Organisation; March to April, lecturing at US universities; April to
May, another relapse; August, Stockholm for meeting of World
Academy of Arts and Sciences, London, Dartington, Italy;
September, *Literature and Science* (his last book); 22 November,
dies in Los Angeles; 17 December, Memorial Service, Friends
House, London.

Acknowledgements and Sources

I should like to express particular thanks to Laura Archera Huxley, Matthew Huxley, and Sybille Bedford who kindly agreed to be interviewed by me and who encouraged me in writing this book. Their reminiscences and critical opinions were invaluable.

I have drawn on the extensive amount of unpublished material which exists in library collections in the United Kingdom, United States and Belgium and would like to thank the following institutions for allowing me access to their collections and granting permission to quote from materials in their care: The Huntington Library, San Marino, California (Huxley collection, oral history transcripts, the diary of Grace Hubble, Isherwood papers); The Harry Ransom Humanities Research Center, The University of Texas at Austin, Texas (Huxley collection, Huxley–Ottoline Morrell correspondence, Huxley–Mary Hutchinson correspondence, Maria Huxley–Ottoline Morrell correspondence, Maria Huxley–Mary Hutchinson correspondence, Hutchinson papers); Archives et Musée de la Littérature, Bibliothèque Royale Albertine, Brussels (Huxley correspondence, Maria Huxley correspondence, Suzanne Nys memoir); University of Southern California, Los Angeles, Charles E. Young Research Library, Department of Special Collections (Huxley collection, Heard collection); The British Library (Huxley correspondence); The Bodleian Library, Oxford, Department of Special Collections and Western Manuscripts (Huxley correspondence); King's College Cambridge Centre for Modern Archives (Huxley correspondence); University of Reading Library, Department of Archives (restricted Huxley–Chatto papers); National Sound Archive (Huxley television and radio recordings); Stanford University, California (Huxley correspondence); New York Public Library (Huxley correspondence); University of Princeton Library, Department of Rare Books and Special Collections (Huxley correspondence); National Library of Wales (Huxley correspondence); Wellcome Institute Library and Galton Institute (Huxley correspondence in Eugenics Society archives); Lambeth Palace Library (Huxley–Dick Sheppard correspondence); Eton College Library (Huxley correspondence). I should also like to thank M. Didier Martina-Fieschi, Service du Patrimonie, Mairie de Sanary Sur Mer; Claude B. Zachary, University of Southern California Archivist and Manuscripts Librarian; Cathy Henderson, Shannon Lawson, Pat Fox,(Harry Ransom Humanities Research Center), Sue Hodson, Romaine Ahlstrom (Huntington Library); Michael Bott (Reading University Library); Hugues Robaye, Amélie Schmitz (Musée de la Littérature, Brussels); Jeff Rankin (UCLA); Jennifer Kerns (Newnham College, Cambridge); Michelle Duke (Random House); Colin Harris (Bodleian Library); John Timson (Galton Institute); Lesley Hall (Wellcome Institute); Michael Meredith (Eton College); Raymond-Josué Seckel (Bibliothèque Nationale de France); Margaret Sherry (Princeton University Library).

I should like to express special thanks to Mr John Deutsch FRCS FRCOphth, Consultant Ophthalmologist, Victoria Eye Hospital, Hereford for his valuable insights into Huxley's eye disease. My research in the United States was significantly extended by the skilful research assistance of my wife, Susan Murray.

I should also like to thank the following individuals who provided assistance, encouragement, advice: Rob Archer (Mira Costa College, CA), Chris Silkin, Professor Cecil Y. Lang, Stan Lauryssens, Professor Bernfried Nugel, Jeremy Lewis, Lord Sackville, Michael-De-la-Noy,

Patrick Trevor-Roper, Pat Krig, Rob Humphrey, Professor James Knowlson, Dr Richard Price.

For permission to quote from the published and unpublished writings of Aldous Huxley I am grateful to Dorris Halsey and the Estate of Aldous L. Huxley and Random House (UK). For permission to quote from an unpublished profile of the Huxleys by Mary Hutchinson I am grateful to Lord Hutchinson QC and for permission to quote from the oral history transcripts at the Huntington Library I am grateful to Professor David King Dunaway, University of New Mexico.

Index